325

SAGE was founded in 1965 by Sara Miller McCune to support the dissemination of usable knowledge by publishing innovative and high-quality research and teaching content. Today, we publish over 900 journals, including those of more than 400 learned societies, more than 800 new books per year, and a growing range of library products including archives, data, case studies, reports, and video. SAGE remains majority-owned by our founder, and after Sara's lifetime will become owned by a charitable trust that secures our continued independence.

Los Angeles | London | New Delhi | Singapore | Washington DC | Melbourne

MINDFUL COMMUNICATION for SUSTAINABLE DEVELOPMENT

Thank you for choosing a SAGE product!
If you have any comment, observation or feedback,
I would like to personally hear from you.

Please write to me at **contactceo@sagepub.in**

Vivek Mehra, Managing Director and CEO, SAGE India.

Bulk Sales

SAGE India offers special discounts
for purchase of books in bulk.
We also make available special imprints
and excerpts from our books on demand.

For orders and enquiries, write to us at

Marketing Department
SAGE Publications India Pvt Ltd
B1/I-1, Mohan Cooperative Industrial Area
Mathura Road, Post Bag 7
New Delhi 110044, India

E-mail us at **marketing@sagepub.in**

Get to know more about SAGE

Be invited to SAGE events, get on our mailing list.
Write today to **marketing@sagepub.in**

This book is also available as an e-book.

MINDFUL COMMUNICATION for SUSTAINABLE DEVELOPMENT
Perspectives from Asia

Edited by
Kalinga Seneviratne

Los Angeles | London | New Delhi
Singapore | Washington DC | Melbourne

Copyright © Kalinga Seneviratne, 2018

All rights reserved. No part of this book may be reproduced or utilized in any form or by any means, electronic or mechanical, including photocopying, recording, or by any information storage or retrieval system, without permission in writing from the publisher.

First published in 2018 by

SAGE Publications India Pvt Ltd
B1/I-1 Mohan Cooperative Industrial Area
Mathura Road, New Delhi 110 044, India
www.sagepub.in

SAGE Publications Inc
2455 Teller Road
Thousand Oaks, California 91320, USA

SAGE Publications Ltd
1 Oliver's Yard, 55 City Road
London EC1Y 1SP, United Kingdom

SAGE Publications Asia-Pacific Pte Ltd
3 Church Street
#10-04 Samsung Hub
Singapore 049483

Published by Vivek Mehra for SAGE Publications India Pvt Ltd, typeset in 10/12 pt Adobe Garamond by AG Infographics, Delhi and printed at Chaman Enterprises, New Delhi.

Library of Congress Cataloging-in-Publication Data

Name: Seneviratne, Kalinga, editor. | Container of (work): Sulak Sivaraksa. Mindful communication for sustainable development.
Title: Mindful communication for sustainable development: perspectives from Asia/edited by Kalinga Seneviratne.
Description: New Delhi, India: SAGE Publications India Pvt. Ltd., 2018. | Includes bibliographical references and index.
Identifiers: LCCN 2017046532| ISBN 9789352805518 (print hb) | ISBN 9789352805532 (e pub 2.0) | ISBN 9789352805549 (e book)
Subjects: LCSH: Sustainable development—Moral and ethical aspects—Asia. | Communication in economic development—Moral and ethical aspects—Asia. | Sustainable development—Religious aspects.
Classification: LCC HC415.E5 M54 2018 | DDC 174/.4—dc23 LC record available at https://lccn.loc.gov/2017046532

ISBN: 978-93-528-0551-8 (HB)

SAGE Team: Rajesh Dey, Alekha Chandra Jena, Megha Dabral, and Ritu Chopra

Contents

List of Figures ix
Preface xi

Introduction 1
Kalinga Seneviratne

SECTION A
Philosophical Perspectives 23

CHAPTER 1
Mindfulness in Communication: A Buddhist Approach 25
Venerable Phuwadol Piyasilo

CHAPTER 2
Mindful Communication for Sustainable Development 29
Sulak Sivaraksa

CHAPTER 3
Buddhist, Hindu, and Jain Contribution to Communication in Asia 34
Binod C. Agarwal

CHAPTER 4
Confucius and Tao of Asian Journalism 43
Kwangsoo Park

CHAPTER 5
Human Dignity and Responsibility to Humanity:
A Buddhist Viewpoint 52
Lim Kooi Fong

CHAPTER 6
"Hindu" Values in Journalism 60
Sanjay Ranade

SECTION B
Training for Mindful Thinking in Communication   79

CHAPTER 7
Thinking Through Practice: Creative Media as a Research
Methodology   81
Jirayudh Sinthuphan

CHAPTER 8
Storytelling with Deep Listening   89
Supaporn Phokaew

CHAPTER 9
New Approach to ASEAN Journalism: From a Thai Perspective 95
Pipope Panitchpakdi

CHAPTER 10
Mindful Communication and Media Training: A View
from Myanmar   108
Cho Cho Thwin

SECTION C
Mindful Communication and Sustainable Development   131

CHAPTER 11
Middle Path Journalism: A Conceptual Framework for
Bhutanese Media   133
Dorji Wangchuck

CHAPTER 12
Philippines: Ignatian Pedagogy and Mindful Communication   150
Evans Rosauro I. Yonson

CHAPTER 13
Mindful Communication for Good Governance: A Buddhist
Approach   161
Sugath Mahinda Senarath

CHAPTER 14
Mindful Communication and Sustainable Development:
The Buddhist Holistic Framework   171
Ananda Kumaraseri

SECTION D
Applying Traditional Practices to Mindful Development Communication   179

CHAPTER 15
A Japanese Path to Mindful Communication: Understanding the Silence of the Japanese   181
Kanako Watanabe

CHAPTER 16
Laos: Traditional Methods of Communication and Their Relevance to Grassroots Community Development—Case Study of Nongviengkham Village   192
Homala Phensisanavong

CHAPTER 17
Cambodia: Mindful Public Relations—From Monastic to Government Communications   212
Nayheak Khun

CHAPTER 18
Crossing Panel Borders: Transnational Constrained Comics Composition and Mindful Development Communication   236
Nicolas Verstappen

SECTION E
Mindful Communication and Contemporary Media   263

CHAPTER 19
Practicing Mindful Communication in a Multicultural Society: Case Study of Malaysian News Reporting   265
Azman Azwan Azmawati, Chai Ming Hock, and Raqib Sofian

CHAPTER 20
Philippines: Beyond the Body Count—Mindful Journalism and the Human-centric Approach to Reporting the Drug War   287
Therese Patricia C. San Diego

CHAPTER 21
South Korea: Compassionate Approach to Journalism—Buddhist True Network   310
Emi Hayakawa

CHAPTER 22
Sri Lanka: Mindful Communication and Reconciliation 317
Ariyarathna Athugala

CHAPTER 23
Mindful Communication for Sustainable Development: A New
Asian Communication Paradigm 332
Kalinga Seneviratne

About the Editor and Contributors 340
Index 344

List of Figures

I.1	What Are the Sustainable Development Goals?	5
18.1	Set of Seven Roughly Sketched Panels Used as a Reference for the Three Professional Cartoonists	247
18.2	Three Different and Final Sets of Seven Panels	248
18.3	Extended Set of Limited and Imposed Panels Based on the Original Set of Seven Panels	249
18.4	First Two Pages of the Four-page Comics Produced by Bigbell	250
18.5	Pages 1–3 of the Four-page Comics Produced by Fon	252
18.6	Pages 1, 3, and 4 of the Four-page Comics Produced by Nick	253
18.7	Pages 1–4 of the Six-page Comics Produced by Top	254

Preface

On September 25, 2015, the United Nations adopted the Sustainable Development Goals (SDGs) that are supposed to end poverty, protect the planet, and ensure prosperity for all by 2030. The SDGs came into force on January 1, 2016. Over the next 15 years, these new goals will mobilize efforts to end all forms of poverty, fight inequalities, and tackle climate change while ensuring that no one is left behind. To achieve these goals, the media has to play a crucial role in mobilizing people and resources—both at national and international levels.

The model of journalism we practice in Asia is an adversarial one driven by conflict reporting—a model we have borrowed from the West. This book is an outcome of a project implemented by the Faculty of Communication Arts of Chulalongkorn University and funded by the International Program for the Development of Communications (IPDC) of UNESCO.

The project incorporates Asian philosophical ideas and communication theories emanating from Buddhist, Hindu, and Confucius teachings for developing a curriculum to train Asian journalists. It is designed to frame a new paradigm of reporting that could form a new approach to development communication. It covers areas such as realizing social harmony, protecting nature and environment, respecting cultural diversity, and encouraging sufficiency economic models. This book focuses on using such a path of communication to promote sustainable development, a priority area of the United Nations known as the 2030 Agenda to promote 17 SDGs.

The new goals are unique in that they call for action by all countries—poor, rich, and middle-income—to promote prosperity while protecting the planet. They recognize that ending poverty must go hand-in-hand with strategies that promote economic growth and address a range of social needs including education, health, social protection, and job opportunities while tackling climate change and ensuring environmental protection. These are all seen as interdependent, and one cannot be solved without addressing the others.

One of the key principles of Buddhist teachings—*pratitya samutpada* or "dependent origination," which sees all things and phenomena as interdependent—is clearly consistent with the interdependent view of these SDGs that are embedded in a complex relationship of cause and effect. Even the

Catholic Church recognizes the interdependencies of the SDGs. In a note addressed to the UN Secretary-General on the adaptation of the SDGs, the Holy See of Rome said[1]: "The pillars of integral human development, namely, the right to life and, more generally, the right to existence of human nature itself, are threatened when we no longer recognize any instance above ourselves or see nothing else but ourselves."

The term "development communication" was coined for communication where the communicator was supposed to wean away the peasants from their traditional lifestyles into a more consumption-oriented society. So tradition became old-fashioned, and greed became synonymous with development/modernization. The East was supposed to embrace the West's wisdom and discard their own mythologies. But today, in the second decade of the 21st century, Eastern "mythology" is becoming modern wisdom. Mindfulness is today the biggest fad sweeping across the West, particularly the USA. We in the East have known this as *Vipassana Bhavana* for the past 25 centuries—be mindful of your actions and its effects.

To achieve the SDGs, the media needs to play an important role in facilitating and promoting the reporting of development issues as interdependent. This may also need a new look at aspects of training journalists to look at issues with less emphasis on conflicts. There needs to be new thinking on how to report on economic, business, environment, and development issues, where Asia's needs, its priorities, and its historical experiences are taken into account. This is where developing mindful communication methodologies that take into account the region's cultural and social norms and traditions will come into play.

Mass communication courses taught in universities across the world are usually based on Western concepts of communication with heavy focus on individual rights and freedom of expression. In Asia, where the protection and promotion of community and social harmony plays an important role in political and social discourse, media practitioners' focusing on individual rights over community harmony sometimes creates unnecessary conflicts that could be avoided by more sensitive and mindful communication strategies that would have the same result of opening up public and community space for more freedom of expression.

The book provides a plurality of viewpoints and pathways to adopt mindful communication methodologies to assist in the promotion of the SDGs. The book is arranged under thematic sections with the first section consisting of

---

[1] See https://www.technocracy.news/index.php/2016/10/20/pope-francis-evaluates-2030-agenda-sustainable-development/ (accessed on October 28, 2017).

six chapters that discuss the philosophical aspects of mindful communication and the concepts behind the SDGs. The chapters are designed to introduce new ways of thinking in terms of communication theory and methodologies bringing in ideas and concepts from Asian philosophy emanating from Buddhist, Hindu, and Confucius teachings.

The second thematic section consists of four chapters that address issues such as human-centric reporting with deep listening, digital storytelling to connect people within ASEAN countries, decolonizing the mind for Asia-centric reporting, reporting a process not as an event, the idea of being a journalist, and some thoughts from Myanmar about incorporating their rich tradition of mindful meditation into journalistic training.

The third thematic section focuses on the links between mindful communication and sustainable development and includes four chapters. It brings you a viewpoint on middle path journalism from Bhutan; a comparative look at the links between liberation theology and mindful communication from the Philippines; a view from Sri Lanka on how mindful communication could promote good governance; and a discussion on how a Buddhist framework could provide a holistic approach to mindful sustainable development communication.

The fourth thematic section presents some interesting and perhaps unusual methodologies on applying traditional practices to mindful development communication. It includes a chapter from Japan about how the Japanese style of indirect, obscure communication and intentionally avoiding direct expressions could be adopted for sustainable development communication. From Laos, a chapter exploring the traditional communication methods between the temple and the community and the current government information systems provides interesting ideas on how the traditional and modern communication systems could synergize to promote SDGs. From Cambodia comes another interesting exploration of how traditional Buddhist communication systems between the temple and the people and modern public relations could synergize as a sustainable development communication process. Finally, the chapter by a Chulalongkorn University lecturer teaching comic arts presents a very interesting take on how this art form, fused with mindful communication concepts, could assist in promoting SDGs.

The fifth thematic section examines the application of mindful communication concepts to the practices of contemporary news media. It consists of chapters from Malaysia on reporting "mindfully" contentious religious issues in a multicultural society; from the Philippines, a chapter looking at the media coverage of President Duterte's "war on drugs" from a mindful communication perspective; from Korea, a chapter on how a Buddhist

TV channel goes beyond the adversarial model of journalism to applying mindful compassionate approach to reporting, especially in the aftermath of disasters/conflicts; and from Sri Lanka, a chapter on how reconciliation issues could be covered mindfully.

The final chapter basically summarizes the book's contents, arguing that mindful communication could herald in a new paradigm of development communication to promote the United Nations 2030 Agenda for sustainable development.[2]

At a time when the current model of capitalist development, which mainly originated and developed in the West, is being questioned for its sustainability—both economic and environmental—it is hoped that this book will inspire a new generation of development communicators who will treat the earth's and human species' sustainability and well-being as paramount while communicating for sustainable development.

---

[2] We would also like to provide the following link to the website that includes model curricula developed for the UNESCO-funded project that would assist in the teaching of "Mindful Communication for Sustainable Development": http://kalingasen.wixsite.com/mindfuljourn/curricula-modules (accessed on September 14, 2017).

Introduction

Kalinga Seneviratne

In a little more than a few decades, mindfulness has gone from being a special element of Buddhist teaching to the front cover of *Time* magazine. It's the must-have app for the stars, courses in it are advertised at the back of all glossies, businesses use it to reduce staff stress and boost productivity. It's even prescribed on the NHS (National Health Service) for anxiety and depression. This is the story of "mindfulness"—from its roots in the Buddhist practice of meditation to today's multibillion-dollar, worldwide industry. Devoted followers hail it as a cure-all for the ills of modern life.

—Introduction to BBC Radio documentary *Mindfulness: Panacea or Fad?*

In the Buddhist philosophy, the real meaning of mindfulness is to remember. Perhaps, mindfulness has to do with memory, but what I will discuss it as is to remember something in any given situation. We have to keep in mind not to let any given situation distract us from what we are thinking. In some ways, this has to do with being in the present moment and not to get distracted from the thoughts and emotions that arise from the present situation.

—Venerable Phuwadol Piyasilo, Yen Boon Forest Monastery, a mass communication graduate from Chulalongkorn University, Thailand

Mindfulness may be a global movement today; it has even been called a fad, especially in the West, where companies are offering mindfulness meditation courses to their employees to boost productivity. Google has introduced it in the workplace, and even doctors could prescribe it under the National Health Service in Britain to treat anxiety. However, mindfulness is an ancient practice; it goes back 2,500 years to the teachings of Gautama Shakyamuni Buddha in India.

When the late Indian–Burmese meditation master S. N. Goenka started popularizing *Vipassana* meditation around the world, beginning in the 1980s, he offered the now famous 10-day retreats free of charge. Today, you can even learn it online. In 2015, University of Massachusetts set up a

Centre for Mindfulness[1] and offered a 5-day residential intensive program of "Mindfulness Tools" for a fee of $625. I learned it at school in Sri Lanka over 40 years ago as part of my Buddhism lessons for the secondary school leaving exam and can still remember answering a question on *Vipassana Bhavana* for my General Certificate of Education (GCE) Ordinary Level (OL) exam. But I never bothered to practice it.

My interest in mindfulness was rekindled when the word started flashing everywhere in the media and in cyberspace in recent years. This led me to propose a project on mindful communication to Chulalongkorn University in Bangkok, and this book is part of that project.

What Is Mindfulness?

Developing mindfulness is at the very heart of Buddhist teachings. Known in Buddhism as "*Vipassana,*" which means to see things as they really are, it is one of India's most ancient techniques of meditation. It was rediscovered by the Buddha in the 5th century BCE and was taught by him as a universal remedy for universal ills (art of living). *Vipassana* (mindfulness) is a way of self-transformation through self-observation.

As Elise Bialylew, doctor in psychiatry and founder of the online meditation campaign "Mindful in May," says[2]:

> Mindfulness is a very ancient practice, it's got its roots 2,500 years old through the Buddhist contemplative practices, but it's really about training our attention to be more present, and through that we develop more awareness about what's going on from moment to moment, both within ourselves, so emotionally and in our thought processes, but also relationally. So in the world, when we are interacting with others, if we are feeling emotionally triggered, we are picking up on that data much more quickly and we are much more able to respond with more wisdom and more effectiveness.

Goenka, who spent over 2 decades introducing *Vipassana* or mindfulness meditation around the world, often had to explain that he is not teaching Buddhism, but a way of life.

---

[1] See http://www.umassmed.edu/cfm/stress-reduction/mindfulness-tools/ (accessed on September 14, 2017).

[2] ABC Radio program "On Being Mindful"—http://www.abc.net.au/radionational/programs/allinthemind/on-being-mindful/6449522 (accessed on September 15, 2017).

I'm not concerned with "isms," I teach Dhamma, that is what the Buddha taught. He never taught any "isms" or sectarian doctrine. He taught something from which people of every background can benefit: an art of living. Remaining in ignorance is harmful for everyone; developing wisdom is good for everyone. So anyone can practice this technique and find benefit ... one must become a good human being; otherwise, one can never be a good Christian, a good Jew, a good Muslim, a good Hindu, a good Buddhist. How to become a good human being—that is most important. (Goenka in Hart, 1998: 18)

Many Buddhists are, however, critical of divorcing the techniques of mindfulness from Buddhist spiritual teachings. Thai Buddhist and social critic Sulak Sivaraksa warns that this meditation practice stripped of its ethical framework can be a form of escapism. "In the teachings of the Buddha, meditation and mindfulness are intended to bring about the elimination of suffering—both of personal internal kinds and that brought about by external factors such as climate change and structural violence," he argues (see Chapter 2).

Venerable Piyasilo is also concerned about the self-centered nature of the mindfulness fad sweeping the world. "Mindfulness practices in the West are usually found to be secular. People there try to practice it without adding any religious value to it," he argues.

This has become problematic because it could manifest itself with the wrong intentions. When you apply Buddhist teachings, mindfulness is accompanied by *panna* (wisdom). Without this moral framework, the practice by itself would not be enough to fast-track us into the right direction. We need to incorporate *panna* into the mindfulness practice itself. (See Chapter 1.)

"A life without wisdom is a life of illusion," argues Goenka. "Being sensitive to the suffering of others does not mean that you must become sad yourself. Instead you should remain calm and balanced, so that you could act to alleviate their suffering" (Hart, 2012: 19).

Bialylew, who was introduced to meditation as a child but came to it later and found it helpful in managing her stress levels, agrees that within the teachings of mindfulness is a sense of developing compassion both for ourselves and others that would help us to handle emotional challenges, when we face them. She notes:

Also it helps us to develop a sense of interconnectedness with other people. So I think naturally as you become more aware of what's going on in the world and you feel more connected, both to yourself and to other people, other humans that you might know or not know, there's just this natural flow-on that makes you actually care. And then from that care there's a natural flow-on that creates a sense of wanting to actually take action, take responsibility. So I do think there is a relationship there, and I think it's quite a strong one.[3]

At the root of the Buddhist philosophy is a path to understanding and guiding your mind toward doing good things. Its teachings are very much centered on the mind because Buddhism does not believe in a creator God.

Guiding your mind also relates to guiding human communications. As the UNESCO's preamble says:

> Since wars begin in the minds of men, it is in the minds of men that the defenses of peace must be constructed.[4]

Sustainable Development—Definitions and Practicalities

After witnessing the exploitation and plunder of their resources by the colonial rulers for over 2–3 centuries, when the postcolonial period began at the end of World War II, the newly independent nations wanted to liberate themselves from the yoke of "underdevelopment" that was imposed on them. Most of them thought that the best way to do it was to emulate the development model of the Europeans. The former colonial rulers also promoted this model with the so-called development "aid." Development and modernization was seen as the process by which individuals change from a traditional way of life to a more complex, technology-driven, and rapidly changing style of life.

Thus, the word "development communication" was coined, where the communicator was supposed to wean away the peasants from their traditional lifestyles into a more consumption-oriented society. So tradition became old-fashioned, and greed became synonymous with development/modernization. The East was supposed to embrace the West's wisdom and discard their own mythologies. In the 1980s, and following the fall of the Soviet Union, the West went full steam ahead pushing their development agenda of free-market liberalism and globalization.

Sivaraksa (2009: 11) argues that globalization and free-market fundamentalism are a "demonic religion" that is imposing materialistic values across the world, "driving individuals to try to earn more to acquire more

---

[3] ABC Radio program "On Being Mindful".
[4] http://www.unesco.org/new/en/unesco/about-us/who-we-are/history/constitution/ (accessed on September 15, 2017).

in a never-ending cycle of greed and insecurity." He alleges that the term "modernization" is racially coded to mean "Europeanization." He accuses the World Bank (WB) and other Bretton Woods institutions of promoting the superiority of industrialization, the monetary economy, and modernity over agrarian lifestyles, subsistence economies, and indigeneity, "making globalization a new form of colonialism" (see Chapter 2 for more analysis from Sivaraksa).

But by the end of the 20th century, our planet had become warmer and natural calamities had increased. Meanwhile, Asians had almost fully embraced the West's economic wisdom, and they were beginning to consume the way the West has been doing for most of the 20th century. Some of them were even threatening to overtake the West in these consumption and development patterns.

Suddenly, development communicators in the West and the East began to realize that this model of "development" cannot work, it is not sustainable, and humankind is galloping toward disaster. So on September 25, 2015, the United Nations adopted the Sustainable Development Goals (SDGs) that are supposed to end poverty, protect the planet, and ensure prosperity for all (Figure I.1).

The SDGs came into force on January 1, 2016. Over the next 15 years, these new goals will mobilize efforts to end all forms of poverty, fight inequalities, and tackle climate change while ensuring that no one is left behind. These new goals are unique in that they call for action by all countries—poor, rich, and middle-income—to promote prosperity while protecting the planet. They recognize that ending poverty must go hand-in-hand with strategies

Figure I.1
What are the Sustainable Development Goals?

Source: United Nations.

that promote economic growth and address a range of social needs including education, health, social protection, and job opportunities, while tackling climate change and ensuring environmental protection. While the SDGs are not legally binding, governments are expected to take ownership and establish national frameworks for the achievement of the 17 goals.[5]

In a note addressed to the UN Secretary-General on the adaptation of the SDGs, the Holy See of Rome said[6]:

> The pillars of integral human development, namely, the right to life and, more generally, the right to existence of human nature itself, are threatened when we no longer recognize any instance above ourselves or see nothing else but ourselves. This can only be remedied by recognition of a moral law that is written into human nature itself, one, which includes absolute respect for life in all its stages and dimensions and the natural difference between man and woman. Human rights derive from a correct understanding of human nature, the human person, inherent human dignity and the moral law.

One of the key principles of Buddhist teachings, *pratitya samutpada* or "dependent origination," which sees all things and phenomena as interdependent, is clearly consistent with the interdependent view of the SDGs that are embedded in a complex relationship of cause and effect. So in the second decade of the 21st century, Eastern "mythology" is becoming modern wisdom.

From a Buddhist perspective, to understand the dependent origination of the SDGs, we need to understand the causes of poverty. The Four Noble Truths that are at the very root of Buddhist teachings could be a guide to developing a communication strategy to address the SDGs.

Each Noble Truth	*Meanings*	*Duties to Deal with It*
1. *Dukkha*	Suffering, dissatisfaction	To comprehend suffering. To know location of the problem
2. *Samudaya*	The cause or origin of dissatisfaction or suffering	To eradicate the cause of suffering. To diagnose the origin
3. *Nirodha*	The cessation or extinction of suffering	To realize the cessation of suffering. To envision the solution
4. *Magga*	The path leading to the cessation of dissatisfaction or suffering	To follow the right path through actual practices

---

[5] See UN SDG website for more details: http://www.un.org/sustainabledevelopment/ (accessed on September 15, 2017).

[6] See https://www.technocracy.news/index.php/2016/10/20/pope-francis-evaluates-2030-agenda-sustainable-development/ (accessed on September 15, 2017).

In terms of development theory, the origination can be understood as follows: what is the cause of underdevelopment? It is poverty. What is poverty? It is *dukkha* (suffering). So we have to be mindful of this suffering.

So what is the origin of poverty? Is it wrong government policies? Is it exploitation of the poor by the more powerful? Is it unjust economic and trade regimes? Is it corruption, which is the ultimate manifestation of greed or craving? So what should we do or advocate for the eradication of poverty? What is the solution?

The role of the development communicator is to understand all these, be mindful of the situation on the ground, and set about to encourage or advocate policies that will lead to the eradication of poverty and suffering. This would lead you to practice compassion and loving kindness.

The note of the Holy See also argued in similar tones. It emphasized that recognizing the poor as dignified agents of their own destiny is an important factor in eradication of poverty.

> To enable men and women to escape from extreme poverty, they must be dignified agents of their own destiny, taking into consideration that integral human development and the full exercise of human dignity cannot be imposed, but rather allowed to unfold for each individual, for every family, in relation to others, and in a right relationship with those areas in which human social life develops.

The note further adds that there should also be a minimum spiritual and material means to enable a person to live with dignity and to create and support a family, "which is the primary cell of any social development."

The Holy See also added that any sustainable development path should be accompanied by a system of justice that requires "concrete steps and immediate measures for preserving and improving the natural environment and putting an end to the phenomenon of social and economic exclusion, with its baneful consequences."

As Islamic Studies Professor Mahmoud Ayoub argues (Hutanuwatr and Manivannan, 2005: 175) that the Hadith[7] gives good guidance on how to tackle corruption and bring justice to the people. He noted the following:

> The Prophet said that any one of us who sees something wrong and indecent must try and change it with our hands, if we can. If we cannot do this, then we must try with our tongue, by speaking against it. If we cannot do that,

---

[7] Hadiths are a record of words and deeds of Prophet Muhammad.

then we must try with our heart. This means to pray and wish that it does not happen again. One can also disassociate oneself from it.

He pointed out that the Prophet has said that the latter is the weakest thing to do and instead one should be more involved in the reform of the society and in safeguarding justice and equality in society.

There is no doubt that you need to be mindful of the need for justice that is required for achieving sustainable development and such a system is created by understanding the root causes of poverty, which is rooted in social and economic injustice and exclusion. This understanding should transcend any religious boundaries.

Asian Wisdom: Democracy and Mass Communication

The study of mass communications has spread rapidly across the world in the past three decades along with the setting up of training institutes. The expansion has been quite rapid across Asia since the mid-1990s. But most of the textbooks used in Asian mass communication programs are mainly written by American scholars, and Asian scholars uncritically pass this knowledge and perspectives to their students, irrespective of whether it is relevant or not. Some see this as necessary in order to achieve higher international rankings for their universities/programs. Thus, inevitably, young Asians are being indoctrinated with the idea that anything worthwhile learning about mass communication, freedom, and justice comes from the West.

People across the globe, including Asia, believe that democracy, mass media, and human rights are European innovations. It is supposed to be common knowledge that democracy originated in ancient Greece in the 5th century BCE, but we are kept in ignorance about the people's assemblies that existed in Vedic societies in India much before that, known as "samitis" and "sabhas" (Misra, 2000).

The Vedic period (1500–500 BCE) was the earliest period where Hindu scriptures, the "Vedas," were composed. It was the time when Indo-Aryans settled in northern India and societies were formed along with the formation of Hindu religious traditions. The societies formed had a chief called "rajan" whose powers were restricted by people's councils called "sabha" and "samiti," which were responsible for the governance of the societies. The "rajan" was actually elected or approved by these bodies. The "sabha" was believed to be meetings of the community leaders/elders while the "samiti' was more like a people's village council. Singh (1998) notes that the two assemblies formed an essential feature of the government in the ancient Vedic societies as described in the Vedas.

> Although it is difficult to distinguish between a "sabha" and "samiti," it appears that "samiti" was the august assembly of a larger group of people for the discharge of tribal (i.e. political) business and was presided over by the king, while the "sabha," a more select body, was less popular and political in character than a "samiti." Although the functions and the powers of "sabha" and "samiti" cannot be exactly defined, numerous passages referring to them clearly indicate that both these Assemblies exercised considerable authority and must have acted as healthy checks on the power of the king. (Singh, 1998: 8)

Isn't it what we today assign as the role of national assemblies, city halls, and village councils in modern democracies? The current system of democracy is becoming corrupted at its roots due to the Western system of multiparty democracy, creating a system of what has come to be known today as "money politics." Its weaknesses have been well-illustrated by the debates that have generated about election funding and its sources during the 2016 US election campaigns and its aftermath.

As nationally syndicated, American daily talk show host Thom Hartmann (2017) noted after the election of President Donald Trump:

> There's a simple reality here: The Republican Party is the wholly owned front for billionaires and transnational corporations. The Democratic Party, since the creation of Al From and Bill Clinton's DLC,[8] have aspired to become the same only for the "white collar" top 10%.

In 1998, in Indonesia, the overthrow of the Suharto regime, which ruled the country with an iron-fist for three decades, heralded a new era of multiparty democracy. A few years into it, there was much concern about money politics corrupting the system. During the rule of Megawati Sukarnoputri, an Indonesian journalist told me that during Suharto's time, corruption was under the table and when democracy dawned it came over the table—"now even the table is corrupt."

With modern democracies in crisis, should we not be looking at those ancient systems of grassroots-based democracies to create a better system of

---

[8] Democratic Leadership Council (DLC) was founded in 1985 by Al From to steer away the Democratic Party from its Leftish views toward the middle to appeal to American middle class. It was dissolved in July 2011 and its records purchased by the Clinton Foundation.

governance at the local level that could gradually filter through to national levels? In some way, China seems to be doing this by tackling corruption at local party level first. The Holy See, in their argument about improving moral values at family and society level (discussed earlier), tend to be promoting such a strategy.

And when it comes to mass media, we teach in universities across the world—including Asia—that it originated with the Gutenberg Bible printed in movable type in the 15th century in Germany. Again, we ignore the fact that six centuries earlier the Chinese had printed the Buddhist Diamond Sutra on the block type (Morgon, 2012). In fact, it was the Chinese who invented paper and printing, and after the Tripitaka[9] was written at Aluvihare in Sri Lanka in the 1st century BCE, it was the written and later printed word that spread Buddhism across Asia.

If the origins of the mass media are about spreading knowledge via the printed text, shouldn't this be the beginning of the mass media? Why is Asia's role in these developments not acknowledged in our mass communication textbooks?

It is important that young Asians are given a balanced knowledge about their own ancient wisdom, especially its role in shaping political systems and communication models. If not, they would be vulnerable to accepting anything that is presented from the West as modernity and will not look into developing indigenous systems of communications that could be more appropriate to local needs and cultural norms to promote SDGs. They would also have a closed mind toward sharing expertise with fellow Asians; rather, they would look up to Western "experts" all the time.

Balancing of Communication Theory

In the past two decades, as mass communication departments and schools across Asia have grown, there has been an increasing debate about de-westernizing communication theory, at least that taught in Asian institutions. It should be called "balancing" rather than "de-westernization." Accompanying this has also been a debate on "Asian values" in journalism.

---

[9] Tripitaka refers to three categories of Buddhist texts that are called the Buddhist cannon. It consists of Buddha's sermons (*sutras*), codes of conduct for monks (*vinaya*), and Buddhist psychology (*abhidhamma*).

What makes a theory "Asian?" As Dissanayake (1988: 6) noted:

> If Asian scholars are to come up with models of communication which bear the imprint of their own cultures and which will enable them to comprehend better and conceptualize more clearly the complexity of human communication, it is indeed imperative that they shake off the influence of the mechanistic Aristotelian model. They need to address their mind to the task of finding out how best they can draw upon the cumulative wisdom of Asian human sciences as a means of formulating theories and models of communication that reflect the cultural ethos of the people, and for that very reason, are more pertinent and heuristically useful.

Asian human sciences are predominantly based on Hindu, Buddhist, Confucius, and Daoist philosophical teachings and ideas. The question here is whether contemporary Asian communication scholars are well-versed in these philosophies.

Wang and Shen (2000) note that even though there is a growing community of Asian communication scholars and journals dedicated to the study of communications in Asia, Asian communication researchers are yet to accomplish the mission to come up with Asian communication theories. While Dissanayake's (1998) book on Asian communication theory helped to shed some light on Asian philosophical thinking and traditions of communication to guide the researchers, there is a need of conducting authentic research and theory construction, which is still lacking.

> Until today there have been few communication theories that can be labeled undoubtedly "Asian." This is serious because theories have a specific role to play in social scientific research: they are not just demonstration of original thinking, but determine the direction and the structure of inquiry. Every time "Western" theories were shown to be inadequate in explaining changes in Asia, and every time Asian values and traditions were mentioned to suggest theoretical development, those in the Asian academic community are confronted with the question, "Where is 'Asian' communication theory?" The inability to come up with a satisfactory answer indicates "mission unaccomplished," thus a lack of substantial contribution to the field of communication from the part of the Asian researcher. (Wang and Shen, 2000: 15)

Though this observation was made over 15 years ago, nothing much has changed. One major impediment may be the mindset of Asian communication researchers who look up to Western researchers and institutions for guidance and recognition. Changing mindsets does not imply outright rejection of Western theories, but examining these critically with a good understanding of our own sociocultural context and its application to such circumstances.

Most of the contemporary media theories were first developed in Europe in the 19th and early 20th century, and later further developed and amplified in the United States. Despite the claims to be universal, these theories were marked by their own cultural context and circumstances of time and place. As McQuail (2000) observes, these theories had a Christian bias, particularly toward the Protestant forms of Christianity, which was associated with capitalism and modernity. Thus, with its predominant attitude of superiority that justified the wonders of industrialism, power of capitalism, benefits of bureaucracy, and the rule of law, they were able to communicate the idea that the Western world's global project of colonialism was legitimate.

Even today, what we call the "global media," which is basically the Anglo-American media, reflects such communication systems of invoking legitimacy on Western-dominated systems and ideas/ideologies.

Earlier in this chapter, we discussed Sivaraksa's criticism of the Bretton Wood system consisting of the WB and the IMF. But this view is not universally accepted. This system is usually seen as working for the good of the world by regulating, monitoring, and guiding the world financial system, even though it was heavily slanted to serve the Western economic interests and their domination. Thus, when China announced plans to launch the Asian Infrastructure Investment Bank (AIIB) in 2015, the Western media's focus was on how the new bank may dilute good governance and anti-corruption criteria practiced by the WB and the Japan–West controlled Asian Development Bank, even though the latter has had accusations of corruption leveled against it for years. McChesney and Herman (1998) describe the Anglo-American global media as "missionaries of global capitalism" for promoting a neoliberal economic agenda.

Another area of obvious bias is in reporting human rights and global conflicts. Today, this global media acts in unison in promoting a gospel of human rights with international human rights organizations that are mainly funded by Western "donor" agencies. They accuse non-Western governments of war crimes, especially in Africa and Asia, but turn a blind eye to worse war crimes in the Middle East and in Afghanistan/Pakistan by the West, often using the term "collateral damage" to describe these acts. Here, the psychology is that the West always acts for the common good of humanity.

Around 2014, when the Islamic terror group ISIS started using sophisticated social media digital technology to reach Western youth, attempts by Western governments to block their websites and pressure Facebook and other new media technology providers to take off their postings were hailed as measures to fight terrorism and protect social harmony. However, when the Chinese (or any other non-Western) government does the same to block youth groups using social media to bring social chaos (which is also a form of terrorism) to the country, it is condemned as infringing on the freedom of expression.

McQuail (2000) argues that to expose Eurocentric bias in Western media, communication researchers need to come up with a set of sub-questions, such as, tracing the sources of Western media bias and forms and levels of expression and solutions to solving such bias. "It is hard to ignore the fact that most media theorizing has been done by 'Western' scholars, living in and observing the media of their own countries and inevitably influenced by their own familiar social cultural context and its typical values" (p. 6).

Asian scholars need to come up with theories to explain the psychology of such thinking (as noted earlier) by the Western media. It is also imperative that Asian scholars take a fresh look at the freedom of expression theories in the context of recent developments globally where the West funds and uses nongovernmental organizations (NGOs) to create chaos in countries whose governments are not subservient to Western interests, using human rights as a cover. The lessons of the "Arab Spring" need to be taken into account, and perhaps, communication theories need to be formulated using Asian philosophical principles of communicating mindfully to promote harmony. Such communications need to be seen in the context of providing justice to socially, culturally, and economically excluded segments of the population through action that are rooted in moral values that generate compassion and kindness, not mobilize restless youth to create social chaos.

The Western model of journalism tends to be too adversarial and creates a negative bias in news reporting. Is the "fourth estate" theory of journalism to blame for this negative reporting? If so, can Asia offer a better theory of journalistic practices that could promote cooperation and harmony rather than focus on conflict?

Gunaratne et al. (2015: 5) espouse a "mindful journalism" path based on Buddhist principles to overcome this negativity and bias. "The aim of mindful journalism is not profit making," he argues, "but truthful reporting without institutional restraints that might defile the clarity of the trained journalist's mind."

In their book *Mindful Journalism and News Ethics in the Digital Age*, Gunaratne, Pearson, and Senarath (2015: 18) described the theory of mindful journalism based on the Buddhist Four Noble Truths thus:

> Mindful Journalism requires the journalist to understand the reasons for sorrow/unhappiness, and to desist from using his/her craft to increase desire (tanha) and clinging (upadana). We extracted this principle from the first and

the second truths. The mindful journalist must distinguish between pleasure and happiness to understand the reality that cyclic existence (samsara) means suffering (dukkha) that one can avoid only by attaining Nibbana or enlightenment. Pleasure is physical and short-lived whereas happiness is mental and long-lasting. The mindful journalist must not mislead the people that lasting happiness is attainable without purifying their minds from defilements. Enlightenment means eradication of all fetters—the mental state of supreme bliss or Nibbana. S/he should understand the reasons for the existence of unhappiness (dukkha), and desist from using journalism to knowingly promote attachment (upadana) and desire (tanha).

Gunaratne et al. make the point that the Western approach to journalism is more concerned with a negative rather than a positive approach and generally means the immunity of the communication outlets from government control or censorship either directly through laws and regulation or indirectly through economics and political pressures.

Park (2015) expresses a similar view and argues that we should change the adversary style of journalism to a more cooperative and active problem-solving style of journalism. In order to do this, journalists should enhance their views broadly and deeply. He quotes Taoist philosopher Chuangtzu's parable of a frog in a well: "You cannot speak of ocean to a well frog, which is limited by his abode." Thus, if we cling to a narrow sphere like a well frog, we will not able to see the great ocean. In the same way, it is necessary for a journalist to keep a non-biased view when reporting on social issues as well as actively solving problems. A journalist need not be hostile toward the government; the role of the journalists could extend to reporting on social problems in our communities in cooperation with government officials and nongovernment specialists based upon clear and concise analyses of contemporary social issues.

"Four Theories of the Press" (Seibert et al., 1956 cited in Nordenstreng, 1997) has for more than half a century defined the role of journalism and the media across the world with its all-encompassing media function theories of Libertarian, Authoritarian, Social Responsibility, and Communist models. The Libertarian theory has underpinned the Western "free" media model of the privately owned media being the "watchdog" of governments' abuse of power—what is known as the "fourth estate" principle.

But lately, with the mainstream media across the world becoming excessively commercial, Edward Herman and Noam Chomsky's "Propaganda Model" and "Manufacturing Consent" of the news media theories have been gaining traction. They argue that

The mass media serve as a system for communicating messages and symbols to the general populace. It is their function to amuse, entertain, and inform, and to inculcate individuals with the values, beliefs, and codes of behaviour that will integrate them into the institutional structures of the larger society. In a world of concentrated wealth and major conflicts of class interest, to fulfil this role requires systematic propaganda.[10]

There are two principles based on Asian traditional thinking that an Asian theory of media function could offer an alternative—taking into account the idea that things are impermanent and subject to change, thus being mindful of this change, and being able to understand, acknowledge, and analyze it to assist people and society to adjust to these changes. The other, which naturally leads from the first, is that social harmony is paramount and journalism should play a more positive role rather than an adversarial role.

A harmonious interdependent relationship is the cardinal idea of the Chinese culture, and Confucianism could give some guidance in formulating an alternative media function theory. Confucianism—which is at the heart of the traditional Chinese culture, the cosmology of yang/yin, and originally used to explain the origin of the universe in Daoism—is the metaphysical basis of philosophy. As Liu (2008) explains, yang and yin are considered as the two forces that regulate the universe with Yang representing masculinity, power, warmth, light, dryness, and hardness and yin representing femininity, passivity, cold, darkness, moisture, and softness.

Thus, Liu argues:

> Everything in the world carries yang and embraces yin and achieves harmony by balancing these two forces. Following this cosmology of yang/yin, Confucianism emphasizes a harmonious society and the appropriate arrangement of social relationships. In contrast to the western individualistic ideology of individual rights, equality and independence, in Confucian ideology, the harmony of society is based on hierarchical and asymmetrical relations between superior and subordinate; and social life is marked by a fundamental relatedness between the self and others, and between the individual and society. Such opposite but complementary forces as superior/subordinate, self/others and individual/society are dialogically interdependent in the process of communication and persuasion. The process of communication and persuasion, in turn, is the key to achieving harmony and to resolving conflicts in everyday interaction.

---

[10] http://www.thirdworldtraveler.com/Herman/Manufac_Consent_Prop_Model.html (accessed on September 15, 2017).

Referring to Confucius's advice to his students, Dan (2006: 22) quotes: "Everybody hopes to live a happy life, but, happiness is only a feeling, which has nothing to do with wealth or poverty, but with inner heart." Thus, the essence of Confucian thinking, she argues, is that you have to be yourself, but at the same time, you have to think about others.

Can this principle be adopted to develop a development communication strategy for sustainable development? How could you communicate a development paradigm that creates the concept of happiness not on material gains but gains of the inner heart?

Ranade (see Chapter 7) argues that *Rasa* is central to Indian communication. It is the nature of how an Indian interprets what is communicated to him/her. It invokes emotions to which one reacts and hopefully makes his/her life better. Information or news is like a performance; one absorbs and reacts to it. An understanding and application of Indian communication design can bring about a change in an individual's ability to live a good life. So should we look at a development communication strategy based on invoking emotions—positive rather than negative—on the receiver in order to absorb the message?

Adhikari (2008), in a comparative study of the Aristotelian model that underlies the Western communication theory and the Sadharanikaran model which she presents as a Hindu communication model, argues that the former is linear while the latter is nonlinear. The mechanistic linear views of the communication stem from rational, mathematical formulas, and Aristotelian models of persuasion and rhetorical analysis. The linear model seeks to represent communication in an oversimplified way. In Aristotle's model, the communicator is actively transmitting messages to a passive audience, who are not communicators, at least at present. The Sadharanikaran model, being a nonlinear model, incorporates the notion of a two-way communication process resulting in mutual understanding of the *sahridayas* (sender and receiver). Thus, the interrelationship between those communicating becomes unique. Its nonlinear structure and inclusion of elements such as context has profound consequences.

> Although the purpose of Sadharanikaran is to achieve commonness or oneness the process itself is an asymmetrical one. There is unequal sharing between communicator and receiver; there is a greater flow of communication from the former to the later.... They are not equal. The source is viewed as "higher" and the receiver as "lower." The relationship is hierarchical and that of "dominance" and "subordination." However, the source is held in high esteem by the receiver of communication, a relationship, idealized and romanticized in guru–chela relationship. Although the source and the receiver are unequal but

they are Sahridayas, which makes even unequal relationship/communication satisfying and pleasurable to both the parties involved. (Adhikari, 2008: 281)

With the advent of social media and community broadcasting across Asia, especially in the Indian subcontinent, it would be the best time to theorize the new communication models that are developing in very localized, rather than national setting. Perhaps, the traditional communication models that Adhikari and Ranade describe could be what is called participatory communication today. Could the concepts of *Rasa* be incorporated into the participatory communication theory?

Asian Paradigm of Development Communication

Filipino Bishop Julio Xavier Labayen argues that consumerism dominates our lives today and it stimulates emotional needs for the acquisition of consumable goods. In other words, it is the culture of consumerism that drives people's emotions and creates the desire for people to crave for goods that they do not need. "As such a culture develops, it eventually generates addiction," he points out. "People cannot distinguish anymore between the goods they 'desire' and goods they really need. The culture of consumerism shifts the point of reference effectively and systematically away from the human person and human relationships, and towards money."

Buddhism attributes people's unhappiness (*dukkha*) to three defilements—desire (*tanha*) and clinging (*upadana*) fostered by ignorance (*avijja*). Bishop Labayen explained these principles quite well in a modern social setting, and he hinted at how modern communications systems—what one would call the "corporate media"—create or foster these defilements.

In his book *Small Is Beautiful*, which he dubbed as *Buddhist Economics*, British economist E. F. Schumacher (1973: 57) argued some four decades ago that modern economists measure economic growth by the rate at which man consumes. "(He) is used to measuring the 'standard of living' by the amount of annual consumption, assuming all the time that a man who consumes more is 'better off' than a man who consumes less," he noted. "A Buddhist economist would consider this approach excessively irrational: since consumption is merely a means to human well-being, the aim should be to obtain the maximum of well-being with the minimum of consumption."

When journalists report about economics, it is often tempered with such data as statistics on economic growth, consumption, disposable incomes, stock market fluctuations, and the like. Rarely do they talk about how this data filter down to the people to impact on their lives and economic circumstances.

On May 9, 2016, Rodrigo Duterte, a mayor from the southernmost island of the Philippines, won a landslide victory in the presidential elections where the incumbent president Benigno Aquino's own candidate was a distant second. Aquino, who cannot stand for reelection under the Philippine Constitution, has presided over an economy that has recorded the most sustained economic growth in recent history, and he has been praised by both the local and international media for "good" economic management. But the "booming" economy has only benefited at most 1 percent of the population; most of the other 99 percent were living in *dukkha* (suffering), and they expressed their feelings at the ballot box, even though Duterte, during his campaign, threatened to kill criminals without going through the due legal process. This alarmed human rights activists, but not a large segment of the population. For them, the reason for their *dukkha* was rampant criminality and corruption. Mindful journalism should have picked up on it by investigating the reason for people's sufferings.

On November 6, 2016, the world was shocked when Donald Trump registered an emphatic victory in the presidency elections of the United States. He carried out a similar campaign to Duterte's, focusing on the *dukkha* of the White working class whose jobs had been slashed by greedy American companies that took their production base to low-wage countries, mainly in Asia. Thus, Middle America has seen a drop in their living standards due to globalization. One of the first acts of President Trump after his election as President of the USA was to pull his country out of the 12-nation Trans-Pacific Partnership (TPP) trade deal that would have taken more jobs out of America. It would also have given greater power to multinational corporations over sovereign governments and tighter protection on intellectual property rights that would have enriched global corporations such as pharmaceutical companies and made essential drugs dearer for the world's people.

The people's movements that are gathering momentum in the West are challenging the free-market globalization economic model. After the 2008 global financial crisis and its mounting social costs, economists in the West are also warming to the Buddhist concept of "gross national happiness" (GNH). Since 1971, the tiny Buddhist Kingdom of Bhutan in the Himalayas has rejected the GDP-based method to measure development and championed the GNH approach to development (see Chapter 11). In 2015, at the UN Climatic Change Conference, the world body adopted Bhutan's call for a holistic approach to development, a move endorsed by 68 countries. A UN panel is now considering ways on how Bhutan's GNH model can be replicated across the globe.

Meanwhile, Thailand's military government is promoting its late King's "Sufficiency Economics" model that was mooted at the peak of the 1997 financial meltdown in the kingdom. To this day, his idea has fallen on deaf ears in Asia. But after taking over the chairmanship of the G77 grouping of developing countries at the UN in 2016, Thailand organized a "Roundtable on Sufficiency Economics" in Bangkok in February, 2016, for G77 members. Prime Minister Prayut Chan-o-cha, in an address to the delegates, explained that this economic model focuses on three components—reasonableness, moderation, and self-immunity—along with two other conditions—knowledge and morality. "The concept emphasizes community development that strengthens the community to the self-supporting level," he was quoted by Thailand's MCOT News as telling the delegates.[11]

It is a lack of mindfulness and insights resulting in a lack of wisdom (*panna*) and compassion that makes the media report about "progress" through data and statistics and not by judging the happiness levels of the people, which is people-centered journalism. This trend is evident also in Europe and the USA, and you don't need to be a Buddhist to gain insights into it. It is there in the Catholic Church's teachings on "Liberation Theology," and Pope Francis has vehemently drawn attention to such economic injustices in the past couple of years.

Nepali journalist Kunda Dixit (1997: 7) argues that with the public service role of the media "being usurped" by business for which the definition of news is something that "has to sell," news has become a commodity rather than a public service. He notes that there is little difference today between selling news and hamburgers or blue jeans.

"Fewer and fewer people control the information we get," he argues. "And they are setting the agenda for the rest of us—how we should behave, what we should buy, which credit card we must use, what we should wear, what movies we can't afford to miss, what we should eat, (and) what we should smoke."

One of the pioneers of development communication, Sri Lankan media critic and journalist Tarzie Vittachi, who trained Asian journalists in development reporting in the 1960s and 1970s, argued in a UNTV interview in 1987 that development journalism is not about the good things governments do, but a "critically appreciative—not a hostile" look at the development process. Almost five decades ago, he challenged journalists to go beyond the headlines to the roots of the problems of poverty and prosperity, and report on them with passion, insight, and professionalism.

---

[11] http://thailand.prd.go.th/ewt_news.php?nid=2801&filename=index (accessed on September 15, 2017).

Dixit (1997) laments that governments hijacked Vittachi's noble intentions by asking their journalists to focus on development journalism, which governments interpreted as "a convenient label under which news agencies in developing countries could file propaganda disguised as news." He argues that this action derailed the struggle of non-Western journalists to develop an alternative paradigm of news to that of the West and "eroded moral argument for a South–South news exchange mechanism to supplement the Western wires."

Dixit made these observations two decades ago, and the struggle still continues as reflected in the contents of this book. In the following chapters, we will look at various aspects of developing a mindful communication strategy for sustainable development, drawing mainly from ideas of Asian scholars. We hope that this book would pave the way for a new development communication paradigm that will grow from Asia and that Asian governments would appreciate and encourage homegrown remedies for tackling problems of modern communication for sustainable development.

References

Adhikari, N. M. 2008. "The *Sadharanikaran* Model and Aristotle's Model of Communication: A Comparative Study." *Bodhi* 2 (1): 268–89.

Dan, Yu. 2006. *Confucius from the Heart: Ancient Wisdom for Today's World*. Beijing, China: Zhonghua Book Company.

Dissanayake, W., ed. 1988. *Communication Theory: The Asian Perspective*. Singapore: AMIC.

Dixit, K. 1997. *Dateline Earth: Journalism as if the Planet Mattered*. Manila: IPS.

Gunaratne, S. A., M. Pearson, and S. Senarath. 2015. *Mindful Journalism and News Ethics in the Digital Era*. New York, NY: Routledge.

Hart, W. 2012. *Vipassana Meditation: The Art of Living*. Igatpuri: Vipassana Research Institute.

Hartmann, T. 2017. "The Corporate Media Isn't Coming Close to Holding Trump Accountable." AlterNet, January 27. Available at http://www.alternet.org/news-amp-politics/corporate-media-isnt-coming-close-holding-trump-accountable (October 28, 2017).

Hutanuwatr, P., and R. Manivannan. 2005. *The Asian Future: Dialogue for Change*. London: Zed Books.

Liu, L. 2008. Yang and Yin in Communication: Towards a Typology and Logic of Persuasion in China. International Council for Philosophy and Humanist Studies. Available at http://dio.sagepub.com/cgi/content/abstract/55/1/120 (October 28, 2017).

McChesney, R., and E. Herman. 1998. *The Global Media: Missionaries of Global Capitalism*. New York, NY: Continuum.

McQuail, D. 2000. "Some Reflections on Western Bias of Media Theory." *Asian Journal of Communication* 10 (2): 1–12.

Misra, S. G. 2000. *Democracy in India*. New Delhi: Sanbun Publishers.

Morgon, J. 2012. "Buddhism's Diamond Sutra: Extraordinary Discovery of the World's Oldest Book." *Huffington Post*, November 12. Available at http://www.huffingtonpost.com/joyce-morgan/diamond-sutra-buddhas-hidden-book_b_1859164.html (October 28, 2017).

Nordenstreng, K. 1997. "Beyond the Fourth Theories of the Press." In *Media and Politics in Transition: Cultural Identity in the Age of Globalisation*, pp. 97–110. Netherlands: ACCO.

Park, Kwangsoo. 2015. "Mindful Communication for ASEAN Integration—Based on the Confucius and Tao of Asian Journalism." Paper Presented at the Chulalongkorn-UNESCO/IPDC seminar "Mindful Communication for ASEAN Integration," December 14 and 15, 2015, Chulalongkorn University, Bangkok.

Schumacher, E. F. 1973. *Small Is Beautiful: Economics If People Mattered*. New York City, NY: Harper and Row.

Singh, U. B. 1998. *Administrative System in India: Vedic Age to 1947*. New Delhi: APH Publishing.

Sivaraksa, S. 2009. *The Wisdom of Sustainability: Buddhist Economics for the 21st Century*. Hawaii: Koa Books.

Wang, G., and V. Shen. 2000. "East, West, Communication, and Theory: Searching for the Meaning of Searching for Asian Communication Theory." *Asian Journal of Communication* 10 (2): 13–52.

SECTION A

Philosophical Perspectives

1

Mindfulness in Communication: A Buddhist Approach

Venerable Phuwadol Piyasilo

I studied mass communication more than 20 years ago as I aimed to be a journalist. But my life took a different turn and I have been a forest monk in a remote area of Thailand for the past 21 years. So when I got this assignment to write about mindfulness in communication, I Googled the word "mindfulness" and came up with 29 million results on the Internet. When it came to mindfulness in communication, there were 25 million results. Thus, if you want to learn about mindfulness, there is a lot of information out there.

Before we understand communication, we have to understand mindfulness. I think the best way to understand mindfulness is to express it. May I ask you to put this book aside and sit still for a few minutes and see if you can bring your mind and your attention to the present moment? Gently bring your attention to your own breath and close your eyes. And try to be fully aware of the present moment. Can you see how your mind works, how thoughts arise, emotions arise? You can pen down your thoughts and emotions.

I think those of us who tried doing this exercise, to express the real meaning of mindfulness, will see that it is not easy to be only with yourself in this present moment. So when we try to find definitions of mindfulness on the Internet, and even among venerable monks like myself, we get different opinions on it. It may seem quite simple to me, but you will find numerous definitions for it.

In the Buddhist philosophy, the real meaning of mindfulness is to remember. Perhaps, mindfulness has to do with memory, but what I will discuss it as is to remember something in any given situation. We have to keep in mind not to let any given situation distract us from what we are thinking. In some ways, this has to do with being in the present moment and not to get distracted from the thoughts and emotions that arise from the present situation.

Lot of people translate *sati* as mindfulness and explain it as awareness. In a lot of instances, particularly in the West now, we have found that mindful practices are very useful, especially for people working in the mental health sector. They see that practicing mindfulness could become very useful in dealing with stress and depression. If you Google it, you will find numerous articles and resources on how mindfulness can work in this area.

But mindfulness practices in the West are usually found to be secular. People there try to practice it without adding any religious value to it. This has become problematic because it could manifest itself with the wrong intentions. When you apply Buddhist teachings, mindfulness is accompanied by *panna* (wisdom). Without this moral framework, the practice by itself would not be enough to fast-track us into the right direction. We need to incorporate *panna* into the mindfulness practice itself. To become successful on the path to become mindful, you need to develop this approach of accompanying mindfulness.

If you look at mindfulness as simply awareness or focusing attention, let us take, for example, the attempt of trying to catch a mouse. The cat would have mindfulness (in plotting to catch the mouse), but we would not consider it right mindfulness (*samma sati*), because the aim is to kill, to cause harm to another living being. So it is important that we focus on mindfulness as something that has to have some moral framework to it. This will then become very useful in working with communication itself.

Another aspect of mindfulness is what we can call self-awareness. You are fully aware of your body sensations and feelings and thoughts that arise in your mind. This is the Buddhist idea of self—that bodily sensations affect our mind. As you can see, it is very obvious that when you are distracted by your feelings and your thoughts, it will not be easy to be objective, to understand something as it is.

In terms of interpersonal communication where we relate to people around us, we can see how we communicate when we have emotions arising in our mind. When you are angry with someone, how can you be mindful and choose the right words in this situation? So you can see how mindfulness or *sati* becomes useful in communication.

Let me apply this to broader media and especially social media that we are now experiencing. One cannot be mindful while being distracted by feelings and emotions. To see the situation as it is, you need to see what is happening, or what you want to happen, or how they think about what is happening. Otherwise this situation becomes a problem in itself.

I had a friend who worried himself when reporting about the numbers of protestors. He had to ask himself why there are so many news agencies and they have such differences in the way they report the numbers of protestors. The situation is there for everyone to see. But one would say that there are 500 people, and another would say 2,000 people. My friend said that the process of crafting the news changes the numbers, because by the time the news comes out in the newspaper the numbers could change from 500 to 2,000. So the way they represent reality does not seem to be the real fact at all because it is clouded by opinions and feelings.

Since we are talking about *sati* and *panna*, we have to develop those into communication. In Buddhist teachings, we focus a lot on suffering. So practicing Buddhism and applying these practices to the communication process, we can look at how we analyze suffering and can help other people to reduce their sufferings, aiming to reduce it in everyday life (in society). So this is something we can contribute by making communication better, not promote conflicts and suffering.

What we see on television, newspapers, and social media is not news that will promote understanding and peace. Without trying to create harmony and bring peace, what the media is doing is making conflicts stronger and leading to misunderstandings. Considering the current conflicts in many countries in the world, and especially Thailand itself, some of you may know about the political conflict between the red shirt and the yellow shirt. I consider this a good example of how not being mindful could cloud the way you present the news and also the way people receive the news.

I have a friend from Isan[1] and I can see how people there receive the news and how they want to see the news. They have ideas on how they want the news to be presented. Even in Bangkok,[2] the facts are there to be seen, but the way to present them is different for both sides. It is about how they feel about it and how they like it to be reported.[3]

I hope that learning to put mindfulness or *sati* into practice, not only at a personal level but also at the level of the media, will help us to promote peace and understanding, and not become part of the problem. Moreover, we need to work more on finding solutions to help others to reduce their suffering.

---

[1] Isan is in the northeast of Thailand, the heartland of the red shirt movement.

[2] Bangkok is considered the heartland of the pro-monarchist yellow shirt movement.

[3] The red shirts are mainly rural farmers from the northeast of Thailand as well as some students, Leftist activists, and some business people who see the attempts by the urban and military elites to control Thai society as a threat to democracy. Thus, their movement started as United Front for Democracy Against Dictatorship. Yellow shirts, known as the Peoples' Alliance for Democracy, is a loose alliance of royalists, ultra-nationalists, and urban middle class.

Much of the suffering comes from misunderstanding. I cannot help the feeling that if some of my friends, from both red shirts and yellow shirts, understand and accept the information from the other side, it will be possible to talk to each other, in spite of having some disagreements.

If you block yourselves from listening, if your mind is wandering around without trying to understand what is being conveyed to you, you would not understand what the other side is trying to do. So you need to listen and try to comment on what you think about what you hear from the other side.

Putting mindfulness into practice is the ability to develop wisdom to often listen to views from both sides and not prejudge other people too soon. This will be a very powerful tool (communication process) to promote peace and understanding. And this would be useful to create a community living in harmony. We could try to help each other with *karuna* (compassion) and *metta* (loving kindness)[4] to reduce our and others' suffering.

---

[4] Loving-kindness is a meditation practice, which brings about positive attitudinal changes as it systematically develops the quality of "loving-acceptance." It acts, as it were, as a form of self-psychotherapy, a way of healing the troubled mind to free it from its pain and confusion— refer to Buddhanet http://www.buddhanet.net/e-learning/loving-kindness.htm (accessed on September 15, 2017).

2

Mindful Communication for Sustainable Development

Sulak Sivaraksa

I would like to give you a perspective of a socially engaged Buddhist as well as that of a historian of Thai Buddhist traditions. I would like to start this discussion with some thoughts on the topic of mindfulness.

Mindfulness has become very popular in recent years, particularly in Europe and North America as well as in other parts of the world. Magazines, journals, television programs, and documentaries have been exploring it and also symposiums and conferences. There is a lot of interest in mindfulness globally. This is becoming fashionable among the middle and upper classes. Many people are coming to the practice of mindfulness for its proven health benefits, for its ability to relieve stress. But from an Engaged Buddhist perspective, these are only secondary benefits not the actual aims of a meditation practice.

This meditation practice stripped of its ethical framework can be a form of escapism. In the teachings of the Buddha, meditation and mindfulness are intended to bring about the elimination of suffering—both of personal internal kinds and that brought about by external factors such as climate change and structural violence[1] (see Box 1.1).

We cannot just run away from the sufferings of the world. We have to face these challenges by combining personal dimensions with work in the world.

We must ask what exactly do we mean when we talk about mindfulness. In its original Pali form, mindfulness comes with *sati*; in various Buddhist traditions, it has a range of implications and meanings. There are aspects of the teachings of the Buddha, that is, ethics and motivation. It is indispensable that when it comes to meditation and mindfulness you have to take it with *sati*. For most Pali words, there are no direct English translations. So we start with the meaning using mindfulness.

---

[1] Watch Sulak Sivaraksa's address to the Economics of Happiness conference in California in March 2012 on the structural violence of the global economy via https://vimeo.com/50242423

The word *sati* literary means remembering or recollecting, or recalling something; the opposite term is forgetfulness. In its original context, spoken by the Buddha, *sati* has a variety of indications, which are not really captured using the term mindfulness. *Sati* or recollections can be remembrance of things in the past, to remember what one is doing at present with awareness in the present moment, and also remembering things for the future, hopes and aspirations. Furthermore, in the context of meditation, mindfulness is a power, the skill that allows one to maintain the awareness of the object of meditation.

In Asia today, the term mindfulness has very different connotations. It is often described as something akin to a state of moment to moment awareness. This understanding of what it means comes partly from an American doctor, who has background in Zen training,[2] but he importantly followed from other traditions in his interpretation of this definition.

It will be a wonderful thing to practice; for some it may bring a lot of benefits. But it has wide meaning in the Buddhist tradition. It cannot be separated from what the Buddha taught in the Noble Eightfold Path, the Buddhist path of enlightenment. Without the rest of the Noble Eightfold Path including ethics, without proper motivation, the motivation to benefit others, to seek enlightenment could be harmful. To seek mindfulness exclusively has the potential to evolve into something unwholesome, something negative.

Recently, we have had McMindfulness. Mindfulness in its current secularized definition is simple, non-judgmental, and ethically neutral. This practice, when de-conceptualized from the rest of the Buddha's path and used for a range of ends, could be sinister. We see this manifesting in big corporate CEOs going for mindfulness (training). When building up empires, taking up this meditation practice without the ethics (wisdom) will not see his mind changing for the better (of humankind) or becoming benevolent, more compassionate, more wise.

Without a sense of universal responsibility, corporate CEO and others will relieve stress and focus their minds so that they can be more clever businessmen and make more money without improving themselves or the world. Mindfulness without ethics will reduce stress and focus their minds to pursue corporate goals including activities that would promote pollution of the

---

[2] Dr Jon Kabat-Zinn is internationally known for his work as a scientist, writer, and meditation teacher engaged in bringing mindfulness into the mainstream of medicine and society. He is Professor of Medicine emeritus at the University of Massachusetts Medical School, where he founded its world-renowned Mindfulness-Based Stress Reduction Clinic (in 1979), and the Center for Mindfulness in Medicine, Health Care, and Society (in 1995).

environment and ultimately result in global warming. These types of practices have the potential to building a world facilitating more greed and delusions.

This type of mindfulness can lead to wrong livelihood contrary to the teachings of Buddhism. The Buddha taught right mindfulness, *samma sati*. Right mindfulness in Buddhism is different to the neutral form of mindfulness that is attracting attention. If mindfulness is ethical, it will help ourselves and others to bring about a peaceful life. *Sila* or ethics are the foundations for uprooting the three poisons—greed, hatred, and delusion—for the elimination of suffering in ourselves and the world.

The Noble Eightfold Path works together as an interdependent system designed to overcome negative qualities and cultivate wholesome positive aspects within ourselves and the world, a system that has compassion, wisdom, and kindness. We should not overlook these principles of Buddhism to work for the benefit of others and cultivate mindfulness in a way that is lacking in *sila* and devoid of right motivation and right effort.

Mindfulness and meditation could be used to build egos to generate greed, hatred, and delusion, bringing us to egohood instead of Buddhahood.

A critical aspect of the Buddha's teachings is the non-wholesome and wholesome state of mind, so that we encourage the antidotes of the three poisons—generosity, compassion, and wisdom. Mindfulness that consists of moment-to-moment non-judgmental awareness may be beneficial to many people, but more than that mindfulness is needed to develop communication to tackle the issues of climate change and environmental sustainability. Mindful communication including mindful speech and deep listening are important. But we must not overlook the role of compassion, wisdom, and critical thinking in communication. We must be able empathize with others to see things from their perspective. We should not continue with our narrow prejudices so that we can start meaningful relationships with others. We can then come more easily to agreement and work together.

Right speech is to get over our fears of telling the truth so not to endanger our friends, brothers, and sisters, truth that will be initially hard to hear but at the end it would be beneficial. Proper education that will help society is essential in order to develop mindful communication. People are not taught the truth about things such as climate change, structural violence, and solutions to deforestation. In a world of lies and deceit, individuals must be able to distinguish facts from fiction, so that they could skillfully work through the solution rather than offering propaganda.

Advertising in the mainstream media promotes useless damaging products and unwholesome ideas which lead people away from meaningful life of contentment and humanity, instead leading to unsustainability and a society of separation from others and our natural world.

Why are the media preoccupied with so many negative things in the world? So many of you know that much of the media exists to make profits, often at the expense of larger humanitarian concerns. Some of the media says that climatic change is a hoax.

Critical (mindful) thinking means deeper understanding of the nature of modern institutions and social structures. You should not be hypnotized and misled by the glamorous garbage that media messages convey to you. Critical thinking is the antidote necessary to prevent some of these disturbing trends in the future.

In conclusion, let me remind you that the three poisons—greed, hatred, and delusion—are at the root of our personal suffering. Mindfulness is not enough; rather, through contemplative meditation on ethics and the rest of the Noble Eightfold Path, the poisons can be rooted out, leading us into generosity, loving kindness, and wisdom. Our minds and hearts have to change, with compassion to the world and sharing with others. The individualistic attitude prevalent today needs to change with the understanding of the interdependent reality.

Box 1.1
Structural Violence—Even Buddhists Cannot Avoid It

> Before talking about structural violence, let me give some background about Buddhism and traditional Buddhist societies in Southeast Asia. Buddhism teaches the elimination of violence entirely, both intra-psychically and interpersonally.
>
> Violence is connected with what Buddhists call the "Three Poisons": greed, hatred, and delusion. Buddhist practice to transform those poisons occurs in the context of the sangha (the spiritual community), set up to make possible the elimination of violence. Members of monastic communities, for example, attempt to live a harmonious life with the other monks and nuns, with the lay people, with the animals, and with the environment. Even lay people avoid professions that are linked to violence, such as trading in arms, intoxicants, slaves, or animals, or being a soldier. Lay people also practice the five ethical precepts (refraining from killing, stealing, harmful speech, sexual misconduct, and misuse of drugs) and try to avoid violence as much as possible.
>
> In simple agrarian societies, the issue of structural violence arises infrequently, although clearly hierarchies according to wealth, power, and gender exist. For example, my wife's grandmother is regarded as a very rich lady in her province in Thailand, but her lifestyle is almost exactly the same as

everyone around her. Her mother had to tend the fields just like any of the poorer people. With the wealth she accumulated, she built a traditional temple to help develop the sangha.

The weakness of Buddhism in Southeast Asia is that Buddhists do not deal with the power structure, which, even in Buddhist kingdoms, has always been guided by Hindu values. That arrangement is based on the theory of the chariot that needs "two wheels"; the wheel of righteousness is represented by the monastic sangha, the wheel of power by the king. Monks would talk to the rulers but refrained from holding power. They gave consolation to soldiers and went on military expeditions, although the Buddha limited such trips by the monks to one week.

The Buddha generally saw the state as being like a poisonous snake. One does not kill it; that would be violence. One deals with it through "skillful means"— being kind, but remembering that it is a poisonous snake! Unfortunately, in the last 100 years, this critical view of the state has not been stressed in Thailand.

The weakness in the separation of the "two wheels" is that a person who avoids power does not understand much about it. The sangha tries to influence the state to be less violent. But at least in the Southern School of Buddhism, the attempt to eliminate violence is entirely on the personal level, occurring ideally through the career of the monks or nuns. There is a minimal understanding of structural violence.

In the last 50 years, the Western model of "development" has largely transformed the traditional rural way of life, centered in the village and temple, and structural violence has greatly increased. In this period, Buddhist alternatives to development have been largely limited to small communities of forest monks who try to have nothing to do with the values and violence of mainstream society. That approach presupposes that violence does not reach the forest and that the forest will be protected. But who nowadays can protect the forest? In the old days, the righteous ruler had to protect the animals and the forest as well as the villages. Nowadays, violence, spread by the greed of capitalism and empire, has become the norm; there is nowhere to go. Even many Buddhists accept this norm.

Source: An excerpt from an interview done by Donald Rothberg with Sulak Sivaraksa in 1997 for the Helen Dwight Reid Educational Foundation. Full interview could be accessed from http://ccbs.ntu.edu.tw/FULLTEXT/JR-EPT/roth.htm (accessed on September 15, 2017).

3

Buddhist, Hindu, and Jain Contribution to Communication in Asia

Binod C. Agarwal

Sixth century BCE, in many ways, was the landmark century in the evolution of spiritual unrest, rebellious thoughts, and advent of two religious philosophies, Buddhism and Jainism within *Sanatan Dharma* or Hinduism (Agrawal, 2015; Radhakrishnan, 1969). Hence, it is important to understand and discuss the concept of mindfulness in the framework of the Indian civilization.

While reviewing the literature on mindfulness in the Indian languages, and during discussion and deliberation, an interesting point emerged. Mindfulness must be viewed and examined within a historical context as it was originally pronounced, deliberated, and propagated in the pre-Christian era. The language of deliberation was Pali, which evolved from Sanskrit as a reaction to *Sanatan Dharma* (Hinduism) on the heels of the hegemony of growing importance of Hindu ritualism and sacrifice. *Sati* in Pali language emerged from the Sanskrit word *smriti*. Inherent in *smriti* is an accumulated wisdom of the past expressed in the present to understand and internalize within the sociocultural milieu of Hindu thought. The two-way, day-to-day verbal conversation and transaction of socially acceptable and desirable information, not necessarily toward achieving a goal, has been the basic form of communication in which verbal, nonverbal, and symbolic methods were followed.

Buddhists coined the concept of *sati* after detailed face-to-face dialogues and debates regarding its essential and inherent content. Whether the Buddha participated in the deliberations has not been ascertained. Hence, it is humbly requested to reconsider whether the translation of *sati* in English as mindfulness is appropriate though well accepted in English. It is important while expanding the scope of *sati* and its meaning.

The intention is not to raise such questions but reflect on the historical evolution and connection of *sati* and *smriti* which is well documented in the Buddhist literature. This viewpoint must be kept in perspective while deliberating on mindfulness and mindful communication. Also, clear distinction must be made between "mindful"—an adjective which means "conscious or aware of something"[1] and "mindfulness" which is a noun.

The concept of mindfulness originated in Buddhism as *sati* and was nurtured in South Asia initially and later spread in Thailand and other parts of Asia. At a much later date, it was introduced and followed in the English-speaking world (Kuan, 2008).

Interreligious Understanding of Mindfulness

The Buddha, while wedded to *Sanatan Dharma* (Hinduism), strongly opposed to the then prevailing ritualism and sacrifices in Hinduism. The Buddha's conception of dharma or righteousness was an imminent order denoting the law of nature and driving principle of the universe (Radhakrishnan, 1969: 341).

On the other hand, Mahavir denied the existence of God but accepted the notion of moksha like Hindus. In Jainism, the idea was propounded that the ability of *atamsamishan* (self-retrospection of soul) is inherent within human self-leading to mindfulness (Desai, 2008). Mahavir's thoughts were at variance with the Buddha, who advanced the concept of nirvana. Mahavir accepted the concept of moksha (Desai, 2008). Hinduism continues to defy any definition or single method of attaining moksha. At micro or village level, the structural basis of Hinduism is *Jati Pratha* or caste system and practiced as a "religious cult" with its multiple gods and goddesses; ritual purity and pollution; and sacred and non-sacred status of human body, object, and surroundings (Srinivas, 1952). Mathur (1964: 60) added, "The correct observance of positive injunctions of dharma is believed to earn spiritual merit for the individuals...." Due to unknown origin of *Sanatan Dharma*, notion of *dhamma* continues to puzzle scholars of religion.

These philosophical arguments tend to throw some new light on the concept of mindfulness within the subcontinent and elsewhere in Asia. Since Jainism remained confined within India, its impact was minimally felt in other parts of Asia and elsewhere in the world. So was the case with the Jain concept of mindfulness and the same holds true in the case of Hinduism, though the philosophical and religious fountain of Buddhism was anchored within *Sanatan Dharma* and its fundamentals. A great deal of research, religious debates, and deliberations have taken place among Buddhist scholars

---

[1] See *The Concise Oxford Dictionary*, Indian Edition (7th ed) (Oxford University Press 1999).

and practitioners on the issue of mindfulness. In spite of differences, Buddhist scholars have accepted the concept of mindfulness, and mindful communication is being practiced in one form or the other. In order to illustrate this point, it is imperative to refer to a scholarly work on the subject.

Buddhist Meaning of Mindfulness

Tse-fu Kuan (2008) has discussed and explained the concept of mindfulness in early Buddhism based on the original texts available in Pali, Chinese, and Sanskrit. Kuan (2008) considered and translated the Pali word *sati* and the Sanskrit word *Smriti* as mindfulness and thinks that "… *Sati* is a function of mind" (Kuan, 2008: 9):

> The scheme of the four satipattanas, establishments of mindfulness, is often used as the paradigm for the practice of sati. It consists of contemplations of four subjects: the body, feelings, mind, and dhammas.

Further, "*Sati* is regarded as *Vipassana* meditation, the authentic Buddhist meditative practice and is even interpreted as the only way to liberation [nirvana]" (Kuan, 2008: 9). However, a widely held opinion in Theravada Buddhism is that serenity meditation is not essential for the realization of nirvana. One of the major dimensions or aspects of *sati* in psychological prospective of Buddhist soteriology is that it functions as a wholesome component of personality and thereby enables us to attain the ultimate religious goal. Ven. Mahasi Sayadaw (1994 cited in Kuan, 2008: 118) says that contemplating the body, etc., externally refers to "contemplation to the life processes of others, by way of inference (*anumana*)."

The intention here is to put forward a view that even after more than two millennia, Buddhist scholars, religious leaders, and philosophers continue to debate about content function and meaning of "mindfulness" that would help achieve nirvana or religious goal as propounded by the Buddha. At the same time, the importance and utility of mindful communication in the contemporary context, in the midst of "digital revolution," has increased manifold. Also, the question of the Judo-Christian method of teaching journalism and media within largely linear conception of time and worldview negates other ways of conceptualizing the communication process largely inapplicable to the ASEAN region. As Kuan (2008: 139) notes, the practice of mindfulness could bring a transformational attitude that could help develop compassionate communication practices.

The practice of mindfulness is not only concerned with oneself, but it can also be altruistic. The process of developing loving kindness (metta) is a type of mindfulness that should be practiced to form one's ethical attitude towards all beings.

Communication Revolution in ASEAN

In the current techno-political situation, it seems essential to introduce the concept of mindfulness and its theoretical and philosophical postulates of mindful communication in teaching and research of journalism and media education in ASEAN. In doing so, communication and media scholars of ASEAN would free themselves from the enslavement of the Judo-Christian positivistic and inductive educational process. Rapid changes are visible in the midst of digital and communication revolution due to manifold increase in connectivity and multiple ways of sharing, storing, and reproducing information in Asian languages. It is imperative to take steps to integrate ASEAN comprising multireligious and multilingual countries, largely steeped in a colonial past, having experience of American, British, Dutch, and French colonial masters who ruled these countries, with the exception of Thailand.

Convergence of information and communication technology has all pervasive influences on education, society, and culture. Convergence of communication technology has drastically influenced journalism education and training in the 21st century world over in varying degrees along with democratic ideology and methods of religious propagation. At another level of communication technology, convergence can be seen the way information and communication technology has largely been integrated in broadcast, reception, and storage forcefully advocated by Euro-American countries and lately by China, Korea, and Japan.

Mindful Journalism and Media

The term mindful journalism has been used along with media given the growing influence of digital media in journalism. Buddhist scholars see change as an eternal element in the religious thought. It is well indicated in the following paragraph.

At the level of society at large, the mindful journalist could facilitate change to reduce the state of *dukkha* in society by exposing corruption among those entrenched in power and by helping people to purify their minds when attachment (*lobha*), aversion (*dosa*), ignorance (*moha*), and other related defilements create conditions that could propel them to commit violence. Mindful journalism might also focus on bringing about institutional changes to remove destructive conditions wrought by environmental destruction, resource depletion, and global warming. It might try to bring about middle-path solutions to lopsided income and wealth distribution, and also call for raising the standard of living of the masses through the cooperative movement and through *shramadanalsarvodaya* movement aimed at promoting self-governance and supply of voluntary labor. (Malikhao and Servaes, 2015: 50)

In the book *Mindful Journalism and News Ethics in the Digital Era*, the editors and the contributors have deliberated on the issue of mindful communication in detail. Malikhao and Servaes (2015: 50–61) have beautifully demonstrated the usefulness of Buddhist mindful communication in teaching journalism. The authors have quoted Thanissaro Bhikkhu who says, "Change is the focal point in Buddhist insight—a fact so well known that it has spawned a familiar bite: 'Isn't change what Buddhism is all about?'" (as cited by Malikhao and Servaes, 2015: 57).

In 2007, UNESCO expert committee formulated "Model Curricula for Journalism Education."[2] According to the UNESCO document, a curriculum in journalism education should include courses like "Foundations of journalism" to promote prerequisite intellectual and craft skills. Following are the foundation courses suggested by the UNESCO:

- An ability to think critically, incorporating skill in comprehension analysis, synthesis, and evaluation of unfamiliar material and a basic understanding of evidence and research methods.
- An ability to write clearly and coherently using narrative, descriptive, and analytical methods.
- Knowledge of national and international political, economic, cultural, religious, and social institutions.
- Knowledge of current affairs and issues and a general knowledge of history and geography.
  (Anonymous, 2007: 8)

The UNESCO attempt has been to create a multireligious journalism education. However, model curricula by and large remained Judo-Christian or

---

[2] Download from http://unesdoc.unesco.org/images/0015/001512/151209E.pdf

Euro-American in approach and incorporated a theoretical and ideological perspective being followed in the West.
Freedman, Rendahl, and Shafer (2009) argue:

> It can be argued that because the Western press model in its various forms is dominant in the most advanced, industrial, and post-industrial countries, it must inherently be the most effective at promoting and sustaining development. Under that argument, which the current UNESCO curricula assumes, that is the desirable model that journalists and news organisations in developing countries should master to further economic and other forms of growth in their own nations. This would seem to be a foundational premise of those who designed the curricula. There is unlikely to be a synthesis between the UNESCO curricula and one that encourages the practice of development journalism. Development journalism has interventionist and intentional characteristics that conflict with the objective and free-market orientations of Western journalism as reflected in the UNESCO curricula. In analysing the UNESCO model, it is evident that intentionality or intervention are omitted as objectives for journalism training and practice, and thus the model is inherently Western in ideology, content, and preferred practice.

The suggested UNESCO curricula lacked Asian cultural specificity needed in a multilingual, multireligious, and multisocial context of ASEAN. There is need to deliberate, discuss, and then develop curricula of journalism and media for learning of mindful communication education. It should be mentioned that the ASEAN academic community has been largely trained in the USA or Europe and followed journalism and media education, though they have differing opinions on the duration of the undergraduate degree and consequently the postgraduate program degree.

Singapore-based Asian Media Information and Communication Centre (AMIC), under a grant from the International Program for the Development of Communications (IPDC) of the UNESCO in 2009, compiled a set of Asian resource material to supplement four of the model curricula compiled by the UNESCO. This included "Media and Society," and three specialized journalism curricula such as development journalism and economic reporting.

Journalism and Media in ASEAN

Historically, Christian missionaries have played a catalyst role in the promotion and growth of journalism and media education with the assistance of the colonial rulers having vested interests. In the postcolonial phase, all efforts have been to promote journalism and media for the development of ASEAN. The cumulative effect has been "explosion" of journalism and media education with little effort to have context/culture specificity in Asia, particularly in ASEAN. Hence, it is appropriate to think of journalism and media education at crossroads in the wake of fast-changing information and communication technologies.

In a study of journalism education in Asia for AMIC, Muppidi (2008: 131) noted:

> In terms of the "philosophy" of what is to be taught, there is a basic confusion with the role and function of journalism itself. The much-brandied terms "watchdog of society", "fourth estate" and other similar functions are used in the same breath as "profit motives" and "audience ratings", now considered to be important in journalism. Some argue there is a shift away from "professional journalism" to "sensationalism" or "rating driven" stories to even promoting one "ideology" over another, religious or otherwise. Across the board, there is a demand for professionally trained journalists but there is no systematic and consistent procedure outlined for doing so for skills, critical ability, and stress on output, rather than process. There is also an increase in advocacy journalism.

Further, it should be kept in view that journalism and media practice and education has been "grafted" in living civilizations of several countries of Asia having multiple faiths and practices, well-established theatrical traditions, and various living forms and methods of preaching religion and religious doctrines (Agrawal, 2015). Also in Asian countries, print media and film remained largely in the hands of private entrepreneurs, whereas colonial governments exclusively controlled and managed radio and telecommunication and imposed the language of the rulers. In the recent past, both government and private companies manage a large part of operations of radio, television, and telecommunications requiring separate training and educational philosophy keeping in mind the requirements.

In ASEAN, there has been unprecedented expansion of cable TV, in country-specific languages of national and transactional private satellite television, and now direct-to-home (DTH) television along with transnational programs in the colonial languages. So is the case with print media, radio, Internet, and telecommunications.

The proposal is to create a professional mechanism to list out all such institutions under the preview of an expert independent body to help the introduction of mindful communication teaching, for its healthy growth, and to meet the growing ASEAN national needs of trained human power.

Need for Research

The last point that must be touched upon relates to journalism and media research in the mindful communication teaching program. Recently, scholars have highlighted the need for culture- and context-specific research for South Asia (Agrawal, 2011). Private satellite television and print media companies have started spending enormous money to find out who is buying their newspapers or keeping FM radio or television on. But little efforts have been made to carry out journalism, media, and communication research to incorporate mindful communication within the Asian cultural domain. It is suggested that all efforts should be made to encourage mindful communication research and the same must be integrated in teaching. The teaching must include research as an essential element of the curriculum. Fundamental research in human communication within ASEAN multireligious worldview is essential for having multimillennia old traditions of oral communication to improve the quality of journalism and media mindful communication education.

In post-World War II Asia, several scholars having strong leanings to Buddhism and *Shantan Dharma* have examined the effects of culture contact with colonial powers. As Dissanayake (1988: 6) argues:

> If Asian scholars are to come up with models of communication which bear the imprint of their own cultures and which will enable them to comprehend better and conceptualized more clearly the complexity of human communication, it is indeed imperative that they shake off the influence of the mechanistic Aristotelian model. They need to address their mind to the task of finding out how best they can draw upon the cumulative wisdom of Asian human sciences as a means of formulating theories and models of communication that reflect the cultural ethos of the people, and for that very reason, are more pertinent and heuristically useful.

Asia's experience of culture contact has not been unique, though the outcome distinctly differed. Changes have been observed in the external appearance without altering the social structure such as family and, to a large extent, religion and language. The process of culture contact, it is believed, has been further stimulated by communication explosion without making further dent in the very core of the Asian civilizations. However, internally directed, planned, and sponsored changes continue to dominate the Asian civilizations such as China, ASEAN, and South Asia. So far, Euro-American owned and regulated transnational television, radio, and print media have marginal role to play in bringing about deep sociocultural changes to homogenize the Asian civilizations by Euro-American education.

Efforts are required to save ASEAN from becoming a cultural colony dependent on ideas and views from the West. It has its own cultural and religious strength, provided mindful communication is introduced in journalism and media education (Agrawal, 2005).

References

Agrawal, Binod C. 2005. "Communication Convergence and the Future of Asian Civilizations: An Analysis of Social Change." Keynote paper presented in the International Conference 2005 on "Mediamorphosis Communication, Technology & Growth" organized by the Faculty of Communication and Media Studies, Universiti Teknologi MARA, Malaysia, July 13–14, 2005.
———. 2011. "Media and Communication Education in India: Some Reflections." Paper presented in the Kushabhau Thakre Patrakarita Avam Jansanchar Vishwavidyalaya, Symposium on "Media Education at the Cross Roads," Raipur, India, April 5–6, 2011.
———. 2015. "Communication, Culture and Buddhism in Asia: Structural Adaptation and Integration of Digital Media." *Journal of the Asian Center for Religion and Social Communication* 13 (1): 83–87.
Anonymous 2007. *UNESCO Model Curricula for Journalism Education*. Paris: UNESCO.
Desai, K. 2008. *Jainism: The Cosmic Vision*. London: Mahavir Foundation.
Dissanayake, W. 1988. *Communication Theory: The Asian Perspective*. Singapore: AMIC.
Freedman, E., Stephen Rendahl, and Richard Shafer. 2009. "Re-examination of Development Communication Theory and Practice: Informing a Critique of UNESCO's Model Curricula for Journalism Education for Developing Countries and Merging Democracies." *Journal of Development Communication* 20 (2): 1–15.
Kuan, Tse-fu. 2008. *Mindfulness in Early Buddhism: New Approaches through Psychology and Textual Approaches of Pali Chinese and Sanskrit Sources*. London and New York, NY: Routledge.
Malikhao, Patchance, and Jan Servaes. 2015. "The Journalist as Change Agent." In *Mindful Journalism and News Ethics in the Digital Era: A Buddhist Approach*, edited by Shelton A. Gunaratine, Mark Pearson, and Sugath Senarath, 50–61. London: Routledge.
Mathur, K. S. 1964. *Caste and Ritual in a Malwa Village*. Bombay: Asia Publishing House.
Muppidi, S. 2008. "Identifying Generic Problems and Recommending Solutions for Improving the Status and Relevance of Journalism Education in Asia." *Media Asia* 35 (2): 131–32.
Radhakrishnan, S. 1969. *Reader: An Anthropology*. General Editors, K. M. Munshi and R. R. Diwakar. Bombay: Bhartiya Vidya Bhawan. (2nd edition, 1988.)
Srinivas, M. N. 1952. *Religion Among Coorgs*, 2nd ed. Bombay: Asia Publishing House.

4

Confucius and Tao of Asian Journalism

Kwangsoo Park

One of the characteristics of modernity is the increasing interconnectedness of humanity and the growing sense of the world becoming a global village. The interdependence of all life on this planet is consciously building "One World." However, every naturally growing phenomenon is accompanied by long-standing problems. In the case of globalization, we hear of cases of poverty, inequality, social disintegration, violence, and terrorism. The world is confronting extreme forms of political and religious extremism endangering "peace" and "security," especially after the terrorist attacks on the World Trade Center in the USA on September 11, 2001.

Globalization's positive potential lies in the possibility of creating a world society that proposes togetherness where all people live together in peace. However, as we enter this new phase of history—globalization—we are increasingly aware of the world's potentials and dangers. These days, the media plays an important role in facilitating and promoting social communication among people around the world. The media contributes significantly to the maintenance of peaceful communication in respecting diversity and raising public awareness.

We are aware of our important mission and role to bring "the social integration in Asian regions" under the theme of "Mindful Communication for ASEAN Integration."

It is important for us to be more open, more diverse, and more inclusive and try to avoid another tragic "holy war," some of which have been the bloodiest wars in the human history. The news media has the key role to play in resolving the problems in our human society in cooperation with governments, nongovernmental organizations, religions, academics, and others. We may raise questions and answer each one step-by-step.

What are the Asian ideas or concepts that can be applied to modern communication and journalism practices?

Concerning this question, we may ask a simple question, "What is the basic principle of communication and journalism?"

Communication is an activity of communicating between people or groups by conveying information. Social networking is an important tool to connect people without being bound by time and space.

Firstly, I argue that bias-free communication requires objective and truthful information sharing. In the words of the Chinese Philosopher Confucius (Ames and Rosemont, 1998: 111): "Following the proper way, I do not forge new paths; with confidence I cherish the ancients—in these respects I am comparable to our venerable Old Peng."

To make this relevant to the contemporary context, it means to say that the proper way of journalism is to keep objectivity and a descriptive approach for the news without falling into bias.

Mencius[1] emphasized the inherent goodness of human beings and he interpreted *jen* (仁) as "the feeling of concern for the well-being of others." He further explained "justice" as the sense of shame and disgust; "propriety" as the sense to treat others with courtesy and respect; and "wisdom" as the sense of right and wrong. According to Mencius, virtues such as *jen*, justice, propriety, and wisdom are not bestowed on us from outside, but are rather already endowed traits in each and every human being. If I borrow the teachings of Mencius, we may say that when we strive for it, we would gain it; if we ignore it, we may lose it.

Secondly, a journalist should keep a public spirit and a sense of universal ethics to benefit human beings in balance with nature. As the human community is becoming more civilized and moving toward an active global and social network, universal ethics and publicness are coming to the fore in the fields of religion and philosophy. Publicness and public ethics are considered practical values and ethics in establishing the relationship between "me" and "others." In this regard, I consider that a journalist should keep the public spirit to respect not only individuals but also the public sphere.

Historically, the concept and perception of publicness was applied differently according to the time and region. "Public" (公) indicates the public area of social groups beyond the area of private individuals such as clans, tribes, nations, and countries. The public sector that was represented by the ruler in the monarchy era extended from the level of the country to the entire civil society in the present time. On the other hand, "togetherness" (共) addresses how to coexist and communicate with each other in relation to individuals, communities, nations, and the world.

---

[1] Refer to http://www.iun.edu/~hisdcl/h425/mencius1.htm (accessed on September 15, 2017).

In regards to publicness, Korean myths are very significant in figuring out religious worldviews and social systems.[2] Several myths were transmitted from the early history of Korea to the present time. We can find interesting subjects and symbols to identify distinctive political or religious leaders as the intimate descendants of the sun, moon, stars,[3] or as the sons of the God/highest being. Among those myths, the Dan'gun myth is considered the paramount foundational myth of Korea and directly relates with the Sun God. Human beings are considered the descendants of Dan'gun and are considered the posterity of Heaven (*Cheonson*, 천손 天孫). The principle teaching of Dan'gun is to practice "the greatest service for the benefit of humanity."

The thought of publicness is also a core idea of new Korean religions and expressed in *gaebyeok* thought, which literally means the Great Opening of a new cosmic era. Discourse about publicness in *gaebyeok* thought provides a spiritual and universal value that contributes to the public wellness of society.

I contend that publicness of journalism requires both recognition of self-identity in relation to others and the awareness of a national identity in relation to the world. As such, a journalist should think of the spirit of publicness in relation to social reformation as well as the coexistence philosophy and practical ethics which show the universal values of publicness by overcoming historical sufferings, such as Western or Japanese imperialism before or after World War II, in order to construct a peaceful civilization in the post-modern era.

How Should We Apply Asian Thought to the Practice of Journalism?

Let us look at some of the issues raised at the symposium at Chulalongkorn University (in December 2015):

1. Is there any aspect of wisdom derived from Confucius/Daoist teachings that can be applied to the practice of journalism?

---

[2] According to Campbell, myth is a "traditional story of ostensibly historical events that serves to unfold part of the worldview of a people or explain a practice, belief, or natural phenomenon." Also, myth is "the secret opening through which the inexhaustible energies of the cosmos pour into human cultural manifestation" (Campbell, 1972: 3).

[3] There is also an animistic belief in Korea to regard sun, moon, and stars as the Great Spirit. In this sense, stars were considered as the lives of heroes. When a hero passed away, a star fell down from the sky.

2. How can Confucius/Daoist ideas contribute to developing journalism practices and help shift the current adversary style of journalism to a more cooperative problem-solving style of journalism?
3. Can Confucius/Daoist teachings be used to develop a better system for reporting on news of poverty and economic development?
4. Can you derive ideas/principles from Confucius/Daoist teachings to report on corruption and good governance?
5. Can Confucius/Daoist ideas help develop a practice of journalism that is uniquely Asian?

These questions relate to how journalism can address and provide solutions for global food, poverty, water, and climate problems. When I attended the General Assemblies of the Parliament of World's Religions (India, 1993, Australia, 2009), the World Conference on Religion and Peace (Religions for Peace), and the Asian Conference on Religion and Peace, these issues were addressed several times.

One of my observations is that a journalist should have broad experience and views.

Let me provide one short example of these meetings, the main theme of the Parliament of the World's Religions 2009 was "Make a World of Difference: Hearing each other, Healing the earth." The theme was similar to the centennial gathering of the Parliament of World's Religions in Chicago in 1993; where a new system of global ethics was adopted to respect other religious beliefs and cultures as we respect our own. The 2009 Parliament featured seven major subthemes of programming that focused on different aspects of the overall mission: Healing the Earth with Care and Concern, Indigenous People, Overcoming Poverty in an Unequal World, Securing Food and Water for All People, Building Peace in the Pursuit of Justice, Creating Social Cohesion in Villages and Cities, and Sharing Wisdom in the Search for Inner Peace.

A journalist has a critical role to convey that faith, communities, and spiritual leaders of the world can play an important role in addressing the enormous problems concerning food, water, and climate.

Although governmental bodies and international secular organizations have initially met their responsibilities to identify areas of concern and have begun to address the problems of starvation and poverty, the food crisis in various regions has led to a vast increase in the millions of newly hungry people in the world, leaving these traditional organizations overwhelmed in their capacity to respond adequately.

Moreover, the recent economic decline dramatically worsened these problems and left a large void in the fabric of support for the poorest of the poor that urgently needs to be addressed. A journalist should report on issues concerning climate change, fresh water access, and human food chain problems. In addition, the role of the journalists extends to reporting on social problems in our communities in cooperation with government officials and nongovernment specialists based upon clear and concise analyses of contemporary social issues.

In this sense, we should be able to change the adversary style of journalism to a more cooperative and active problem-solving style of journalism. In order to do this, a journalist should enhance his/her views broadly and deeply.

The Taoist philosopher Chuangtzu (莊子) provided a parable of a frog in a well (井中之蛙): "You cannot speak of ocean to a well-frog, which is limited by his abode. You cannot speak of ice to a summer insect, which is limited by his short life. You cannot speak of Tao to a pedagogue, who is limited in his knowledge." If we cling to a narrow sphere like a frog of a well, we will not able to see the great ocean. In the same way, it is necessary for a journalist to keep a non-biased view when reporting on social issues as well as actively solving problems.

Secondly, I would like to suggest that the journalist should keep their interests in new ethical values to benefit the weak and poor people in the global economy. What would be a proper treatment for the symptoms of financial crisis in our society? It is necessary for all of us to change our lifestyles in the global financial crisis.

Nowadays, we are confronting a very difficult situation given the circumstances of the economic crisis starting from the mortgage crisis in the United States of America (USA), spreading to Europe, that is, Ireland, Ukraine, Iceland, Greece, Spain, and other countries. In Asia, the Asian financial crisis started in Thailand with the financial collapse of the Thai Baht beginning in July 1997, which raised fears of a worldwide economic meltdown due to financial contagion.

The current global situation has been a clash of the traditional 20th century powerful elite and the newly emerging 21st century economies. There is a major battle brewing where each country is seeking its own financial benefit through reforming the global financial system. For example, the US Federal Reserve's fresh round of bond purchasing to boost the US economy will generate broad opposition from Asia and the EU. Europe has joined Asia and other big emerging economies by protesting America's $600 billion new cash infusion in 2010. They are rightfully worried that this influx of cash will put upward pressure on their own currencies, create asset bubbles, and eventually impair growth, already destabilized at a worldwide scale.

Because of near-zero US interest rates and China's rigid currency regime, emerging countries are faced with massive inflows of capital, which push their currencies higher. Furthermore, recent unilateral actions by countries such as Japan, Brazil, and South Korea to curb the value of their own currencies have fueled concerns of a looming war on global foreign exchange markets. There are several important issues to be discussed in detail and on a deep level to solve the current financial crisis of the world.

What Are the Symptoms of Financial Crisis?

There are many critical problems in the financial crisis such as: Over-inflated property markets resulting in a major slowdown; monetary policy—central banks may soon restart printing money to buy government bonds; liquidity crisis; quantitative easing—creates a gross distortion in the world economy as investors rush into emerging economies in search of higher yields; and brewing international currency war—currency intervention and capital control.

What Is the Cause of the Current Financial Crisis?

There are many reasons for this crisis such as asymmetric information (distorted and incorrect financial information), moral hazards in economics in general, a demand for transparency of information (for example, Lehman Brothers, Goldman Sachs, Enron and other financial centers), and exorbitant investment in risky assets such as derivatives and mortgage loans, which originates from the tendency of investors to seek maximization of their profits. Also, excessive greediness is accountable for this crisis.

I suggest a global ethics of capitalism with Asian thought as its foundation. During the 2009 Parliament of World's Religions, in Melbourne, Australia, when I attended the session dealing with "How Interreligious Dialogue Can Address Global Food, Water and Climate Problems," speakers discussed the critical role that faith, communities, and spiritual leaders of the world can play in addressing the enormous problems concerning food, water, and climate.

Although governmental bodies and international nongovernmental organizations have initially met their responsibilities to identify areas of concern, and have begun to address the problems of starvation and poverty, there are still millions of malnourished people suffering from this food crisis. Moreover, the recent economic decline dramatically aggravated these problems and left a large void in the fabric of support for the poorest of the poor that urgently needs to be addressed. The new economic crisis causes countries to become more inward, and donations are beginning to dry up, whereby countries are focused more on sustaining their own economic growth and could care less about other poorer countries.

In order to avoid the increased fear and the prospect of poverty amid the global economic crisis which might cause outbursts of social unrest, firstly, it is very important for us to build a global ethics in economics to avoid a global economic crisis and to enhance mutual benefit. Secondly, profit maximization should be based on public interests and mutual benefit. Thirdly, people, particularly in the USA and other leading countries, have to rethink their lifestyle. We have to reduce spending, increase savings, so that we are self-reliant in economic activities, and act logically and morally when dealing with finance.

This should not only be focused on by the developed richer countries, but should also be spread to poorer economic regions of our world. Many leading countries with economic and political influence should work toward making poorer countries more self-reliant through basic structural economic investment in infrastructure and sound economic management.

Excessive human desire seeking personal gain for maximum profits only causes an exploitation of natural resources that destructs the natural environment and degrades human life. As a small example, fair trade between the strong and the weak in a broad sense should be well practiced in all countries to protect the exploitation of child labor, women, or poor workers. Proper working conditions should also be provided for foreign workers to be treated equally.

What Role Can Journalism Play to Bring About Financial Reform in Proper Ways?

The first problem that needs to be dealt with is currency reform. The major economies need to balance their currencies in such a way that benefits all. This may sound easy, but it will be difficult to enforce. The world's economies need to limit debt and bad lending. Leading countries have to be more fiscally responsible.

There has to be a morally biased lifestyle change of personal and national expenditures. Moreover, there needs to be systematic, structural, logical financial support for smaller micro-loan projects that would greatly benefit underdeveloped nations around the world. For example, Muhammad Yunus, a Bangladeshi economist and founder of the Grameen Bank who received a Nobel Peace Prize in 2006 provided micro-credit (small loans to poor people possessing no collateral) to help its clients establish credit worthiness and financial self-sufficiency.

Then, how can we recover credit with our faith in the financial market? It is very important to recover credit and faith in our financial system. A globalized model based on capitalistic exploitation cannot harmoniously bridge the world into one. Mutual benefit is necessary to create worldwide peace and achieve prosperity of humanity. Nowadays, the powerful countries (or strong multinational corporations) use their political, military, economical, and cultural power to suppress or influence the weaker countries into being subordinates. Currently, America, China, and other powers are trying to monopolize the world's natural resources for their own benefit. Without changing this kind of antagonistic relationship between the strong and the weak, as well as the rich and the poor, we may not be able to solve current global problems. These leading countries must take responsibility for the prosperity of human society, not just their own.

A goal of journalism is to stimulate harmony among people by encouraging them to celebrate diversity while at the same time realizing the common thread that connects them all.

When Confucius discussed ambition with his students, he did not suggest that the higher your ambition is, the better it is. As Dan (2009: 156) noted in reflecting on Confucius teachings:

> Let us build a wisdom of the soul, founded on the wisdom that comes from self-knowledge; let us enter into the wisdom of Confucuis, so that we too can be his peaceful students, overcoming the changes and turmoil of the ages to see his serene, steady, peaceful face today ... in fact, in our modern era, the serenity we find in Confucius every day concepts, the clarity and truth of his ideas, and the strength we find within them should encourage us to cherish our inner hearts, and recognise that the roots of all our ambitions and goals are found deep within us.

For Journalism in the contemporary era, Asian values can help balance material civilization and spiritual culture. It is my hope that we all nurture our spirituality and common sense to utilize globalization as a means to consciously work toward building a world of peace and engaging in economic cooperation. We should be able to implement righteous, ethical, and financial reforms in a practical manner in our home, companies, and nations, and eventually extend these virtues to the world.

References

Ames, R. T., and H. Rosemont, Jr. 1998. *The Analects of Confucius*. New York, NY: Ballantine Books.
Campbell, J. 1972. *The Hero with a Thousand Faces*, 2nd ed. Princeton, NJ: Princeton University Press.
Dan, Yu. 2009. *Confucius from the Heart*. London: Macmillan.

5

Human Dignity and Responsibility to Humanity: A Buddhist Viewpoint

Lim Kooi Fong

All human beings are born free and equal in dignity and rights. They are endowed with reason and conscience and should act towards one another in a spirit of brotherhood.

—Article 1 of the Universal Declaration of Human Rights[1]

The Buddhist view of human rights and religious liberty arises from the conviction that human beings are born with complete freedom and responsibility. The celebration of human freedom runs through Buddhist practices, institutions, and doctrines. Human beings, as individuals, are free to choose their own course of action for achieving liberation. Religious teachings should not prevent human beings from taking individual action for their liberation.

The historical Buddha strongly affirmed that human beings have their destiny in their hands. Emphasizing self-reliance of each individual, human equality in dignity and rights is clearly recognized. Buddhist texts such as the *Sampasadaniya Sutta*[2] stress the importance of personal effort, human endeavor, strength, and responsibility. Buddhahood itself is open to all human beings without any limitation.

Fundamental Buddhist Ethical Principle

The fundamental Buddhist ethical principle that underpins the concept of human rights is that "all life forms have a basic desire to safeguard themselves." This ethical perspective gives validity and strength to the

---

[1] http://www.un.org/en/universal-declaration-human-rights/ (accessed September 19, 2017).
[2] *Digha Nikaya* III: 113.

principle of universal love (*metta*) advocated by all Buddhists. Buddhist texts assert this crucial ethical standpoint in various ways: for example, the *Dhammapada* states that all beings desire happiness and that life is dear to all living beings.

> Whoever harms with force
> those desiring happiness,
> as seeker after happiness
> one gains no future joy
>
> (*Dhammapada*, Verse 131)

The above verse says that people who like to be happy and are in search of pleasure hurt others through various acts of violence for their own happiness. These victims too want to be happy as much as those who inflict pain on them. Those who inflict pain do not achieve happiness even in their next birth (Buddhanet, 1996).

> All tremble at force,
> dear is life to all.
> Likening others to oneself
> kill not nor cause to kill
>
> (*Dhammapada*, Verse 130)

The above verse points out that all are frightened of being hurt or any threat to one's life. To all life is dear. Seeing that others feel the same way as oneself and equating others to oneself refrain us from harming or killing.

This Buddhist ethical position proposes to compare one's situation with that of another and avoid resorting to violence and depriving another of its right to life. From this Buddhist perspective, the ideal life is one in which one lives with friendliness and compassion toward all beings.[3]

Dignity of Human Person

As in many other world religions, there is no doubt that Buddhist teachings also can be drawn to support the view that religious liberty is firmly grounded on a conception of the dignity of the human person. In addition, however,

---

[3] *Digha Nikaya* I: 70.

Buddhist doctrines maintain that the free exercise of "will" is the key for both material and spiritual well-being of the human person, who is "free to choose and open to seek" an individual program of religious regiment that enables each individual to taste the fruit of liberation.

The best illustration of this unconditional acceptance and recognition of liberty and human freedom is found in the *Kalama Sutta*.[4] Here, the Buddha advises on how one should design their religious enquiry by transcending any biases that come into play when human persons make critical decisions in adopting a religious tradition or practice. The historical Buddha advised the *Kalamas* (a group of critically minded people) "not to accept anything on the grounds of revelation, tradition, or hearsay," not to

> accept because they are mentioned in the collections of the scriptures or because they are based on reasoning or because they are in accordance with logical arguments or because they conform with one's own preconceived notions or because of inadequate reflection on them or because they fit to a context or because of the prestige of your teacher.[5]

The historical Buddha's provoking statement here is an illustration of religious freedom that the Buddha himself advocated in relation to his own teachings as well as those of other religious teachers.

The *Kalama Sutta* provided 10 points to guide one's life as follows (Dhammananda, 1987):

1. Do not simply believe what you hear just because you have heard it for long.
2. Do not follow tradition blindly merely because it has been practiced in that way for many generations.
3. Do not be quick to listen to rumors and hearsay.
4. Do not confirm anything just because it agrees with your scriptures.
5. Do not foolishly make assumptions.
6. Do not abruptly draw conclusions by what you see and hear.
7. Do not be fooled by outward appearances.
8. Do not hold on tightly to any view or idea just because you are comfortable with it.

---

[4] *Kalama Sutta* is a discourse of the Buddha contained in the *Anguttara Nikaya* of the Tripitaka, and it is often cited as the Buddha's "charter of free inquiry."
[5] *Anguttara Nikaya* I: 189.

9. Do not accept as fact anything that you yourself find to be logical.
10. Do not be convinced of anything out of respect and deference to your spiritual teachers.

As Dhammananda (1987: 2) points out, the Buddha's advice to the *Kalama's* could be very valuable to guide modern communication practices:

> Buddha's advice is not to accept anything based upon mere reports, traditions or hearsay. Usually people develop faith after listening to others. They unthinkingly accept what others say about their religions or what is recorded in their religious books. Most people seldom take the trouble to investigate, to find out whether what is said is true or not.

The Buddha recognized the importance of living, working, and cooperating with all human beings in an integrated society. Compassionate attitudes extended toward others and nonviolent values translated into positive mental, physical, and social actions are extremely important for religious harmony and social progress. One's spirituality depends on and is enhanced by a positive contribution of the other.

A healthy, open, and conducive environment in which ideas and practices can be studied, discussed, critiqued, and appropriated for positive human action in the wider community is absolutely essential for modern democracies. In the *Parinibbana Sutta*,[6] the Buddha outlined seven conditions for community growth, which are:

- hold well-attended gatherings frequently,
- assemble and disperse peacefully,
- enact or repeal laws constitutionally,
- respect and seek the counsel of elders,
- uphold the honor of women and maidens,
- respect and honor existing places of worship as their forefathers have done, and
- protect and honor the holy ones.

"Buddhism is a religion which teaches one to understand that man is not for religion but religion is for man to make use of. Religion can be compared to a raft a man uses to cross a river. Once he has arrived at the other bank, he can discard it and carry on with the journey" argues Dhammananda

---

[6] *Digha Nikaya* II: 74–75.

(1987:9). "A man should use religion for his betterment and to experience freedom, peace and happiness."

Facilitating Between Extremes

One of the core philosophical tenets of Buddhism, in fact, is to avoid taking the extreme position. The Buddha himself is a product of extreme conditioning. He was a prince, wealthy and luxuriant, before deciding to give it all up to become a practicing ascetic. Doing so, he starved himself to the point of death. Only then did he realize that salvation is found neither in luxury nor in self-annihilation, but in cultivating a balance or centeredness in practice.

In this, he expounded the "middle path" (*majjhima patipada*), the path of enlightenment that spurns both the extremes of nihilism and existentialism. The Buddha advises against personal cultivation up to the point of personal destruction (the anti-social stance) and wanton materialism (the anti-spiritual stance). The well-rounded individual, as Buddhism espouses, is one who takes upon him or herself the personal liberty to advance spiritually while maintaining a mindful circumspection of society at large.

As discussed earlier, a healthy individual is predicated upon a healthy community and vice versa. If a community allows for the development of mindful and contemplative individuals—that is, in terms of spiritual substance rather than outward forms of religiosity—such individuals in return can help to nurture the evolution of a community which encourages conducive environments that support spiritual development.

Such evolved communities, by their natural tendencies, can play a role in preventing destructive elements from taking hold—elements forewarned by the Buddha as destructive to human and society endeavors are greed, hatred, and ignorance (the three evil roots).

It is not surprising that today's clamor for religiosity in general has heightened because of the perceived threat of wanton capitalism and unfettered openness. In some ways, religious extremism and the rising face of terror is somewhat linked to this ubiquitous display of unlimited liberties. It can even be said now that what we are seeing is the confrontation of one extreme with another, that is, *the clash of nihilism and existentialism.*

On the one hand, we have people who would be driven to destroy their lives to make a point, such as the Arabian terror group Daesh or ISIS.[7] On

---

[7] Daesh is an acronym for an Arabic phase that means "Islamic State of Iraq" and the Levant that has basically replaced the other acronym ISIS.

the other hand, there is the tactless and materially driven culture, promoting gross vulgarity in the name of free speech, such as those demonstrated by the equally crude and immoral *Charlie Hebdo*[8] publishers.

Asian Values and Human Rights

Such views lead us to the center of what in the international human rights debate of the last years has come to be known under the term "Asian values." During the 1990s, political leaders of various Asian states, headed by Malaysia and Singapore and markedly supported by China, have repeatedly criticized the human rights idea as being too Western and contended, in particular, that the individualism on which it is based is opposed to the community-oriented "Asian values" (see Sen, 1997).

For some countries like China, Vietnam, Myanmar, and others it is only too obvious that this argument is used in order to distract from considerable violations of human rights within their own states or for withdrawing them from international criticism.

"The championing of Asian values is often associated with the need to resist Western hegemony," argues Nobel Laureate Amartya Sen (1997). "The linking of the two issues, which has occurred increasingly in recent years, uses the political force of anti-colonialism to buttress the assault on basic political and civil rights in postcolonial Asia."

Sen (1997) noted:

> The fact that individual liberty and freedom may have been championed in Western writings and even by some Western political leaders can scarcely compromise the claim to liberty and freedom that people in Asia may otherwise have. As a matter of fact, one can grumble, with reason, that the political leaders of Western countries take far too little interest in issues of freedom in the rest of the world. There is plenty of evidence that the Western governments have, by and large, tended to give priority to the interests of their own citizens engaged in commerce with the Asian countries and to the pressures generated by business groups to be on good terms with the ruling governments in Asia. It is not so much that there has been more bark than bite; there has in fact been very little barking either.

---

[8] *Charlie Hebdo* is a French satirical weekly magazine featuring cartoons, news reports, polemics, and jokes that came into global prominence after they published a controversial cartoon of Prophet Muhammad in 2005 and their offices were attacked in 2011 and 2015 by terrorist groups.

And yet, without doubt, this is not the last word on the topic of "Human Rights and Asian Values." Underlying some of the Asian voices is the genuine concern that a liberal individualistic ethos in conjunction with a legalistic, aggressive, and consumerist attitude does not meet traditional values of Asian societies, that is, values such as social harmony, respect for family and authorities, and, in particular, emphasis on duty and responsibility rather than on claimable rights.

Such concerns should not easily be dismissed. The Indian–British scholar of political science Bhikkhu Parekh (2002) has rightly pointed out that on the one hand emphasizing "Asian values" is vulnerable to the collectivist danger and unlikely to create a culture conducive to the development of individuality and choice, but that on the other hand a one-sided liberal stress on rights is hardly able to nurture the spirit of community and social responsibility.

This statement marks a good starting point for understanding that both sides, the representatives of "Asian values" and the defenders of a "Western liberalism," could learn from one another and, in a sense, complement each other.

To guard the freedom of the individual against the force of powerful communities and institutions, those "rights" need not only be on exactly the same level but—it is a big "but"—need to be on a legal level providing minimal protective rights. It is true that emphasizing such individual protective rights is not enough for promoting moral sensitivity and social responsibility. Responsibility exceeds that what can be secured legally.

For this reason, it makes a lot of sense to identify, in addition to the declaration of human rights, an "intercultural and interreligious basis" for a declaration of human responsibilities as it is intended within the context of "global ethics." This is crucial for Sustainable Development Goals (SDGs; as discussed in the Introduction), providing socioeconomic equity that includes protecting human dignity and cultural heritage protection.

Thus, human responsibilities and human rights should complement, not supersede, one another. Emphasizing social and moral responsibility must not lead to a removal of that basic intuition of human rights that seeks legal protection for the individual's freedom of self-determination. On the other hand, this right cannot prevail without any limitations. It finds its limits, as already stated in the human rights declaration from 1948, in the rights of others and "the just requirements of morality, public order and the general welfare." Community well-being must not be crushed by unfettered individual liberty. This is the basis and foundation for the development of a healthy and sustainable integrated community.

References

Buddhanet. 1996. Treasury of Truth: Chapter 10. Punishment. *The Illustrated Dhammapada*. Buddhanet.Net. Available at http://www.buddhanet.net/dhammapada/d_punish.htm (accessed on October 25, 2017).

Sri Dhammananda, K. 1987. *How to Choose a Religion*. Wisdom Series no. 47. Kuala Lumpur, Malaysia: Buddhist Missionary Society.

Parekh, C. 2002. *Rethinking Multiculturalism: Cultural Diversity and Political Theory*. Cambridge, MA: Harvard University Press.

Sen, Amartya. 1997, May 25. *Human Rights and Asian Values*. Annual Morgenthau Memorial Lecture Series. Available at https://www.carnegiecouncil.org/publications/archive/morgenthau/254.html (accessed on October 25, 2017).

6

"Hindu" Values in Journalism

Sanjay Ranade

This chapter looks at mindful communication from the Indian perspective. I am contesting the term "Hindu" values, the explanation for which is included in a separate section within the chapter. I suggest the term "Indian values" instead. I argue that for mindful or conscious communication, one has to be up to date on the media and communication environment that we are dealing with, and one has to look at how this environment evolved and what were the influences that shaped it.

In this chapter, I look at the values and principles that shaped the Indian media and communication environment over the centuries. While I have tried to cover as vast a review of literature as possible for a comprehensive understanding of the issues, I have had to assess, based on my own experience and observations and my constant interactions with journalists, media educators, and media students from 1989 onward, the probability of how things stood, how they stand now, and what shape they may take in the future.

I argue that within the context of journalistic values, the study of three specific areas needs to be included in journalism curricula. The three areas are essential to an understanding of why and how Indians communicate, what are the forms of narratives used, and how ultimately is knowledge generated from this activity. These areas are Indian epistemology, the theory of *Rasa*, and Indian narratology. Before we go into a discussion on why these three areas are important, it would be necessary to understand the media and, more, specifically news media access and consumption scenario in India.

Unity in Inequality[1]

Mass media, whether news or entertainment, requires a social, economic, and political environment to sustain itself and thrive. We now look at the social and developmental situation in India as of today. The following statistics

---

[1] I am grateful to Dr Kavita Rane, one of my PhD scholars, for this input.

indicate both the rural–urban divide and the gender disparities in the vast country (Dreze and Sen, 1996):

- There are only 940 females in India per 1,000 males.
- Only 65 percent of female population is literate compared to 82 percent of literate males. Half of the literate females have not completed even 10 years of their schooling.
- The share of women in total organized employment is just about 20 percent.
- Only 11 percent of the MPs are women. Moreover, in 2011, five states of the country had zero female participation in the Lok Sabha (lower house of the Indian Parliament) as well as Rajya Sabha (upper house of the Indian Parliament).
- Thirty percent of the Indian population lives in abject poverty. Rural poverty figures are much higher than the urban poverty figures. Poverty estimates for rural areas for 2009–2010 were 34 percent for rural areas and 21 percent in urban areas. Urban dwellers need to earn twice that of the rural dwellers to survive.
- During 2009–2010, the per capita per month average household expenditure was ₹1,984 for urban areas. At the same time, the rural Indian could afford to spend only ₹1,054 per month. This does not imply that all the urban dwellers earn more than rural farmers or laborers.
- A mere 30 percent of India's population contributes to more than 80 percent of the GDP.
- Sixty percent of the population depends on agriculture for their livelihood but contributes only 20 percent of the GDP. Agricultural and industrial sectors in India are weak, and the unorganized sector provides employment to 90 percent of the population.
- More than 90 percent of the villages have been provided with primary schools but everybody from parents to scholars worry about the quality of education provided in the public schools. The Annual Status of Education Report (ASER)[2] survey 2011 showed that in rural India more than 40 percent of the students studying in Class 3–5 could not read Class 1 text. Top schools in metro cities do not show any improved picture either. WIPRO-EI Quality Education Study 2011 surveyed 20,000 students in 83 "top schools" in five

---

[2] Available at http://www.asercentre.org/ (accessed on December 7, 2015).

metro cities.[3] They found that reading and basic mathematics skills of Class 4 students were below the international average. Basic facilities are luxuries in government schools.

- Only 55 percent of government schools are provided with toilets and 32 percent with electricity supply. About 90 percent of the school children have not seen computer in their schools.
- Moving from a government school to a private school requires huge increase in the family income.
- There is only one primary health care center for a population of 50,000. Of these health care centers, 60 percent are provided with a functional operating theatre, but 36 percent of them have no regular electricity supply.
- Of the total households, 50 percent are opting for open defecation, causing severe health challenges.
- Of the children below five years, 40 percent are undernourished—the lowest performance in the world. Food continues to remain the first priority for 90 percent of the household budget. Food expenditure of the average Indian accounts for 50 percent of his/her total income.
- A bad monsoon has the power to swing India's GDP growth rate by over 1 percent.

This environment of endemic poverty and social and economic inequality is reflected in the access and usage of mass media as well. It has to be borne in mind that this inequality is not recent but has been around for centuries, and it will continue to remain so for a long time. According to the 2011 census, there were 248 million households in India, housing a population of 1.2 billion.[4] According to 2014 report by the media and entertainment industry, India has 161 million TV households, 94,067 newspapers of which 12,511 are dailies, approximately 2,000 multiplexes, and 214 million Internet users of which 130 million are mobile Internet users.[5]

Given the above scenario, it is clear that there are large portions of the population who are yet to access mass media content in India. This holds true for the mass news media too.

---

[3] Available at http://www.wiproeducation.com/?q=qes and http://www.thehindu.com/todays-paper/tp-opinion/learning-by-rote-prevalent-in-top-schools-too/article2707562.ece (accessed on December 7, 2015).

[4] Available at http://www.censusindia.gov.in/2011census/population_enumeration.html (accessed on December 7, 2015).

[5] FICCI-KPMG Indian Media and Entertainment Industry Report 2014.

Mass News Media and Journalism Values in India

Journalism has arguably been a tool to inform, educate, and entertain the masses. These Reithian values[6] have had an overarching influence on journalism apart from the ideology of journalism that revolves around autonomy, objectivity, being fair and balanced, telling the truth, and shouldering a social responsibility. This influence has its moorings in a Euro-American view of the world. These influences have been shaping journalistic practices and values in covert and overt ways as much in India as all around the globe.

Let us pause here to briefly look at how the processes and values of journalism in India have probably been shaped from the first newspaper onward. The Irishman James Augustus Hicky introduced the design[7] of journalism to India in the 18th century. Hicky used his journalism for personal invective more than anything else. The Christian missionaries used journalism for proselytization of Christian values.

A series of newspapers followed. These were mostly in English, owned and run by Englishmen. They wove a narrative of British Rule and presented its various aspects, yet, as Chaudhuri (1955: 291) notes, news writing was adopted long before the British arrived in India:

> In the Moghul period, news writers were appointed to various administrative units in their territory, and were charged with the function of sending reports to the headquarters of the administration. The East India Company also requisitioned the services of news writers for the same purpose as Moghul emperors.

Sukeshi (2011) argues that although the publications the British established were called newspapers, the journalism was rhetorical and focused more on building public opinion than providing news. The Indians who took up journalism during the British rule adopted their design—the form, layout,

---

[6] A stern Scottish Presbyterian, John Reith was the first director general of the British Broadcasting Corporation (BBC) and more than 75 years after he joined the BBC, initially with the humble title of general manager, the term "Reithian values" has become a byword for public service broadcasting (refer to http://news.bbc.co.uk/2/hi/526855.stm; accessed on October 28, 2017).

[7] Design invents something of use by bringing together the human and the technical, or the technological using knowledge. Design also creates new knowledge, and it brings together intuition, instinct, and intent. It involves creativity and taking decisions and responsibility. Journalism design would involve the process of putting content on a media platform for use by the receiver.

purpose, and the values by which the activity of journalism would be driven and evaluated. They had just awakened to the reality of colonial exploitation. The first important milestone in reforming the design of journalism in India was the implementation of the Indian Penal Code in 1860. The second was adopting the Constitution of India on November 26, 1949. The Euro-American influence on the values of journalism, as practiced in India, was set in motion by these two significant events. Both these provided definitions to the various elements that were involved in the practice of journalism. They defined the roles and functions of individuals and institutions involved in the venture. They marked out what would be good journalism and what would be bad and what activities would be punishable under the law. The Indian Penal Code that was implemented soon after the first Indian revolution of 1857 had specific sections that defined when it would be criminal to publish anything.

The Euro-American framing of World War II and the Cold War in later years further shaped the moral and ethical values of journalism around the world and in India. This was especially significant in the English language press where journalists tried to measure up to what they believed were international or global standards of journalistic values and practices. The Hutchins Commission[8] report (1947) and the MacBride Commission report[9] (1980) were considered as a landmark in setting and evaluating journalistic principles, practices, and values.

> Too much of the regular output of the press consists of a miscellaneous succession of stories and images which have no relation to the typical lives of real people anywhere. The result is a meaninglessness, flatness, distortion, and the perpetuation of misunderstanding. The press emphasizes the exceptional rather than the representative; the sensational rather than the significant. The press is preoccupied with these incidents to such an extent that the citizen is not

---

[8] The Hutchins Commission (whose official name was the Commission on Freedom of the Press) was formed during World War II, when Henry Luce (publisher of *Time* and *Life* magazines) asked Robert Hutchins (president of the University of Chicago) to recruit a commission to inquire into the proper function of the media in a modern democracy. Available at https://archive.org/details/freeandresponsib029216mbp (accessed on November 7, 2017).

[9] *Many Voices One World*, also known as the MacBride report, was a 1980 UNESCO publication written by the International Commission for the Study of Communication Problems, chaired by Irish Nobel laureate Seán MacBride. Its aim was to analyze communication problems in modern societies, particularly relating to mass media and news, consider the emergence of new technologies, and to suggest a kind of communication order (New World Information and Communication Order) to diminish these problems to further peace and human development. Available at http://unesdoc.unesco.org/images/0004/000400/040066eb.pdf (accessed on November 7, 2017).

supplied the information and discussion he needs to discharge his responsibilities to the community. (Hutchins' Commission Report, 1947)

The press—the Fourth Estate, as it came to be called—established itself as an integral part of the modern constitutional state, in which governments normally changed as a result of elections and not simply through manoeuvers within an elite or at the whim of a monarch. Also, newspapers were now strong enough to defy pressure from authorities; the idea that they had a right, and indeed a duty to maintain their independence became accepted doctrine. However, this, in itself, was not always accompanied by equal independence from the private interests that controlled it. (MacBride Commission Report, 1980)

Shaping public opinion through rhetoric dominated providing news and information and was the main purpose of journalistic activity throughout the struggle for Independence and after (Iyengar, 2001). In the 1970s, when Prime Minister Indira Gandhi declared a "State of Emergency" and a clamp down on journalistic activity followed, freedom of speech and expression zeroed in on a more specific freedom of the press, and it was argued that freedom of the press meant a more resilient and effective democracy (Sorabjee, 1977).

Large portions of the press had been affected by the clamp down and for the first time ever, journalists in India rallied around to some sort of unified purpose and value. For the first time, values from the Indian language press emerged to influence the overall values of the press in India. Thus far, the press was in the hands of the private sector and the government controlled the electronic media, that is, television and radio. Soon after, technology and commerce combined to change "press" into "media." Color printing, television, the World Wide Web (www), and finally the mobile digital devices, on the one hand, and the emergence of the private sector as the main advertiser, on the other, coupled with a rapidly growing "fifth" estate[10] ensured that all content vied for a multimedia presence. This also meant that the government control over media reduced considerably.

We have seen how the processes and values of journalism probably evolved in India and what were the main influences that shaped journalism design in India. These values were Euro-American, chief among them being the Reithian values—media for information, education, and entertainment. This was as true of the private media as it was of the government-controlled

---

[10] An undefined space within media that includes public relations professionals, advertisers, bloggers, citizen journalists, etc. who are not formally associated with a news media organization but cast an influence on the content.

news media. Both the state controlled television and radio, Doordarshan and All India Radio, were modeled on the British Broadcasting Corporation.

However, while the news media and journalism began to take shape, India's masses largely remained illiterate and poor. When India gained Independence, four out of five of her citizens could not read. The population then was approximately 350 million. As of 2015, India is talking of literacy of around 73 percent and approximately 300 million Indians are still illiterate.[11]

How then does journalism reach out to the masses if at all? Who are the target audience of journalism in India? How do Indians understand information, education, and entertainment?

Let us look at the communication and media environment of Indians today.

Relevance of Mass Media in Life Decisions

For my doctoral thesis (2012), I studied the recipients' point of view of political news in India. I surveyed readers of eight major newspapers, four English and four Marathi, in Mumbai. I found that a large majority of these readers were in a subliminal multimedia space. All of them consumed more than one newspaper and more than one media for political news. Political news itself was getting marginalized and the readers' interests included sports, lifestyle, etc. As part of the study, I also found that the believability of newspapers was eroding and that people preferred to believe news that they could counter check with other people.

In my studies, I found further that communication continues to be predominantly aural/oral in India, and access to and validation of information and knowledge continues to remain at an interpersonal level for a majority of Indians even today. Major economic decisions taken by families and households are based on interpersonal interactions and an epistemology grounded in family or community. Even the most casual survey of Indians produces the same consistent result when it comes to media relevance in day-to-day living and decision-making. I have been conducting such studies every year.

Even while writing this chapter, I did a small survey. The question was—How many of our life decisions are helped by mass media? Both the news

---

[11] Available at http://censusindia.gov.in/Census_And_You/age_structure_and_marital_status.aspx, http://pib.nic.in/archieve/lreleng/lyr2003/rsep2003/06092003/r060920031.html (accessed on December 7, 2015).

media and the entertainment media in India are completely irrelevant to the life of an Indian. I gave respondents the following options: (a) completely disagree, (b) partially disagree, (c) partially agree, (d) completely agree, (e) can't say. I posted this on seven WhatsApp groups. Three of these are groups of postgraduate students of communication and media, one group of media educators, one group that is passionate about language and culture, one group of finance analysts, and one group of students and teachers of psychology. Altogether, there are approximately 400 men and women of varying ages, interests, educational qualifications, social status, and political leanings on these groups. Between 6.25 PM and 9.15 AM, I received 110 replies. Of these, 9 completely disagreed, 12 partially disagreed, 61 partially agreed, 21 completely agreed, and 7 couldn't say. The options "partially disagreed" and "partially agreed" were deliberate. The intention was to find the leanings of the respondents.

As we go deeper into the data, some very significant variables emerge. The influence of mass media reduces significantly with access to media—lesser the access, lesser the influence. However, once access is possible the consumption of media is shaped by social and cultural factors. Those with access to media but belonging to a socially, educationally backward class do not get as influenced by media when it comes to life decisions.

The combined scheduled caste and Scheduled Tribe population of India according to the 2011 census was close to 25 percent.[12] The Other Backward Classes, although not separately enumerated in the census, are anywhere between 40 and 50 percent of the total population. It needs to be clarified here that for the unmarried youth (youth being from 20 to 30 years of age) in India, education and career decisions followed by who and when to marry were life decisions, whereas for the married youth in India, food, shelter, clothing, having children, and getting them a good education was a life decision.

It is also significant that India has the largest proportions of population in the younger age groups in the world. It would appear then that a large proportion of India's population is either without access to mass media or is not influenced by it.

A BBC report[13] on five ways in which Indians use mobile phones provides significant insight into this phenomenon. According to this report,

---

[12] Available at http://censusindia.gov.in/Census_Data_2001/India_at_glance/scst.aspx (accessed on December 7, 2015).

[13] Available at http://www.bbc.com/news/world-asia-india-26028381 (accessed on December 7, 2015).

India is the world's fastest growing market for mobile phones with 900 million subscribers. Here are the five unusual ways in which Indians use the technology:

1. Giving missed calls where the caller disconnects is hugely popular and often used as a way to pass on the "message" without being charged for a call. Children and employees use the facility regularly to communicate with parents and employers. They are also used for marketing purposes and some television channels offer a missed call service to viewers who wish to be alerted about specific show timings. Even political parties use this for recruitment. The Aam Aadmi Party, which now rules Delhi, is India's newest political party, and through a missed call drive, the party claimed to have added more than 700,000 members in less than a month.
2. The mobile phone is used as a torch in India especially on roads and poorly lit public spaces.
3. The mobile phone as radio is another use that is peculiar to India, which has over 200 private FM channels. The government sponsored All India Radio too has now developed a mobile application.
4. The phone is used as an alternative to YouTube. This is used by NGOs in India who offer a call-in service to poor farmers and the rural poor. If the Internet is not working, then all the user needs to do is call up a number, choose a video put up by the NGO, and request a call back to listen to just the audio.
5. Lastly, the mobile phone is being used as a scanner/copier. The culprit again is lack of electricity coupled with short supply of photocopier or scanning machines.

Age was another significant factor that determined the degree of influence. Those above the age of 30 tended to agree with the proposition. Some of these demonstrated a skeptical or even a cynical attitude toward the mass media.

To completely disagree or completely agree with the given statement would assume a very interesting media environment for the individual. For an individual to completely disagree with the proposition, one would have to be living off mass media, otherwise it would be impossible for mass media to play an absolute role in life decisions. Mass media may provide options or evaluative comparisons within the options but it would be far-fetched that a decision was based only on mass media input. The probability of other factors such as family, social status, and income would come into play. On the other hand, to completely agree would lead to the assumption that one was not influenced or even touched by mass media. Given that all respondents were social media users, the latter could not be completely true. Yet those who completely agreed were more than twice those who completely disagreed with the proposition.

I have been doing this exercise consistently since 2010 and found that even among media users, the believability or credibility of news media is low. My own studies show that media, and especially mass news media, does not have much of a role to play in the lives of close to 55 percent of Indians accessing modern mass media. Close to 20 percent of these appear to be uncomfortable with even this marginal role that the mass media seems to play and highly skeptical of mass media content.

Significantly, All India Radio, the national broadcaster, has 414 stations across India covering 92 percent of the country's area, reaching 99.19 percent of the total population with programs in 23 languages and 146 dialects. Doordarshan, the national public service broadcaster, has a three-tier program service—national, regional, and local. The service covers 90 percent of the Indian population through a network of more than 1,416 terrestrial transmitters and 67 studios.[14] However, despite their fantastic reach, these two media outlets are not the preferred channels for people.[15] The reasons are viewer skepticism about the content since both channels are controlled by the government, bad quality of the content, and, most importantly, with respect to Doordarshan, lack of continuous flow of electricity.

Despite the severe limitations of the Indian mass media, its democracy has remained robust and active. Except for the small period during the national Emergency, democracy in India has shown itself as able to deal with all kinds of challenges whether within India or from outside (Ganguly, Sumit, and Plattner, 2007).

This discussion leads us to the following questions:

- How do Indians learn about their world?
- What do Indians call knowledge and what are the processes employed for knowing?
- How do Indians evaluate information and how do they narrate it, conserve it, and use it to their advantage?
- What role does mass media and specifically mass news media play?

---

[14] Available at http://prasarbharati.gov.in/AIR/Information/Pages/default.aspx (accessed on December 7, 2015).

[15] Available at http://www.thehindubusinessline.com/opinion/dont-let-doordarshan-die/article4425191.ece (accessed on December 7, 2015).

Before we delve into these questions, we must first address the question of who are the Hindus today and are there "Hindu values" or are these "Indian values."

Defining the Hindus and Their Values

Before we go any deeper into this discussion let us look at the word Hindu. When we say the Hindus and their values, whom are we speaking about?

In a reply to a query under the Right to Information Act filed by Neemuch (in the state of Madhya Pradesh) resident Chandrashekhar Gaur, the Union Home Ministry replied that the Central Public Information Officer (CPIO) did not have any information regarding the meaning and definition of the word Hindu.[16] The situation might seem odd especially given the fact that that there are Acts passed by the Indian parliament that are called Hindu Marriage Act, and "Hindu" law is also recognized in India.

For the purposes of this chapter, we will look at the definition of Hindu and Hindus provided in the Hindu Marriage Act. This is being done because marriage is still considered an important rite of passage into adulthood in India but more importantly the Act gives a very good idea of what we are up against when we use the word Hindu or Hindus.

The Hindu Marriage Act 1955 applies to any person who is a Hindu by religion in any of its forms or developments including Virashaiva, a Lingayat or a follower of the Brahmo, Prarthana or Arya Samaj. It also applies to any person who is a Buddhist, Jain, or Sikh by religion, and to any other person domiciled in the territories to which this Act extends who is not a Muslim, Christian, Parsi, or Jew by religion. Nothing contained in this Act applies to the members of any Scheduled Tribe within the meaning of clause (25) of Article 366 of the Constitution unless the Central Government, by notification in the Official Gazette, otherwise directs. This means that not all Scheduled Tribes[17] are Hindus. The Act further states that the expression

---

[16] Available at http://www.thehindu.com/news/national/govt-does-not-have-info-on-definition-of-hindu/article7750000.ece (accessed on December 7, 2015).

[17] The Scheduled Castes and Scheduled Tribes are various officially designated groups of historically disadvantaged indigenous people in India. The terms are recognized in the Constitution of India and the various groups are designated in one or other of the categories. During the period of British rule in the Indian subcontinent, they were known as the Depressed Classes. The percentage of people in scheduled castes is essentially the percentage of people in the lower part of the Indian society (Wikipedia).

"Hindus" in any portion of the Act shall be construed as if it included a person who, though not a Hindu by religion, was, nevertheless, someone to whom the Act applied by virtue of the provisions contained in the Act. It is significant that the way the Hindu or Hindus have been defined in this Act follows from the very extensive discussions on the Hindu Code Bill, 1951.

When, as the Law Minister, Dr B. R. Ambedkar first introduced the Hindu Code Bill in 1951, Sardar Hukum Singh objected to the Sikhs being included in the Bill. Dr Ambedkar's reply is significant. When the Buddha differed from the Vedic Brahmins, Dr Ambedkar argued that he did so only in matters of creed, but left the Hindu legal framework intact. Dr Ambedkar said that the same was true of Mahavira and the Sikh Gurus. He argued that in India although religions changed, the law remained one.[18]

Thus, what we find is that in India one can be legally a "Hindu" while following any of a number of sects or philosophies. This does not apply to the Christians, Muslims, Parsis, the Jews, and to some Scheduled Tribe communities. However, coupled with this definition of the Hindus, when one looks at the highly syncretic behavior of Indians (Burman, 1996) as a whole in all matters of philosophy and religion, it is more probable that Indians have a shared epistemology (Das, 1995).

The principles, values, and practices of Indians have seamlessly flowed into each other in such a way that identity for the individual is subliminal. To put it more colloquially, all Indians are in a "semi" identity—semi Hindus, semi Christians, semi Buddhists, semi Jews, semi Muslim, and so on and so forth. There is a very high probability of a shared worldview and a shared epistemology among Indians whether legal Hindus or belonging to any other religion, caste, creed or sect, who owe their allegiance to the principles and values enshrined in the Constitution of India today. What we need to do then is to substitute "Hindu values" with "Indian values."

Indian Epistemology

Epistemology is concerned with the origin, nature, limits, methods, and justification of human knowledge. Epistemic relates to knowledge more generally and to the conditions for acquiring it. Concerns about personal epistemology focus on how the individual develops conceptions of knowledge

---

[18] Available at http://www.ambedkar.org/ambcd/64B1.On%20the%20Hindu%20Code%20Bill.htm (accessed on December 7, 2015).

and knowing and utilizes them in developing an understanding of the world. This includes beliefs about the definition of knowledge, how knowledge is constructed, how knowledge is evaluated, where knowledge resides, and how knowing occurs.

Our beliefs about knowledge and knowing influence our encounters with new information, be it from a newspaper, a television show, the classroom or the family or parliament. As the amount of information increases and the tools of access change rapidly, there is an increasing urgency to understand the meaning-making process of individuals and societies. We need to develop an understanding of personal epistemology and its relation to learning (Hofer and Pintrich, 2002).

The classical Indian approaches to knowledge and justification focus on occurrent knowledge coupled with a theory of "mental dispositions" called saṃskāra.[19] Epistemic evaluation of memory is seen to depend upon the epistemic status of the occurrent cognition or awareness or awarenesses that formed the memory, that is, the mental disposition. Occurrent knowledge, in turn, must have a knowledge source, *pramāṇa*.[20]

For the Indians, knowledge, thus, is a cognition generated in the right fashion.[21] Each of these terms requires a very intense and deep understanding of Indian philosophical approaches to knowledge. The six shastras or schools of thought—*Sankhya, Yoga, Nyaya, Vaisheshika, Poorva Mimansa, and Uttar Mimansa*—are the sources of Indian epistemology.

The epistemological values in these schools of thought were disseminated to the layperson, who, as we have seen, lived in a media and communication environment that was predominantly oral and aural, through performance and narration.

At this stage, it is important to see how Indians have narrated themselves because the tools and processes used by Indians throughout their centuries-long history give us the insight into how Indians have gained knowledge and conserved it and in all probability continue to do so.

The two ways in which Indians have gained, conserved, and passed on knowledge have been through performance and narration of all they learnt. The performance was done through the principles of communication

---

[19] Saṃskāra is a concept that all beings have past impressions resulting from previous lives and/or experiences that judge or guide one's present actions, shape one's personality, and direct one's life.

[20] *Pramana* is a theory of knowledge, and it encompasses one or more reliable and valid means by which human beings gain accurate, true knowledge

[21] Available at http://plato.stanford.edu/entries/epistemology-india/#KnoKnoSou (accessed on December 7, 2015).

enumerated in the *Natyashastra* and the *Yogashastra*, and the narration followed the principles and processes of Indian narratology.

Indian Narratology

Let us look at some of the features of the Indian narratology first.

Interiorization is the process by which a distinction, a contrast or even a contradiction is affected between the surface features of a text and its internal essence. The notion that there is in a text something like a counter-text may help a reader decide on the best approach to a text. In this sense, every tale seems to contain a complex tissue of interiorized tales that is unraveled by the audience. Indians prefer to serialize their narrative in an apparent neverending series of episodes instead of a unified, single-strand, streamlined course of events, centering around a single hero or heroine.

This episodic looseness allows for variations in tone and style in the middle of the work; even gaps are provided for as part of the system; and wherever necessary, a song or dance or variety show could be inserted to fill the gaps when it is felt necessary.

The Indian mind has always questioned the nature of reality and often transformed apparent reality into invisible or intangible legend or myth. The plasticity of legend or myth makes for the interplay of imagination encouraging the dominance of fantasy. The vedas, puranas, epics, fairy tales, and folktales are primarily perceptions of the imagination and only secondarily those of the rational mind—the very grammar of communication is heavily weighted in favor of fancy and fantasy.

Indian narrators treat time and space as nonlinear and, thus, they assume that all tales are recycled even as living organisms are themselves recycled perpetually in the natural world. Whether this is primarily an aspect of religious belief or philosophical concept, for the Indian narrator it has come a handy device for stringing together any number of tales in a particular narrative formula—it is a feature of sophistication rather than the absence of it.

To invest inanimate objects as well as non-human creatures with the capacity to feel, think, and speak probably stems from the animistic or atavistic beliefs of early times, and the Panchatantra is the best example of this. The use of the frame story, the practice of emboxing (seemingly putting the narrative into a box, boxing it in) stories, the emphasis on moral values, the introduction of subtales, the element of soft satire, and, above all, the lively presentation of animal characters are important features of the allegorization attempted in the Indian narrative.

The *Apauruseya*—not personal, impersonal, universal, collective manner of narrating—was meant to merge the subjective self of the narrator in the collective readership so that ideally the narrator and the audience are one. Narration itself is rendered elastic by making time more psychological than logical, whereas space is more specific. Thus, the narration implies selection, elaboration, and condensation with regards to time while the scene becomes more crucial in the unfolding of the plot. Indian narratology uses both stylization as well as improvisation. The former enforces discipline of form and structure allowing the audience to step into the performative space, while the latter allows for freedom for the performer to express and experiment at the same time (Paniker, 2003).

Now we shall look at the theory of *Rasa* to understand in brief what *Rasa* is, and why its values and principles are essential to mass media practice in India.

The Theory of *Rasa*

The aesthetic theory of *Rasa*, the fruit of nearly 2,000 years of Indian contemplation on art, drama, and poetry, is not only a theory of aesthetics or literature but a living principle governing the whole of the life of an Indian (Prasad, 2007). *Rasa* is one of those quintessential words in Sanskrit that sums up a whole philosophy or even a civilization (Gokak, 1949). It is the crystallization of art, philosophy, and psychology. No meaningful idea is conveyed, if the *Rasa* is not evoked. The most ordinary action is a performance. We perform when we breathe, when we work, when we live. The goal of all performance in India is the formation of the *Rasa*—from ordinary cooking in the kitchen to a sophisticated classical dance in a temple. From a news story to a reality show, everything is a performance in India.

In his seminal work *Performance Theory*, Richard Schechner (2003) gives a very exhaustive and comprehensive explanation of the theory of *Rasa*. Theatricality in the Western tradition is located in eyes and to some degree in the ears. Seeing requires distance, engenders focus or differentiation, encourages analysis or breaking apart into logical strings—privileges meaning, theme, narration. In the Indian tradition, the mouth or better said the snout-to-belly-to-bowel—the route through the body managed by the enteric nervous system—is the "where" of taste, digestion, and excretion.

The snout-to-belly-to-bowel is the "where" of intimacy, sharing of bodily substances, mixing the inside and the outside, emotional experiences, and gut feelings. Quoting from the *Natya Shastra,* Schechner answers the question of what is *Rasa.* Because it is enjoyably tasted, it is called *Rasa.*

How does the enjoyment come? Persons who eat prepared food, mix different condiments and sauces if they are sensitive, enjoy the different tastes, and then feel pleasure; likewise, sensitive spectators, after enjoying the various emotions expressed by the actors through words, gestures, and feelings feel pleasure. This feeling by the spectators is here explained as the "*Rasas* of Natya." *Rasa* is aromatic, it fills space, drawing the outside to the inside. Food is actively taken into the body, becomes part of the body, and works from the inside. What was outside is transformed into what is inside. An aesthetic founded on *Rasa* is fundamentally different than one founded on the "theatron," the rationally ordered and analytically distanced panoptic (visible in one single view).

Rasa is realized when an emotion is awakened in such a manner that it has none of its conative tendencies and it is experienced in an impersonal mood (Chaudhary, 1953). The theory of *Rasa* rests on two very important concepts—*bhava* (sentiments or emotional states) and *sahridaya* (literary being of similar heart). These are everyday measures of a good life for an ordinary Indian.

For the Indian mind, *Rasa* is Rama, *Rasa* is destiny, *Rasa* is God, *Rasa* is divinity, *Rasa* is good, and bad *Rasa* is ugly and beautiful. The *Rasa* is located in the heart of the person experiencing a performance making the receiver of performative content at once a performer and the audience—a *sahridaya.*

It is in this social, cultural, and psycho-philosophical frame that an Indian consumes media content including news media. This probably explains why Indian news and entertainment content appears almost similar in terms of color, pitch, sound, and overall design.

Communicating for Sustainability

This takes us to some very important insights into how communication is viewed in India. The first is the recognition of the nature and role of consciousness. It is so much richer and meaningful, a solid foundation, compared to the materialist and reductionist theories and methods propounded otherwise.

The theory of *Rasa* explained in the *Natyashastra* and the *Yogashastra* contains a perfectly coherent theory of knowledge. The Indian communication design, reflected in the folk media of the subcontinent, is equipped with rigorous and effective techniques to arrive at valid and reliable insights into communication. It covers a wide range of subjects such as philosophy, psychology, aesthetics, dramatics, poetics, linguistics, phonetics, human development, and motivation. More importantly, an understanding and application of Indian communication design can bring about a change in an individual's ability to live a good life.

Like the *Rasa*, the narrative is ubiquitous in Indian communication. From literature to everyday communication between a vegetable vendor or a tea vendor and the customer, the narrative dominates. This narrative is not merely aural/oral but also is a performance with the individual at the center of this world. It is stylized and improvised at the same time. It is this narratology that is used in India to make meaning of everyday world and to evaluate it.

The 13th chapter of the Bhagvad Gita elaborates on the Indian epistemological thinking on territoriality and sovereignty. The body, the mind, the intellect, and the soul are what every human being owns, possesses, and is. The body interacts with the environment through the senses, the mind through the emotions, the intellect through thought, and the soul through faith. Each has its role to play, and together these provide us the doorway to our environment and allow the environment to interact with us. These interactions are constant and ever changing. As human beings, we narrate this interaction all the time. The *Natyashastra* speaks of *anukaran* (doing after) and *anukirtan* (saying after). We mirror our environment and our environment mirrors us as we do after and say after. The end product of this constant mirroring is empathy. This empathy is what leads to one becoming *sahridaya* (of one heart) with one's environment. Significantly, the Indian thought emphasizes that the body, the mind, the intellect, and the soul too are part of "our" environment.

Humans narrativize and string together events in a natural psychological and neural process through *anukaran* and *anukirtan* and achieve *sahridayata*, an empathy, with everything that constitutes them and their world. This is an important way in which human beings define themselves and their world. This is important for journalism to perform its functions of social responsibility, of providing that institutionalized objectivity through which the consumers of news can look, understand, analyze, and interpret their world, of providing not just education but learning by empathizing with themselves and their environment. In a globalizing world, journalism can only ignore these values at its own peril.

References

Bijapurkar, Rama. *We Are Like That Only.* New Delhi: Penguin Books India.
Burman, Roy. 1996, May 18. "Hindu-Muslim Syncretism in India." *Economic and Political Weekly* 31 (20): 1211–15.
Chaudhary, Pravas Jiwan. 1953. *Studies in Comparative Aesthetics.* West Bengal, India: Vishwa Bharti.
Chaudhuri, R. 1955, February 26. "The Story of the Indian Press." *The Economic & Political Weekly.* Available at "http://www.epw.in/system/files/pdf/1955_7/9/the_story_of_the_indian_press.pdf" http://www.epw.in/system/files/pdf/1955_7/9/the_story_of_the_indian_press.pdf (accessed on December 7, 2015).
Das, N. K. 1995. *Cultural Diversity, Religious Syncretism and People of India: An Anthropological Interpretation.* Available at "http://www.bangladeshsociology.org/BEJS%203.2%20Das.pdf" http://www.bangladeshsociology.org/BEJS%203.2%20Das.pdf (accessed October 28, 2017).
Dreze, Jean, and Amartya Sen. 1996. *India: Development and Participation.* New York: Oxford University Press.
Ganguly, Sumit, L. Diamond, and Marc F. Plattner. 2007. *The State of India's Democracy.* Baltimore, MD: Johns Hopkins University Press.
Gokak, V. K. 1976. *An Integral View of Poetry—An Indian Perspective* (1st ed). New Delhi: Abhinava Publications, quoted in Gupteshwar Prasad. 2007. *I.A. Richards and Indian Theory of Rasa.* New Delhi: Sarup and Sons.
Hofer, Barbara K., and Paul R. Pintrich. 2002. *Personal Epistemology: The Psychology of Beliefs about Knowledge and Knowing.* Mahwah, NJ: Lawrence and Erlbaum Associates.
Iyengar, A. S. 2001. *Role of Press and Indian Freedom Struggle: All Through the Gandhian Era.* New Delhi: A.P.H. Publishing Corporation.
Paniker, K. Ayyappa. 2003. *Indian Narratology.* New Delhi: Indira Gandhi National Centre for the Arts.
Prasad, Gupteshwar. 2007. *I.A. Richards and the Indian Theory of Rasa.* New Delhi: Sarup and Sons.
Schechner, Richard. 2003. *Performance Theory.* London: Routledge.
Sorabjee, Soli. 1977. *The Emergency, Censorship and the Press in India, 1975–77.* London: Writers and Scholars Educational Trust.
Sukeshi, Kamra. 2011. *The Indian Periodical Press and the Production of Nationalist Rhetoric.* Basingstoke and New York: Palgrave Macmillan.

SECTION B

Training for Mindful Thinking in Communication

7

Thinking Through Practice: Creative Media as a Research Methodology[1]

Jirayudh Sinthuphan

The nation, which in the modern age has been formalized as a nation-state, depends on ideologies and practices of clear-cut borders and requires the formation of identities and communities within defined borders and territories. Like the European Community, the ASEAN Community was conceptualized with the goal of deterritorializing national political boundaries and encouraging greater cooperation among Southeast Asian nations. Yet there is still a key contradiction in the position of the nation in our times. While culture and communication become increasingly deterritorialized and transnational, the national political boundaries have also become increasingly reinforced.

Mahathir Mohamad (1970: 5), in his book *The Malay Dilemma*, noted in looking at the May 1969 racial riots in Malaysia between the Chinese and the Malays that there was never true racial harmony in his nation-state. "There was a lack of interracial strife. There was tolerance. There was accommodation. There was a certain amount of give and take. But there was no harmony. There was in fact cacophony, muted but still audible."

This condition creates a rupture between the politics of a nation and the human condition within the nation and even more so for those human subjects who cross national boundaries, especially through migration and transcultural flow.

Since almost every country in ASEAN was colonized by European powers, it is important to look at how relationships between various races were before and after this period, what impact colonization had in fermenting today's ethnic or religious conflicts, and its impact on the contemporary nation-state identity.

Looking at the relationship between the Chinese and the Malays before and after the arrival of European colonizers, Mohamad argues this gives a

---

[1] This chapter is based on the "Digital Storytelling and ASEAN Citizenship" research project, which is funded by the Ratchadapisek Sompoch Endowment Fund (2013), Chulalongkorn University (CU-56-596-AD).

true reflection of the reasons for racial conflicts occurring in today's societies in the region. He points out that whenever the Chinese are in a minority they avoid provoking the majority, in Malaysia's case the Malays. Before the Europeans arrived and colonized the land, the Chinese who migrated and settled in the country acquired not only the local language (Malay) but also the way of life of the Malays. Therefore, the conflicts were rare and never sustained. But when the Europeans brought Chinese and the Indians to Malaya their impermanent status made them live apart, never really coming in contact with the Malays.

"This lack of contact minimized conflicts, although in the later part of British rule the Malays became more and more conscious of the danger the Chinese and Indians posed to their political power in the country," Mohamad (1970: 6) points out.

> People who live apart need not like each other. If there was no conflict, it was because there was no occasion for confrontation. There was only a consciousness of each other's existence, and this consciousness was sufficiently unpleasant to prevent any desire for closer relations.

Such complex intercultural relationships (or lack of it) within countries due to colonial policies of forced migration and imposed transcultural flows that have created postcolonial faultlines and conflicts are common to the region. Indonesia, Myanmar, Vietnam, Philippines, Laos, Cambodia, and Singapore face these in one form or another. It is a formidable challenge to address issues of community building and intercultural communications as ASEAN embark on a regional community building phase.

"Digital Storytelling and ASEAN Citizenship" is a practice-related research project that seeks to explore the role of digital storytelling and narrative arts in the deterritorialization of national boundaries and in establishing a transcultural connection between people of the Southeast Asian nations. The project has brought 30 participants from different communities in the region to work together and to think, through the process of media practice, about the issues of politics, cultures, and identities of this emerging community.

The Task Ahead: Politics, Culture, and Identities

The ASEAN Community should rank as the most diverse regional community in the world, linguistically, spiritually, and culturally. The largest religious communities are Buddhists and Muslims who constitute almost over 90 percent of the population, equally divided. Philippines is predominantly Christian while there are significant Christian minorities in many of the other countries as well as a unique Hindu majority in Bali, as well as substantial Hindu populations in Malaysia and Singapore. There are diverse populations of indigenous people scattered as marginalized communities across the ASEAN region. In terms of language, almost every country has its own unique language with a rich history drawn from the Indian and Chinese civilizations.

After the colonial era, many of the ASEAN countries went through a period of authoritarian rule and it is only in the past two decades that the region has started to democratize somewhat reluctantly. Many countries such as Singapore, Laos, and Vietnam still have strong authoritarian political systems.

Former Indonesian President Abdurrahman Wahid believes that to develop a national identity, the use of a national language is very important. "The use of the national language is so widespread in Indonesia," he says. "Almost everyone can use and understand it, except a few, who may constitute only 5 percent of the population, mostly immigrants. The language we use in IT is going to be the national language of our country" (Hutanuwatr and Manivannan, 2005: 242).

Sivaraksa (2005: 107) describes the difference between the cultural attitudes of the East and West thus:

> In the West, people are taught that more is better; one should seek more of everything every day. In the East, we are taught from the cradle that we can constantly reduce our attachments or wants. In the West, the quality or quantity of personal gain and possessions marks the good life. In the East, good life simply means successfully overcoming the attachment to gains and possessions. Lastly, in the West, most people near the end of their lives simply want to lead a carefree lifestyle unburdened by work or stress. In the East, we hope to have successfully extinguished all worldly attachments by the twilight of our lives, preparing ourselves for the next world.

However, Sivaraksa argues that Thailand began to uncritically absorb the Western concepts of progress and civilization during the reign of King Rama V, and as a result, the traditional way of life began to be seen inferior and as the source of the country's backwardness. "We looked down on our value and culture without really understanding their roots or virtues," he argues (2005: 110). "We have retained Buddhism, we have not adopted Christianity. But, willfully accepting the Western notion of civilization is even more dangerous than converting to a spiritual system that is not rooted in our heritage."

Wahid, who was the leader of Indonesia's biggest religious and political organization, Nahdlatul Ulama (Rise of Islamic Scholars), before he became the president of the country (October 1999 to July 2001), explained in an interview with Thai social activist Pracha Hutanuwatr that there are many people in Indonesia who want to make Islam the state ideology in the country with the world's biggest Muslim population. "In my opinion, this follows from the narrowness of their idea of panchasila," he argued (Hutanuwatr and Manivannan, 2005: 238). "Indonesia has only one state ideology: Panchasila. To try to usurp this is wrong. However, the assumption is widespread that the growth of Islam in this state will be as an alternative to Panchasila."

Wahid argues that to maintain the plural character of Islam cannot become the state ideology because it will then have the same function of nationalism, socialism, and other isms. However, he argues that Islam teaches the roles and responsibilities of strong leader that creates a strong, obedient, and loyal community. To accomplish these goals, a leader has to establish a just and prosperous society.

Filipino Catholic Bishop Julio Xavier Labayen (Hutanuwatr and Manivannan, 2005: 200) describes the vision and goals of an ideal society as:

> We dream of a society where everybody will have the opportunity to grow into a fuller life and humanity. We dream of a society where there will be an ecological system that will provide in abundance the resources we need to sustain our lives and those of all humanity. We dream of an ideal society where there will be compassion, love, justice and sharing that bears fruit in solidarity and peace. We dream of a society where there will be perfect harmony among peoples and with the ecological environment. In short, we dream of a society where fuller life, fuller humanity and the integrity of creation will be a living reality.... It is almost becoming an impossible task to realize our dream.

Thus, Bishop Labayen argues that we need to create a counter-culture that does not promote wasteful consumerism—a simple healthier way of life that will nurture harmony with the environment, where we take care of the earth and its resources. "It is not media as such that are wrong," he argues. "It is how they are used; for what objective. Unfortunately, the media promotes chiefly a culture of consumerism."

So, can we change the media practices that could contribute to building a better ASEAN Community that could live in harmony with nature and avoid a conflict-driven economic model? What type of media practice, through research, could be created to produce such an "ideal" society as discussed above?

Media Practice as Research

In recent years, "practice" has become an important element in research activities in international higher education, especially in the fields of humanities and social sciences. The premise is that "practice" is not just a way of creating something, but it is also a way of thinking by doing through the body. There are two types of practice-related research: practice-based and practice-led.

Practice-based Research: This is an original investigation undertaken in order to gain new knowledge partly by means of practice and the outcomes of that practice. Claims of originality and contribution to knowledge may be demonstrated through creative outcomes in the form of designs, music, digital media, performances, and exhibitions. Whilst the significance and context of the claims are described in words, a full understanding can only be obtained with direct reference to the outcomes.

Practice-led Research: This is concerned with the nature of practice and leads to new knowledge that has operational significance for that practice. In a doctoral thesis, the results of practice-led research may be fully described in text form without the inclusion of a creative work. The primary focus of the research is to advance knowledge about practice, or to advance knowledge within practice. Such research includes practice as an integral part of its method and often falls within the general area of action research.

"Digital Storytelling and ASEAN Citizenship" is primarily a practice-led research that focuses on the theory and process of transcultural media education. At the same time, its creative outcomes that include digital designs, short films, and documentaries will also make it a practice-based research that seeks to promote transcultural connectedness among ASEAN citizens.

Cultivating Transculturalism

Transcultural connectedness or transculturalism is often defined as "seeing oneself in the other" (Cuccioletta, 2002), to which we would also add "seeing the other in oneself." Although this concept has its roots in the field of diaspora studies, transcultural connectedness is not singularly the property of the diaspora and as such it also has wider implications, especially in transcultural media practice. Similar to a person's identity, a piece of storytelling is shaped in a location and a space. Each space is attached to a shared thought and memory, as well as to a shared sense of belonging and longing.

Whereas in the diaspora context in the West, transcultural media practices may mean the migrant groups trying to establish a cultural identity in a foreign land, in the Asian context it has to be seen in the context of local communities trying to preserve or even nurture their cultural heritage from threats from outside, such as globalization and transnational media companies.

Transcultural media practice seeks to establish a link between two different sets of identities from two different spaces that are interconnected, but sometimes distinct and competing. Each identity depends on shared myths and memories, as well as upon a sense of belonging in an imagined community, which has some continuity and relevance across time and space (Georgiou, 2010).

According to Fernando Ortiz, who introduced the concept in the 1940s, transculturalism is a process of de-culturalization with the past and reinventing a new common culture based on the meeting and the intermingling of the different peoples and cultures. Contrary to multiculturalism, which most experiences have shown reenforces boundaries based on past cultural heritages, transculturalism is based on the breaking down of boundaries and on the recognition of the other, based on a culture of the mix. In other words, one's identity is not strictly one-dimensional (the self) but is now defined in terms of a mosaic of identities (the others).

But in the ASEAN context, as the earlier discussions reflects, the practitioners may need to be extremely mindful of cultural sensitivities, the need to establish cultural identities after ravages of colonialism or onslaught of globalized media or the political currents that pulls states between developing a national identity or protecting that identity from pressures of globalization and migratory currents.

Through the process of the AIMS workshop, participants are invited to reflect upon their own identities and to observe elements of themselves in fellow participants. They shared their stories, discussed their ideas, confronted with contrasting perceptions, and looked for the missing links between seemingly disparate worldviews, in order to reimagine the pluralistic identities of a shared community.

Reaching a Wider Audience

What started as an experiment—an experiment in the methodology, in the concept, and in the way that the project involves researchers across the Faculty of Communication Arts—"Digital Storytelling and ASEAN Citizenship" has a far-reaching impact, more than what we have thought. Since the project launch, we have been invited to give workshops in many ASEAN countries and to form a panel in upcoming International conferences.

Everywhere we went, we were greeted with enthusiastic participants and excited audience. This is a proof that a practice-related research in the humanities and social sciences can also have a wider impact in the society, as well as in the academia. Above all, this research project has demonstrated the power of storytelling and creative media in capturing the audience's imagination and in fostering a sense of belonging to the ASEAN Community.

Conclusion

A community, as Benedict Anderson (1991) has proposed, is imagined. It is psychologically constructed by those who share interests and mutual identification, rather than being simply bound by locality or face-to-face interaction. It is possible for people to maintain a sense of connectedness with those outside their geographical area. Such a sense of connectedness, as Walter Fisher illuminates, is forged and maintained through the use of stories. Fisher also recognizes that "communities are co-constituted through communication transaction in which participants co-author a story that has coherence and fidelity for the life that one would lead" (Fisher, 1989).

In light of these arguments, the future of the ASEAN Community exists equally in the stories that its human subjects recount about their own community and themselves as it does in its administrative policies. Transcultural media practice like "Digital Storytelling and ASEAN Citizenship" can provide an interconnected space for reflection, dialogue, and a complex articulation of the Us and the Others. It is a way of thinking by doing—through the body and through the use of imagination. It is an interpretative tool to make sense of events and phenomena that would otherwise be disparate and apparently unconnected. In other words, transcultural media practice is a gateway to globality in one's own consciousness.

Bibliography

Anderson, B. 1991. *Imagined Communities: Reflections on the Origin and Spread of Nationalism*. London: Verso.
Brah, A. 1996. *Cartographies of Diaspora*. London: Routledge.
Cuccioletta, D. 2002. "Multiculturalism or Transculturalism: Towards a Cosmopolitan Citizenship." *London Journal of Canadian Studies*, 17: 1–11.

Fisher, W. R. 1989. *Human Communication as Narration: Toward a Philosophy of Reason, Value, and Action*. Columbia, SC: University of South Carolina Press.

Georgiou, M. 2010. "Identity, Space and the Media: Thinking through Diaspora." *Revue Européenne des Migrations Internationales*, 26 (1): 1735.

Hinchman, L. P., and S. Hinchman. 1997. *Memory, Identity, Community: The Idea of Narrative in the Human Sciences*. Albany, NY: State University of New York Press.

Hutanuwatr, P., and R. Manivannan. 2005. *The Asian Future: Dialogue for Change*. London: Zed Books.

Mohamad, M. 1970. *The Malay Dilemma*. Singapore: Times Books.

Mouw, R., and S. Griffioen. 1993. *Pluralisms and Horizons*. Grand Rapids, MI: Eerdmans.

Sivaraksa, S. 2005. *Conflict, Culture, Change: Engaged Buddhism in a Globalising World*. Bangkok: Suksit Siam.

8

Storytelling with Deep Listening

Supaporn Phokaew

Often peoples' minds get blocked when we talk about religion, but when we talk about mindful communication, it should not be blocked by religion at all. It is about right and careful thought about so many things.

When I got this assignment to write the chapter, I thought about how we practice journalism and the way we think. It is based on the way we grow up, how we practice things influenced by the people surrounding us. These are, in turn, influenced by our teachers, and when I think of the teachers, I come back to Buddhism. I have grown up and learned something like this through the Buddhist perspective. When I talk about something like this, it does not mean I'm promoting Buddhism, but, this is part of my identity.

It is a part of the way I think, and when we go into defining mindful communication, these influences could come in the way we look at how to apply mindful communication to sustainable development. Mindful communication and sustainable development could go well together.

Communicating for Sustainable Development

So sustainable development would be the core of my argument. If we look at how we communicate for sustainable development, mindful communication should come into the frame, which could even redefine sustainable development as well.

There has been a global movement for sustainable development for some time, and now the United Nations has set up Sustainable Development Goals (SDGs) as their post-2015 millennium development goals (MDGs). Starting from 2016, SDGs are going to be key issues for the world. We need to go back and see why we have to set this up as a global agenda.

When I look back on almost four decades of the global sustainable development movement and the serious environmental problems that have come into existence in the past years, for me it is a question of why the global movement has not been effective. They now talk about "green growth" in terms of economic growth. Economic growth has become a vicious circle of development.

We talk about economic growth, but depletion of the environment and social culture is not covered in the discussion on economic growth. From this perspective, it seems like a circle. Thus, we have a crisis situation with human society.

Economic Growth and Social Crisis

This economic growth focus has led to political catastrophes that are leading us to social crisis. These are reflected in exhausted resources, epidemics, diseases, environmental wars, conflicts, and so on. I see that when we talk about economic growth, it is driven by consumption growth, even when we try to apply the concept of sustainable development. We still believe that economic growth and "green growth" can go together. I have no answer to how they can go together. But I'm trying to find out how this jigsaw could be solved or how these two could work together when we are talking about sustainable development.

Missing Elements in Sustainable Development

Some missing elements in sustainable development may be more crucial than those we talk about—economy, society, and environment—but something that I think is crucial is human mind and spirit. We do not talk much about these and we think they are separate from sustainable development.

I would like to define sustainable development from my own perspective. Sustainable development, if driven by human spiritual development, could develop humans (mind) to be happy. What that means is less attachment to unnecessary desires and material things that lead to unreal consumption and resource utilization. Compassion for others and living in harmony and peace is also important. This is how sustainable development could be redefined with mindfulness.

When we talk about mindful communication, we could apply that to redefine everything around ourselves. Let me start with how I redefine sustainable development in this way.

I need a reference to spiritual teachings for me, but I can open this up to others. To prepare this chapter, I read from both Theravada and Mahayana thoughts; so I bring perspectives from both traditions of Buddhism into defining what we mean by sustainable development under the concept of mindfulness.

Paticcasamuppada is about interdependence. It is not about ourselves, but self with others with something surrounding us. These writings talk about interdependent co-arising or dependent origination. We see environmental phenomena as interdependent and arising from multiple conditions. It is clearly consistent with the sustainable development concept of the environment embedded in a complex relationship of cause and effect.

This provides a very useful guidance to human beings to behave politically and responsibly and in harmony with nature and our universe. If individuals, organizations, agencies, communities, and nations continue to destroy environment, humanity will suffer. It is happening now with pollution, loss of biodiversity, deforestation, desertification, and climatic change.

Sustainable Development Is About Human Beings

From this perspective, sustainability concerns ecology, economy, and political regime. Therefore, the main core of sustainable development is to develop human being to decrease their greed, be less selfish, and learn to live in harmony with their environment. If humans are educated correctly, they can be expected to behave responsibly toward nature and environment and will act accordingly.

To deal with sustainable development is not to set up a policy for the supply side, but to look at the demand side as well, in terms of our consumption. Also important is how we interpret and develop both sides together. Ven Payutto (1998) also talks about these things in his book. He says that in terms of sustainable development, development should be realized through the principle of *madhyama pratipada* or middle path. He talks about the practice of moderation that we humans have to train ourselves on to improve our mind through wisdom. He links this with sufficiency—how one can improve the quality of life with his/her mind and wisdom.

This type of development is to improve the happiness, and this does not cause environmental degradation. However, we have to be concerned of the three defilements—greed, hatred, and delusion. To reach happiness, these are the obstacles that human beings come across and have to discard.

So, we have to emphasize peoples' values as human beings are part of nature. Under the cause and effect concept, people are the same as nature.

Therefore, human beings can lead their lives together in harmony with nature. Ven. Payutto (1998) says:

> A correct relation system of the development of mankind is an acceptance of the fact that human beings are part of the existence of nature and to its ecology. Human beings should develop itself at higher capacities to help its fellows and other species in the natural domain. To live in a harmonious way, and lessen exploitation, in order to contribute to a happier world. The concern to be living in harmony with nature is likely to be driven by inner happiness obtained by wisdom and understanding of the interdependence of living with all kinds of beings and nature, as well as happiness from less use of resources and less on materials.

Inner Happiness and Development

We need to get people to learn about and develop inner happiness. We need to put emphasis on human spiritual development as a key factor of sustainable development. Given the conventional idea that sustainable development has long been used in a not so sustainable way, it may be time to change the development mindset and rethink about the sustainable development framework with the right path and right views. This could take a new direction for effecting sustainable development. Considering inner happiness as the key of driving sustainable development can make a critical change.

This will involve promoting inner happiness with moderate consumption. In line with "middle path" economies lies the holistic sustainable development approach. Spiritual or inner happiness focus of sustainable development can be considered as a direction for advanced human development encouraging humans to move on the path of happiness on a more basic level than getting happiness from some material dependency. The higher level is happiness in your mind with wisdom. This is the happiness level we have to inculcate because we have been accustomed to material life. We need to see the happiness inside ourselves.

This is to promote happiness in humans at a higher level, which is more independent with sustainable type of happiness and can help in effecting sustainable development. Bringing in Buddhist teachings, I have learned that we can bring in compassion and loving kindness to achieve this. You have to open your heart and have compassion and loving kindness toward all species, humans and other sentient beings.

Bringing Compassion into Development

If we look at everything around us in a friendly manner, then we are giving *metta* (compassion) and *karuna* (loving kindness) together not only to our social networks but also to all humans and living kinds that surround us. We share not only our suffering with others but accept sufferings of others because of unsustainable actions. Thus, compassion and loving kindness could mobilize action to overcome situations that have destroyed the ecology and created the environmental crisis.

A lot of the forest monks in Thailand mobilize the people, especially who live in the forests, who suffer from disrupting logging. The monks and the people get together and do a ceremony to protect the remaining forests and the environment of the country as well. If you travel in the countryside, especially in forest areas, you may see trees that are wrapped in monks' robes. People will then not cut down these trees. When people do that, they start to love and be concerned about the environment, and they try to protect it.

When we talk about mindful communication, we have to be mindful to sustainable development as well. We have to set up mindful development, starting with the mindset. We have to shift the mindset toward sustainable development to include compassion and kindness in it. Moreover, the idea that we are sharing something together needs to be included in sustainable development. We have to translate spiritual development into the meaning of happiness, that is, when people do not see in material terms anymore.

I think that mindful communications does not happen accidently; you need to practice it, and it is part of human development as well. While mindfulness is something we all naturally possess, it is more readily available to us when we practice on a daily basis. Whenever you bring awareness to what you are directly experiencing via your senses, or to your state of mind via your thoughts and emotions, you are being mindful.

Deep Listening

The key for the media in order to practice mindful communication is deep listening. Deep listening is to be very open, an open mindfulness. In universities that teach mass communications, practice of listening is rarely taught. In our universities, we start by talking and teaching about how to write and how to speak, but listening, we think, comes automatically. I think listening is something we need to practice in classrooms, and students have to learn about open heart; we become very sore and diligent of things.

Deep listening involves listening, from a deep, receptive, and caring place in oneself, to deeper and often subtler levels of meaning and intention in the other person. It is listening that is generous, empathic, supportive, accurate, and trusting. It is an ongoing practice of suspending self-oriented, reactive thinking and opening one's awareness to the unknown and unexpected. So to learn deep listening you need to start by listening yourself silently—being silent. The more important thing is that we need to practice listening to others and being patient while doing so. The keyword is deep listening for me, and that is the path to practice mindful communication.

Second is that we must think in terms of the level of society as well. The aim of mindful communication is that we should facilitate change and that at the end we have to reduce the state of suffering for the people in the society. That is the big picture. We do not just talk about ourselves, we listen to other. When we say "listen to other," as what Sulak Sivaraksa argued in Chapter 2, you need to listen to the people about the impact of development on them. You listen and learn from them.

In mindful communication, by listening and thinking about the bigger picture, we try to reduce the suffering of the people. In the Buddhist Eightfold Path, we first understand suffering and then find a way to solve it and then practice that path. So for the mindful media, we can explore how to practice the Eightfold Path to help achieve happiness and sustainable development.

In training journalists, these principles could be adopted in workshops, taking a given situation to develop a mindful communication path to achieve sustainable development. It is important that spiritual ideas (teachings) and secularism come together in devising this new development/mindful communication path.

We have to promote how to live a meaningful life and that sustainability is achieved on mindful training. We need to deconstruct something and change into something new. By embracing change, media could embrace the practice of the "middle path," and media should promote harmony with nature and contemplate on the usefulness of services and products before consuming them. Media should promote mindfulness over consumption.

Reference

Payutto, P. A. 1998. *Buddhist Economics*, 5th ed. Thailand: Buddhadhamma Foundation.

9

New Approach to ASEAN Journalism: From a Thai Perspective

Pipope Panitchpakdi

Focus on individual expression is the basis of what we define as news values. Those who have been trained formally try to introduce this public idea of freedom of expression (FOE) and news values. If you look at news in mainstream media, it is about personal interactions, people killed, raped, violated, some "stupid" officials who take bribes, and so forth. It's not about the structure of society.

In the Thai context, what is valuable as far as news is concerned has something to do with someone, not the situation or the structure. So you see the localization of most issues. Floods we tell through the story of some village or one person. Many times, it is good because it can reach the heart of the reader, but at the same time, the news story is simplified. Because Thai society is heavily individualized as a person and they want news at a personal level.

For me, FOE is an act of politics, where someone wants to change something and use that expression to mobilize change. If you look at mainstream or social media, FOE is to say things that one wants to express casually, but sometimes I think there are things that should not be said in public.

Conformist Society and News

There is a saying that it is safe to stay in a safe place. So the bubble in Thailand is very large. We believe that the best person is the person who does not say anything. There is a proverb in Thai which translates as "If you are quiet, you get more money, but if you express yourself, trouble would come to you." That is why we are seemingly conformist and do not stand up for things we feel are important.

But that may be an old thing. One thing about Thailand is that it is insular, as the country is in the middle of trade routes from olden days, the Silk Route, so people from many backgrounds interact here, since hundreds of years ago. From that we developed a way of not saying what we think. We would not tell a Muslim that pork is good; it is tasty. At certain times, we can be flexible.

I do not know if conformist is a real word to describe the Thai society. We are really adaptive. This ability to adapt can be interpreted as double speaking, double dealing. Finding a good balance is important. Sometimes we can be violent, as seen in color shirts conflicts in recent years.

The conflicts between the so-called "red shirts" and "yellow shirts" gripped the Thai nation between 2006 and 2014. These two bitterly divided camps staged street protests, occupations, and many other protest campaigns that pitted Thais against each other.

The red shirts began as supporters of deposed former Prime Minister Thaksin Shinawatra, who was ousted by a military coup in September 2006. This support transferred to Thailand's Pheu Thai Party led by his sister, Yingluck Shinawatra, who was also ousted by a military coup in 2014. The yellow shirts represent those opposed to Mr Thaksin and they were the force behind the street protests that led to the 2006 and 2014 coups.[1]

Just prior to the 2014 military coup, in January 2014, *Al Jazeera* reported that Thailand is no stranger to "political tumult," and since the absolute monarchy was changed in 1932, the Kingdom has experienced 18 coups, 23 military governments, and 9 military-dominated governments. Thus, they observed:

> In 2014—like 2013, 2010, 2008 and 2006—demonstrators filled Bangkok's streets, demanding the government step down. With a beloved king in fragile health, a still-powerful military at odds with the current government and no love lost between the leading political parties, stability is not likely to come to Thai politics any time soon. A clear pattern of protest and unrest has emerged since the ouster of former Prime Minister Thaksin Shinawatra eight years ago. In November 2013, anti-government protesters took to the streets of Thailand's capital, and by December the raucous crowd had grown to over 200,000. (Shay, 2014)

Being confrontational is a human trait. Thailand, despite being a predominantly Buddhist country, has been a diverse community since long. When I say so, this diversity is not necessarily based on religion. There are many other factors that affect the structure of Thai society such as socioeconomic diversity. Thailand's controlling center is really loose. It is trading that makes Thai what it is. But it has to be open to new things.

---

[1] For more background, refer to http://www.bbc.com/news/world-asia-pacific-13294268 (accessed on October 27, 2017).

Yellow and red shirts were about the concept of monarchy. That is what they were debating about. However, on the outside it might be seen as being about democracy. It was something we were trained not to debate about—the concept of monarchy.

Adversarial News Model and Thai Journalism

I think news has to be critical, but being critical does not have to be confrontational. Being critical is looking at things objectively, but the approach of doing it does not have to be negative. We have to find a concept of finding a solution to journalism that is currently based on the adversarial model of journalism borrowed from the West.

It may be quite suitable for Thailand to create a dialogue—something more than a discourse, more than words—an ongoing dialogue as a news piece.

People like bad news so long as it is about other people. They can derive warning from these types of news for themselves and their families so as not to fall into the same trap. Second, it provides a kind of entertainment. When we talk about negativity, the news by itself is not negative, but it is the way that news is approached and explained. I will call a news positive if it has the value of bringing a positive change, even if it is reporting on a bad situation.

Take the reporting of floods for example. It sounds like bad news if you report people are being flooded, government did not go and help. But if what is reported is why help from the government was delayed, what caused the floods, and its multiconditions, and if news can maintain that complexity and at the same time have good narratives, that is what we need. That is very important in Asian culture. We have our roots in Ramayana, which is a complex story and we can still get information out of it. Why don't we do that?

I think the recent news reporting approach in Thailand is like this because we took the Western tabloid attitude. People in industrial society do not want complicated stories. They prefer to hear that their position in society is okay and bad things happen to other people. I have a strong suspicion that this is the reason why news reporting in Thailand is the way it is.

Decolonizing the Mind

I think it will be a shame if we make mindful communication an anti-Western sentiment. The real problem is extreme capitalism and colonization that are ongoing processes. The industrialization that developed in the West, from

Europe, has marginalized many, and mass communications systems we know of today are product of that extreme capitalism.

Thailand is at the crossroads of many cultures. When a Western academic comes here and sees us, they say we are heavily Indianized. You see the mindset of the academic? It has to be conquered; it has to be taken. They do not say that the Thais have borrowed a lot of wonderful things from India. Part of being mindful is to look at it that way. If an Indian academic is going to write a book on Thailand, unless he is very westernized, he will surely say there is a lot of coercion (mixing) going between many cultures here. We do not talk much about our diversity because it comes naturally to us.

When it comes to communication, we need to change the whole concept. Since I am a media practitioner, rather than going into too much theory, I will discuss how these communication theories apply to our practice in producing contents. We are really saturated with notions of how we should talk. Our Asian values are based on:

- Being non-judgmental
- Pragmatism and coercion
- Acceptance of differences
- Celebrating blissfulness
- Compassion and kindness

We are non-judgmental and pragmatic. These mean that anything goes as far as it does not hurt us, and we can coexist. We can go and eat other peoples' food without much questioning, accepting differences. It is interesting that we eat this Muslim (Malay) dish *satay* with pork—Muslims will not eat it that way. It is coerced culturally and it creates something new. This shows respect for the original culture with bean sauce and the way to do it. Then they adapt to what is appropriate to their tongue, because Chinese trend of Buddhism is not eating beef. Accepting our differences is a strong point and it can be witnessed everywhere.

Celebrating blissfulness is to be seen everywhere and it is not about full-moon parties where you let go of stress. Being blissful has to do with a lot of our narratives and storytelling skills, but we have been trained to get agitated and excited, that is the wrong way to communicate in our own terms. It does not mean we are emotionless and being mindful does not mean we are sedated.

Many people think that being mindful is moving slowly here and there and having no fun. Sense of happiness is the feeling of being able to have compassion and kindness. During industrialization, Thais were considered too slow, unindustrialized, and tardy. Thai people like to laugh and giggle, and this too was frowned upon. Actually, laughing is healthy. People should laugh and smile. Now, in the post-industrial era, these are the qualities that I would like to call "Suvarnabhumi" culture.

Suvarnabhumi culture is in the middle with India to the west and China to the northeast, and we have been borrowing from both. Nobody owns anything; it is a mutual flow of commerce, knowledge, religion, and culture. It has been an ongoing process for 1,600 years.

Kalama Sutta Path to New Journalism

When it comes to news production, the West would think that it is an act of acquiring facts. They are always occupied with material things that materialism has created. But when we are mindful, we have to be aware of things that minds create. The process that goes hand in hand when we produce contents is that first we like to be there. We do not want to visualize or imagine things. We like to be there before we speak.

We have the *Kalama Sutta*[2] in Buddhism, which is a handy tool to verify the truth. Lot of people say that Thais are not concerned about the truth. I think they are concerned about the truth, and they also have a reason that the truth has to be carefully managed. When you go there, you not only ask questions about what is going on, but you should also be encouraged to feel (for the people). For example, when we go to an earthquake-hit area, at first we feel sad for the victims, then we empathize, and think that leads to compassion. If we do not inculcate this as a quality, we will think that Western journalism, as we learn from school, prohibits us to think that way.

Actually the new mindful journalist must be encouraged to think from the heart. And think long into the past to understand why it has happened—the inequality, disaster, the injustice, that may be going on. And the last, which is uniquely Asian, is to reflect. Through the means and tools you have in hand, you should try to produce knowledge. This ongoing process of being there, to feel, to think, to reflect, is not taught in journalism schools.

We talk about news positions, which is about primary resource and secondary resource, but, the working of the mind of the person as the agent of producing reality and narratives has not been really talked about. We look at it as if it is things people do anyway.

I am in the television industry and we produce contents in three stages: pre-production, production, and post-production.

---

[2] See http://www.buddhanet.net/e-learning/kalama1.htm (accessed on September 19, 2017).

In pre-production, that is, before we start the filming, the Western media is really into dramatic form. The dramatic form is one of many forms of storytelling formats that exist in the world. It was really glamourized during the restoration age when Christians came into the theater during the Shakespearian time. Coming to our Ramayana, it is a totally different type of storytelling. You do not have those good guys and bad guys. We have the so-called epic storytelling.

In epic storytelling, you cannot really say who is good and bad; it just happens. You interact without being concerned about who is going to be a hero before doing the deeds. It took 200 years for Batman to say "just judge me from what I do." Actually, the epics did this for many centuries, 2,000 years.

You cannot tell a dramatic story without the contents and that is why journalism is so conflict-based. You have to have a conflict to tell a story and eventually you have the good guy and the bad guy. This good guy and the bad guy have to fight for something and in the end someone will win. If someone wins, according to some religions, something needs to be wiped out. That is what is going on politically.

The concept of having this dramatic approach is very dangerous and the Indian culture and Chinese culture have known it for thousands of years. That is why they encourage the epics of storytelling. So you have stories that are really fragmented. You will have this guy and something is going on and anything can happen to this guy. If you go through all this structures, you get the feel of the mind. I think this is mindfulness as a storytelling method.

The Western media is often into speculation and forecasting. That is not the way we do investigation. We go there, taste it, we talk to the person, and we chase the bad guy. The social media is totally an American way of communication—individualization and free speech; say whatever you want and if you do not like it and are frightened, well you still say it.

For us, groundedness is important. That is why our presenter becomes famous as a news anchor. Because the viewers see that this person actually goes there. Sometimes, news anchors use graphics to show that they were there, but that is not the way to do it. You have to do the news stories through the direct experience of someone and I call it groundedness.

Reporting as a Process, Not an Event

Filming and deep listening go hand in hand. I learned it from my experience of doing tsunami stories. My wife is from Songkla; I lost someone close to my family there and I had to go there and work as a journalist myself. They were no longer victims; they were kins, they were my family. Filming could be a process that could be healing for both, those who are being filmed and those who are filming.

This is a good style of doing things and this is suitable for mindful communication. You have the right concept and right mind when you are not going to do it in a dramatic form. You are trying to be helpful rather than useful in portraying it in a dramatic form. Try to be grounded rather than being speculative, and be collaborative and have the right intention. This practice is very important in mindful communication.

Interviewing is not to be filming something as a product. It is the act of being there while you have this interaction. In recording, one is telling you the truth and you are listening to it. Let it be lengthier than the usual media slot and create this together. To use it later or not and in which way is another matter. The point is being there and listening to someone. I think every journalism school must focus on this, or else you fall back in the trap of just producing products.

About a year after the tsunami, I did an interview with a Sri Lankan television producer and communicator, Nalaka Gunawardene,[3] and this is how he reflected on the way Western (mainstream) media crews went about reporting the event and its aftermath:

> As the tsunami happened on a lean news day, the media took some time to ultimately get into the multiple scenes of devastation. By that time, in fact the first few hours of coverage was done by the holidaymakers and those labeled as "amateurs" by the mainstream media. This is interesting that the mainstream media had to rely on so-called "amateur" coverage to devastation taking place and unfolding. As soon as the media crews and TV reporters arrived on the scene of the devastation, they were overwhelmed, the national as well as the foreign television crews. Because the scale of the disaster and the magnitude of the impact is not something the journalists and the camera crews were used to in the typical normal working lives. So they took time and I think they did a commendable job in coping with very hard working conditions that prevailed in all the tsunami hit countries and locations.

> But, as the days passed we realized there was a certain superficial nature, the coverage was largely looking at death, destruction, and devastation. Yes there was that element in the tsunami, in any major crisis or disaster there would be that element. But also there was an important aspect that we felt

---

[3] Refer to https://nalakagunawardene.com/2009/12/25/looking-back-at-asian-tsunami-of-2004-and-media-response/ (accessed on October 27, 2017).

the mainstream media did not cover, that was how the affected people, the individuals and the communities, coped with the enormous problems that prevailed immediately after. On the one hand as we know the search and rescue operations that took place in the first few days, and then disposal of bodies, the missing locations of friends and relatives, and a whole range of these stressful and very problematic issues that prevailed, and how there was human ingenuity, there was resourcefulness, and there was resilience, and these stories which were unfolding in many tsunami towns, villages and locations, these were not picked up enough of the times in the media.

Media had two or three headlines topics, how much aid was being pledged around the world, which was very good, but, that was not the only story and then the media had particular preoccupation with Western tourists who have been unfortunately affected by the disaster, again I would say that was legitimate news coverage but sometimes one wonders whether the Western media news coverage was disproportionately focused on the Western tourists that were affected by the tsunami. So like that we felt that while we watched the coverage over time, over a few days and weeks, we felt there was more to this disaster and more to the recovery from the disaster. We also knew that the typical attention span of the major news networks would not last very long....

We wanted to look at some of those unfolding stories of human survival and human resilience. We were looking at a way of doing this and we had the option of doing the traditional documentary with facts and figures and interview clips and location filming. That was an option we considered and then we realized that there will be enough other documentaries that will be made about this. We wanted to find a new and different way of covering this important story, important for a number of reasons for Asians and for the world.

That's when in January 2005, we at TVE Asia Pacific had an internal brainstorming session and thought we will look at the recovery process through the personal stories of tsunami affected children, and their families. That we wanted to happen through locally based filmmakers, we as a regional organization did not want to be going and filming at each of these locations. Having decided the concept then we looked for like-minded filmmakers and TV journalists who could do this in the four countries hit by the tsunami. India, Indonesia, Sri Lankan and Thailand. We were very fortunate in finding like-minded TV producers in these countries who can cover this tsunami recovery process in a different way. This was the genesis of the children of tsunami initiative.[4]

---

[4] Available at https://www.youtube.com/playlist?list=PLE3CAC0F15EC7C0C2 (accessed on October 27, 2017).

As Gunawardene explained, the Asian Tsunami was a huge news event because its images fitted very well with the Western news model. But if news media is really going to make an impact on society, what is important is how we report the process that could take years to rebuild these communities and heal the affected families. As the Asian Media Information and Communication Centre (AMIC) (Seneviratne, 2006) said in the introduction to its book *Media's Challenge: Asian Tsunami and Beyond*:

> The tsunami demonstrated that modern journalism can do more than just bring unfolding stories to the world. One of the biggest lessons of the tsunami that is unraveling is that the modern journalist can also help to heal communities, rebuild lives, keep families intact and raise funds. The media should also keep an eye on government and relief agencies, helping to ensure that aid gets to the people that need it, and that those who deliver the goods remain accountable to the donors and practice ethical standards of aid delivery. It is in the rehabilitation or healing process that the media face the most challenging task. In this endeavor, democracy and the freedom to gather and disseminate information may not be enough.

Reporting the Role of Religious Charities

In the AMIC publication, which was based on location research by local researchers 2 years after the Asian tsunami, on how the media reported the issue then, it was observed that there was a critical factor in the relief effort that went largely unreported, especially by the international (i.e., Western) media. This was the role of religious organizations in seemingly unethical aid practices. The report noted (Seneviratne, 2006: 243):

> A critical issue in the aftermath of the tsunami disaster was the role religious organisations played in raising money for relief work and delivering the relief quickly. Communities in the tsunami hit areas in Asia were predominantly Muslim, Buddhist or Hindu, but religious organization of many denominations—Buddhist, Muslim, Christian, Hindu, etc.—raised millions of dollars and actively went about delivering this aid. But, there were also many evangelical groups who tried to exploit the disaster for their own gains, through proselytizing in "unreached areas" which exacerbated existing religious conflicts or created new ones. Thus the tsunami experience has made it imperative that the media play a more active role in not only exposing corruption in the aid delivery mechanism, but also exposing the unethical activities undertaken by religious organisations through their proselytizing in affected areas.

I reported in Nation[5] about proselytization where a certain group came and converted sea gypsies to Christianity. The reaction by Thai readers was that we should not bring up religion in our news reporting. Even though there is a difference now with the Dhammakaya issue,[6] a lot of what we see in newscasts and newspapers is reflecting what people want. Certain things are not to be spoken about, and if it has to, it needs to be spoken at an individual level.

For example religion should not be reported, but if there is this bad monk, proven no doubt he is bad, then ok. Issues like he going out as a civilian at night and coming back as a monk in the daytime cannot be reported. But critical questions about Buddhism itself—that will be a tough task reporting. Thus, what may be happening in poor communities, regarding "unethical" activities of Christian organizations, may go unreported.

Challenges of Reporting About the Structure

In Thailand, I have found that if you report on a personal level about a person then you are pretty safe. When you go to the structural level, not about a bad doctor but about the bad medical system, it will not only be risky for the journalist but it will lack interest. Structural or process reporting does not touch the heart.

As discussed by Sulak Sivaraksa in Chapter 2, a major reason for poverty and dissatisfaction is the structural violence of the global and local economic system. Thus, it is in human interest, in my understanding, that structural problems are addressed first. You need to bring a face to the structure, to relate to the bigger problems. But what is popular in Thai media is focus on the individual.

Once I got funded by the Thai Development Research Institute (TDRI) to do a program on poverty. We did it through the Nation TV. There were five episodes; the first was about the poor—one poor guy who works in a city and goes back (to the village). This gained in the most popularity. We were immensely praised for it, but when we went to the community and tried to report on the invisible structure of poverty, it did not get any attention at

---

[5] Nation Group is Thailand's largest media organization.

[6] Wat Dhammakaya is a leading Buddhist temple and religious sect in Thailand that is patronized by Thailand's rich elites. As of early 2017, political tensions were raised to a dangerous level when the military surrounded and cordoned off the temple area. The religious sect, whose former abbot, Phra Dhammachayo, is facing money-laundering charges, is said to have strong links with senior Pheu Thai members and some of the Shinawatras. The military was trying to arrest him to face charges.

all. People wanted to watch the story of the poor guy but they did not want to go there and change the structure that made him poor. They wanted to give money to that particular poor man.

That series we did for TDRI spun a new TV program called "pun pun pun," man search for man type of stories, but it did not touch on the structural problem. The stories focused on one "hard luck" person and people wanted to donate to that but the real motive of TDRI and us was to show the poverty problem through the individual guy. After that I stopped doing this one-person story, even though it brought me a lot of program commissions.

Moving to Community Media

I think the Thais need to shift their approach a little: from the individual to the community. If you do programs/reports on structural issues, only the intellectually educated may watch it, like those who tune to Thai Public Broadcasting Service (TPBS), and their ratings are very low. Yet there should be a way to articulate those structural problems. We journalists must care about the people, but the structure of the system should be important in telling the story. There must be a different way to get their attention; just showing infographics or the likes does not work.

The craving for one-person stories and dirty laundry has proved to be very successful in the mainstream media, but from my experiments in the field, community interest is also very attractive when the viewers have a community. The problem with mass media is when we communicate to a mass crowd, there is no such thing as a community. A community story could be highly popular if it is broadcast in a place where there is a community. So the place where community model works for me is in the rural areas. Or even in an inner city, you can define a group of viewers (community). It is not a broadcast anymore, it is a narrow cast that could bring real change. That is my interest these days.

Why Do We Want to Be Journalists?

We want to be in journalism not for a job, but because we want change, we want better lives. We want something to make our lives better. So I am into this narrow casting from community to community, and then bringing the community story to the interest of the larger public. If you wanted to do this 10 or 15 years ago, it would not have been viable at all, but we have digital technology today. With Internet, with social media, with mainstream media that could be scaled down a lot—to a level that you do not need a lot of money—it can happen.

Earlier we had human-interest stories, so now I propose community-interest stories. It will be able to prosper and grow because of technology today. I use smartphone as the main platform to go out and make the community aware of issues. Community will become interested to learn from the experience of others (in the community).

Thailand has regular floods and during these disasters, mainstream media will report on celebrities going to communities or rains developing in Vietnam or so on. But community media will look at the floods in your area and how you manage them, how nearby community, which is not flooded, comes in and helps.

They use live Facebook feeds, and those consuming it are nearby communities. A community that had this type of experience somewhere else will learn from it and get empowered. A network of help is created, with people coming in and sharing techniques for preventing floods or getting flood water out of their houses, and this they watch through mobile phones. Today, studies have shown that people watch TV more through their smartphones than on their TV screens. That gives some hope and this gives the people an idea of the potential of social media to promote broader community interests and reforms to unjust social and economic structures.

I think this is a new kind of mindful communication through the availability of technology. Without Internet and without locals having easy access to smartphones nowadays, it wouldn't have happened. Mainstream TV will still do human-interest stories about someone who lost his mother or so, but community TV don't do that. They would do stories on how a group of people are doing something to help each other. This also gets a lot of viewers. It is not true that one-person stories get the most attention. It only happens where the community has collapsed and you only have the mass audience.

Bibliography

Ng, E. 2015. "Who Gets Mindfulness 'Right'?: An Engaged Buddhist Perspective." ABC Radio, Australia, March 12. Available at http://www.abc.net.au/religion/articles/2015/03/05/4191695.htm (accessed on October 25, 2017).

Rakasaseri, K. 2016. "What Lines Can, and Cannot Be Crossed in the Name of News?" *Nation*, January 26.
Seneviratne, K. 2006. *Media's Challenge: Asian Tsunami and Beyond.* Singapore: AMIC.
Shay, C. 2014. "Explainer: In Thailand, Why Yellow and Red Clash." *Al Jazeera*, January 24. Available at http://america.aljazeera.com/articles/2014/1/24/explainer-in-thailandwhyyellowandredclash.html (accessed on October 25, 2017).

10

Mindful Communication and Media Training: A View from Myanmar

Cho Cho Thwin

It is undeniable that university subjects do effect and reflect the setting of educational goals and objectives which are intended to best serve the society in the specific field and area. Nowadays, public relation and information are of critical importance to every society, and they have precipitated the entry of multimedia into educational content.

Representatives of 19 nations at UNESCO's 1982 International Symposium on Media Education[1] held in Grunwald, Germany, acknowledged the critical role of parents, teachers, media personnel and decision-makers in developing public awareness. The final declaration said:

> Rather than condemn or endorse the undoubted power of the media, we need to accept their significant impact and penetration throughout the world as an established fact, and also appreciate their importance as an element of culture in today's world. The role of communication and media in the process of development should not be underestimated, nor the function of media as instruments for the citizen's active participation in society. Political and educational systems need to recognize their obligations to promote in their citizens a critical understanding of the phenomena of communication.

Communication is a key element of mass media, and the development of communication technology allows getting news and information rapidly within the society and achieving interaction between different communities. In addition, journalism acts as an essential tool in conduct of mass media in every society.

Mindfulness in the field of communication has mainly been considered in terms of how consciously people plan their approach to a communication exchange or the extent to which they identify and respond to relevant

---

[1] Available at http://www.unesco.org/education/pdf/MEDIA_E.PDF (accessed on October 27, 2017).

or irrelevant information in a given situation (Folkes, 1985). Furthermore, Goldstein (1993) asserted that the increased awareness afforded by mindfulness makes it possible to initiate effective communication without getting caught in reactive judgments.

Media training provides a framework of theories and practices about understanding public affairs and the process of particular events such as economic, political, and social by using appropriate methods, structure, and measures (Loo, 2013). Moreover, mindful communication has been recognized as a social imperative for education development and understanding of the ethical responsibilities in a society. Therefore, it is strategically important to plan mindful communication concepts that could be adopted in developing curriculum for media training and practice.

Myanmar's Pioneering Role in Popularizing Insight Meditation

Myanmar is one of the few countries in the world where Theravada Buddhism still survives in its original form (Bischoff, 2003). The Buddha himself tells us in *Satipatthana Sutta* about establishment of mindfulness that serves as the cornerstone of the whole system of insight meditation expounded and popularized by Ven. Mahasi Sayadaw. The Buddha himself found the right middle path which is conductive to the opening of the eye of wisdom and to the attainment of wisdom itself by avoiding the two extremes of sensual pleasure and self-torture, and developing the eight practices: (a) right view, (b) right thinking or resolution, (c) right speech, (d) right action or right conduct, (e) right living or livelihood, (f) right effort, (g) right mindfulness, and (h) right concentration (Mahasi Sayadaw, 1981; Mahathera Ledi Sayadaw, 1965). This middle path enables extraordinary knowledge and insight knowledge that discerns matters being difficult to know. The eye of wisdom means the act of knowing in this regard (Mahasi Sayadaw, 1981).

The Buddha has given the guidelines or instructions on how to train in morality, develop concentration, and become wise (Bhikkhu Moneyya, 2015). Accordingly, it has been recognized that mind and matter are impermanent things. These impermanent things have to be meditated seeing them as they really are, as being impermanent. They rise and pass away and keep on oppressing, so they are considered as dreadful sufferings. They are processes lacking in a personality, a soul, and a self. In fact, these are all matters of personal knowledge and not beliefs held out of deference to one's teachers or blind beliefs accepted out of reverence for the Buddha. That is why the Buddha's teaching is praised as the *Dhamma* comprising morality, concentration, wisdom, and deliverance that can be personally experienced if practiced (Mahasi Sayadaw, 1981; Pa Auk Sayadaw, 1998).

Owing to its truth and accuracy, the Buddha's teaching is better, fresher, and brighter than ever (Mahasi Sayadaw, 1981). Almost without exception, meditation is needed as a dietary supplement for proper assimilation of the Buddha's teachings (Ba Khin, 1991). Mahasi Sayadaw (1904–1982) founded, in 1947, one of the main *Vipassana* insight meditation traditions in Myanmar, and many people have benefited from the mindfulness practice of his meditation training. Mahasi Sayadaw (1981) thoroughly explained the noble teaching of the Buddha emphasizing the importance and value of *Vipassana* insight meditation as well as describing how this meditation may be undertaken. *Vipassana* meditation means observing every phenomenon occurring at the six-sense doors. It is suggested that one should begin with observing the few phenomena that are of a pronounced character. For example, every time one breathes in and breathes out, his or her abdomen moves, and its rising and falling is quite plain and easy to meditate on. If, while noting the rising and falling of the abdomen, any thought or imagination comes up, he or she may note "imagining," "thinking," etc., and subsequently achieve contemplation of his or her mind. By continuing to meditate on whatever comes up, one's concentration becomes very strong (Mogok Sayadaw, 1967).

In Mahasi Sayadaw's explanation, there are seven factors of wisdom including mindfulness, investigation of the *Dhamma*, energy, joy or rapture, repose, concentration, and equanimity. However, these factors of wisdom do not come up to the beginner in meditation. They come only to one who has attained the knowledge of arising and passing away of things. When a person notes the arising and passing away, he or she will be mindful of it, and consequently at the time of being mindful, he or she will also be aware it is mindfulness. Being thus aware, one's concentration gets especially stronger. With every act of seeing, hearing, touching, or knowing, whatever is experienced is only psycho-physical phenomena recognizing how cause brings effect and how this cause and effect relation goes on. It is also personally experienced that there is no permanent self-entity (Mahasi Sayadaw, 1981; Pa Auk Sayadaw, 1998).

A critique of *Vipassana* meditation was presented by S. N. Goenka (Singh, 2007). He explained that *Vipassana* is subtly described as the one true path to liberation. Due to the significance and rationale given to dispassionate observation of the bodily sensations, other techniques are considered as only being able to reform the surface mind, whereas *Vipassana* is claimed to change the unconscious layers of the mind as well. He also advised the students to fully concentrate on the task at their hand while doing their jobs.[2]

Concepts of Mindful Communication

Mindfulness or *Vipassana*, as it is known in the Buddhist tradition, is often described as seeing things as they really are, and this concept was popularized globally by S. N. Goenka (as discussed above and in the Introduction). "To observe reality as it is. No imagination, speculation, belief or disbelief is allowed. When people start realising the truth of their body and minds, how they work, they come out of misery," argues the Burmese-born mindfulness guru.[3]

According to studies, mindful communication literacy has been centered on five core competencies: understanding what you believe and why; accepting that your perceptions are always limited; bringing your empathy, however weak, to every communication; starting recognizing the role your judgment plays in how you communicate; and linking our intentions to subsequent outcomes (Louise Altman, 2013). Barker (2000) and Spencer-Oatey (2013) mentioned the key concepts of mindfulness that have initially developed by Langer, Blank, and Chanowitz (1978) such as the nature of mindfulness was presented by creating new categories, showing openness to new information, awareness of more than one perspective, categorizing is a fundamental and natural human activity, and it is the way we come to know the world in more detail.

The other perception of a successful communication strategy is based upon 10 approaches for a better communicator suggested by Jennifer Mellon (2016). These include: (a) give a valuable takeaway; (b) be a good listener; (c) pick an opportune time to speak; (d) be the unifying voice; (e) keep your responses succinct; (f) do not be the person who need to comment on everything; (g) cut the fluff; (h) prepare ahead of time; (i) smile; (j) validate, then share.

---

[2] For further knowledge, refer to http://www.h-net.org/reviews/showrev.php?id=44558 (accessed on October 27, 2017).

[3] Refer to the interview with S. N. Goenka—http://www.awaken.com/2013/03/interview-with-sn-goenka/ (accessed on October 27, 2017).

According to Triandis (1994), the key concepts of mindful behavior mainly include: developing cultural flexibility (learn culturally valued activities and accommodate them), learning to communicate (use others' rules for verbal and nonverbal communication), managing conflict (learn a collaborative style not an aggressive one), learning to suspend judgment (take time to understand), showing cultural sensitivity (search for cultural explanations for behavior), developing tolerance (for differences among people).

> "Mindfulness can be of many things. You can be mindful of the outside thing, you can be mindful about others, you can be mindful even about your body," argues Goenka,[4] pointing out that the mindfulness thought in his Vipassana technique "is (to be aware of) the inner reality, because that's related to our misery. One is to come out of misery."

Mark Pearson (2014) mentioned mindful journalism in his study focusing on Buddhism's "Noble Eightfold Path". He explores its applicability to Fourth Estate journalism in the modern era. It takes each of its elements— understanding free of superstition, kindly and truthful speech, right conduct, doing no harm, perseverance, mindfulness, and contemplation.

In the book *Mindful Journalism and News Ethics in the Digital Era*, Gunaratne, Pearson, and Senarath (2015) describe not only background and critique of the prevailing Western-centric media ethics and practices but also demonstrates evidence of how "mindful journalism" restores the lost professional standards through purification of an individual's mind (Murthy, 2016). This book also offers a comprehensive theoretical framework of dependent co-origination relating to journalistic practices explaining how a journalist helps media to end a conflict and promote peace/harmony, and how Buddhism supports the journalist to adhere to the principles of naturalness or spontaneity. In fact, mindful journalism does not treat the "news" as a commodity and discourages promotion of anger, greed, conflict, lust, etc., through the unlimited consumption of "news about suffering" (crime, rape, seduction, kidnap, murder, extortion, etc.).

Ethics has been defined as "moral philosophy [which is] the study of the general nature of morals and of the specific moral choices to be made by a person." Ethicist Michael Josephson says that there are two aspects of ethics; the first involves the ability to discern right from wrong, good from evil, and propriety from impropriety. The second involves the commitment to do what

---

[4] Refer to the interview with S. N. Goenka—http://www.awaken.com/2013/03/interview-with-sn-goenka/ (accessed on October 27, 2017).

is right, good, and proper. Ethical journalists are mindful of such potential vulnerabilities and either look for alternative sources or take considered steps to minimize the impact of their reportage (Pearson, 2014).

Actually, the Eastern traditions and contemporary secular applications of mindfulness emphasize the nonjudgmental role which plays in opening one's awareness and letting go of the initial tendency to blame others that often arises during difficult interactions. Recognizing emotional reactions and positively reappraising the conflict appear to be central to choosing a productive and satisfying response (Huston, Garland, and Farb, 2011).

As Sulak Sivaraksa warned (in Chapter 2), mindfulness practiced stripped of its ethical framework can be a form of escapism. Thus, mindfulness practices are intended to bring about the elimination of suffering, both of personal internal kinds as well as suffering brought about by external factors such as climate change and structural violence.

Thus, it could be argued that one of the definitions of mindfulness is paying attention to someone's life with kindness and curiosity. The practice of mindfulness teaches students how to pay attention, and this way of paying attention enhances both academic and social-emotional learning (Saltzman, 2010). The idea of mindfulness, in this context, highlighted that as human beings we have the unique capacity to pay attention to and be aware of our internal and external worlds and the interactions between the two.

Basically, the teaching program of mindful communication has been composed of student's learning interest, content, and understanding of searching processes. Furthermore, critical thinking, analysis, synthesis of skill, and problem-solving ability are considered as the criteria for improving teaching and training of mindful communication (Moore, 2008). There are some potential benefits that the students can gain from mindfulness practices: (a) The students can be able to build a learning community and became aware of social environment; (b) mindful writing helped students generate new thoughts and become aware of their thinking; (c) mindfulness facilitated the learning process, cultivated creativity and intelligence; (d) mindful cooperative learning provided the students with an opportunity to discover their awareness, learn from others, reflect, and think critically (Wang and Liu, 2016).

An understanding of ethics, social responsibility, and cultural diversity provides students with the ability to consider the impact of their conduct and actions. For instance, students are required to behave ethically and responsibly in relation to cheating in examinations or assessment items, acknowledging the intellectual property rights of others, falsifying or improperly obtaining research data, and assisting other students to cheat.

Burgoon, Berger, and Waldron (2000) argued that the mindful communication is also a medium for the development of local and cross-cultural understanding, educational opportunities, and collaborative effort among persons with different traditions and cultures. On an individual level, it promotes personal fulfilment, social inclusion, employability, and adaptation to change.

As Ananda Kumaraseiri argues,[5] because of our culturalization, we tend to look at problems in a physical form because that is how we have been taught. That's how our education system is. And because we see in a physical form, we are not able to see the root of the problem. We only see manifestations of the problem, and when we see manifestations of the problem, we tend to only address the manifestations. We do not address the root of the problem. If you do not address the root of the problem, the problem will still continue such as effects of climatic change or violence in society.

Seneviratne (in Gunaratne, Pearson, and Senarath, 2015: 184) argues that reporting on human rights and democracy are two areas that need deeper thinking about root causes. A mindful journalist needs to analyze, dissect, and review the proclivity of West-centric media to bundle human rights and multiparty democracy in a "one-size fits all" formula. They could bring in the Eastern principles of harmony, consultation, and consensus rather than superficially focusing on human rights and democracy. This means going beyond conventional truth in a deeper journey to discover ideational/absolute truth and at least getting to the point of intuitive truth.

For example, one of the regional media, Singapore's *Strait Times*, in December 2016,[6] expressed the plight of Rohingya in Myanmar focusing on how the Muslim has galvanized opposition in Muslim majority states in the region, such as Indonesia and Malaysia, and as a result, it could undermine support for a delicate ongoing peace process in the country (Chan, 2016). In contrast, the *New York Times* in January 2016,[7] presented that the new government of Myanmar led by Nobel Laureate Aung San Suu Kyi may respect the human rights of all people and is already taking action to end festering conflicts between Myanmar's military and armed ethnic groups, and promises to strengthen the fragile democratic institution and bring economic opportunity to the Myanmar people (Munita, 2016). However, the *Times*

---

[5] Refer to https://www.youtube.com/watch?v=-Q0AfXnJiMI (accessed on October 27, 2017).

[6] See http://www.straitstimes.com/opinion/rohingya-crisis-may-spur-militant-response-in-s-e-asia (accessed on October 27, 2017).

[7] See https://www.nytimes.com/2016/01/25/opinion/ending-the-horror-of-myanmars-abuse-of-muslims.html?_r=0 (accessed on October 27, 2017).

pointed out that while there are political challenges, what has been done to Rohingya is a crime against humanity.

According to Stein (2013), a Swiss peace report acknowledged that the violence and discrimination between Rakhines and Rohingyas have also affected Kamans, an officially recognized ethnic group which also practices Islam. As violence spread across the country, communal violence has evolved beyond the Rakhine–Rohingya cleavage. To overcome communitarian violence and ongoing armed ethnic strife, Myanmar's citizens may have to consider what vision of a country will allow Myanmar to successfully accommodate multiple languages, religions, traditions, and ethnicities.

Hayward and Walton (2016) mentioned that in Myanmar, religious freedom for non-Buddhists was severely limited. Christians, Muslims, and others faced restrictions on free movement, ability to construct buildings, and public worship. Religious difference, like ethnic difference, marked individuals and groups as potential threats to the integrity and stability of the country.

Graeme Swincer (2016) also explained that Muslims of Myanmar, numbering perhaps 4 percent of the population, have struggled, and sufferings seem to be increasing in spite of the political movement toward democratic rule and international pressure. The plight of the Rohingyas has become quite well known, but hundreds or thousands of non-Rohingya Muslims, who live mainly in other parts of Myanmar, have also faced great difficulty in relation to both their citizenship and their place in society.

Most of these comments and reports reflect a viewpoint that does not take into account the fears of the majority Buddhists that have been precipitated by the rise of political Islam across the world. The recent inquiries triggered by poor journalism and ethical practices have demonstrated that journalism within the libertarian model appears to have lost its moral compass and consequently it needs to explore new ways to recapture this situation. We should educate journalists, serious bloggers, and citizen journalists to adopt a mindful approach to their news and commentary accommodating a reflection upon the implications of their truth-seeking and truth-telling as a routine part of the process (Pearson, 2014).

Mindfulness training may foster awareness of the emotional impulse to react and blame others as well as promote a positive reappraisal of the situation, and ultimately result in more effective communication. This study is aimed to examine the effects of teaching mindfulness in an introductory mindful communication course at a media training institute through positive reappraisal among students who are expected to become skillful journalist in the future.

Why Is Mindful Communication Important in Myanmar?

In the Myanmar context, this could be the ideal time to draw upon its *Vipassana* meditation tradition to apply mindfulness to addressing great social inequalities, conflict, and social divisiveness the country is facing.

For a long time and especially in the past two centuries, Myanmar (known as Burma) has been a popular center of *Vipassana* meditation training which has attracted students from overseas, including the West. The Mahasi Sayadaw tradition has been the most popular.

Intensive *Satipatthana Vipassana*, as taught by the late Mahasi Sayadaw, emphasizes the continuity of moment-to-moment awareness of all physical and mental phenomena. The primary objects of mindfulness are the physical elements (rising and falling of the abdomen during sitting, or lifting and placing of the feet during walking); mindfulness of non-physical elements (mental states, thoughts, perceptions, etc.) is also cultivated. The sequence of meditative experience involves (a) recognition of the object in the field of awareness, (b) the deliberate mental noting of the object, and (c) the observation or experience of the object through its duration.[8]

This method of developing mindfulness could be very useful in journalism/communication training. The key question for those concerned with designing curriculum of mindful communication for media training is how to incorporate these traditional knowledge and training methodologies to nurture a concept and practice of media training.

Myanmar is the second largest country in Southeast Asia and an ethnically diverse nation (Smith, 1994). It has been officially recognized that there are 135 distinct races and 117 languages in the country. These races are mainly grouped into Kachin, Kayah, Kayin, Chin, Bamar, Mon, Rakhine, and Shan. Most of the ethnic minorities are grouped according to region rather than linguistic or ethnic affiliation, such as Shan includes 33 tribal groups and the Chin includes more than 60 ethnic tribal groups.

According to a census report (Myanmar Information Management Unit, 2014), there has been an estimated 57 million population speaking over 100 distinct languages and dialects in Myanmar. Among them, about 68 percent of the population belongs to the Bamar, while 9 percent is Shan, 7 percent is Karen, 3.5 percent is Rakhine, 2 percent is Mon, 2.2 percent is Chin,

---

[8] See http://www.buddhanet.net/medburma.htm (accessed on October 27, 2017).

1.5 percent is Kachin, 0.75 percent is Kayah, 4.5 percent is Others group, 2.5 percent is Chinese, and 1.25 percent is Indians. Each of these groups practices their own cultures, languages, and religions. Most of the non-Barmar ethnic minorities are living along the country's mountainous frontiers.

Any region and state in the Union is home to all ethnics and not for a single ethnic group specifically. For example, more than 1.6 million of population are living in Kachin State with 29.2 percent of Bamar, 23.6 percent of Shan, 18.97 percent of Jaingphaw, 7 percent of Lisu, 5.5 percent of Rawam, 3.33 percent of Lawwan, 2.89 percent of Lacheik, 1.57 percent of Zaikwa, and 8 percent of the other ethnics in population ratios in line with the census enumerated in 2014. Kayah State has a population of over 260,000, in which Kayah accounts for 59.45 percent, Shan 16.9 percent, Bamar 15.44 percent, Kayin 7.04 percent, and other ethnics 2.02 percent. More than 5.8 million population are scattering in Shan State with 35.23 percent of Shan, 11.44 percent of Bamar, 8.94 percent of PA-O, 7.06 percent of Palaung, 6.41 percent of Wa, 4.46 percent of Danu, 3.22 percent of Kokang, 4.05 percent of Lahu, 2.35 percent of Jaingphaw, and 16.84 percent of other ethnics. Some ethnics have larger population and some have lesser.

The majority religion of Myanmar is Buddhism and religion plays a vital role among the people of Myanmar. Buddhism was first introduced in around 241 BC. In Myanmar, 85 percent of the population professes Theravada Buddhism, 6 percent Christianity, 4 percent Islam, 1 percent Hinduism, and the remaining 1 percent consists of Mahayana Buddhism, Vajrayana Buddhism, and Animism.

The ethnic minority languages and literatures were taught for five years in the primary schools before 1964. However, during the socialist period, they were taught for three years. The promotion of ethnic languages and literatures plays an essential part in respective ethnic cultural identity. But today, many young ethnic minorities cannot speak or write in their own languages. Today, Burmese language has become the official common language of all ethnic groups and it is also the only medium of instruction for all education in Myanmar.

With such a diverse population, the media needs to play a very important role in not fermenting conflict but helping to promote social harmony. The adversarial role of the media emanating from the Western libertarian media function model may not be fully compatible with Myanmar's needs or appropriate to addressing these. Thus, it is essential that mindful communication principles and strategies are adopted in designing new journalism and mass communication curriculum for Myanmar.

Before discussing specific aspects of designing new media training curriculum for Myanmar, let me draw your attention to various challenges that Myanmar faces due to its diverse ethnic and religious minorities.

In Myanmar, all the young people, including diverse ethnic and religious minorities who live all over the country, are allowed to enter into schools and universities without any restriction. However, what must be considered in designing a new media training curriculum for Myanmar is that some students who strongly believed in their own religion looked uncomfortable when the subject of Buddhism was mentioned in the classroom.

Challenge to Having Different Ethnic Armed Groups

Ethnic armed groups in Myanmar have their own detailed constitutions and administer their areas with systems akin to those of one-party states. They establish their own demarcation and mapping systems, often with little or no resemblance to those of the government.

In Myanmar, the multiparty system is at nascent stage and more than 70 political parties were legally registered with the election commission at the end of 2014. Among these, the National League for Democracy (NLD) and Union Solidarity and Development Party (USDP) stand out as major nationwide parties. Apart from these bigger parties, the ethnic party landscape is in flux, since a lot of them are newly formed and already discuss possible mergers and alliances.

The main armed groups in Myanmar are the Kachin Independence Organization (KIO), the Kachin Independence Army (KIA), the Karen National Union (KNU), the Democratic Karen Benevolent Army (DKBA), the Karenni Nationalities Progressive Party (KNPP), Border Guard Force (BGF), the New Mon State Party (NMSP), Arakan Army (AA), Arakan Liberation Army (ALA), Shan State Army-South (SSA-S), Shan State National Army (SSNA), and Pa-O National Army (PNA).

Major Conflicts Facing the Government in Myanmar

The civil conflict in Myanmar is considered as one of the longest ongoing conflicts in the world. Since 1948, the two largest insurgent factions were the communists, led by the Communist Party of Burma (CPB), and ethnic Karen insurgents, led by the KNU. Both groups had fought the government prior to independence (BTI, 2016). During the post-independence period, the KNU favored an independent state administered by the Karen people. The proposed state would be forged out of Karen State (Kayin State) and Karenni State (Kayah State). The KNU has since shifted their focus from full independence to regional autonomy under a federal system. Armed groups have fought to change the overarching structure of Myanmar and obtain the freedoms they seek. The main actors in the conflicts are mostly ethnic armed groups and the most recent clashes are occurring between the Tatmadaw and the armed groups from the Kachin state.

On November 19, 2014, government forces attacked the KIA's headquarters near the city of Laiza. Between February and May 2015, government forces launched several military operations in the Kokang area of Northern Shan State. Insurgent groups of the Chin, Rakhine (also known as Arakanese), and Rohingya ethnic minorities have fought against the government for self-determination in Rakhine State since the early 1950s.

In Rakhine State, the Rohingya problem is no more than the problem of unregistered illegal immigrants as claimed by the official newspaper *Working People's Daily* on January 25, 1992. Additionally, the use of the ethnic term "Rohingya" for Arakanese Muslims is rejected by the state and the government has officially announced that there are no ethnics called Rohingya in Myanmar. So, the government does not even recognize the Rohingya as citizens among all ethnic groups in the country and does not give them citizenship (Horsey, 2015). In May 2016, the US government defied the call from the Myanmar government to not use the name Rohingya for referring to the Muslims in Rakhine State.[9] In November 2016, BBC reported quoting a UN official that Myanmar wants ethnic cleansing of the Rohingyas by driving them across the border to Bangladesh.

While the international media projects the Rohingyas as one of the most persecuted minorities in the world, the general perception of Rohingya within Myanmar is that they are Bengali immigrants from Bangladesh. The violence between Rakhine Buddhists and Rohingya Muslims started in July 2012. Myanmar Buddhists view them as recent Bengali migrants who compete for scarce resources and want to expel them. Animosity toward the Rohingya is widespread and deep-seated. Thousands of Rohingyas have fled across the border into other neighboring countries seeking refuge (BNI, 2014).

---

[9] Available at https://www.theguardian.com/world/2016/may/11/us-defies-myanmar-government-rohingya-muslims (accessed on October 27, 2017).

In Rakhine State, unidentified insurgents attacked border posts on the Myanmar–Bangladesh border—Maungdaw Township—on October 9, 2016, and clashes continued. On December 15, 2016, International Crisis Group (ICG) with headquarters in Brussels released a report warning Myanmar that "a well-organised, apparently well-funded group" has been behind the recent attacks on the armed forces in Myanmar. ICG says:

> The insurgent group, which refers to itself as Harakah al-Yaqin (Faith Movement, HaY), is led by a committee of Rohingya émigrés in Saudi Arabia and is commanded on the ground by Rohingya with international training and experience in modern guerrilla war tactics. It benefits from the legitimacy provided by local and international fatwas (religious judicial opinions) in support of its cause and enjoys considerable sympathy and backing from Muslims in northern Rakhine State, including several hundred locally trained recruits. (ICG, 2016)

Nationwide Ceasefires Agreement

The Nationwide Ceasefires Agreement (NCA) was signed by the Government of the Republic of the Union of Myanmar and armed ethnics groups with the aim of restoring a durable eternal peace through all-inclusive political dialogues. Under the new constitutional reforms in 2011, state-level and union-level ceasefire agreements were made with armed actors. Out of 17, 14 of the largest ethnic arm actors signed a ceasefire agreement with the new reformed government. According to the Myanmar Peace Monitoring Group, clashes between KIO, its allies, and the government have displaced hundreds of thousands of people and have created another severe humanitarian crisis in Kachin and Northern Shan State.

Since 2011 and 2012, the government agreed to ceasefires with the KNU, DKBA, and KNPP (Jolliffe, 2015). The KIA was inactive between 1994 and 2011, but the ceasefire was broken with clashes between the Tatmadaw and KIA forces in 2011. The violence is a result of a call by the KIO for autonomy and ethnic rights in the face of increased economic and strategic interests for the Kachin lands and decreased interests for the welfare of the population. SSA-S maintains bases along the Myanmar–Thailand border and signed a ceasefire agreement with the government on December 2, 2011. In October 2015, after two years of negotiations, the government of Myanmar announced that it will finalize and sign a ceasefire agreement with eight insurgent groups, including the KNU.

Development of the Media Sector in Myanmar

The developments or reforms in the Myanmar media sector need to be analyzed in the context of the various threats facing the nation as discussed earlier.

Myanmar's first newspaper, the *Maulmain Chronicle*, was introduced for a handful of English-speaking readership in 1836 in the city of Moulmein in British-held Tenasserim. During the colonial period, Myanmar had dozens of newspaper in Burmese, English, Chinese, and several Indian Languages. After independence, several major newspapers were nationalized and many private newspapers were closed down, and there were about 40 new publications including four English versions, nine Indian versions, and a Chinese newspaper in 1962. The government established the first state-owned newspaper, the *Working People's Daily*, on October 1, 1963. During this period, the government established only six newspapers. After 1988, the assumption of the state responsibilities by the Tatmadaw government, the *New Light of Burma, Myanma Alin,* and *Kyemon* (the *Mirror*) dailies continued to be published. In 1990, the print media industry had revitalized and the country allowed foreign investment. The first private weekly and monthly journals were permitted and this sector strengthened in 2000.

In 2011, exiled media companies and ethic media groups returned to Myanmar and established print publications such as the *Irrawaddy* and *Mizzima*, and the broadcaster Democratic Voice of Burma (DVB). Ethnic media (Shan newspaper, Karen newspaper, and Mon newspaper) also continued to grow, and adding to the plurality of the media were British Broadcasting Corporation (BBC), Voice of America (VOA), and Radio Free Asia (RFA) Burmese Services. During 1962–2012, media sector also did not have freedom of the press and most of the newspapers were government owned.

In 2012, the media landscape in Myanmar changed dramatically when the Press Scrutiny Board ceased prior censorship of print media. Journalists continued to practice self-censorship. This development was full of both opportunity and risk. The removal of prior censorship also led to a proliferation of daily newspapers, which greatly increased the plurality of print media, and the Ministry of Information (MOI) continued to control the registration. In July 2012, after a picture of Buddhist women who had allegedly been raped was circulated by private media, incidents of physical violence occurred in Okkan, Meiktila, Lashio, Thaton, and elsewhere of the country. Sometimes, the media may even promote conflict and social divisiveness.

As of 2014, there were 20 private Burmese language daily newspapers and four state-owned Burmese language daily newspapers registered under the MOI. *Myanma Alin* and the *Mirror* newspapers have the largest circulation of all print media at 138,756 and 180,000 copies, respectively. Due to fierce competition within the media industry, only seven of the original 20 private daily newspapers are still in circulation. Ethnic print media outlets are beginning to gain some momentum and print information in a variety of languages (UNESCO and IMS, 2016). Due to the country's weak road infrastructure, print media circulation is mostly limited.

Given the circulation constraints faced by print media, many citizens rely on broadcasters for their information and entertainment needs. Broadcasters in Myanmar are represented by two state-owned (MRTV and Myawaddy) and joint ventures between the State and private companies. At present, there are two joint-venture TV broadcasters, namely, the Forever Group and the Shwe Than Lwin Group. Private, public, and community broadcasters do not yet exist in Myanmar, although the MOI did a draft of Public Service Media Bill in 2014.

Myanmar also has seven joint-venture radio stations (Mandalay FM, Shwe FM, Padamyar FM, FM Bagan, Cherry FM, Pyinsawaddy FM). Over the country, joint-venture radio broadcasters tend to cover two or three states or regions each.

Joint-venture broadcasters offer subscription services, but a large proportion of the population cannot afford to regularly access them. Free-to-air channels are more commonly viewed, particularly in rural areas where incomes are lower. Both state broadcasters offer free-to-air channels. Joint-venture TV broadcasters offer a total of five free-to-air channels. In 2013, MRTV launched the National Races Channel (NRC), which broadcasts a total of 17 hours of news per day in 11 ethnic languages. MRTV has opened news bureaus in 13 locations across the country to collect the news. MRTV, which is still operated by the MOI, has announced plans to go public service broadcasting.

Under President Thein Sein's government, the most notable developments have been a significant drop in the price of mobile SIM cards and an improving telecommunications network across the country. Internet censorship has also been widely removed. These changes have significantly improved media workers' access to information via the Internet, especially through mobile phone applications. Currently, in Myanmar, Internet is the primary medium for communication, and Internet access on mobile phones is more easily available in urban areas than in rural areas.

Although social media have been used for peace building at the same time, it also exacerbated ethnic and religious tensions and helped spread misinformation and rumor. Hate speech has proliferated online, including reinforcing negative stereotype about both Muslims and Buddhists (Dolan and Gray, 2014). Unfortunately, social networking sites and blogs have become a spawning ground for anti-Muslim hate speeches in Myanmar. Moderate and unbiased reporters are needed to improve the quality of the various media environments.

Media Training in Myanmar

Most journalists benefited from their media training. The majority of training events within the country cover basic journalism skills. Many of these training courses touch tangentially on subjects such as human rights or democracy but do not go into great depth. International media development organizations such as Internews and International Media Support (IMS) often provide thematic training events related to democratic principles. One of the organizations, Myanmar Egress was a notable forerunner in providing training on democracy and human rights. Its mass communications course had a strong focus on human rights and democratic principles as do many of the other courses that they continue to offer.

Internews played a large part in this process by opening the "J School" in 2004 to train Myanmar journalists in Chang Mai, Thailand. The Yangon Journalism School started providing training courses as early as 2003. The Yangon Journalism School and the Myanmar Journalist Network have provided on-site training in a handful of state and regional capitals. Occasionally media international nongovernmental organizations (INGOs) conduct thematic workshops in these institutes. Topics have included media management, human rights, newsroom management, investigative journalism, and other subjects.

Center for Myanmar Media Development Journalism School started in 2012 and it offers the basic journalism course. BBC Media Action provides distance training via an online portal and a journalist mentorship program. Myanmar Institute of Theology also offers an elective course in journalism, thereby broadening the available additional elective courses, and laying the foundation of a potential department of journalism for the Liberal Arts Program (LAP) of undergraduate students.

National Management Degree College (NMDC)

The NMDC's department of journalism started in 2007–2008 academic year and offers students a four-year bachelor of arts in journalism (National Management Degree College, 2016). It is the only academic institution in Myanmar to offer a degree in media. It includes practical work, either at the student newspaper or local media internships, early into their programs. Most of the course materials are provided in English, but the language of instruction is both Burmese and English. The NMDC is a state-run entity, operating under the Ministry of Education (MOE).

Myanmar Media Development Center (MMDC)

The MMDC is one of the few institutions within Myanmar to provide technical broadcast training. MMDC offers a 10-month Diploma in TV broadcasting. This includes six months of classroom-based work and four months of studio-based, hands-on learning (Media Development Center, 2016).

Myanmar Journalism Institute (MJI)

Recognizing the limited supply of academic courses in the media field, a consortium of international donors and 39 local media organizations established the MJI in May 2014. Although the MJI is not an academic institution in the traditional sense, it does offer a 10-month diploma in multimedia journalism. The language of instruction is both Burmese and English. This program is offered to individuals who are new to the media industry as well as media professionals who want to improve their skills through additional training.

Developing Curriculum

What is needed today in media training is how to shape the curriculum to help students to think in terms of assisting in developing their communities. The syllabus for the department of journalism's degree program was developed in coordination with the UNESCO. As such, the syllabus mirrors that of most internationally accredited journalism programs covering such topics as media law and ethics, human rights, democracy and the rights of the citizen. The curriculum also includes specialized courses such as economic reporting, public affairs, environment and health, political science, etc. The courses also incorporate components of the modern communications such as use of audiovisual equipment and new online technologies into scheduling training and practice.

MMDC also offers individual production management, communication skills, presentation and interview techniques, audio and lighting technique, media management, and broadcast engineering. Although the broadcasting diploma does include a section on journalism, the course focuses mainly on the technical aspects of broadcasting.

MJI also offers individual courses covering the basic journalism, radio news, photo journalism, digital media, TV news, media ethics, media law, environment, and feature writings, method of using equipment (camera, video camera, and recording instrument). Some INGOs have provided short training courses on peace and conflict, and human right but mindful communication journalism courses are absent from academic curricula.

As mentioned earlier, Myanmar needs to develop a journalism practice that is less adversarial and more geared toward promoting social harmony in the community. This may also require a new look at the human rights aspects of the media with less emphasis on voices of dissent and more emphasis on crafting the story with mindfulness to tackle the root causes of problems such as poverty with deep understanding of social and cultural norms and realities in the community. What mindful journalism could add is a dimension from eastern philosophical thinking of balancing the ying and yang as thought in Confucius philosophy (discussed in the Introduction).

Curriculum content needs to explain to the students how such mindful communication is conducted, what information is contained in those messages and how to relate to your own communities via this form of thinking. Students need to learn communication concepts and behavior to act on their thoughts and emotional reactions and decisions about how to respond to challenging situations. Students will become aware of the communication requirements in response to a full range of incidents concerning the political, economic, and social events they are reporting about with knowledge of local cultural, historic, socioeconomic, and political trends.

Upon completion of a training course, students would be able to explain the mindful communication requirements of the media organization, and how it could have a positive impact on the community, as well as its vulnerabilities. Mindful communication could be applied to planning and conducting public relations, how the media could work in conflict management, and how such a relationship can benefit the people where new media and other communication technologies could become a change agent. In addition to a general overview of communication theory and scope, the course would address the various interactions that may be required between managing a conflict and a full spectrum of relevant stakeholder interactions in the communication process.

Sugath Senarat discusses in Chapter 13 how Buddhist wisdom and moral values could be adopted in crafting stories to tackle issues of good governance and why the current thinking on good governance is too focused on development literature. He argues that although today's advanced digital technology enables the media to reach the people rapidly, most media fail to target their content toward human development. Thus, to tackle the problems of a complicated world we live in today, the high value we give to purely economic development rather than moral development may need a rebalance. This is where, especially in teaching business or economic reporting, we would need to bring in ideas of "sufficiency economic" that was discussed in the Introduction, where the three poisons of greed, hatred, and delusion need to be understood by the students.

The course structure needs to be illustrated with examples and case studies as appropriate with such examples coming from closer to home than from far away. Students need to be able to identify and feel empathy with such case studies, so that students could contribute to interactive class discussions. Such courses will provide the development of social–emotional qualities essential for skillful journalists and media professionals who are paying attention to the public relation with mindfulness concepts.

To sum up, the diversity of race or religion, the existence of different ethnic armed groups, and conflicts between the military of government and ethnic armed groups can be seen as the major reasons for the need of substantial mindful communication and media training development in Myanmar. It is, thus, essential that students understand the historic, socioeconomic, cultural, religious, political, and geo-political dimensions of these issues and how freedom of expression concepts need to be mindfully navigated with these complexities in mind.

Deep listening, understanding, feelings and emotions, empathy with the subject, and developing compassion—these are part and parcel of mindfulness (as discussed in the earlier chapters) and need to be incorporated into designing a new journalism curriculum. As discussed earlier in this chapter, there are many aspects of traditional wisdom from the Burmese Buddhist culture that could be drawn into this curriculum. This would need some real thinking "out of the box" from Myanmar educational policy makers, especially those involved in developing mass communication programs.

References

Altman, L. 2013. *Five Practices for Mindful Communication: The International Workplace.* Available at https://internationalworkplace.com/ (accessed on October 25, 2017).
Ba Khin, Sayagyi U. 1991. *Dhama Text*, Series 1. Wiltshire, UK: The International Meditation Centre. Available at www.internationalmeditationcentre.org/ (accessed on October 28, 2017).
Barker, V. 2000. *Mindful Communication in Cross-cultural Organizations.* Available at www.valeriebarker.net/ (accessed on October 25, 201).
Bhikkhu, Moneyya. 2015. *Teaching & Training.* Singapore: Pa-Auk Forest Monastery, Pa-Auk Meditation Centre. Available at http://www.buddhanet/.../teach-train3rd.pdf (accessed on October 25, 2017).
Bischoff, R. 2003. *Selected Discourses of Webu Sayadaw.* Dhamma Text Series 3. The International Meditation Centres, In the Tradition of Sayagyi U Ba Khin. Kandy: Buddhist Publication Society. Available at http://www.internationalmeditationcentre.org/ (accessed on October 25, 2017).
BNI. 2014. *Deciphering Myanmar's Peace Process: A Reference Guide.* Available at http://myanmaypeacemonitoring.blogspot.com (accessed on October 2, 2017).
BTI. 2016. *Myanmar Country Report.* Available at http://www.bti.projectorg (accessed on October 25, 2017).
Burgoon, J. K., C. R. Berger, and V. R. Waldron. 2000. "Mindfulness and Interpersonal Communication." *Journal of Social Issues.* Available at https;//www.researchgate.net/...227645064-mindfulness-and-interpersonal-commu (accessed on December 14, 2016).
Chan, F. 2016, December. "Outlook 2017: Rise of Muslim Hardliners." *The Strait Times.* Available at http://www.straitstimes.com/.../ (accessed on January 15, 2017).
Dolan, T., and S. Gray. 2014. "Media and Conflict in Myanmar: Opportunities for Media to Advance Peace." Available at https://www.usip.org/publications/2014/01/media-and-conflict-myanmar (accessed on October 28, 2017).
Folkes, V. 1985. "Mindlessness or Mindfulness: A Partial Replication and Extension of Lange, Blank, & Chanowitz." *Journal of Personality and Social Psychology* 48 (3). Available at https://pdfs.semanticscholar.org/97c8/d34bd9f9ffe/54f959938/d128893b//3d.pdf (accessed on October 25, 2017).
Goldstein, J. 1993. *Insight Meditation: The Practice of Freedom.* Boston, MA: Shambhala Publications. Available at http://www.shambhala.com/insight-meditation.html (accessed on October 25, 2017).
Gunaratne, S., M. Pearson, and S. Senarath. 2015. *Mindful Journalism and News Ethics in the Digital Era.* New York, NY: Routledge.
Hayward, S., and M. J. Walton. 2016. *Advancing Religious Freedom and Coexistence in Myanmar, Recommendations for the Next U.S. Administration.* Available at https:/ora.ox.ac.uk/.../ATTACHMENT01 (accessed on December 14, 2016).
Horsey, R. 2015. "New Religious Legislation in Myanmar." Online Burma Library. Available at www.burmalibrary.org/.../ (accessed on December 14, 2016).
Huston, D. C., E. L. Garland, and N. A. S. Farb. 2011. "Mechanisms of Mindfulness in Communication Training." *Journal of Applied Communication Research* 39 (4): 406–421.
ICG. 2016. "Myanmar: A New Muslim Insurgency in Rankhine State." Report No. 283/Asia. Brussels: International Crisis Group. Available at https://www.crisisgroup.org/asia/south-east-asia/myanmar/283-myanmar-new-muslim-insurgency-rakhine-state (accessed October 28, 2017).

Jolliffe, K. 2015. "Ethnic Armed Conflict and Territorial Administration in Myanmar." *The Asia Foundation*. Available at https://asiafoundation.org/.../... (accessed on December 14, 2016).

Langer, E., A. Blank, and B. Chanowitz. 1978. "The Mindless of Ostensibly Thoughtful Action." *Journal of Personality and Social Psychology* 36 (6): 635–642. Available at jamesclear.com/wp-content/uploads/2015/03/copy-machine-study-ellen-langer.pdf (accessed on December 14, 2016).

Loo, E. 2013. *Bridging the Cultural Gaps in Journalism Training and Education in Asia*. Singapore: Konrad-Adenauer-Stiftung. Available at www.kas.de/medien-asien/en/ (accessed October 28, 2017).

Mahasi Sayadaw. 1981. *Mahasi Abroad: Lectures by Mahasi Sayadaw on his World Missionary Tour 1979*. Rangoon: Boddhasasananuggaha Association.

Mahathera Ledi Sayadaw. 1965. *The Vipassana: Dipani, the Manual Insight*. Kaba-Aye, Rangoon: Union Buddha Sasana Council. Available at elibrary.ibc.ac.th/files/.../index.html (accessed on January 15, 2017).

Media Development Center. 2016. *Curriculum of MMDC*. Myanmar. Available at mmdcmyanmar.com/index.php?page (accessed on December 14, 2016).

Mellon, J. 2016. *10 Ways to Be Better Communicator*. Available at https://twitter.com/jenmellon/ (accessed on December 14, 2016).

Mogok Sayadaw. 1967. *Practical Application of Paticcasamuppada on the Cessation of the Cycle of Rebirths*. Rangoon, Burma: The Society for the Propagation of Vipassana.

Moore, P. 2008. "Teacher Training Curricula For Media and Information Literacy Report." Paris: UNESCO House, UNESCO. Available at portal.unesco..org/.../12212271723 Tech....Group Meeting (accessed on November 14, 2016).

Munita, T. 2016, January. "Ending the Horror of Myanmar's Abuse of Muslim." *The New York Times*. Available at mobile.nytime.com/2016/.../ (accessed on December 14, 2016).

Murthy, C. S. H. N. 2016. "Mindful Journalism and News Ethics in the Digital Era: A Buddhist Approach." *Asian Journal of Communication* 26 (5): 252.

Myanmar Information Management Unit. 2014. *Myanmar Population and Housing Census*. Republic of Mogok the Union of Myanmar. Available at http://www.themimu.info/census-datMyanmar (accessed on November 10, 2016).

Myanmar Journalism Institute. 2016. *Curriculum of MJI*. Myanmar. Available at www.cfi.fr/.../setting-myanmar-journalist (accessed on December 14, 2016).

National Management Degree College. 2016. *Curriculum of NMDC*. Myanmar: Department of Journalism, Ministry of Education.

Pearson, M. 2014. "Towards 'Mindful Journalism': Applying Buddhism's Eightfold Path as an Ethical Framework for Modern Journalism Religion." *The International Journal of Communication Ethics* 11 (4). Available at www.communicationethics.net/.../feat1.p... (accessed on December 14, 2016).

Saltzman, A. 2010. *Mindfulness: A Guide for Teachers*. The Center for Contemplative Mindfulness. Available at www.contemplativemind.org/... (accessed on December 14, 2016).

Sayadaw, Pa Auk Tawya. 1998. *The Practice Which Leads to Nibbana (Part 1)*. Available at www.buddhanet. Net/pdf.../nibbCEna Myanmar (accessed on December 14, 2016).

Singh, H. 2007. *A Critique of Vipassana Meditation, as Taught by Mr S N Goenka*. Available at http://harmanjit.googlepages.com/vipassanacritique.pdf (accessed on December 14, 2016).

Smith, M. 1994. *Ethnic Groups in Burma: Development, Democracy and Human Rights*. Human Rights series. Anti-Slavery International. Available at http://www.ibiblio.org/obl/docs3/Ethnic_Groups_in_Burma-ocr.pdf (accessed on October 25, 2017).

Spencer, Oatey H. 2013. *Mindfulness for Intercultural Interaction*. A compilation of quotations: GlobalPAD Core Concepts. GlobalPAD Open House. Available at http://go.warwick. ac.uk/globalpadintercultural (accessed on October 25, 2017).

Stein, S. A. 2013. *Presentation of the Report of the Inquiry Commission on the Sectarian Violence in Rakhine State*. Zurich: Center for Security Studies, ETH Zurich Available at http://www.swisspeace.ch (accessed on October 28, 2017).

Swincer, G. 2016. *Citizenship and Discrimination Issues of Muslims in Myanmar*. Available at www.bmrsg.org.au/.../Citizenship..., (accessed on January 15, 2016).

Triandis, H. C. 1994. *Culture and Social Behavior*. New York, NY: McGraw-Hill. Available at eyewitness.utep.edu (accessed on October 28, 2017).

UNESCO and IMS. 2016. *Assessment of Media Development in Myanmar*. Available at https://www.unescobkk.org/communication-and-information (accessed on June 10, 2016).

Wang, Y., and C. Liu. 2016. "Cultivate Mindfulness: A Case Study of Mindful Learning in an English as a Foreign Language Classroom." *The IAFOR Journal of Education* 4 (2). Available at iafor.org/.../2016/.../Cultivate-Mindfulness (accessed on December 14, 2016).

SECTION C

Mindful Communication and Sustainable Development

11

Middle Path Journalism: A Conceptual Framework for Bhutanese Media

Dorji Wangchuk

In June 2016, the Bhutan Media Foundation (BMF) convened the first national-level media conference to discuss the way forward for the Bhutanese media. Given the dire strait that the Bhutanese media was in, some invitees joked that the meeting was called to organize a solemn funeral. The Bhutanese media had seen a slump with some media agencies folding up—a fatal blow to the young and nascent industry. Still, during the course of the two-day conference some level of optimism returned with several senior journalists reaffirming their commitment to the profession. Among many new ideas floated was the adoption of the concept of middle path journalism as a white paper for the way forward. The conference also agreed that there was the need to relook at the existing media from every aspect—business, capacity development, legislation, licensing and the free-market policy.

Even globally, the explosion of the social media and new technological platforms coupled with the decline of the traditional mass media have forced some fundamental changes and rethinking in the media landscape. In the case of Bhutan, the new democratic era that the country has embarked upon is seeing more openness in the way news and information are being shared. Thus, these new realities, developments and circumstances necessitate major rethinking in the way media and communications are carried out.

This chapter offers a conceptual framework on middle path journalism. The proposed media model draws from the core philosophy of Gross National Happiness (GNH) and the social values. It proposes a four-dimensional model based on community, compassion, commitment, and contentment.

Middle path journalism strives toward building consensus and communities through a more human-centric approach instead of thriving on conflicts, controversies, and commercialism. A media model such as these could offer a better narrative for a small country like Bhutan. This article provides the theoretical groundwork for further discussions, deliberations, and eventual application. Middle path journalism adds to discussion in the area of mindfulness communication—first put forward by Gunaratne, Pearson, and Senarath (2015) together with contributions from other scholars.

Bhutan: The Context and Background

In September of 2009 a devastating earthquake hit Eastern Bhutan. The whole country shook for almost a minute. Houses crumbled, lives were lost and mountains gave away. I was then serving as the Media Director to His Majesty the King. News of untold destructions and deaths started pouring in every minute. I was on the phone getting information on a continuous basis. But after few days I was getting tired. Not for working 24 hours per day but with the deluge of only bad news. So I called up the Kuensel Correspondent in the area and asked if there was nothing good happening there. I was definite that there would be help and humanity going around in such times. There could be some good things happening there like people helping other people who had lost more. Two days later, a news article appeared in Kuensel about a health worker who saved a child from a house that was crumbling and had killed rest of the family. The health worker risked his life. The story of heroism and humanity lifted the whole nation. Coincidently, that's one story that I remember from that tragic event. In the days after the earthquake, His Majesty the King visited the area. I ensured that what we released to the mass media were not again stories of agony and misery but stories of hope, strength and resilience—and stories of restoring laughter and joy and stories of reconstruction and reassurance. (Wangchuk, 2015)

Bhutan is a small country with a population of 768,577 (National Statistical Bureau, 2016) and wedged between India and China. This small nation also has 19 different languages spoken in as many ethnic groups with distinct cultures, traditions, and history (Phuntsho, 2013). Adding to these complexities is the fast-changing mindset brought about by the country's socioeconomic development activities since 1961, and, in recent years, with the introduction of television and Internet. A large percentage of the population (60 percent) is under the age of 24.

The Bhutanese media has its genesis in the modernization process that began with the launch of the First Five-Year Plan in 1961. As a tool to keep the people informed of the new development plans and projects, *Kuensel*, the national newspaper, was started in 1967 as an official gazette. The fortnightly publication carried official announcements, important appointments, movement of high-level officials, etc., that were mainly aimed at the growing civil service and officialdom in Thimphu (the Kingdom's capital).

Radio National Youth Association of Bhutan (NYAB) was followed in 1973 as a youth radio with a weekly 30-minute broadcast and run by volunteers. In 1979, the Royal Government of Bhutan, recognizing the importance and the power of radio for mass dissemination of news and information, embraced the radio under the Ministry of Communications. Then in 1986, it was upgraded to become the national broadcaster and renamed as the Bhutan Broadcasting Service (BBS).

Both *Kuensel* and BBS had the mandate to inform, educate, and entertain the Bhutanese people alongside the country's overall goal of modern socioeconomic development (Wangchuk, 2007). In addition to these two organizations, there were two other related agencies—the Government Press and the Development Communication Centre. The four agencies were grouped together to form the Department of Information & Broadcasting under the Ministry of Communications.

In 1992, a royal decree from His Majesty the King removed BBS and *Kuensel* from the government bureaucracy and were granted autonomous status making way for independent media in Bhutan. In 1996, the Development Communication Centre, which had a strong video production capacity, was merged with the BBS in preparation for BBS TV that was launched three years later in 1999. Internet was also introduced in Bhutan almost on the same day as the television.

In 2006, as a part of the preparation for the first parliamentary elections in 2008, two newspapers, *Bhutan Times* and *Bhutan Observer*, were licensed. The two papers hit the newsstand in April and in June, respectively. The two newspapers were the first independent media outlets in Bhutan. Two years later, in 2008, the Constitution of Bhutan was adopted ushering the mass media into a new era. The Article 7 of the constitution explicitly guaranteed the freedom of the press, information, and expression. This new development gave rise to a proliferation of independent mass media taking the figures to 12 privately owned newspapers and four commercial FM radio stations.

New Era. New Responsibility. New Reality. New Model?

The Bhutanese media practiced development journalism prior to the advent of democracy in 2008. The media was an institution that assisted the government and the people in the overall process of nation-building. In the post-2008 era, the media quickly moved to its new role of advocating openness and transparency and as a check on power (the watchdog model). However, some agencies even went on overdrive mode adopting a very confrontational approach with the government. They took the "radical role" (Christians, Glasser, McQuail, Nordenstreng, and White, 2009). This was not a big surprise, as most of the journalists were trained in India. However, the older section of the society viewed such confrontational approach as being very *un*-Bhutanese. Young TV anchors were often derided for "questioning" ministers and bureaucrats who were older and in "higher" positions.

Then, around 2011, the government, faced with severe budget deficit, slashed the media spending. It was not clear as to whether the move was intended to punish the media. But the impact was huge. Media agencies soon realized that there was also a bigger issue to attend to: financial sustainability. Operating in a small market with an underdeveloped advertising culture, the media outlets, especially the newspapers, depended heavily on government advertising and announcements. The budget allocations for such activities further saw a decline as government departments decided that they fulfilled the obligation of "informing" the public by using their websites and social media pages. Hence, as quickly as it rose, the traditional media began to fall. It found itself at a crossroads (Tshering, 2014). Quality and reach were compromised in favor of balance sheets. Many senior journalists left their full-time jobs. Meanwhile, the two older agencies—BBS and *Kuensel*, went into a greater state of confusion trying to decide whether to be a public service media or commercial entities. Simply put, the Bhutanese media went from development communication model to a model-less journalism.

As the last nail in the coffin there was the social media. The number of newspaper readers and radio listeners saw a downward curve as more and more people depended on new technological platforms that offered uncensored "news" and information. The media impact studies conducted in 2010 and in 2013 and the circulation audit in 2014 clearly gave some depressing numbers for the traditional media. The new reality, thus, calls for a serious reflection and the search for a new media model and business approach. This paper attempts to address the former.

Two important considerations have to be made with regards to the search for an appropriate media model for Bhutan. First of all, it must be noted that Bhutan's thrust into democracy has come in an unconventional manner. It was introduced as an initiative by the institution of monarchy (Sinpeng, 2007). Hence, it is obvious that the media models postulated under different social, cultural, religious, political, and historical evolutions and circumstances (Hao and Datta-Ray, 2006) won't be fully applicable to Bhutan.

The famous Fourth Estate concept, the basis of western media, was enunciated by Edmund Burke in 1787 (Hampton, 2010) in a predominantly Protestant Britain and France with imperial entanglements. Closer to Bhutan, the anti-establishment model was adopted by the Indian press in the late 19th century as a voice against the mistreatment of locals by colonial rulers (Datta-Ray, 1996). In the post-independence era starting from 1947,

Mahatma Gandhi blessed the mass media to continue its role as a watchdog on the government, with his famous dictum that "the national cause will never suffer by honest criticism of national institutions and national policies" (Datta-Ray, 1996).

The widely acclaimed *Four Theories of the Press* (Siebert, Peterson, and Schramm, 1956) does not describe the Bhutanese media. In fact, even the authors seem to agree that the media should reflect the prevailing philosophy and political system where they operate (Park and Curran, 2000). Perhaps the *Theory of the Social Responsibility of the Press* by the same authors would come close. However, even this theory was postulated as a response[1] to the atrocities of World War II and media's failure to prevent it. Hence, as Park and Curran (2000) argue, every society should shape its media taking into consideration its history, cultural traditions, economic development, national configuration of power, and state policies.

Secondly, media as an important state institution and as one of the pillars of democracy owes it to the society to work toward, and assist in, achieving the overall national vision. In fact, in the words of the patron of Bhutanese democracy, His Majesty the King Jigme Khesar Namgyel Wangchuck, the current monarch, democratic governance is a "means" toward the country's greater aspiration of overall well-being. Media as one of the means to democracy, thus, becomes a means to a means (democracy) to an "end" (overall well-being). The ultimate goal of the media is, therefore, the overall well-being of the people.

Lastly, it is also worth noting that the Judeo-Christian worldview is based on the concept of the Original Sin, which all humans are believed to inherit (Wiley, 2002) and carry until the Judgment Day and the eventual salvation. In contrast, the Buddhist worldview, especially in the Himalayan Buddhism, is positive—in that it teaches that all sentient being have Buddha-nature[2] (Norbu, 2001) and thus are inherently good. Hence, there is a real fundamental difference between the two origins of the worldviews. Would this explain why the traditional media, all over the world, has increasingly thrived on negativity?

Even in Bhutan, newsrooms are increasingly on the lookout for corruptions, controversies, and conflicts in a country where the people are generally easy-going, optimistic, and content. Some of the newspapers even tended

---

[1] The theory was formulated following a recommendation of the Commission on the Freedom of Press established in 1949 in the United States.

[2] Known as the concept of *Tathagatagarba* in Sanskrit and *Jangchubsemba* in Bhutanese, this attribute does not discriminate between a wrongdoer and the victim. Both possess the Buddha-nature. It is because of one's ignorance, jealousy or greed, and karmic consequences that this true nature is clouded.

to flesh on gossips, rumors, and sensationalism.[3] Yet as the above opening story shows, humanity is still not lost. There is still space and time for good and positive stories. Good news can also be news; and news need not always be bad to garner audience or to improve the ratings.

Middle Path Journalism—Definition

Although the concept is still a work in progress, middle path journalism could be defined as a human-centric model that takes into account the values and vision of a country in the practice of media and communication. Middle path journalism strives to avoid the extremes by finding the delicate balance (the middle path) in the practice and use of all forms of media as well as in the consumption and analysis of media contents.[4]

Middle path journalism is, thus, anchored in two concepts—values and vision. Values are a set of principles or standards of human behavior that determines one's judgment and belief of what is important in life within one's place in society. Vision, on the other hand, is the long-term stated goal of a nation that provides the strategic direction of what is to be achieved collectively—and as a nation.

Earlier, we saw that every society should redefine the role and the model of its media based on the social, cultural, religious, historical, and political structure. The sociocultural structure can be represented by the values that a society holds dear while the historical and political circumstances are distilled into a vision.

While the definition of middle path journalism is up for further refinement, what is definite is what *actually* it is not. Middle path journalism is not another set of code of ethics for journalists. It is also not a substitute for existing communication theories and other genre such as peace, restorative, positive, deliberative, citizens, or civic journalism. And while middle path journalism is a conceptual framework for Bhutan, the model can be applied to any society as long as people have a common understanding of the vision and values.

The term middle path or middle way (Sanskrit—*madhyama pratipad*, Tibetan/Dzongkha—*umelam*) is not only one of the most profound

---

[3] In 2007, *Bhutan Times* was fined by the regulatory authority for publishing a sensational story titled, Abi Khawmo, which was untrue.

[4] Media is to be understood as any form of mediated communication in traditional media, social media, and in the new technological platforms.

philosophies in Buddhism but also an established concept found in other great civilizations. Aristotle's doctrine of the Mean and the Confucius Golden Mean in the Chinese civilization (Dickson, 1988) are just some of the examples. The term middle path is also often confused, or simply understood, as being in the "middle" or to make a compromise. The meaning is far deeper than that. Finding the middle path is a search for the ultimate and perfect balance between the extremes in every situation, circumstance, or event. Just like the principle of Golden Mean, middle path philosophy also emphasizes moderation and pluralism and the "nothing in excess" approach.

The Vision of "Gross National Happiness"

We have earlier mentioned the role of the Bhutanese media as a means to a "means" (democracy) to an end—overall being. The "overall well-being" has often been encapsulated in the concept of GNH—a development philosophy enunciated by the Fourth monarch, King Jigme Singye Wangchuck in 1979.[5] The concept of GNH has been subsequently promulgated as the overarching goal of policies of development (Ura, 2005).

GNH proposes a more holistic development (Phuntsho, 2013) with a more human-centric and inclusive approach. In other words, the model puts humans at the center of development and growth (Givel, 2015). His Majesty the Fifth King, Jigme Khesar Namgyel Wangchuck, defined GNH as "development with values" (Beaglehole and Bonita, 2015). A lot of work has been done in recent years in the field including a GNH index and GNH screening tool (Adler, 2009) to test the "GNHness" of all major projects and policies in the country.

In this chapter, I will move beyond the conventional wisdom of GNH and go back to the core principle of GNH, which, I believe, is not happiness (especially, not as it is understood in the West) but contentment.[6] Happiness is very often taken as pleasure, delight, exhilaration, excitement,

---

[5] In an interview to a group of reporters in Bombay Airport in 1979, the King stated that for Bhutan, gross national happiness was more important than gross national product. The statement was later reiterated in an article "The Modern Path to Enlightenment" by John Elliot (1987).

[6] In one of the sessions at the 2014 Mountain Echoes Literary Festival, Her Majesty Queen Dorji Wangmo Wangchuck is believed to have confirmed that GNH is contentment. No reporters were present and so the revelation went unreported. *Kuensel*, the national newspaper, now uses that definition and mentions in this article that "the ultimate goal is contentment". Available at http://www.kuenselonline.com/celebrating-a-kings-life/ (accessed on November 24, 2017).

etc. Happiness is also subjective—differing from person to person. It is also transitory. One moment you are happy, the next moment you may not be. Thus, the statement GNH is more important than "gross national product" and has to be understood in totality instead of selectively pulling out just one word—happiness. In an interview to the *Financial Times* in 1987, the King remarked that the overall national goal should be "contentment and happiness" (Elliot, 2008). And by contentment and happiness it means that as long as the people are generally satisfied these are the true measurement of a country's progress.[7] Therefore, GNH as a development philosophy is more for state institutions to create enabling conditions for people to be content and happy. This requirement was later included in the provisions of the Constitution of the Kingdom of Bhutan.

Contentment can be defined as a deep sense of fulfillment, happiness, and satisfaction in life. Being content is to treasure and cherish with what one has and with what one is. The goal of contentment as human pursuit is not new either. Several great religious traditions and civilizations have voiced out the need to pursue contentment (Cordaro, Brackett, and Anderson, 2016). However, down the ages it has lost its prominence in every public discourse and rhetoric, overtaken by the more visible concept of happiness and more measurable indicators such as the gross domestic product (GDP).

Traditional Bhutanese society has put more emphasis on contentment. This is evident from the numerous folktales, and songs, proverbs, everyday language, etc., were used to further the concept of contentment and other values (Kinga, 2001; Penjore, 2005). Popular sayings such as *tsham tshay shey na khebhi tah* (if you know how to limit yourself, it is a sign of smartness) are widely used. Equally popular are folktales such as the story of *Memay Helay* (*memay* means grandfather), which tells a story of an old man who finds a large turquoise while working in his field. He decides to sell his treasure and ends up bartering each time by going for something of lesser economical value, but that which enhances his contentment. He ultimately ends up with a song, which he sings joyfully as he returns home from his trading mission.

Another example is the folk song, *kokaray ko*, in which a rooster sits on the rooftop of a dzong (temple fortresses) comparing his physical attributes to beautiful objects that he sees—such as the governor's golden pen, a monk's

---

[7] The statement by the King was also made in response to a question by the reporter who told the King that he did not know anything about Bhutan and if the King could start by providing the gross national product (GNP) *per capita* of Bhutan. Former Indian Ambassador, Dalip Mehta, who was a diplomat on protocol duty to His Majesty the King at Bombay Airport, confirmed this during an informal conversation at the Mountain Echoes Literary Festival 2015.

headdress, etc., but concludes every time that "I would neither sell, nor barter off my body. I am happy with what I am and what I have."

Values in Bhutanese Society

Earlier we defined GNH as development with values. Values are a set of principles and standards of behavior that also define one's judgment and beliefs of what is important in life. Values help people negotiate their lives through the eternal dilemma of what is socially acceptable and what is not. They are acquired through socialization, religion, and education—both formal and parental. Values are also deeply rooted in society's history and philosophical traditions.

The Bhutanese society derived its social values primarily from the Buddhist culture (Phuntsho, 2013). Two concepts—*lay-judrey* and *tha-damtsi* are the anchors of Bhutanese values (Wangyal, 2001). *Lay-judray* can be roughly translated as "ways predestined by karma." It is based on the belief that whatever we are, whatever we do, and whatever happens to us, in this lifetime, are all because of our karma from our past lives. Hence, if we have been good, we will deduce good things, and if we have been bad, we will inherit the bad merits (Wangyal, 2001). This value is derived from the belief that all phenomena are interconnected and interdependent within the wheel of *samsara* (births and rebirths). No events and incidents occur in isolation or out of nothing.

The value of *tha-damtsi* establishes one's commitment and obligation toward others. Kinga (2002: 156) defines it as a "commitment and obligation of love, honour and loyalty in one's relationship with other people." This social value is best exemplified by the five pairing of duty and obligation such as *pha da bhu gi damtshig* (parent and child), *lobey da lobtu gi damtshig* (teacher and student), *nyen da drok gi damtshig* (husband and wife), and *poen da yok gi damtshig* (master and subordinate) (Wangyal, 2001).

Tha-damtsi can also be understood as one's commitment and loyalty toward one's job, task, or profession. In fact, *tha-damtsi* is used by the elders and superiors to encourage the younger generation by saying *tha-damtsi tehndhichha zhugho* (serve with commitment). Phuntsho (2013) also argues that in recent times the concept has also become intertwined with the notions of loyalty to the country.

Tha-damtsi is also translated as "moral integrity" (Phuntsho, 2013) that requires a person to live by his or her principles. Journalism is one profession where moral integrity is a necessary attribute. This is because people shape their beliefs, opinions, and views by consuming media products. While there seems to be a general consensus that the value of *Tha-damtsi* has its roots in Buddhism, Kohn (1994) claims that this set of moral principle was earlier practiced in Brahmanism and later was adopted in Buddhism, which then made its way to China in the first centuries CE and infused with Daoism. Hence, this value has universal appeals, origins, and usages. A study by Evans (2008) shows that Bhutanese values are still strong. However, conventional wisdom is that they remain severely challenged by increased living standards and independence, rural–urban migration, and fragmentation of communities and clans and less dependence on the state.

The belief in *lay-judrey* entails important and practical concepts and behaviors such as *nyinjay* (compassion–empathy–altruism) and *maang* (community) among others. Compassion may be defined as sympathy, pity, and concern by a person for the sufferings or misfortunes of others, while a community is a group of people living in a same area or sharing a common ancestry or interests or beliefs. A community could also be sharing a common public space or resources leading them to pursue some collective activities and goals.

While middle path journalism proposes the promotion of social values as its strategy, the intention is not novel. For generations, traditional Bhutanese society has used the medium it had such as art and folktales to transmit these values (Kinga, 2001; Penjore, 2005). For example, all these values are captured in one story of *thuenpa puenzhi*,[8] the "four friends." The story is rendered as an iconography and adorns the walls of private homes and public spaces in Bhutan.

The Four Dimensions of Middle Path Journalism

Based on what we have seen so far in terms of vision and values, we can summarize that the four dimensions of middle path journalism are contentment, community, compassion, and commitment. In this section, we will delve into these four dimensions and explore how they can be applied to the practice and consumption of media and communication.

---

[8] The story is about four animals, an elephant, a rabbit, a monkey, and a bird, who disputed over the ownership of a tree on which all of them happened to feed. The elephant claimed that it was his because he saw it first. The monkey said it was his because he had been feeding on the fruits of the tree. The rabbit claimed that he had been feeding on the leaves of the tree when it was a small sapling. The bird, who was watching the argument, told that the tree would not have grown if it had not spit out the seed from fruit it had eaten. The elephant, monkey, and rabbit, all then bowed to the bird and regarded it as their eldest brother. The four animals became friends and decided to share the tree together in peaceful harmony, fraternity, mutual care, and respect.

Contentment

The traditional Bhutanese society advocated the concept of *tsham tshay*. *Tsham tshay* is not contentment, which is rendered by another word, *chhokshay*[9]—but it is loosely translated as "limit or boundary." Practicing *tsham tshay* means limiting one's desire, greed, or other emotions. Interestingly, it is also to encourage moderation of both emotions—positive and negative. A person will be advised to practice *tsham tshay* if he or she exhibits excessive desire or no desire at all, or behaves cruelly or even too generously, or lead a hedonistic or an ascetic life. *Tsham tshay* promotes the value of "everything in moderation." It is derived from the concept of middle path philosophy.

The mainstream and the social media could advance the concept of *tsham tshay* in several ways:

1. **Limiting greed and desire:** Just as the media has been used to dilute one's self-esteem and contentment by offering images of perfect body, beauty, and wealth (McDonald, 2004), it can also be used to celebrate life and physical appearances as they are and instill respect and self-confidence.

    The mass media, especially the public service media, should not promote desire or unwanted or excessive needs. The public service broadcaster BBS, which is fully subsidized by the State, should refrain from carrying commercial advertisements and rather focus on practicing journalism. Similarly, *Kuensel*, which has been established through government funding and foreign donor support, should have a predictable revenue stream so as to fully focus on news and information. There is also another compelling reason for a country like Bhutan.

    The Royal Government, because it was headed by the King until very recently, is still sacrosanct in the minds of many people. Hence, between an official announcement and a Coca Cola advertisement, the audience takes them both as a *ka* (sacred command) of the Royal Government and hence many are left wondering why they should drink the fizzy stuff. Scholars such as McDonald (2006) have proposed banning advertisements from Bhutanese television altogether. He makes a compelling case against television advertisements if Bhutan were to achieve GNH.

---

[9] The word is in *chhokay*—the classical Tibetan, used in, and by, the monastic community.

2. **Human interest stories:** We have earlier mentioned that middle path journalism would take a more human-centric approach. This approach entails placing people at the center of the story and not the person's status, power, or wealth. For example, we could have more stories that celebrate community, family, solutions, and healings, which lighten the human hearts and carry the human spirits forward. Stories of ordinary people like in the opening story rarely make it to the news because these people are not "prominent."

Middle path journalism is diametrically opposite to the corporate media where celebrity gossips are sold; and pictures of politicians opening bridges and hospitals (actually built by ordinary people) flood the screen. The media impact studies in Bhutan have shown that the media contents today are too capital-centric and elitist. Middle path journalism will seek to correct this imbalance.

Community

Traditional Bhutanese society is communal (Phuntsho, 2013) where families and communities work toward, and in the interest of, the community itself. Individual rights, unless they were violated beyond the basic human rights, were hardly featured in the public discourses. The word *maang dhen* (community interest) was considered acceptable while the individualistic *raang dhen* (personal interest) was almost a social taboo. If the person worked only toward his personal interest, he or she would often become an outcast—a severe social justice handed down by the community.

A community also considers a person as acceptable and honorable if he or she took care of the family and communal matters. On a more spiritual–philosophical level, a person is also respected in the community if he or she performed acts of devotion for all sentient beings, such as sponsorship of religious monuments or events, which are believed to benefit not just the human beings.

One of the errors that the governments and multilateral agencies made during this modernization process is not recognizing community as an institution. In other words, a development activity or a project would be implemented directly by the central government without factoring the community's wisdom or local knowledge. At the most, a local coordinator would be appointed from the community and in some cases there would be "consultations" if they were required by the donor agency.

The breakdown of communities has brought the problems inside people's homes where families are increasingly becoming nuclear; divorces in urban areas are very common (Yangdon, 2017). A joke got circulated among the Bhutanese twitterati some time back where a man messaged to a friend, "Sorry bro! Couldn't make it to your wedding. Will try next time." Middle path journalism will work toward restoring or rebuilding that sense of community.

1. *Seeking balance:* In the decades since Bhutan joined the international community and the globalized world, ideas and influences such as individualism and human rights crept in. As a Buddhist nation, where right to life is a given—not only for humans but also for all sentient beings—these imported concepts were not really necessary because they were either misread or misused. While no sociological studies have been done, one could speculate that individual rights have overtaken community interest in many parts of the country. The advent of democracy made the case even worse. Even individual freedom took the front seat as opposed to the ideals of democracy—which is consensus building in national and local governance.

    Middle path journalism could seek to restore the balance between community and individual rights. This is not to mean that violations of laws or human rights should be silenced; rather the modus operandi for the media is to give more voice to the community on issues and development activities and adopt a middle path between community interest and individual rights.

2. *Celebrate family and community:* Middle path journalism could reinforce the importance of the institution of family and family networks. In eastern Bhutan, for example, there used to be, and there is still, the tradition of extended family. Such traditions can be celebrated rather than be stereotyped as orthodox or outdated. More space in the mainstream media could be given to village festivals and religious ceremonies such as *ngyun ney*, which actually are ceremonies that bring communities and families toward reconciliations and healings. Social events and traditional festivals such as the lunar New Year could be promoted instead of encouraging imported traditions such as Valentine Day or Christmas.

Compassion

The concept of *lay-judray* assumes a practical form in our daily lives in the form of compassion for all sentient beings. This is so, even in cases where it may not seem to be appropriate such as homicides—the most unacceptable act by human beings. Bhutanese, however, believe that such unfortunate incidents are because of *ken* (roughly translated as karmic misfortune), and that even the perpetuator would not have prevented it. A person does what he does, or is subjected to fortunate or unfortunate incidents, because of karmic consequences. No one exudes sheer malevolent intentions but things happen because of reasons going to one's past karma. Hence, everyone deserves some level of compassion. The offender cannot be vilified beyond a certain point, while the victim need not be overly sympathized or victimized either.

A real incident occurred few years back in Bhutan where a teacher had accidently killed a young student. The traditional media reported dutifully—even using the word "murder" instead of "manslaughter." Users on Facebook made bigger outcry—some even calling for capital punishment. A young blogger who was also a former student of the teacher surprised with an appeal on behalf of the teacher calling for some sympathy and compassion. Yet in another similar incident in 1997, a local governor in the eastern district of Mongar accidently shot a person, when his gun misfired. People were outraged obviously by the news but many older people concluded that it was *ken* and the persons were pre-destined to be involved in such an unfortunate accident.

Under the middle path journalism approach, journalist could practice and promote compassion in his or her line of duties by avoiding the extremes while calling for justice and at the same time, healings and forgiveness could be encouraged. The parties could be encouraged and guided to move forward.

Commitment

Earlier, we have explained the value of *tha-damtsi* as social commitment and responsibility. We have also qualified that *tha-damtsi* can be a value that an individual can possess to reaffirm one's sacred duty toward one's family, community, and the country. Compared to the other three dimensions, *tha-damtsi* is an equally, or if not more, important value. As Whitecross (2010) claims, *tha-damtsi* plays an important role in the creation of a sense of moral identity among contemporary Bhutanese. And this identity, when extrapolated to a nation, becomes the national identity and a hallmark of what it truly means to be a Bhutanese.

This fourth dimension of middle path journalism, therefore, ensures that a journalist is committed to the job and the profession and works toward achieving the core function of a journalist: seeking the truth and playing the normative roles (Christians et al., 2009) in the overall process of nation-building and well-being of the people. This value is also important for it can be argued that the other three dimensions of contentment, community, and compassion could lead to complacency, compromise, and clemency, respectively. After all, being content could also mean being happy with mediocrity; taking the community interest into consideration could mean compromising individual's rights and freedom, and being compassionate could entail forgiving and thereafter leading to unwanted implications and consequences. Middle path journalism, therefore, does not seek to compromise or to be in the middle. It is about seeking the perfect balance by staying committed to one's vocation.

Retrieving the Past to Improve the Present

In medieval Tibet, if someone stole something from a person, he (assuming that thieves were men) was imposed a fine payable to the State plus he was also made to cleanse his bad karma (Whitecross, 2008). This even entailed being sent to work for the victim for a certain period of time—depending on the nature of the theft. The judge in doing so was not only dispensing the justice but was also ensuring that he did not accumulate any negative karma against that person.

As countries became "modernized," western legal practices were to replace such indigenous methods, although Dubgyur (2003) claims that the ancient Buddhist legal system was quite advanced. For example, the system of having defense lawyers is well illustrated in the 14th century rendition of the Judgment of Dead (*Bardo Thodrel*)—a masked dance that is still performed in religious festivals even today. The switch to the western legal system has, however, not resulted in decrease in crimes whatsoever. Instead, the number of prisons proliferated in every country around the world.

The point is—there were different ways of doing things. But where have we lost them? Can we retrieve such practices and integrate them with the existing systems? Traditional values have been passed down the generations using communication tools and knowledge that a given generation had in its hand. It is, therefore, the duty of this generation to use modern tools such as the mass media and films and newer communication technology to pass these timeless values to the next generation. And, of course, the media and journalism should recognize their important role as state actors that can work toward the overall goal of nation-building and not be too carried away by the imported methods and models that were postulated under different sociopolitical circumstances.

References

Adler, B. A. 2009 "Gross National Happiness in Bhutan: A Living Example of an Alternative Approach to Progress." *Social Impact Research Experience Journal*. Available at http://repository.upenn.edu/cgi/viewcontent.cgi?article=1003&context=sire (accessed on October 25, 2017).

Beaglehole, R., and R. Bonita. 2015. "Development with Values: Lessons from Bhutan." *The Lancet* 385 (9971): 848–49. doi: 10.1016/S0140-6736(15)60475-5.

Christians, C. G., T. L. Glasser, D. McQuail, K. Nordenstreng, and R. A. White. 2009. *Normative Theories of the Media: Journalism in Democratic Societies*, vol. 117. Chicago, IL: University of Illinois Press.

Cordaro, D. T., M. Brackett, L. Glass, and C. L. Anderson. 2016. "Contentment: Perceived Completeness Across Cultures and Traditions." *Review of General Psychology* 20 (3): 221. doi: 10.1037/gpr0000082

Datta-Ray, S. K. 1996. "Press Freedom and Professional Standards in Asia." *Media Asia* 23 (3): 131–33. Singapore: AMIC.

Dickson, S. H. 1988. "The 'Golden Mean' in Journalism." *Journal of Mass Media Ethics* 3 (1): 33–37. doi: 10.1080/08900528809358307

Dubgyur, L. 2003. "The Influence of Buddhism on the Bhutanese Trial System." In *Conference on Buddhism*. Available at http://www.judiciary.gov.bt/publication/buddhism.pdf (accessed on October 25, 2017).

Elliot, J. 2008. "Bhutan's King Told Me About His Plans for Gross National Happiness." *Riding the Elephant*, November 5, 2008. Available at https://ridingtheelephant.wordpress.com/2008/11/05/bhutans-king-told-me-about-his-plans-for-gross-national-happiness/ (accessed on October 25, 2017).

Evans, S. 2008. "Bhutan National Values Assessment." *Journal of Bhutan Studies* 18: 95–115.

Givel, M. S. 2015. "Gross National Happiness in Bhutan: Political Institutions and Implementation." *Asian Affairs* 46 (1): 102–17. doi: 10.1080/03068374.2014.993179.

Gunaratne, S. A., M. Pearson, and S. Senarath. eds. 2015. *Mindful Journalism and News Ethics in the Digital Era: A Buddhist Approach*, vol. 12. London: Routledge.

Hampton, M. 2010. "The Fourth Estate Ideal in Journalism History." In Stuart Allan (ed), *The Routledge Companion to News and Journalism*, pp. 3–12. Oxon: Routledge.

Hao, X., and S. K. Datta-Ray, eds. 2006. *Issues and Challenges in Asian Journalism*. Singapore: Marshall Cavendish.

Kinga, S. 2001. "The Attributes and Values of Folk and Popular Songs." *Journal of Bhutan Studies* 3 (1): 132–70.

———. 2002. *Changes in Bhutanese Social Structure: Impacts of Fifty Years of Reforms: 1952–2002*. Chiba, Japan: Institute of Developing Economies.

Kohn, L. 1994. "The Five Precepts of the Venerable Lord. *Monumenta Serica* 42 (1): 171–215. doi: 10.1080/02549948.1994.11731253

Penjore, D. 2005. Folktales and Education: Role of Bhutanese Folktales in Value Transmission." *Journal of Bhutan Studies* 12: 47–73.

———. 2013. *The History of Bhutan*. NOIDA, India: Random House.

McDonald, R. 2004. "Television, Materialism and Culture: An Exploration of Imported Media and its Implications for GNH." *Journal of Bhutan Studies* 11 (1): 68–89.

———. 2006. "Selling Desire and Dissatisfaction: Why Advertising Should Be Banned from Bhutanese Television." In *Media and the Public Culture, Proceedings of the Second*

International Seminar on Bhutan Studies, pp. 188–207. Thimphu: The Center for Bhutan Studies.

Norbu, T. 2001. *White Sail: Crossing the Waves of Ocean Mind to the Serene Continent of the Triple Gems*. Boston, MA: Shambhala Publications.

Park, M. J., and J. Curran. 2000. *De-Westernizing Media Studies*. New York, NY: Routledge.

Siebert, F. S., T. Peterson, and W. Schramm. 1956. *Four Theories of the Press: The Authoritarian, Libertarian, Social Responsibility, and Soviet Communist Concepts of What the Press Should Be and So*. Chicago, IL: University of Illinois Press.

Sinpeng, A. 2007. "Democracy from Above: Regime Transition in the Kingdom of Bhutan." *Journal of Bhutan Studies* 17: 21–47.

Tshering, K. 2014. *Media at the Crossroads*. Bhutan News Network. Available at http://www.bhutannewsnetwork.com/2014/05/media-at-the-crossroads/ (accessed on October 25, 2017).

Ura, K. 2005. "Gross National Happiness." *Sociological Bulletin* 54 (3): 603–07. Available at http://www.jstor.org/stable/23620628 (accessed on October 25, 2017).

Wangchuk, D. 2007. "Media in the New Political Order." In *Media and Public Culture: Proceedings of the Second International Seminar of Bhutan Studies*, 274–96. Thimphu: The Centre for Bhutan Studies.

Wangchuk, D. 2015. "Middle-path Journalism: A Conceptual Framework [Weblog post]. Available at http://dorjiwangchuk.blogspot.com/2015/10/middle-path-journalism-conceptual.html (accessed on November 25, 2017).

Wangyal, T. 2001. Ensuring Social Sustainability: Can Bhutan's Education System Ensure Intergenerational Transmission of Values. *Journal of Bhutan Studies* 3 (1): 106–31.

Wiley, T. 2002. *Original Sin: Origins, Developments, Contemporary Meanings*. New York, NY and Mahwah, NJ: Paulist Press.

Whitecross, R. W. 2008. "Transgressing the Law: Karma, Theft and Its Punishment." *Revues d'études Tibétaines*, 45–74. doi: 10.1.1.540.1284

———. 2010. "Virtuous Beings: The Concept of Tha Damtshig and Being a Moral Person in Contemporary Bhutanese Society." *HIMALAYA, the Journal of the Association for Nepal and Himalayan Studies* 28 (1): 6. Available at http://digitalcommons.macalester.edu/himalaya/vol28/iss1/6 (accessed on October 25, 2017).

Yangdon, S. 2017. Monetary and Matrimonial Cases Top the List. *The Bhutanese*. Available at http://thebhutanese.bt/monetary-and-matrimonial-cases-top-the-list/ (accessed on October 25, 2017).

12

Philippines: Ignatian Pedagogy and Mindful Communication

Evans Rosauro I. Yonson

This chapter will look into the Ignatian Pedagogy as it is applied in the education and practice of development communication in Xavier University—Ateneo de Cagayan, in the Mindanao island of the Philippines. I will try to relate how this pedagogy is related to mindful communication in the context of the delivery of instruction and the application of communication by key players in the community.

The Jesuits—A Background

The Society of Jesus, popularly known as the Jesuits, was founded by St Ignatius of Loyola in 1534 with St Francis Xavier, St Peter Faber, and six other companions in Paris, France. In 1540, Pope Paul III officialized the organization in a papal bull containing the "Formula of the Institute." Today, the Jesuits are in 112 nations all over the world engaging in evangelization, apostolic ministry, and education. The Jesuits' work in education has brought about the founding of schools, colleges, universities, and seminaries, the conduct of scientific and intellectual researches, and cultural efforts.

In its efforts to standardize the Jesuit educational system, the society came up with *Ratio atque Institutio Studiorum Societatis Iesu* (The Official Plan for Jesuit Education; in short, *Ratio Studiorum*) in 1599. The first Ratio Studiorum was based on the Holy Scriptures, scholastic theology, cases of conscience, philosophy, moral philosophy, mathematics, the humanities, and Latin and Greek languages. A better version was introduced in 1832, still with the classical subjects but now considering the native languages of the students, history, geography, and natural sciences.

In 1986, the Society of Jesus came up with *The Characteristics of Jesuit Education*, a document that has given teachers, administrators, students, and parents a sense of identity and purpose. More popularly called the Ignatian

Pedagogy, it provides for new methods of imparting knowledge in the modern times not only for Jesuit schools, colleges, and universities but also for every form of education service inspired by the teachings and writings of St Ignatius and the *Ratio Studiorum*. Thirty-one years later, the Ignatian Pedagogy remains a staple of Jesuit education throughout the world.

The Jesuits in the Philippines and Mindanao

The Jesuits arrived in the Philippines in 1581 led by Fr. Antonio Sedeño, SJ, from the Jesuit Province of Mexico.[1] Sedeño founded the Colegio de Manila (later known as Colegio de San Ignacio) in 1590. Not long thereafter the Jesuits established themselves in several missions throughout the archipelago. However, in 1767, Spanish King Charles III banished the Jesuits from the islands. In 1859, the Jesuits returned to the Philippines with a special purpose—the missions of Jolo and Mindanao.

In Cagayan de Oro (Northern Mindanao), Fr. James T. G. Hayes, SJ, founded the Ateneo de Cagayan in June 1933 with 17 high school students. Five years later, under the administration of Fr. James Haggerty, SJ, Ateneo de Cagayan became a college. At the end of March 1940, the first college diplomas were conferred. The Ateneo's repute as an educational institution in Southern Philippines had grown such that it had students coming from all over the country.[2] When World War II broke out, the Ateneo had to close down until the country's liberation from the Japanese. In 1953, Fr. William F. Masterson, SJ, founded the College of Agriculture. He wrote:

> The College [of Agriculture] itself was set up with the aim of forming men and women of scientific competence and social responsibility who ... would return to the land to improve production, and to provide the rural areas with the concerned leadership so despe[r]ately needed.

On August 27, 1958, the Ateneo de Cagayan was granted university status with numerous offerings—basic education, liberal arts, education, commerce, agriculture, pre-engineering, pre-legal, law, and graduate studies. In changing its name to Xavier University (XU), the Ateneo de Cagayan aimed to

---

[1] *Jesuits in the Philippines*. Available at https://www.phjesuits.org/portal/the-jesuits/jesuits-in-the-philippines/ (accessed on October 25, 2017).

[2] *Brief History of Xavier University*. Available at http://www.xu.edu.ph/about (accessed on October 25, 2017).

demonstrate the soul of all Ateneos—the spirit of learning and service, and the spirit of purposeful scholarship.

In the years that followed, several other units and programs were introduced: the Southeast Asia Rural Social Leadership Institute (SEARSOLIN) in 1963, the Museo de Oro (1968), the Institute for the Development of Educational Administrators (1972), the College of Medicine and the Center for Industrial Technology (1983), the College of Nursing (1988), and the McKeough Marine Center (2014), among others. These offerings have made XU the leading Catholic university in Mindanao.

Introduction of Development Communication

Nora C. Quebral (2007), former Chairperson of University of the Philippines—Los Baños' Department of Agricultural Communication defines development communication as:

> An art and science of human communication is applied to the speedy transformation of a country and the mass of its people from poverty to dynamic state of economic growth that makes possible greater social equality and the larger fulfillment of the human potential.

In 1976, the College of Agriculture introduced the Development Communication (DevCom) program with the aim of producing a pool of communication experts to help out in extension services of the College in Mindanao.

In XU, the DevCom program is a four-year undergraduate curriculum, which aims to equip students with the knowledge and skills necessary in the teaching, management, and implementation of communication programs for development. As a program in a Jesuit institution, DevCom is in the pursuit of forming development communicators of character who will become catalysts for change, following the characteristics of a Jesuit education.

Mindanao—The Land of Promise and Mission

Mindanao, the second largest island in the Philippine archipelago, has valuable human resources with a high literacy rate, abundant natural resources with its lush forests and vegetation, and rich biodiversity. With six regions,

Mindanao has an estimated population of 22 million (2010 figures from Philippine Statistics Authority, 2016) with a poverty incidence of 28.8 percent. Of the top 10 poorest provinces in the Philippines, five are found in Mindanao—Lanao del Sur, Maguindanao, Zamboanga del Norte, Sarangani, and North Cotabato. The island is replete with corruption and injustice, infighting between and among tribal peoples, Christians, and Moslems, and exploitative businesses, among others.

In 2016, the Philippine Province of the Society of Jesus issued the Philippine Province Roadmap after conducting a series of meetings, consultations, and conversation all over the country. The roadmap renews the Jesuits' commitment and responds to the urgent and critical challenges that Mindanao faces today, which include:

- harnessing current apostolic presence and impact in the island through its various engagements;
- pursuing strategic collaboration and partnerships within the society (among province ministries) and externally with local churches and other organizations;
- strategizing how Manila and other non-Mindanao Jesuit institutions can engage in the island; and
- continuing discernment and conversation within and across the province.

One of the strategies that the Provincial Roadmap will employ is strengthening institutions in Mindanao like XU through education, working with indigenous peoples, disaster risk reduction and management, sustainable agriculture and rural development, and research and social outreach for the marginalized. The roadmap also calls for engagement in awareness-raising, immersion, and capacity-building activities on the Mindanao situation and realities.

The Ignatian Pedagogy

The goal of Jesuit education is best described by Fr. Peter-Hans Kolvenbach (Kolvenbach and Jesuit Conference, 1989):

> The ultimate aim of Jesuit education is, rather, the full growth of the person which leads to action—action, especially, that is suffused with the spirit and presence of Jesus Christ, the Son of God, the Man-for-Others. This goal of action, based on sound understanding and enlivened by contemplation, urges

students to self-discipline and initiative, to integrity and accuracy. At the same time, it judges slipshod or superficial ways of thinking unworthy of the individual and, more important, dangerous to the world he or she is called to serve.

Kolvenbach added that a Jesuit-schooled graduate is "well-rounded, intellectually competent, open to growth, religious, loving, and committed to doing justice in generous service to the people of God." These students are taught an education, through careful reasoned investigation, that will form or reform their usual attitudes toward other people in his/her community, in particular, and the world, in general. When these students finish their education, they are expected to become leaders in service, in imitation of the Christ, men and women of competence, conscience, and compassionate commitment.

The Teacher–Learner Relationship

In Ignatian Pedagogy, the teacher takes the center stage but always taking into consideration the learner in the process. The teacher facilitates the learner's quest for truth. He/She, with his/her expertise in the field of study or interest, provides for knowledge and skills for the learner to experience, reflect, and act on the situations that they have been exposed to. This cyclical paradigm is further divided into five steps: context, experience, reflection, action, and, evaluation.

The teacher begins instructions with the basic principles and truths of the subject matter. He/She then creates the conditions where the students gather and recollect information from the experiences in order to grasp the subject matter cognitively with the sensation of affective nature. These human experiences may either be direct or vicarious in nature. The direct interpersonal experiences include conversations with real people, field trips, and immersions in communities. Vicarious learnings may be done by showing films, role-playing, and simulations.

The teacher formulates questions for the learner to reflect on how all the basic principles and truths and experiences relate to one's existence and being. This part of the process becomes a deepening, formative, and liberating one, where the learner is given the chance to discern the significance of all these that lead him/her to undertake action. The action may involve two steps: interiorized choices and externally manifested choices. These choices may lead the student to do something consistent with his/her new conviction.

Evaluation, an integral process in Ignatian Pedagogy, is done periodically throughout the semester to check on the learners' achievements and shortcomings. These evaluations may include periodic quizzes and reports. But the teacher needs to be observant of the learner's growth or lack thereof, during class discussions, attitude, and participation. For this to be effective, the teacher creates a relationship of mutual respect with the learner.

The Development Communication Program of Xavier University

The DevCom program has general education courses that include philosophy, religious and social studies, statistics, history, languages, and pure sciences; and technical and social science electives, such as farm accounting, crop production, food technology, animal science, peace education, cultural anthropology, and community organization.

The DevCom student takes communication courses such as communication theories, communication research, development journalism, educational communication, community broadcasting, communication and society, interpersonal communication and participatory development communication, multimedia production, radio/TV production, and undergraduate thesis. Most of the courses offered by the DevCom Department are production classes that require final products/outputs. The final product/output is considered as the students' final examination. In these communication courses, the Sustainable Development Goals (SDGs) of the United Nations are considered as topics of interest for the students to take on for their projects.

The first communication course that the students take is Introduction to Development Communication (DC 20) where concepts on development, Philippine situation, literacy, poverty, employment, women, indigenous peoples, and the marginalized, among others, are discussed.

The highlight of the course is a three-day immersion program that will expose the students to an underdeveloped community. The learners will live with their host families and commune with them. At the end of the immersion, they will pool the information about their host families and come up with a summary report. They will then identify and recommend possible projects and programs that may be done for the community.

The recommendations made by the students will then be used for another course, Strategic Communication in Development (DC 28). In this course, the concepts of social marketing, KAP (knowledge, attitude, and practices) survey, and community's demographic information are discussed. The students will go back to the same community for another longer immersion.

Children from the tribe perform a traditional song of welcome to the XU DevCom students. (Photo by Jerome Torres)

This immersion will now be the application of several courses: Interpersonal Communication and Participatory Development Communication (DC 29), Photography in Development (DC 41), Fundamentals of Educational Communication (DC 25), and Development Journalism (DC 24).

This could be compared to the mindful communication approach discussed in Chapters 2 and 8 where deep listening and becoming more aware of the circumstances of peoples' sufferings could lead one to develop compassion which will reflect upon the production of development communication contents/messages.

In Ignatian Pedagogy, empathetic listening is relevant and important for both the teacher and learner. It requires actively listening to one to understand them. Pope Francis (2014), himself a Jesuit, puts it best what listening is in his message:

> Listening is never easy. Many times it is easier to play deaf. Listening means paying attention, wanting to understand, to value, to respect and to ponder what the other person says. It involves a sort of martyrdom or self-sacrifice, as we try to imitate Moses before the burning bush; we have to remove our sandals when standing on the "holy ground" of our encounter with the one who speaks to me (cf. Ex 3:5). Knowing how to listen is an immense grace, it is a gift which we need to ask for and make every effort to practice.

Philippines: Ignatian Pedagogy and Mindful Communication 157

As part of the XU DevCom Department's social outreach program, the students give out something to the community. In the picture, the XU DevCom student hands out a water container to schoolchildren. Potable drinking water is a major concern for the schoolchildren in rural Philippines. (Photo by Jerome Torres)

With this value of empathetic learning, the learner will begin to understand the plight of the community to which he/she is exposed to. He/She abandons his prejudices and starts to process his/her experience from the point-of-view of the community. This adds greater significance and meaning to the student's exposure to the community.

The various outputs produced from this immersion will have to be presented back to the community: an information–education–communication (IEC) campaign on matters concerning the community such as health, food and safety, and voters' education; a photography exhibit and a coffee-table book featuring the community and their everyday dealings; training modules for local residents; and local news articles that will be turned into a community paper.

For the Undergraduate Research in Development Communication (DC 31) requirements, the students are advised to take on social phenomena that may be found in the community and conduct research on it. The results of the research are then given back to the community. The same is the case with the Radio/TV Production (DC 44) and Development Writing (DC 43); the students identify possible topics that may be investigated for their final 30-minute documentary film for airing on TV.

All these efforts are under supervision and guidance by several faculty of the DevCom Department. Throughout the four-year academic life of the students, only one community is adopted to measure the students' impact on the lives of the community members. In order to facilitate learnings, regular consultations and evaluations are done with the community leaders and faculty-in-charge.

XU heeds the call made by Pope Francis (Vatican, January 24, 2016):

> Communicating means sharing, and sharing demands listening and acceptance. Listening is much more than simply hearing. Hearing is about receiving information, while listening is about communication, and calls for closeness.

"Compassionate" Engagement with Community

At the end of the four-year engagement, the students and the community will have communicated very well and built partnerships through the conduct and outputs of various activities at the community level. Such closeness will have a greater impact in the development of the learner and at the same time, the community. The learner applies what he/she has learned in the classroom to the community. In the process, he/she becomes the teacher and sees meaning of all these experiences.

Central to a Jesuit education, the learner must be able to exhibit the following characteristics: *magis*; men and women for and with others; *cura personalis*; unity of the heart, mind, and soul; *ad majorem Dei gloriam*; and forming and educating agents of change.

Literally translated "more," *magis* has been inculcated in the learner from the start. This elusive concept to do more comes from the Jesuit motto *ad majorem Dei gloriam* ("For the Greater Glory of God"), which is a challenge for the DevCom students (and graduates) to strive for excellence in each of their endeavors, whether for their general education courses or their core courses. Whether it is for a small class activity or a major course requirement, the students are challenged to give their best. The more, the better, the greater for God.

But giving more is not only confined in the four corners of the classroom. More importantly, an XU DevCom student is shaped to become a man or woman for others. As such, students are molded to have the desire to share their gifts, pursue justice, and have sincere concern for the poor and marginalized.

At XU DevCom, this is manifested in the students' engagements in the marginalized communities. Their various encounters with the community through their courses expose the students to communities, allowing them to better understand the locals' lives and inculcate the need for development to improve the lives of these people. The same is the case for the students' other core courses, whose emphasis is on using effective communication materials to address their needs.

Shaping men and women for others begins though by caring for the "whole person." This Jesuit education characteristic called *cura personalis* commits to care for the whole person, which includes the soul. Thus, in addition to the general education courses, students also take up religious studies and philosophy courses. This education goal is to develop the whole person; these added courses integrate all aspects of the students' lives, achieving *unity of heart, mind, and soul*. Additionally, these students are taught behaviors reflecting critical thought and responsible action on moral and ethical issues. This is reflective in the students' roster, which are centered in investigating on social issues relevant in today's time. This forming and educating catalysts of change is what makes DevCom students with Jesuit education stand out.

Today, the DevCom Department has produced numerous graduates who are working with various international, national and local nongovernmental organizations, government agencies, civil society organizations, people's organizations, media companies, and local government units. But the majority have remained in Mindanao holding positions as project officers, writers/researchers, production crew, journalists, planners, and consultants in development-related projects that have made strong impact at the community level.

The Ignatian Pedagogy calls for the teacher to be a living example of the ideals of St Ignatius of Loyola. With the teacher as the leader, it is then expected that the learner will follow suit, thus creating a cycle of learning that will be handed down to the next generation.

References

Farrell, Allan P., trans. 1970. *The Jesuit Ration Studiorum of 1599*. Conference of Major Superiors of Jesuits, 1717 Massachusetts Avenue, NW, Washington, DC.

Kolvenbach, Peter-Hans, and Jesuit Conference. 1989. *Assembly 1989: Jesuit Ministry in Higher Education*. Rome, Italy: The Conference.

Philippine Province of the Society of Jesus. 2016. *Philippine Province Roadmap 2016*. Available at https://taborasj.files.wordpress.com/2016/05/philippine-province-roadmap-final-may-2016.pdf (accessed on October 25, 2017).

Philippine Statistics Authority. 2016. *Philippines in Figures 2016.* Available at http://web0.psa. gov.ph/sites/default/files/PIF%202016.pdf (accessed on October 25, 2017).

Pope Francis. 2015. "48th World Communications Day: Communication at the Service of an Authentic Culture of Encounter." *Vatican,* January 24. Available at http://w2.vatican.va/ content/francesco/en/messages/communications/documents/papa-francesco_20140124_ messaggio-comunicazioni-sociali.html (accessed on October 28, 2017).

———. 2015. "49th World Communications Day—Communicating the Family: A Privileged Place of Encounter with the Gift of Love." *Vatican,* January 23. Available at http:// w2.vatican.va/content/francesco/en/messages/communications/documents/papa-francesco_20150123_messaggio-comunicazioni-sociali.html (accessed on October 25, 2017).

———. 2016. "50th World Communications Day: Communication and Mercy: A Fruitful Encounter." *Vatican,* January 24. Available at http://w2.vatican.va/content/francesco/en/ messages/communications/documents/papa-francesco_20160124_messaggio-comunicazioni-sociali.html (accessed October 25, 2017).

Quebral, Nora C. 2007. "Reflections on Development Communication: Update on Development Communication." In *Philippine Communication Today,* edited by Crispin C. Maslog Quezon City, Philippines: New Day Publishers.

13

Mindful Communication for Good Governance: A Buddhist Approach

Sugath Mahinda Senarath

Governance is not a new concept. Its history goes as far back as human civilization.[1] The World Bank formulated the concept of "good governance" in 1992 (Singh, 2014). The bank defined the concept as the "[m]anner in which power is exercised in the management of a country's economic and social resources for development" (World Bank, 1992: 3). The phrase "good governance" may be literally defined as the system of "good control," "good administration," or "good management," which is universally accepted by all as an ideology for running a government, an organization, or a firm (Bodhiprasiddhinand, 2009). The word *Dhammappasāsana* in Pāli (or *Dharmaprasāsana* in Sanskrit) means "good governance": *Dhamma* (virtue/law/righteous) and *Pasāsana* (governance), which means the law of governance (Singh, 2014).

The United Nations Economic and Social Commission for Asia and the Pacific (UNESCAP) states that good governance has eight major characteristics:

> It is participatory, consensus-oriented, accountable, transparent, responsive, effective and efficient, equitable and inclusive, and follows the rule of law. It assures that corruption is minimized, the views of minorities are taken into account and that the voices of the most vulnerable in society are heard in decision-making. It is also responsive to the present and future needs of society. These eight characteristics reinforce each other, and a proper governance strategy needs to take cognizance of each. (Singh, 2014)

Buddhist Perspective

Buddhism believes in the innate goodness not only of human beings but also of every creature in the world. It identifies all humans as *manussa* because of their better developed brain or mind (*mana/manasa*). Therefore,

---

[1] Refer to http://www.unescap.org/sites/default/files/good-governance.pdf (accessed on November 10, 2015).

in human society, we discover men and women purposefully and meaningfully engage in work. They are motivated to work for various reasons, particularly personal individual reasons. Collective reasons also exist (Sri Dhammavihari, 2006: 108).

The *Agganna Sutta* of the *Digha Nikaya* explains the Buddhist theory of the origin of the humans and also their social and political institutional ground. The Buddhist theory debunks the divine creation of human society. The *Agganna Sutta* confirms the cosmic law based on the principle of impermanence (*anicca*) and the law of cause and effect (*paticcasamuppada*). At the beginning of human society, people owned land as common property. But as a consequence of greed (*tanha*), they turned this common property into private ownership, which gave rise to individualism. This situation engendered a new situation in society that brought about stealing, selfishness, and punishment. Thereupon, people assembled together to discuss the moral standards they needed to install and to select the most capable person as the guardian of those morals. They assigned the selected person the responsibility to maintain justice among the group. Because the entire society elected this person, he was named *Mahasammata* (the Great Elected). Additionally, he was called *Khattiya* (the Lord of the Field), and because he had to please everyone, he was also called *Raja* (One who Pleases), the one responsible for maintenance of *Dhamma*. Thus, Buddhism regards society totally as a human institution that depends on human beings.

Agganna Sutta contains a theory of a democratic conception of both the state and the law based on the premise that all human beings are born with equal rights, socially and politically. In origin, all human beings, in the words of *Agganna Sutta*, were "like unto themselves and not unlike" (*aññesam sadisaññeva no asadisanam*) though class distinctions and the like were to arise later among them. Of course, Buddhism does not deny differences (*vemattata*) among individuals resulting from other factors" (Perera, 1995a: 5).

The Brahmins held that the birth is the sole criterion that can be used when deciding the caste to which an individual belongs. The Buddha rejected that outright, and instead argued and proved that highness or lowness of an individual has to be judged on his behavior (*Vasala Sutta, Sutta Nipata*) (Nanayakkara, 1995: 72).

> *Na jacca vasalo hoti - na jacca hoti brahmano*
> *kammana vasalo hoti - kammana hoti brahmano*

[One does not become an outcast by birth or genius by birth; one will be an outcast by deed or will be genius by deed]

Even though individual differences due to heredity, genes, environment, or *karmatic* factors could occur, their essential nature remained the same. As Sri Dhammananda (1993: 231) points out:

> While recognizing the usefulness of separating religion from politics and the limitations of political systems in bringing about peace and happiness, there are several aspects of the Buddha's teaching, which have close correspondence to the political arrangements of the present day. Firstly, the Buddha spoke about the equality of all human beings long before Abraham Lincoln, and that classes and castes are artificial barriers erected by society. The only classification of human beings, according to the Buddha, is based on the quality of their moral conduct. Secondly, the Buddha encouraged the spirit of social-cooperation and active participation in society. This spirit is actively promoted in the political process of modern societies. Thirdly, since no one was appointed as the Buddha's successor, the members of the Order were to be guided by the Dhamma and Vinaya, or in short, the Rule of Law.... Fourthly, the Buddha encouraged the spirit of consultation and the democratic process. This is shown within the community of the Order in which all members have the right to decide on matters of general concern.

In contemporary society, huge accusations come from civil society on bribery and corruption of politicians and officials. When implementing law and order, double-standard measures can consist in bribery and corruption between politicians and/or those who have more political and economic power, and the powerless. The Buddha once said:

> When the ruler of a country is just and good, the ministers become just and good; when the ministers are just and good, the higher officials become just and good; when the higher officials are just and good, the rank and file become just and good; when the rank and file become just and good, the people become just and good (*Anguttara Nikaya*).

Buddhism is concerned with "all beings" (*sabbe sattā*).

In the *Cakkavatti Sihanada Sutta* (Tang, 2008), which continues from where the *Agganna Sutta* ends, the Buddha said that immorality and crime could arise from poverty, but it is futile to eradicate crime through force. In the *Kutadanta Sutta,* the Buddha shows economic development as the precious way to reduce crime. According to Buddhism, nothing can be called a "just war," which is only a false term coined and put into circulation to justify and excuse hatred, cruelty, violence, and massacre (Rahula, 1996: 84).

From the Buddhist perspective, the ruler must follow the *Dasa Raja Dharma*, the 10 rules the Buddha prescribed for a good government:

1. Be liberal and avoid selfishness.
2. Maintain a high moral character.
3. Be prepared to sacrifice one's own pleasure for the well-being of the subjects.
4. Be honest and maintain absolute integrity.
5. Be kind and gentle.
6. Lead a simple life for the subjects to emulate.
7. Be free from hatred of any kind.
8. Exercise nonviolence.
9. Practice patience.
10. Respect public opinion to promote peace and harmony.

In the *Cakkavatti Sihanada Sutta*, he further advised (Sri Dhammananda, 1993: 233):

- A good ruler should act impartially and should not be biased and discriminate between one particular group of subjects and another.
- A good ruler should not harbor any form of hatred against his subjects.
- A good ruler should show no fear whatsoever in the enforcement of the law, if it is justifiable.
- A good ruler must possess a clear understanding of the law to be enforced. It should not be enforced just because the ruler has the authority to enforce the law. It must be done in a reasonable manner and with common sense.

Buddhist literature suggests that Buddhism would uphold democracy as the ideal form of polity (Perera, 1995a). "Buddhism would agree with Jean Jacques Rousseau that the assumption of man's responsibility for his own governance is of the essence of human dignity" and that "no man can without degrading himself beneath the level of humanity, be denied a personal share in the making of political decisions" (Perera, 1995a: 5). Being empirical in approach, Buddhism views all problems. Buddhism accepts economic security (*atthi-sukha*). But the Buddha did not consider the formulation of a comprehensive economic theory. His concern was more on the ethical aspects of the economy rather than on the theory or subtle mechanisms involved in it (Nanayakkara, 1995: 16).

The *Milinda Panha* states: If a man, who is unfit, incompetent, immoral, improper, unable, and unworthy of kingship, has enthroned himself as a king or a ruler with great authority, he is subject to be tortured ... to be subject to a variety of punishment by the people, because being unfit and unworthy, he has placed himself unrighteously in the seat of sovereignty. The ruler, like others who violate and transgress moral codes and basic rules of all social laws of mankind, is equally subject to punishment; and moreover, to be censured is the ruler who conducts himself as a robber of the public.

> The king always improves himself and carefully examines his own conduct in deeds, words and thoughts, trying to discover and listen to public opinion as to whether or not he had been guilty of any faults and mistakes in ruling the kingdom. If it is found that he rules unrighteously, the public will complain that they are ruined by the wicked ruler with unjust treatment, punishment, taxation, or other oppressions including corruption of any kind, and they will react against him in one way or another. On the contrary, if he rules righteously they will bless him: "Long live His Majesty." (Sri Dhammananda, 2006: 234)

Buddhism measures human affairs in terms of a Universal Norm and also holds that a good end can only be reached by good means (Perera, 1995b). "Ethical perfection advocated by Buddhism has not only a personal but also a social dimension" (Nanayakkara, 1995: 37).

Buddhist Way of Life

The *Sigāla Sutta* shows the great regard and respect the Buddha had for the layman's life, his/her family, and his/her social relations. A young man named *Sigāla* used to worship the six cardinal points of the heavens—east, south, west, north nadir, and zenith—in obeying and observing the last advice given to him by his dying father. The Buddha told the young man that in the "noble discipline" the six directions were—east: parents; south: teachers; west: wife and children; north: friends, relatives, and neighbors; nadir: servants, workers, and employees; zenith: religious men.

Buddhism is a way of life, and what is essential is following the Noble Eightfold Path (Rahula, 1996: 81). The Eightfold Path consists of eight factors. These eight factors can be divided into three easily remembered dimensions:

Sila (Morality) = Right Speech, Right Action, and Right Livelihood

Samadhi (Mental Culture) = Right Effort, Right Mindfulness, and Right Concentration

Panna (Wisdom) = Right Understanding and Right Thoughts

Right understanding (*Samma Ditthi*) is the knowledge of realizing the Four Noble Truths (Chandawimala, 2014; Sri Dhammananda, 1993). When someone has right understanding he/she acquires right thought (*Samma Sankappa*). This factor is sometimes known as right resolution, right aspirations, and right ideas (Sri Dhammananda, 1993: 81). Right speech (*Samma Vaca*) is refraining from lying, frivolous speech, and harsh speech. Right action (*Samma Kammanta*) is refraining from the three bodily unwholesome actions of killing, stealing, and sexual misconduct (Chandawimala, 2014). Right effort (*Samma Vayama*) is refraining from evil conduct for livelihood. Right mindfulness (*Samma Sati*) is good consciousness. "It is fourfold as mindfulness of contemplation of the body, mindfulness on all feelings, mindfulness on state of consciousness and mindfulness on all objects" (Chandawimala, 2014). Right concentration (*Samma Samadhi*) is the practice of developing one-pointedness of the mind on one single object (Sri Dhammananda, 1993), either physical or mental (Chandawimala, 2014; Sri Dhammananda, 1993).

Buddhism suggests that the best way is to lead a balanced way of life (*samajīvitatā*). This balanced life gears toward not only the happiness of deftness (*ananasukha*) but also helps enjoy economic stability (*atthisukha*). In this regard, everyone should be aware of limiting his/her needs to bare necessities (*appicchatā*) (Nanayakkara, 1995).

In the teachings of the Buddha, the middle path (*majjhima patipada*) is not a condition between two extremes. The middle path means choosing the correct one when two extremes exist, abandoning both of them. "The Buddha's Middle Path means the most effective way leading to the cessation of *dukkha* (unsatisfactoriness) that lies between the extremes of searching for happiness through the pleasure of senses, and the other extreme searching for the same through self-mortification in different forms of asceticism" (Senarath, 2015: 130–31). The middle path is the way of transcending both extremes.

Good Governance and Buddhist Thinking

In "good governance," the king/queen or the government must spread the four sublime states of mind for all living beings: *mettā* (loving kindness), *karunā* (compassion), *muditā* (sympathetic joy), and *upekkhā* (equanimity). *Digha Nikaya* (III, 182,288) says the king who rules the country must avoid the four biases or prejudices (āgati) against his subjects: *chandagati* (biases of like), *dosagati* (biases of dislike), *mohagati* (biases of dilution), and *bavagati* (biases of fear).

Buddhism also mentions 14 unwholesome negative traits or characteristics of mind:

1. Hatred (*krodha*) is the ill will arising with the desire to hurt others.
2. Enmity (*upanàha*) is repeatedly occurring old hatred. It is also called hate and opposition.
3. Ingratitude (*makkha*) is forgetting the support rendered by others.
4. Malice (*palāsa*) is the nature of considering oneself the same as the virtues. "Those who are not intelligent enough to assess themselves and are immoral equate with moral, unwise equate with wise, weak equate with powerful, poor equate with the rich" (Chandawimala, 2014: 98).
5. Jealousy (*issà*) is the nature of disliking the prosperity of others.
6. Stinginess (*maccarā*) is the nature of unwillingness to part with your property for others to receive any benefit from it.
7. Fraud (*màyà*) is the nature of misleading people by pretending to be virtuous while performing various unwholesome acts.
8. Treachery (*sàtheyya*) is the nature of deceiving others by showing false loving kindness.
9. Inflexibility (*thambha*) is the nature of not bowing down to *Dhamma* and individuals who deserve respect.
10. Impetuosity (*sàrambha*) is the nature of working to overcome and be above others.
11. Conceit (*mana*) is the nature of estimating oneself to be someone not to be discarded as refuse but someone of value and respectability.
12. Arrogance (*atimàna*) arising from factors such as power, higher economic background, education, profession, caste that causes the normal conceit to develop into a strong conceit and consider others to be low.
13. Infatuation (*mada*) is the intoxication caused by haughtiness arising from riches, education, higher birth, and power.
14. Heedlessness (*Anarakkhata, Pamatta, Avimansakarita, Asamikkhakarita*) is the nature of forgetting and not performing wholesome acts but enjoying fivefold pleasures and performing unwholesome acts (Chandawimala, 2014).

The rulers and people of the country should be protected. The *Pañcha sila* (five precepts) constitute *the minimum moral obligations of a lay Buddhist* (Rahula, 1996). These precepts are: not to destroy life, not to steal, not to commit adultery, not to tell lies, and not to use intoxicants. Buddhist principles also require adherents to avoid four wrong paths: the paths of greed, hate, cowardice, and dilution (*Candā dosā bhayā-yo dhammaṁ ati vattati Nibhīyati tassa yaso-kālapakkheva candimā*).

If someone acts surpassing propriety due to greed, hatred, cowardice, or dilution, his/her fame will deteriorate like the fading moon (Chandawimala, 2014: 103) and will face 10 defilements (*kilesa*), namely, greed, ill-will, dilution, conceit, wrong view, skeptical doubt, sloth, restlessness, lack of moral shame, and lack of moral dread.

The Buddha clearly explained 10 wholesome acts, which are very important not only for personal development but also for social development:

> *Dānaṁ sīlaṁ ca bhāvanā-veyyāvaccāpacāyanā, Pattānumodanā pattidānaṁ -dhammassa desanā, Savanā ditthijjukamma-miccevaṁ dasadhā*

> [Alms giving (*dāna*), morality (*sīla*), meditation (bhāvanā), respectfulness (*apacāyana*), service (*veyyāvacca*), transferring merit (*patti dāna*), receiving merit (*pattānumodanā*), listening to *Dhamma* (*dhamma sevana*), delivering *Dhamma* (*dhamma desanā*), development of right view (*ditthijju kamma*)]

Buddhist Attitude to Legal Dispensation

The Buddhist attitude toward law in general and toward legal dispensation, in particular, stems from two conceptions: (a) that of the "rule of the righteousness," since sovereign authority in the Buddhist context is represented by the "wheel," which is symbolic of the ongoing and expanding process of law and justice in the world, and (b) that of the "happiness and well-being of mankind" (*bahujanahita, bahujanasukha*), which is unique to Buddhist thought (Perera, 1995b: 66–67):

> *Devo vassatu kalena - sassa sampatti hotu ca*
> *phito bhavatu loko ca - raja bhavatu dhammiko*

> [May the rains be on time, may the farmers have successful harvests, may the ruler be just, and by these happenings may the people prosper]

Good Governance and Buddhism

"Good governance" is now mostly used as a concept in discussing development literature. But it is not a new concept. As discussed in this chapter, Buddhist literature clearly shows an emphasis on good governance. The Buddhist polities highly valued moral conduct in politics.

Now we are living in a very complicated world. We highly value economic development rather than moral development. Consequently, money has become a powerful tool when tackling social problems. Bribery, corruption, crime, mental depression of people, individualism, over-consumption, etc., have become common problems in all countries around the world.

Religious fundamentalism and political fundamentalism are also playing critical roles in the world. The Buddhist *majjhima patipada* (middle path) offers a precious way to solve most of the problems. Also known as the Noble Eightfold Path, it provides a valuable roadmap to reach development goals. The mass media, including social media, have become an integral part of contemporary society. Although today's advanced digital technology enables the media to reach the people rapidly, most media fail to target their content toward human development. It is quite evident that media-generated emotion has significant implications for actions and interactions within the larger social world (Nabi, 2014: 12).

References

Bodhiprasiddhinand, P. 2009. *Notes on Buddhism and "Good Governance,"* 58–78. Available at http://www.bodhinand.com/ download/ bodhinand_com/Notes% 20on%20 Buddhism%20Good%20Governance.pdf (accessed on November 20, 2017).
Chandawimala, R. 2014. *Handbook of the Buddhist.* Pokunuwita: Sri Chandawimala Dhamma Treatises Presentation Board.
Nabi, R. 2014. "Emotion, Media, and Our Social World." In *Media and Social Life*, edited by M. B. Oliver and A. A. Raney, p. 12. New York, NY and London: Routledge.
Nanayakkara, S. K. 1995. "Economics." In *Encyclopedia of Buddhism: Extract No. 3*. Colombo: The Department of Buddhist Affairs.
Perera, A. D. T. E. 1995a. "Democracy." In *Encyclopedia of Buddhism: Extract No 3*. Colombo: The Department of Buddhist Affairs.
———. 1995b. "Human Rights." In *Encyclopedia of Buddhism: Extract No 3: Social Dimensions of Buddhism*. Colombo: The Department of Buddhist Affairs.
Rahula, W. 1996. *What the Buddha Taught.* Dehiwala, Sri Lanka: Buddhist Cultural Centre.
Senarath, S. 2015. "The Journalist and the Middle Path." In *Mindful Journalism and News Ethics in the Digital Era: A Buddhist Approach*, edited by S. A. Gunaratne, M. Pearson, and S. Senarath, pp. 130–31. New York, NY and London: Routledge.
Singh, R. S. 2014. *The Teachings of Buddha and Good Governance in Modern India: A Socio-Economic Analysis.* Buddhism and Australia: International social Conference on Buddhism Available at http://buddhismandaustralia.com/index.php?title=The_Teachings_of_Buddha_and_Good_Governance_in_Modern_India:_A_SocioEconomic_Analysis_by_Ravi_Shankar_Singh (accessed on November 10, 2015).

Sri Dhammavihari. 2006. *Dharma: Man, Religion, Society in Buddhism.* Dehiwala: Buddhist Cultural Centre.
Sri Dhammananda, K. 1993. *What Buddhists Believe,* rev. ed. Kuala Lumpur: Buddhist Missionary Society.
Tang, F. N. Y. 2008. *Cakkavatti Sihanāda Sutta* [The Discourse on the Lion-roar of the Wheel-turner]. Translated by P. Tan. D 26/3:58-79. Available at http://dharmafarer.org/wordpress/wp-content/uploads/2010/02/36.10-Cakkavatti-Sihanada-S-d26-piya.pdf (accessed on December 7, 2015).
World Bank. 1992. *Governance and Development.* Washington, DC: The World Bank. Available at http://documents.worldbank.org/curated/en/604951468739447676/pdf/multi-page.pdf (accessed on November 10, 2015).

14

Mindful Communication and Sustainable Development: The Buddhist Holistic Framework

Ananda Kumaraseri

We have discussed a great about mindfulness in this book so far. I do not wish to be repetitive but to try and inject some fresh insights into the discussion. In particular, I would like to introduce some cogent reasoning, even fundamental factors, that we should take cognizance of and address urgently with a view to finding lasting solutions. In respect to the subject matters of mindful communication and sustainable development, I am inclined to think that it is practical and more effective to avoid an academic approach. This is because, generally speaking, academics tend to over-theorize and get into all kinds of knotty issues such as in splitting hairs on definitions, debate as to who is right, and finally end up in talking at cross-purposes. At the end of the day, nothing is solved, only that a great deal of hot air is let out, intellectual masturbation is performed, and confusion and distraction continue to roost. In all due respect to academics, such indulgences are a recurrent phenomenon, which is best avoided in the deliberation of mindful communication and sustainable development, or for that matter on most mundane issues confronting the contemporary world. In any case, the subject matters of mindful communication in relation to sustainable development involve the masses and it would be prudent not to theorize as we will then be talking well above their heads which will be of little purpose, if any at all.

Briefly, I am of the view that a holistic effective approach is preferred that would take into account some key paradoxes, and a diagnostic approach should be adopted in keeping with the letter and spirit of the Buddha's framework for overcoming mundane human problems. This would allow the masses of ordinary people to understand and appreciate the pertinent issues and related factors involved. They would then become mindful that the subject matters impact their welfare and well-being directly. It is more likely for us then to expect positive responses in addressing the pertinent issues/problems under discussion.

The first point I would like to draw attention to is that because of our acculturation, we tend to look at problems, issues, and challenges, including wholly mundane ones, as environmental degradation, climate change, and deep ecology in the physical form or perception. That is to say, peoples' understanding of a problem or issue is commonly perceived along physical or tangible parameters. This is simply because that is how we have been taught from infancy and how mind generally perceives problems and issues and challenges them. Further, it is to be noted that our essentially cognitive-based education system reinforces the physical orientation in our conceptualization of problems, issues, and challenges. The point to note here is that since we conceptualize in a limited or restricted physical orientation, we fail to recognize the "root" of the problem, issue, or challenge. We invariably tend to see only their physical manifestations. As a consequence, we address only the symptoms. The problem thus persists. The Buddha's scientific approach of addressing the very root of a problem or issue should be adopted as a cardinal principle of our strategy. So, let us go beyond the manifestations to the very root/roots in addressing mindful communication in the context of sustainable development.

The second paradox is that we tend to view problems, issues, and challenges as though they are very distant from us. People, in general, tend to regard the challenge of say sustainable development as someone else's onus and as if it has nothing to do with them. So they remain uninvolved in addressing the challenge. We have to confront this fixation of indifference. While the Buddha consistently advised us to always "look within ourselves first" and to observe the "pedagogy of teaching by example" as the most effective teaching and learning process, the mental training and culture of introspection and a holistic education which goes beyond *pariyathi* (knowledge/theory or cognitive learning) to include *patipatti* and *pativeda* (affective and psycho-motor learning) are greatly wanting. Indeed, these inputs are imperative across all levels and sections of society and should most certainly include academic circles.

Concept of Sustainable Development Is Not Novel

Yet another paradox is the notion that sustainable development and deep ecology is something that was introduced in contemporary times and that this is a Western notion or wisdom. However, the Buddha had already recognized, more than two and a half centuries ago, the consequences of the transformation of human society from a tribal stage of hunters and gatherers to a sedentary society where the individual became more important than the group, and the environment was left to be exploited according to one's whim and fancy.

The Buddha pointed out that when property was individualized in contrast to the hitherto community ownership, insatiable materialistic desires are automatically whetted. His sublime teachings of moderation, contentment, balance, etc., are encapsulated in the teachings of *majjhima patipada*, that is, the middle path of avoiding extremes of self-indulgence of our senses and self-mortification. However, because of the way we look at things, we think that these are modern phenomena, whereas it is actually an anthropological evolutionarily outcome of human society from being hunters and gatherers to one of a sedentary property-owning society.

Briefly, this then is the origin of the problem of ecological degradation and climate change. The only difference is that the scales and corresponding repercussions have taken on far larger dimensions, especially since the agricultural revolution and later on with the industrial revolution. Today, we are beset by the dynamics of modern technology and globalization that have further exacerbated the challenge of deep ecology and sustainable development. But if we fail to understand these pertinent facts and the other foregoing fundamental realities, we would fall short of addressing the challenges set before us.

Yet another underlying fundamental factor that I would like to stress upon is that environmental degradation and consequential climate which has given rise to the call for sustainable development are caused by human beings. National and international dialogues, meetings, and conferences persist without stressing the fact that these issues are created by human beings. The solution, therefore, lies in human beings and not in any external being or power as some religious advocates have propagandized as a fear tactic. We need to disabuse those who believe that these challenges are acts of God or any external being or power. More specifically, the primary cause is "human greed," as the Buddha had pinpointed more than 2,550 years ago. But are the global dialogues addressing the key factor? We can make a difference if this dialogue focuses on the foregoing parameters and on the "human being."

Mind Is Paramount: Imperative of Cultivating Wholesome Mental Culture

Yet another telling paradox is that we talk about—mindfulness; we talk about mindful communication, but we fail to talk about the "mind" per se. Indeed, mindfulness is born out of the root word mind. How can one promote mindful communication without first understanding what exactly is the "mind". Beyond question, the mind is central to our deliberations, and yet paradoxically, we tend to overlook, if not leave out, this crucial factor.

It is imperative that we understand what the mind is. We are talking about human beings, yet we do not look at the mind despite it being so central to our discussion. Furthermore, the mind is highly complex. We need to understand that there is a logical mind and there is an emotional mind; there is a conscious mind and a subconscious mind, and so on and so forth.

It is with a sound understanding of the working of the human mind and its complexities that we are to proceed to eradicate its defilements. Simultaneously, we need to purify the mind through *bhavana* (the cultivation of a wholesome mental self-culture), commonly referred to as mindfulness or mindfulness meditation.

Another important feature of the mind is that it is a super duper computer. We need to recognize this reality. Whatever we experience is mind-made and mind-orientated. The Buddha stressed that the mind is the forerunner of all of our thoughts, all of our speech, and all of our actions. Irrespective of what you believe or where you come from, whether India, America, China, or Africa, this is a reality of all human beings.

Cultivation of the Mind from the Fetal Stage

A related reality that has been sadly overlooked is that the mind begins to function and is alive right from the fetal state. It is not during childhood, or adolescence when a child attends school, or when she or he is an adult, or after marriage that the mind starts functioning, but right away at the fetal stage while growing in the mother's womb. Thus, the cultivation of the mind, which we need to adopt as a principal strategy, therefore, has to commence in the mother's womb. Otherwise, the mind is in all likelihood going to be negatively impacted. (These scientifically and medically validated facts are more fully explained in my book *Mothercare and Parenting: Key to Social Structuring*.[1]) Given the limitation on wordage, it would suffice to note that the Buddha's guidelines for the cultivation of a wholesome mind from the fetal stage are referred to as *Gabbha Parihara* (*Gabbha Shastra* or *Gabba Sanskar* in Sanskrit).

---

[1] You may also refer to our website livebybuddhism.com for more free resources and insights on these subject matters.

The holistic development of the fetus ensures not only the baby's physical development, but the equally important mental, spiritual, psychological, and emotional development of the yet-to-be-born baby as well. In Chinese, this is referred to as *Tai Cheow*, in Korean as *Tekiyo*, and in Japanese as *Taikyo*. So we have a rich heritage of cultivating a wholesome mental culture in a person from the fetal stage. Regrettably, however, contemporary society has not understood and appreciated this heritage. Much less are these guidelines being observed among modern nuclear families. We are not mindful of the origins of human problems such as greed and fail to recognize their connectivity to the problems/issues that manifest later on in life. So let us make a dramatic difference by getting to the "root", as I stated earlier, that is, by the cultivation of a wholesome mental culture.

The second critical stage of the development of the mind is the first five to six years of a child's development. This is the period when the mind develops the fastest, after that it plateaus off. A significant factor that has to be noted is that in the modern social environment, whether we like it or not, a child is invariably bombarded with negative influences right from infancy. So it is imperative that parents conscientiously cultivate a wholesome mental culture in their child from infancy in the home, well before he/she goes to school. The Buddha defined this key duty of parents as *Pubbha Archariya*. This is to underline that parents are the first and foremost teachers, and the home is the first and foremost school. Today, "home education," for want of a better coinage, is virtually non-existent. Both parents usually have careers and the TV or maid or iPad has replaced this vital parental responsibility. These core factors obviously have to be squarely addressed as an integral strategy of sustainable development and mindful communication. Otherwise, we would face a far more complex task of having to deprogram the mind at adulthood to rid it of its accumulated defilement.

Media and the Mind

In focusing on mindful communication, we have to recognize three factors. Firstly, people have become conscious of the challenge of environmental degradation, climate change, deep ecology, and sustainable development largely because they are sensationalized by the media and also because of the publicity generated by leaders, policy makers, government officials, and political leaders. Otherwise, not much attention is given by the general public to these subject matters. Secondly, the public is at the same time constantly enticed toward a culture of consumerism. The media, especially its advertising arm, focuses on promoting indulgences in sensual pleasures with a view to enhancing sales and greater profit. As a result, a culture of crass materialism is constantly being reinforced and is flaunted across all levels of society. Thirdly, though the public has a choice not to respond to media publicity enticing greater use of goods and services, in reality public responds in large numbers and thereby add to the aggravation of the challenges.

A major challenge of mindful communication thus is: How to get the media to encourage moderation, balance, and abstinence in certain matters, as guiding life principles?

Understanding the Human Being

An underlying common denominator of the three segments identified is that the targeted audience compromise human beings. The question that arises is: Do we understand what a human being is? The human being is at the heart of the challenge of sustainable development and mindfulness commmunication. It is only logical, therefore, that we should first have a thorough understanding of the human being.

The Buddha referred to human beings as *manussa*, which is derived from the word *mano* or *mana*, meaning a being which has a mind that can be developed to its highest potential. So it is up to us now to try and develop a wholesome mental self-culture that is not going to respond positively to the negative stimuli from the media and other channels. Once people possess a wholesome self-culture, they are self-regulated and would respect and safeguard the environment and nature as integral to their welfare and wellbeing. A principal task of mindful communication should be to foster the cultivation of a wholesome mental self-culture among all segments of society.

Long-term Solution

Education is another key factor. For none of the things we have been talking about can be sustained unless we have a holistic education system in place. Our discussion so far, however, has been confined to education in the context of mass communication. It is imperative that we ensure a holistic system of education as a whole. The fact is education systems all across the world are generally a failure. Otherwise, we would not have unprecedented crimes and serious social ills in the contemporary society, as education is expected to make students better human beings.

The Buddha is an unparalleled teacher. It is imperative to incorporate his pedagogy in the education systems. We need to introduce a holistic education system that would embody the foregoing concerns outlined and help to reinforce the cultivation of wholesome mental cultures among students.

The Pedagogy by Example

The most powerful pedagogy you can think of is to teach by example. We fail to do this and we fail to understand and appreciate the importance of teaching by example. We ourselves must set the examples. Our leaders must set the examples. Those of us who are advocating mindful communication must set the examples in everything that we do so that this becomes a culture or second nature and would rub off on others to follow suit.

SECTION D

Applying Traditional Practices to Mindful Development Communication

15

A Japanese Path to Mindful Communication: Understanding the Silence of the Japanese

Kanako Watanabe

Japanese culture is known as a "high-context" culture. "High context" and "low context" are terms presented by the anthropologist Edward T. Hall (1981: 91) to explain cultural differences. In his book, *Beyond Culture*, he states the following:

> A high-context (HC) communication or message is one in which most of the information is either the physical context or internalized in the person, while very little is in the coded, explicit, transmitted part of the message. A low-context (LC) communication is just the opposite; i.e., the mass of the information is vested in the explicit code.

In a high-context culture, people must have a good understanding of others' feelings based on their history, their relationships, and their shared culture. People involved in a conversation are always expected to be able to sense the hidden words behind the spoken letters.

Japanese communication style is indirect, very obscure, and intentionally avoids the direct expressions, where truth or important information is often hidden behind spoken words. Hall (1981: 114) writes the uniqueness of Japanese novels as follows: "Japanese novels are interesting and sometimes puzzling for Westerners to read. To the uninitiated, much of the richness as well as great depths of meaning pass unnoticed, because the nuances of Japanese culture are not known."

Thus, foreigners and many *Kikokusijyo*,[1] returnee children who lived under the foreign educational system for a certain period of time on account of their parents, are often confused and struggle with this complex communication

---

[1] According to "Annual Report of Statistics on Japanese Nationals Overseas" (2016) by Ministry of Foreign Affairs of Japan, 859,994 Japanese are living abroad and 78,312 are children of school age.

style as they are not capable of "reading between the lines" and consequently judged as a *KY* person. *KY*[2] is a Japanese expression that is short for *Kuuki Yomenai*, a term literally translated as "can't read the air." It is a word used to label a person who has difficulty reading their surrounding social situations. This is a typical example of the unique Japanese communication culture, where one is expected to read between the lines. If a person is *KY*, it means that they are incapable of sensing a situation or understanding unspoken information, such as facial expressions, silence, etc., and they also lack common sense or are insensitive to others' feelings.

For those who grew up in direct and individual culture, it is extremely difficult to adjust to the Japanese society where there is an expression, *honne to tatemae* or *ura omote* to describe the gap between the "true intentions" and the "stated words." In her book, Hendry (1995: 163) writes as follows: "The ability to adjust runs alongside the necessity always to make distinctions between the front (*omote* or *tatemae*) appropriate for a particular situation and the real opinions (*ura/honne*) which lie behind it." Being brought up in such linguistic culture, it is one's nature to sense *honne* or *ura*, behind *tatemae* or *omote*, in order to have a polite and mature relationship in the society.

Shinto and Buddhism in the Japanese Culture

Shinto is the traditional Japanese religion; it is the largest religion in Japan[3] and it has a strong influence on Japan's cultural identity. *Shin*, could also be read *kami*, means "gods," and *to* means "the way." Although *Shin* literally translates to gods, gods are called *yaoyorozu no kami* in Japanese, literally meaning "eight million gods," which is a reference to natural features such as mountains, waterfalls, seas, animals, and even human beings.

The spirit of Shinto is based on gratitude toward other people, surrounding nature, and all living things. *Okage-sama* is a frequently used word in Japan. It literally means "thanks to you," and is a phrase used to express one's gratitude to others. The concept of "caring for others" stems from the Shinto belief, and it strongly influences the Japanese cultural identity.

---

[2] Nominated as 1 of 10 buzzwords of the year 2007 for U-Can New Words and Buzzwords Awards announced by the Jiyukokuminsha publishing house.

[3] According to "Religious Statistical Survey" (2015) by the Ministry of Education, Culture, Sports, Science and Technology, the numbers of adherents are: *Shinto* 89,526,176 and Buddhism 88,719,287.

Since the 6th century CE when Buddhism was introduced to Japan, the Japanese have accepted Buddhist belief, and it has merged with Shinto belief. Both religions have influenced each other, which has resulted in the coexistence of the two; hence Buddhism and Shinto have become the two major religions in Japan. *Shinbutsu-shūgō*, which is the syncretism of Shinto and Buddhism, literally "syncretism of *kami* and Buddha," has continued until the government developed a policy, *Shinbutsu-bunri*, "separation of Shinto and Buddhism," in 1868 during the Meiji period (1868–1912) to separate the two religions.[4] However, many Japanese are still confused about the difference between the two religions, although many follow the religious rituals for ceremonial occasions with deep respect. People generally distinguish between the two religions by having weddings at Shinto shrines and funerals at Buddhist temples.

Itadakimasu, is a phrase used before dining, and it is considered as one of the important table manners. It has more meaning than the simple phrase "enjoy your food," or "let's eat." *Itadakimasu* literally means "I humbly receive" showing gratitude for the lives sacrificed, for the people who cultivated the food, and for those who cooked by using words to express one's modesty. *Gochiso-sama* is also an important phrase used after the meal, expressing the gratitude and respect for the efforts of a person who cooked and people that cultivated. These philosophies of appreciation—toward food or person—derive from of Jyodo Shinshu belief, a Buddhism sect, which is the largest sect practiced in Japan.[5]

Ishin-denshin is a common Japanese four-character idiom called *Yojijyukugo*, reflecting the style of nonverbal communication. It means "to communicate from mind to mind," similar to "sympathy" or "telepathy" in English. This concept derives from a Buddhist sect called Zen Buddhism, which symbolizes Japanese cultural identity to convey the force without spoken words:

> Zen Buddhism is a practice that needs to be experienced, not a concept that you can intellectualize or understand with your brain. Zazen [Zen Meditation] is an attitude of spiritual awakening, which when practiced, can become the source from which all the actions of daily life flow—eating, sleeping, breathing, walking, working, talking, thinking, and so on. [Thus] Zen Buddhism is not a theory, an idea, or a piece of knowledge. It is not a belief, dogma, or religion; but rather, it is a practical experience.[6]

---

[4] *Shinbutsu Hanzenrei*; the Kami and Buddha Separation Order (1868).
[5] According to "Religious Statistics Japan" (2015) by the Ministry of Education, Culture, Sports, Science and Technology.
[6] Available at http://www.zen-buddhism.net/ (accessed on October 27, 2017).

Famous 20th century Japanese Zen master Taisen Deshimaru described the essence of Zen as: "You must concentrate each day, as though a fire were raging in your hair."[7]

Gift Giving in Japanese Culture

Gift giving or gift exchanging is a common Japanese tradition, which originates from Shinto ritual. In early days, people sent offerings to gods as the expression of one's respect or appreciation. This is the origin of Japanese gift-giving custom.

There are various gift-giving occasions in Japan. After a trip, one is expected to bring back *omiyage*, a local souvenir, usually a box of sweets, from the place you have visited to give out to superiors or to colleagues in the office, or to your friends for maintaining good relationships. *Temiyage* is a gift one should bring at the first visit to the client's company or when one is invited to someone's home. Gift-giving custom in business is especially important and this makes the future relationship smoother.

Ochugen, which translates as a "mid-year gift," and *oseibo*, "a year-end gift," are both important and are well-known gift-giving rituals, and are used to express gratitude to relatives, superiors, colleagues, or acquaintances for their support. Such gifts are usually beautifully decorated with a piece of *Washi* paper *called Noshi*, a small ceremonial origami attached to the gift, considered a token of good fortune, and tied with *mizuhiki*, a traditional Japanese cord usually in red or black color depending on the occasion or intention, in order to express that the gift is highly formal.

In this Japanese gift-giving tradition, series of actions from choosing the appropriate gift to its form of wrapping are more important than the actual gift, showing care and appreciation to others.

Like its communication style, there are many unspoken rules under strict manners in gift giving that confuse the people from outside the Japanese culture. When preparing a gift, Japanese consider the wrapping of a present more significant than what is actually inside.

A social anthropologist, Joy Hendry, argues in her book *Wrapping Culture* (1995: 27):

> A western perception of the practice prepares us to regard wrapping as a means to obscure the object inside, whereas in a Japanese views it would seem that

---

[7] Available at http://www.zen-buddhism.net/famous-zen-masters/taisen-deshimaru.html (accessed on October 27, 2017).

the function of wrapping is rather to refine the object, to add to it layers of meaning which it could not carry in its unwrapped form.

Japanese people value the gift received based on its wrapping, such as the type and color of paper used and the manner in which it is wrapped. As Hendry (1995: 27) also discusses, "Perhaps it is rather in the wrapping that we should seek most of the significance of a Japanese gift;" wrapping is more than just a box or layer protecting the material inside that is merely waiting to be torn open immediately after giving the gift. This is because in Japan, the wrapping implies respect, care, or appreciation toward the receiver. Hendry (1995: 39) notes "wrapping may well indicate something about relationship between the people, close friends using little more than that necessary to enclose the object or objects, more distant relations preparing a package suitable to the formality of the occasion."

Usually, in most department stores a customer can ask for wrapping free of charge and, quite often, the sales person may even ask you if the purchase is a gift or for the customer's own use, so that they can wrap the item for the customer, if required. Many do not realize the uniqueness of this tradition until they travel outside of the country. Japanese travelers abroad are commonly amazed or shocked by the way a gift is treated in different cultures, where people do not see the sense of the wrapping itself.

Wrapping Culture and Environment

In recent years, this custom of wrapping has been debated in terms of its environmental impact because of the waste of materials involved. The Ministry of Environment established a law, "Basic Law for Establishing a Recycling-based Society,"[8] to reduce the environmental load caused by wasting natural resources, including the tradition of excessive wrapping, through the "3 Rs Initiative": Reduce, Reuse, and Recycle. Although the law has increased the nation's awareness of Japan's over-wrapping culture and environmental responsibility, there is a conflict between traditional cultural customs and the recent environmental movement.

However, the attitude to feel and express appreciation or respect others is deeply rooted in Japanese daily lives in forms of manners, traditional customs, and rituals. These days, *Furoshiki*, a traditional Japanese wrapping cloth, known to have originated during the Muromachi Period (1392–1573), when

---

[8] Refer to http://www.env.go.jp/recycle/low-e.html (accessed on October 27, 2017) for translated copy of the law.

people spread it out in place of a bath mat or wrapped one's clothes with it, is now regaining its value as a recyclable, reusable, and more ecological form of wrapping material.

As *Furoshiki* is one sheet of cloth, it is very flexible in shape and various items could be wrapped in many different ways. Common usage of *Furoshiki* is to wrap *Bento*, a lunch box to carry to the school or to the office. In launching the product, in April 2006, Japan's Environmental Minister Yuriko Koike[9] said:

> The *Furoshiki* is so handy that you can wrap almost anything in it regardless of size or shape with a little ingenuity by simply folding it in a right way. It's much better than plastic bags you receive at supermarkets or wrapping paper, since it's highly resistant, reusable and multipurpose. In fact, it's one of the symbols of traditional Japanese culture, and puts an accent on taking care of things and avoiding wastes. It would be wonderful if the *Furoshiki*, as a symbol of traditional Japanese culture, could provide an opportunity for us to reconsider the possibilities of a sound-material cycle society.

Mottainai-Furoshiki is a unique *Furoshiki* introduced by Ms Koike. It is made of a fiber manufactured from recycled PET bottles, and has a birds-and-flowers motif drawn by Ito Jakuchu, a painter of the mid-Edo era.

Washi—Traditional Handcrafted Paper

Washi is a traditional handmade Japanese paper, first used for copying Buddhist scriptures or for writing records or rituals by Shinto priests. *Washi* is still produced in Japan, and many people who make *Washi* follow the traditional papermaking methods using the fiber of Japanese native trees such as Kozo, Gampi, and Mitsumata as raw materials. In 2014, three types of *Washi*-making traditions were registered on UNESCO's list of the Intangible Cultural Heritage as the "Craftsmanship of Japanese hand-made paper."[10]

During the Heian period (794–1191 CE), when *Washi* was a luxury good, it was only limited to religious ceremonies or rituals. Later on, as *Washi* was used to wrap offerings, people came to practice folding and presenting offerings in beautiful ways, giving birth to ceremonial folding. *Washi* is an

---

[9] Ms Yuriko Koike, a former Minister of the Environment, has created the "Mottainai Furoshiki" as a symbol of Japanese culture to reduce waste. She presented it at the Senior Officials Meeting on the 3R Initiative held in Tokyo in 2006. Refer to https://www.env.go.jp/en/focus/060403.html (accessed on October 27, 2017).

[10] See http://www.unesco.org/culture/ich/en/RL/washi-craftsmanship-of-traditional-japanese-hand-made-paper-01001 (accessed on October 27, 2017).

important Japanese culture since it has also been used and integrated into the Japanese lifestyle. In *Washitsu*, or the traditional Japanese-style rooms, one can see many examples of the incorporation of *Washi*. For example, *Shoji* are sliding screens with *Washi* mounted on each side, and *Fusuma* is a sliding door with *Washi* attached on the surface and used for Japanese lanterns. The Japanese still use *Washi* to wrap kimonos to absorb moisture from the air.

Upon its declaration as a "tangible heritage" by the UNESCO, *Japan Today*[11] quoted an unnamed UNESCO official as saying: "Handmade 'washi' paper has not only helped promote the continued cultivation of mulberry trees throughout Japan, but it has also ensured the longevity of traditional artistic techniques and cultural knowledge, allowing for an interconnectivity between regional communities for generations."

Art and Symbolism of Origami

When *Washi* became less expensive, its use shifted from religious ceremonies and rituals, and people started to enjoy *Washi* as a type of hobby called origami, the practice of folding paper. Its popularity spread among people during the middle of the Edo period (1603–1868 CE), and it initially began as a winter pastime activity.

Origami has become a well-known technique for producing various shapes such as animals or flowers by folding a piece of paper. The activity is popular among all, from children to the elderly, and is passed down in families from parent to child and from grandparent to grandchild. Although origami itself is theorized to be of Japanese, Spanish, or Chinese origin, it is not necessarily a Japanese tradition exclusively.

There is a folk belief called *Senbatsuru* which literally means "thousand paper cranes," which states, if one folds a thousand paper cranes, a symbol of longevity, one's wish for a long life or for recovery from illness will come true. Therefore, collections of one thousand cranes are often given as gifts to people who are hospitalized.

Senbatsuru came to symbolize a wish for peace after the atomic bomb was dropped on Hiroshima, and Sadako Sasaki,[12] who died of radiation

---

[11] Available at https://www.japantoday.com/category/national/view/washi-paper-added-to-list-of-unesco-intangible-heritage-items (accessed on October 27, 2017).

[12] Born in Hiroshima city, January 7, 1943; she was two years old when the exposure occurred. At the age of 12, she was diagnosed with leukemia from the radiation, and she spent her time in hospital until she passed away on October 25, 1955.

exposure, folded cranes to pray to extend her own life. When the "Great East Japan Earthquake" occurred on March 11, 2011, hundreds of thousands of bound *Senbatsuru* were delivered to the disaster-struck region, sent from all over the world with thoughts of compassion and support for the well-being of those affected. Many people have been encouraged by the soulful messages symbolized by the *Senbatsuru* as both requiem and praying for revival. Japanese people have often projected their sentiments onto objects or actions beyond language.

Today, the Japanese word origami has spread around the world as a type of traditional Japanese handicraft, and it has gained fans in many countries including those in the West. This is largely due to the efforts of Akira Yoshizawa,[13] who is considered as the grandmaster of origami. He has created more than 50,000 models throughout his lifetime and has developed a system or a way to teach folding origami models with symbols, arrows, and illustrated diagrams.

> My origami creations, in accordance with the laws of nature, require the use of geometry, science, and physics. They also encompass religion, philosophy, and biochemistry. Overall, I want you to discover the joy of creation by your own hand ... the possibility of creation from paper is infinite.[14]

Yoshizawa served as an international cultural ambassador for the Japanese government by holding many exhibitions or lectures in Oceanian and European countries. He also put forth much effort to spread origami worldwide by lending his own origami models to other exhibitions around the world. Eventually, his name became famous worldwide along with the Japanese word origami, and he was invited to various countries as an origami lecturer.

In 1983, Emperor Hirohito awarded him the Order of the Rising Sun, one of the highest honors given in Japan. Origami was popularized throughout Japan and the Western countries through him and his work. Today, there are many origami organizations or societies existing not only in Japan, but around the entire world. People learn and share origami work, beyond their cultures and languages to simply enjoy their time together.

---

[13] A Japanese origamist born on March 14, 1911 in Tochigi prefecture, Japan. His first oversea exhibition was held at Amsterdam, in 1957. Many significant folding techniques were developed by him including wet folding, which is famous among many origamists. He died on March 14, 2005 in Itabashi Ward, Tokyo.

[14] By Akira Yoshizawa. See http://www.azquotes.com/quote/1223037 (accessed on October 27, 2017).

Origami Developing Mindfulness

Origami was introduced to kindergarten education when kindergartens were established in 1876 under the Meiji government. Soon after that, it was also introduced as a teaching material for elementary schools. The idea is that neatly folding paper in a set sequence improves concentration and patience. It may look like a solitary activity, but children teach one another, what one child does can spread throughout the class, and everyone makes the same item and progresses together. Origami can, thus, be said to be an effective mindful communication tool. Origami also trains the mind to "treat things with care" as the creations can tear or break if the paper is not treated gently and carefully.

In recent years, people in Japan have become familiar with origami from a variety of angles, not just as an activity for leisure. The creativity and potential of origami allow us to illuminate various problems deeply related to our lives, such as depressions and dementia. In the age of alternative medicine, there are many forms of therapies including music therapy, art therapy, color therapy, sand play therapy, expressive therapy through exercise, and yoga. These can be broadly grouped into art therapy, play therapy, behavior therapy, and meditation. Among these, origami is often used in the rehabilitation of patients suffering from cranial nerve disease, and in recent years, it is used in the treatment of depression for its therapeutic effects.

Because origami effectively stimulates the brain, it is expected to be enormously effective in preventing and improving dementia. For that reason, origami is being widely used in Japan as an art therapy recreation activity in nursing homes. It operates by engaging people in work to produce various forms like cranes and flowers, moving the fingers while visually enjoying multicolored paper, memorizing the process of how to fold things, and actually moving the hands to make them. Using different brain functions such as confirming balance with every sequence and thinking about colors to evoke a sense of the seasons, origami leads to prevention of dementia.

New origami creations stimulate the brain by making it work hard to remember something new. Furthermore, it is effective in rehabilitating the fingers by encouraging nerve concentration in the fingers in order to fold the paper. It is also possible to change the level of difficulty in creating origami pieces. Selecting seasonal or nostalgic models can also be anticipated to inspire a reflective mood.

"Mindfulness" is about being aware of or focused on the present moment, which originates from Buddhist philosophy. Through the practice of mindfulness, studies show a decrease in depression symptoms. When involved in origami, one has to concentrate on the folding process to create the expected model. One has to memorize steps and fold a piece of paper precisely. During such process of folding, one's mind cannot be distracted. This being in the moment denotes a state of "mindfulness."[15]

"Mindful communication" also has its roots in Buddhism teachings. It means to listen and speak with kindness and awareness toward others (see Chapters 1 and 2). To communicate effectively, such mindfulness mentality is required in communication. These concepts of care and being thoughtful of others are naturally embedded in the Japanese cultural identity mainly because of the "high-context" linguistic characteristic and religious influence of Shinto and Buddhism. For the improvement of mindful communication, origami can also be a useful tool as people discuss what to make, show finished pieces, and share thoughts through communication. It is said that origami is more effective when done while talking with others, in places such as nursing homes or classrooms, rather than doing it sitting quietly alone.

As discussed above, Japanese cultural identity, such as ethical values, philosophy, or morality, has been strongly but unconsciously influenced by the linguistic character of the "high context," the religious beliefs of Shinto and Buddhism to care for and appreciate others, and the habit of projecting sentiments onto objects or actions such as origami or gift-giving traditions. These mentioned examples are only few of many other examples seen in the Japanese culture. The communication style associated with mindfulness is naturally embedded in Japanese people who are born and brought up in the country, since such philosophy can be found or required everywhere in their daily life. However, interestingly, Japanese themselves are less aware of the traditional aspects of such mindfulness communication style of their own.

In a cross-cultural situation, a lack of knowledge of the other culture's background leads to misunderstanding or misinterpretation. When involved in an environment where participants hold different values or philosophies, one is required to interpret not only the language but also the other participants' behavior as it is linked to, or influenced by, their cultural identity in order to communicate better and to establish a good relationship beyond culture and language barrier. However, most important of all, one needs to be aware of one's own cultural identity to avoid unnecessary confusion or misunderstanding while communicating with people of other cultures.

Thus, for Japanese to raise awareness of their own unique or rather distinctive style of communication, it is very useful to get over the difficulty of

---

[15] Please go back to the Introduction for the definition of mindfulness.

cross-cultural communication. The Japanese must understand that there is always a philosophy of care for others and should foster the ability of figuring out the true intention of the unspoken, which underlies the behavioral patterns of the Japanese. To be aware of one's own cultural behavior could be as important as to put efforts to understand other's cultural identity when facing people from different cultures.

Bibliography

Cotton, G. 2013. *Say Anything to Anyone, Anywhere: 5 Keys to Successful Cross Cultural Communication.* Hoboken, NJ: John Wiley & Sons.
Elwood, R. 2008. *Introducing Japanese Religion.* New York, NY: Routledge.
Hall, E. T. T. 1981. *Beyond Culture.* New York, NY: Anchor Books.
Hendry, J. 1995. *Wrapping Culture: Politeness, Presentation and Power in Japan and Other Societies,* 2nd ed. Oxford: Oxford University Press.
Jackson, K., M. Tomioka, and Y. Akashi. 2004. *The Changing Face of Japanese Management.* Edited by Keith Jackson. London: Routledge.
Yoshimura, N., P. Anderson, and N. Yoshirmura. 1997. *Inside the Kaisha: Demystifying Japanese Business Behavior.* Boston: Harvard Business School Press.

16

Laos: Traditional Methods of Communication and Their Relevance to Grassroots Community Development— Case Study of Nongviengkham Village

Homala Phensisanavong

Laos is a predominantly Buddhist nation in Southeast Asia. Theravada Buddhism is at the heart of Lao people's culture and traditions because it has been the dominant religion in Laos for more than 660 years (Phetmeuangkhuan, 2016), and most Lao people are devout Buddhists today visiting a Buddhist temple regularly.

Most of Lao people like to donate food and other useful items to the Buddhist monks to gain merit and improve their karma. The Buddhist temples in Laos are likely to be the education institutions for novice monks as well as for the general public. Lao novice monks are highly respected and revered in Lao communities. Traditional methods of communication based on Theravada Buddhist teachings imparted by the temples can be considered as norms or traditions that should be followed by Lao people to ensure that the Lao culture remains alive and the national identity is maintained.

This also helps to support community development and to help Lao people to live peacefully in harmony within their own community, outside their community as well as in the world community. This issue is explored and examined in the case study presented in this chapter of Nongviengkham Village, Xaythany District, in the Vientiane Capital in the Lao People's Democratic Republic.

Introduction to Nongviengkham Village

The present Nongviengkham Village used to belong to Saphangmuek Village, but it has its own small community temple separated from Saphangmuek Village, which was established in 1968. After establishing Lao People's Democratic Republic in 1975, the village's population increased by about

14–15 families, so it was separated from Saphangmuek Village and was named "Nong Noi" which means a small pond village.

Due to a small land area of its temple, approximately 2 Rais (3,200 square meters), the village authorities requested from the people who had land area near the temple to donate some parts of those lands to this community temple in order to meet the needs of the new local community. As the temple is the center of village activity, it is important that the temple has enough land area to serve a bigger number of people in this community as well as other communities to join in Buddhist events or activities.

Luckily, there were two villagers who heartily donated land wishing it to be a "dana" (merit making gesture of generosity). It is believed that performing a *dana*[1] of land to a temple makes a great deal of merit for the donor. The two donors were Madam Viengsong who donated 2 Rais (3,200 square meters) and Mr Khamphet who also donated a land area of 2 Rais. From that time, Nong Noi Village Temple has had land area of 6 Rais in total. Besides that, Nong Noi Village also had got the new name "Nong Vieng Kham," and the temple got the name "Vat Siviengkham Photharam."

Now Nongviengkham Village is one of the eight villages in Dongdok group under Xaythany District authorities. This district has a land area of 2,048 square meters, 435 families, 430 houses, with a combined population of 2,255 people, out of which 1,411 are females. People in this village community have different professions with about half of them government employees, 22 percent pupil-students, about one-fifth traders, 5 percent physical workers, and 2 percent farmers. Village office is located in the middle of the village.

Except normal services such as factories, hotels, guest houses, restaurants, Internet shops, and pharmacies, there are also many important institutes in this village/district community such as Agriculture–Forest Research Institute, Land Area Control Department, SEA (South East Asian) Games Village (now students' dormitory of the National University of Laos), two military camps, one government kindergarten–primary school, two private English colleges, two private kindergartens, one vehicle driving school, and two temples.

The main village authorities are one village general party secretary, one head of village, two vice-heads of the village, and five supportive units.

In this chapter, we will examine the personal support to grassroots community development by the donation of the land to the community temple. This is a big part of our discussion as it relates to our ancestors who had purity of mind, were very generous in charity, and used to lend a helping hand to Buddhist concerns in order to develop their community, even though they had lived with limited facilities compared with our modern

---

[1] *Dana* (generosity), *sila* (morality/ethics), and *bhavana* (meditation/mindfulness) are known as the three pillars of Buddhist practice.

society. Our ancestors performed their *dana* with kindness, compassion, and empathy. Thus, their names have remained in this community of the "Nongviengkham" village.

Nongviengkham Village Temple

The first temple of Nongviengkham Village is Vat Ban Nongviengkham (Nongviengkham Village Temple) named "Vat Siviengkham Photharam," but local people here like to call it "Vat Ban" which means it is in the village. Vat Siviengkham Photharam has 22 monks, which is a big number compared with other temples in the capital city of Vientiane. This may be due to its location near the National University of Laos, Dongdok Buddhist High School, and other colleges.

Phra Achan Khamphan Sengmany, the abbot of Vat Siviengkham Photharam,[2] said that Vat Siviengkham Photharam has a great relationship with the community. From among the novice monks in this temple, 12 are studying at Dongdok Buddhist High School, 1 monk at the English college and 7 are studying at National University of Laos, which is very close to the temple.

There is also very clear working structure for the novice monks in this temple as they are divided into five groups, and each group has different

Phra Achan Khamphan Sengmany, the Abbot of Vat Siviengkham Photharam (Vat Ban)

---

[2] Personal interview with the author, October 16, 2016.

temple responsibilities as well as the work with its community. The temple effectively functions as a center of community with traditional Buddhist festivals held here the whole year. The novice monks are regularly invited to chant in private houses, government offices as well as in some private companies during important traditional events such as while moving into a new houses or company premises or when someone passes away. While the monks support the needs of any traditional community Buddhist activity, the community also supports the temple actively. "As our community has developed in many modern ways, our temple also has erected its own constructions, developed a temple management system and working cooperation with the bigger community as well as Lao Buddhist Association," the abbot said.

Nongviengkham Jungle Temple

Vat Pa Nongviengkham (Nongviengkham Jungle Temple) is formally named "Vat Pa Samakhi Xayaram," but local people here like to call it by the short name "Vat Pa" because it is located in the jungle area of the village.

Phra Achan Vatana Budpasa, the abbot of Vat Pa Samakhi Xayaram,[3] said that Vat Pa Samakhi Xayaram was established on July 6, 2007, with building work led by Phra Achan Buala Phangao and Nongviengkham villagers with

Vat Pa Samakhi Xayaram (Vat Pa)

[3] Personal interview with the author, October 16, 2016.

land area around 3,200 square meters. At the beginning, there were only 7–8 novice monks with 1 abbot (*Phra Achan*), 1 vice-abbot, and novices. The abbot said that after the building construction was completed in 2012, the temple can now serve local people very well.

Vat Pa Samakhi Xayaram is located in the far corner of the village. Therefore, it has borders with many other nearby villages such as Nathom Village, Huideanmueang Village, and Donenoun Village, and there is also the Nongviengkham Village cemetery. So nowadays, this temple mainly functions as a funeral place for Nongviengkham villagers as well as villagers nearby, as "Vat Ban" does not.

At present, there are 1 *Phra Achan* (chief monk), 6 *Phras* (ordained monks), and 18 novices, so there are all 25 in total. Almost all of these novice-monks are from other provinces, staying here for the purpose of their studies. There are 5 *Phras* and 6 novices studying at National University of Laos and 12 novices studying at Dongdok Buddhist High School. The present abbot completed his bachelor degree at National University of Laos. He feels happy and comfortable to be here in this community because the villagers in this community as well as in the communities nearby trust him (*Satha*); moreover, he helps the temple without any regrets and discriminations. Thus, he can help to develop both temple and this community.

Vat Pa and Vat Ban cooperate to serve the needs of local people in their Buddhist activities because only Vat Ban cannot fully accommodate all Buddhist people from this area, especially during important occasions such as *Boun khao phansa* (to celebrate the beginning of Buddhist Lent), *Boun Ho khaopadapdin* (to make offerings to the dead spirits of ancestors), *Boun Ho khaosalark* (to make offerings for some Chosen dead spirits of ancestors to obtain merit), and *Boun Ok Phansa* (to celebrate the end of Buddhist Lent).

Lao Traditional Communication Methods: The Institutions

Small Community Temple

This case study shows how Lao people relate to Theravada Buddhist teachings in their daily lives. Even a small community that belonged to a village did try to build the temple just for their small community. Presently, we can see a variety of examples of how villages have two or three temples, such as Donenoun Village and Saphangmuek Village that have two temples each.

Khamdone Sanaphone, 63 years old, the head of Lao Front for National Construction[4] of Nongviengkham Village, said,

> In the past as well as at the present, we cannot separate the temple from the village because we are used to it. We experience many important events in our daily, monthly, or yearly life—traditional (Buddhist) activities like "heed 12-khong 14" (12 traditional festivals in all 12 months in each year—14 rules for Buddhist people). We cannot do any of these activities without the Buddhist temple.

He added that "I really rely on the Buddhist temple. I spend approximately equal time at home and in the temple; nearly all of my life activities relate to the Buddhist temple, Buddhist community and Buddhist friends."

Yes, he is right because he is the head of Lao Front for National Construction of this village; without his functioning, Buddhist villagers may not be sure how to act or perform in each Buddhist temple activity. I am, as one who lives near the Vat Ban temple, very familiar with his announcements, like talking to the temple members through a microphone about Buddhist traditional activities, which help us a lot in following the regulations while performing these activities.

Community Temple Building Fund

We examined how the funding of Vat Siviengkham Photharam was achieved in a comparatively poor community, where neither the villagers nor the temple paid any money for expanding four more Rais of temple land area. They got donation from two nearby villagers.

According to the Theravada Buddhist *Dhamma* (teaching), a temple is a center for Buddhist people to perform traditional activities, so it is always expected to be big enough to accommodate buildings such as *kuti* (monks quarters), *kuti ho jeak*,[5] *sim*,[6] *ho kong*,[7] toilets, and wide court for

---

[4] Personal interview with the author, September 14, 2016.

[5] *Ho jeak* is a big central building where monks eat, organize all temple activities, and gather many people in it. Ho = building, jeak = *dana* = merit = donation.

[6] *Sim* is a building where people do *sang kha kam* = make someone a monk. Monk has a higher position, title, or age than a novice. To make someone a novice is much more simple, can organize wherever. However, to be a monk, it must be done in *sim*. Not every temple has a *sim*. The temple has *sim* means that the temple is complete and has full function as a temple.

[7] *Ho* = building, *kong* = drum. So *ho kong* is a building where you put a drum. Usually there is only one big drum.

community activities. Moreover, there should be more big trees to provide shelter from the hot sun while doing any outside activities, because the weather in Laos is hot.

"We as Buddhist followers always think that temple must be bigger, larger, and more open or servable for the community than our private houses, and also more accessible for everybody," Khamdone Sanaphone pointed out. He agreed that our community ancestors did it well for us, so we could have this for our people in our generation. Had they ignored tradition or not expanded it, we cannot be sure that we could have done this in our generation, because the land in this area is horribly expensive. He thinks most people today may not be able to donate land as in previous generations. Thus, he expressed lots of gratitude to the ancestors.

One important point here is about the name of the village; after getting four more Rais of land area for expanding the previous temple, they combined three important names. The first part is from the first word of the previous village's name "Nong Noi." The second and the third parts are from the first syllable of the names of two donators "Vieng thong" and "Kham phet." So to combine these three segments "Nong–Vieng–Kham," we have got the full name of this village "Nong Vieng Kham" written as "Nongviengkham."

Analyzing how to name this village can give us many interesting ideas concerning naming traditions in Lao culture. Firstly, it provides a historic background information of this village. Secondly, people in the past did not give *dana* with money as we do nowadays because money as bank note was rarely used in the past. However, they did perform *dana* in their own way with material things or home products as in this example. To donate a piece of land area for the temple, it can remain more concretely and visibly forever, as there is one Lao idiom: "*dana* water will enable a millionaire, *dana* without any regret will be able to become a Buddha (*Nibbana*)," and we can hear this idiom often said among Lao Buddhist followers.

Thirdly, the name of temple land donors could be incorporated to the name of the village. This provides a link to the community ancestry. Thus, the community will remember this history, respect the relatives of these donors, and their next generations could continue doing good deeds for the community and society in general. Finally, this would often remind us how ancestors of one family of our community had donated land to expand the temple. And what we can do with such generosity to help develop our community is "Be more giver than receiver," as advised in the Buddhist *Dhamma*. If everybody in our present society could apply the same teachings, our society would be better and more livable.

Novice Monk Students

As mentioned earlier, many novice monks from these two community temples stay here in order to get their education. Most of them come from poor families of other provinces and have no money to pay for the accommodation, study, or even living expenses. That is why these temples are the only refuge for them, because they are located near the National University of Laos, some private colleges, and Dongdok Buddhist High School. So the novice monks staying here do not have to pay for their traveling to school every day as other lay people, as some can walk and some use bicycles.

After completing their study, most of them disrobe (leave monkhood) and become lay people and work in many different government offices and some in private sector. However, both these temples still continue to support poor countryside novice monks to live there to get further education. This has happened generation to generation and this is one type of supporting grassroots community development.

Expenses such as staying, eating, and learning material for novice monks and their robes are supported by the temples as they can get these from the people's *dana*. Looking at novice monks' daily routine or their activity schedule, we can clearly see that it is not so complicated for them to operate or accomplish. The schedule for the normal days and full moon days are to some extent different, but villagers say that the novice monks follow their schedules well.

In the normal working days, novice monks wake up early, go on their alms-collecting rounds to certain village houses according to their planned map, after that they have breakfast and go to study. After morning school time, they come back to the temples to have lunch and go back to school again for the afternoon session. On full moon days, these novice monks do not go for alms-taking, as people bring food to the temple. Besides this, we hear monk groups chanting in the early morning and late night too.

We found that the novice monks in both temples attend to the needs of the Buddhist traditional activities of the local people, like being invited for alms-taking in villagers' houses, preaching or chanting for some events like opening ceremonies of new houses, offices, company premises, banks, restaurants, shops, and so on. As Phra Achan Vatana Budpasa said, he and other monks from his temple were invited to preach at Buddhist traditional activities many times a year; the most meaningful one is preaching on *Dhamma* advice to high school children based on the high school curriculum of Ministry of Education and Sport. This is one of the methods or ways to teach teenagers and youngsters in order to guide them to behave appropriately at school with teachers, staff, and friends, at home with parents and relatives, with general people in the community, as well as in the society at large.

This could be compared to the educational role public service broadcasting (PSB) is required to play under the theories of such broadcasting in modern society. Claude Ondobo, Deputy Assistant Director General and Director of Communication and Information Department of UNESCO, described the public service role of PSB in 2001 as (cited in Banerjee and Seneviratne, 2006: 9):

> Public service plays an irreplaceable role providing citizens with information, education and entertainment free of commercial, state or political influences ... public service must enable each citizen to become a stakeholder in society, participating fully in the life of the community to which they belong and actively involved in its organization.

If Buddhist teachings are properly imparted, such communication should include the concepts of mindful communication we have discussed in other chapters in this book.

It should be pointed out here that being a novice monk, such students would be able to get a more rounded education—learning both technical/academic school curriculum and *Dhamma* from the temple such as practicing their mind cultivation or meditation, as part of the monastic training. This can inculcate a good model of behavior for oneself, which can serve local people according to the Buddhist traditional needs.

In other words, monks with a disciplined mind and behavior, with a lifestyle based on sufficiency economics (satisfied with what you have), functioning as the communication medium for the community, could help to shape a community that is not affected by the three poisons taught in the Buddhist teachings—greed, hatred, and delusion.

Lao Traditional Communication Methods: The System

Temple-centered Community Activities

It is often argued that a good public service broadcaster or a community broadcaster is one that addresses community needs and serves as the link to the community to convey/transmit information, education, and entertainment.

Let us see how this theory works out in the context of the relationship between the temple and the community we are focusing on in this chapter.

There are many Buddhist traditional community activities based on "heed 12-khong 14" concept as explained earlier. This brings the village community together at the temple with the temple acting as the communication, education, or even the entertainment (when fairs are part of the temple festivals) conduit.

This idiom has very important meaning for Lao Buddhist people as it guides us on how to conduct an activity and how to act or to behave in our society as well as in the world society in order to live peacefully and in harmony. It has no meaning if we do anything that contradicts the "heed 12-khong 14" concept, as it may bring some negative effect to us or our society.

"Heed 12" is 13 traditional festivals spread over the 12 months of the year[8] from January to December and are as follows:

1. Deuan Jieng: *Boun khao kam* (Monks are on meditation)
2. Deuan Ngii: *Boun khoun lan khao* (Celebrate rice harvest ceremony)
3. Deuan Sam: *Boun khao chii* (Celebrate rice ceremony offering to the heavenly spirit and later to the monks)
4. Deuan Sii: *Boun phravet* or *Boun Mahaxat* (Great Birth Sermon)
5. Deuan Ha: *Boun Pimai* (Lao New Year)
6. Deuan Hok: *Boun Bangfai* (Rocket festival, praying for rain)
7. Deuan Jet: *Boun bouxa mahesack lackmueang* (Respect guardians' spirits around living places)
8. Deuan Pet: *Boun khao phansa* (Celebrate the beginning Buddhist Lent; there are three months of enhanced religious practices, heightened moral conduct, and meditation).
9. Deuan Kao: *Boun Ho khaopadapdin* (to make offerings to the dead spirits of ancestors)
10. Deuan Sip: *Boun Ho khaosalark* (to make offerings for some chosen dead spirits of ancestors to obtain merit)
11. Deuan Sip et: *Boun Ok Phansa* (to celebrate the end of Buddhist Lent after monks' three-month fast and retreat during rainy season; it is also called the Boat racing festival)
12. Deuan Sip Song: *Boun Kathin* (to make offerings of robes to the monks)
13. *Boun That Luang* (festival of the Grand Stupa)

---

[8] Lao lunar calendar is about 10 to 15 days ahead of the international calendar.

These traditional festivals covering all 12 months of the year are held in the temple; there are also many other activities which are held in the temple each month such as Buddhist holiday alms-giving approximately two times a month, village meetings to announce government policies, government's annual meetings with the community[9] or election, village authorities elections, village vaccination campaigns, aid delivery to the local people, and so on. All such activities of the village are always organized in the temple.

There are many reasons why all of these must be held in the temple as Bualin Buaphalakone,[10] party secretary-head of Nongviengkham Village, said. Firstly, the village office is located in the middle of the village; it is very convenient. However, it is in the corner of a T-junction with very small land area; it cannot contain many people for any meeting purpose, while the land area of the temple is bigger. Secondly, villagers, especially elderly people, head of each family, and temple as well as female authorities concerned wish it to be in the temple as they are familiar and feel comfortable with this location; it has become their life routine. Thirdly, some of them usually go to temple every morning as they take breakfast for monks known as *pai jung han*, and the activity like these meetings are usually held in the morning at around 8:30 and it is the right time after monks' breakfast; so these people can stay there for other activities. Fourthly, a Buddhist temple is considered as a cultural and respected place for village people to listen to their leaders' speeches, advices, announcements, or people's agreement. Finally, community meetings held in the temple reflect the harmony and unity of the village community based on Buddhism.

For villagers, the temple is a familiar place to meet, sit, talk, discus, and worship, and coming to attend something held in the temple, some people are likely to sit properly in the Lao sitting style in front of the main Buddha, putting flowers in front of the Buddha, burning incense and natural bee wax candles, and prostrating three times to show their respect to the Buddha, *Dhamma*, and sangha. These are the ways our ancestors used to follow and that have led our community to live in harmony until the present time.

---

[9] There is an organized government's annual meeting with the community once or twice a year, especially at the district level, the focus of each meeting is different. It really depends on the situation in each village or the national trends.

[10] Interview with the author, September 14, 2016.

Lao Traditional Communication Methods: Modern Impediments

Novice Monks and Continuity as Communicators

As discussed earlier, the temple has made an investment of sorts in helping to educate and train novice monks (known in Lao as *Mea Cee*[11]) to serve as educators and communicators within the community as they grow and mature. But in the modern day with increasing opportunities and choice for young people, this institution is facing some threats.

Someone may want to be a novice monk permanently or temporally depending on their circumstances, yet there are others who become a novice monk "unexpectedly" because of many necessary reasons. As can be seen from the interviews with the abbots and some monks of both temples, some Lao Buddhist children pleased their parents by becoming novice monks in their early childhood as they saw the life of monks in their hometown. Some of them get education as a result, and some do not. Also, while some may prefer to be monks for their entire life, others may go back to live a lay person's life after completing their study and get a job in government service or private sector. There are both female novice monks (wearing white robes) and male novice monks (wearing yellow/orange robes).

One reason for this may be that from their birth, people of Laos learn what may be translated to English as the "life cultural activity circular." So the mainly Buddhist population of the country wish to follow these activities at least once in their lifetime in order to learn Buddhist *Dhamma* (teachings) like *dana* to practice generosity by helping others, *sila* to cultivate morality by observing the precepts (of Buddhism), and *bhavana* to acquire wisdom through meditation. These are known as the three pillars of Buddhism in the Theravada tradition.

Moreover, this is also a way to appreciate the parents' goodness, according to Phosynoi Khampad, the head of Technology Data Academic Unit of Dongdok Buddhist High School. In the Buddhist tradition, there is a belief that "to be a novice, one has to express gratitude (make merit for) not only for mother's goodness but for the father's as well." This is because lay Buddhist people worship Five Precepts (*Panchasila*)—to abstain from

---

[11] *Mea Cee* are females wearing white with no hair.

harming or killing any living beings, to abstain from taking what is not given, to abstain from sexual misconduct, to abstain from lying and false speech, and to abstain from the abusive consumption of intoxicants and drugs. *Mea Cees* follow Eight Precepts, senior novices (male monks) follow Ten Precepts, and fully ordained monks follow 227 precepts (known as "Vinaya code"). These facts differentiate the daily practices of lay Buddhist people, from a novice, a *Mea Cee*, and a fully ordained monk.

Moreover, it is said that a male "who hasn't been a monk, is an uncooked person," meaning that a person is naive, not adult, and not ready to build up his own family, because he will not be able to lead his family in a proper Buddhist way of life. That is why most Lao Buddhist males are likely to spend some time as a novice monk in order to live peacefully with each other in their society. Males can become a novice monk at whatever time is suitable or convenient for them like during school holidays, after completing their education, before joining the job market or before getting married, or even sometime later on.

However, there is also the possibility of becoming a monk unexpectedly in Lao society as well as in this community. The abbots of both Vat Ban and Vat Pa said that both temples experienced such cases with some boys, especially secondary school boys. "These secondary school boys relied on their friends, lacked interest in their study and in some cases couldn't complete the study and so on," the abbots added. So, their families brought them to listen to the *Dhamma* advice, to participate in temple activities, and to learn how to behave properly in our community.

One of the useful and fruitful advices is hell and heaven that makes an impression on young peoples' minds. As one of the abbots said, this *Dhamma* advice works well in some case in this community, especially with the high school children. This is because the *Dhamma* advice says: "After this life, who is doing good and avoiding evil will go to the heaven; whereas who is doing bad will go to the hell." This tells them that where they are reborn will depend on how they conduct themselves in this present life. Some of them are really afraid of going to the hell after their death. Some of them even say that their current lifestyle is not the heaven, neither hell, but they still suffer in their everyday life. Thus, they wonder how their life would look like if they go to the hell after this life and how much more suffering they may undergo.

By listening to these advices/sermons, some of them may reform, yet others may want to go further and become novice monks. This is what the abbots call "unexpected" ordinations. Living, studying, and also following a Buddhist monk's way of lifestyle could help them to focus more on their study, develop more concentration, become calm, and avoid doing any inappropriate activities which can create social problems.

However, this depends on each family, and the temple council can only help to meet the needs of the families, relatives, teachers, or other authorities concerned. Both temples in this community agreed that the Lao society is in the process of changing like everywhere in Asia and it is becoming more complicated, fast moving, and materially focused.

One of the abbots added:

We are lucky that we are Lao and live in this community that still has a traditional system of communication, Lao traditional atmosphere and living style that makes permanent residents here to know each other well and can get help from the village temple council quickly and effectively.

Nearby Educational Institutions

As mentioned before, there are also many important institutes in this village community. The National University of Laos has over 36,000 students studying there and close to 3,000 of them stay in the SEA Games Village (Students' dormitory of National University of Laos). Another important educational institution for this community is Dongdok Buddhist High School which has 816 students studying from level or grade 1 to 7. Southi Sythatphouthorn,[12] the vice-director of Dongdok Buddhist High School said that 95 percent of these students are from poor families in the countryside, they lack sufficient support and need help from the Buddhist temple. "I am very proud of them and happy to have the chance to help them," Southi said.

The Lao Government stresses that by educating monks, Buddhist high schools can help to maintain a national cultural identity. With such an influx of students, especially from different parts of Laos, one may think that it could create many social problems. Interestingly, the village can live peacefully with this influx from outside.

Kita Keomany,[13] a 21-year-old female student at Archeology Faculty, National University of Laos, who lives in SEA Games Village, said that the Buddhist traditions they practiced in their own village are also practiced here, and taking part in these makes them feel at home. "Our students here are mainly from Buddhist families," she noted; "participating in Buddhist traditional festivals is always in our heart, so we often join events here like alms giving in the temple." She and some of her friends in the dormitory also

---

[12] Interview with the author, September 21, 2016.
[13] Interview with the author, September 30, 2016.

like to wake up early for street alms-giving as they feel good for the rest of the day after doing so, as they used to do before when they were with their families in their hometowns.

Vongsavanh Duangsavanh,[14] a 21-year-old female student at Sirimoungkhoun English College, who lives in this village with her relative because her hometown is in Savannakhet province, said that she never misses any Buddhist traditional festival that is held in this community because both temples are very close to her relative's house that she lives in. "I'm familiar with the way of organizing Buddhist traditional festivals here as it is not so different from my hometown, and the most important thing is I like and always feel good doing it," she added.

One more important thing to point out is that whenever these university or college students had any problem, burden, or difficulty such as exam or health issue, they prefer to go to the temple to do merit making, meditation, donations, or even just to sit in front of the Buddha and pray.

Traditional Methods of Communication in This Community

As can be gathered from the above discussion, the traditional methods of communication in this community would be very similar to many other communities in Laos because the people here are mainly Buddhists as are those in other communities. Thus, Buddhism provides that common identity, something which public service broadcasters set out to do in the postcolonial era in many developing countries.

As people in this community have the heads and vice-heads of the villages, *Silavat* (village-temple coordinator), temple abbot, different novice-monks cooperative working groups, they can all communicate with each other in their own traditional ways. For example, after any meetings or agreements, the above authorities would use traditional methods of communicating these messages/information to their community such as beating drums to call a temple meeting, announcing on the loudspeaker from the temple or from the village office, handing out notices to each house, hanging posters in some important community locations and/or an inviting orally.

---

[14] Interview with the author, September 30, 2016.

When you hear a beating of a drum, it reminds you that there will be a meeting to be held in the temple, but you do not know exactly its contents. When you hear the drum, the head or the representative of each family is likely to go to that meeting. Going to participate in a meeting when you hear the drum beat is compulsory according to the Lao traditional communication method.

An announcement on the loudspeaker from the temple or from the village office is one method of community communication. The speaker needs to speak the message clearly for it to be understood by the villagers. The message should briefly provide the contents, time, location, and so on. This message, however, would have its limitations and people in the next village may not hear it. Bualin Buaphalakone, party secretary and head of Nongviengkham Village, said that such announcements could be about government policy, government's annual meeting or election, village authorities' elections, village vaccination, aids to the local people, spreading out of some disease like malaria or dengue fever, any problem about electricity or running water, local road construction, someone passing way in the community, or about any urgent accident. Bualin said that every day before going to sleep he has to prepare about what is necessary to be announced to his community early in the morning the next day. It needs to be done by 6:30 AM, so he has to wake up early and start announcing at around 6:00 AM and it may last only 15–30 minutes.

Bualin has functioned as a head of this village as well as the familiar announcer in the community for many years. People are familiar with his announcing; they trust him and listen to him. One important announcement is "Saturday Village Cleaning Day." This activity is done approximately twice a month. This announcement may be done a bit earlier to inform the community that the coming Saturday is the village cleaning day and one or more members of every family must join it. Moreover, the details of the cleaning schedule, location as well as the family groups divided for each specific place are given in the announcement.

Another method of this community communication is handing out notices to each house, which would include a "merit making" notice list or a government notice list. This cannot be announced as it must be written, and then the copies are delivered to each house by someone. According to Bualin, this method has its drawbacks as some may not bother to read it or one could leave it the house and forget to read.

Next method of this community communication system is putting up posters in a clearly visible community location where people are likely to gather for activities such as eating, drinking, smoking, and chatting. "Through this method, we may not reach every house member as the notice location may not be his or her familiar place," Bualin said.

The last method of this community communication is an oral invitation by a person. Bualin said that some of the villagers in this community still like to use oral invitation by a person, especially the elderly people. Bualin added:

> I used to tell them that they do not need to come to see me personally, they can use a phone call or just send me the invitation card through someone. But they said that they feel happy, accessible and secured for their events every time after talking to me or inviting me personally.

Khammeung Philavan,[15] a 76-year-old woman, called "Mea Tou Mee," one of the elderly of Nongviengkam village, said that she feels accessible when she has the chance to go and invite villagers in each family to her home for merit making as she can talk to them, chat with them, and let them know about her personal family purpose of organizing such things. By sending only an invitation card without any talk, she says that it is a modern way of communication not the real invitation from the depth of the heart of people in her generation; it is artificial, not seems to be the real root of merit making. "In my previous life, I used to talk or invite people face to face. By using this face to face talking, I can guess, recognize and realize how those people accepted my invitation, are they likely to support me in doing such things or not," she explained. "Entering people's houses nowadays is not so polite or appropriate method anymore because it is said that we might disturb their privacy and I am afraid of doing it too," she said.

Traditional Methods of Communication and Public Service Broadcasting—A Comparison

Sundeep Muppidi (Muppidi and Manvi, 2012: 9) argues:

> The mass media is presumed not only to have certain objective effects on society but also to serve a social purpose. This means that some of the effects that have been observed are both intended and positively valued. These include the effects of disseminating information, expressing different voices and views, helping public opinion to form on issues and facilitating debate. The many entertainment and cultural activities of the media can also count as approved purposes. Where effects are intended we can usually identify who is behind them, in this case primarily those who own or direct the media and work in

---

[15] Interview with the author, September 15, 2016.

them, as well as those for whom the media provides channels of communication, including governments, authorities and individual communicators.

The role of the media in shaping modern societies is a hotly debated topic in the mass communication discourse today. The well-known "four theories of the press" by Siebert Peterson, and Schramm (1963) have been held up as the theories that explain the function of the media in any given society. But with the advent of new communication technologies in the past two decades, there are question marks as to how valid these theories are to describe today's communication systems.

In the context of the traditional methods of communication between the temple and the community in Laos, which has been discussed in this chapter, it will be interesting to carry out a comparison between the above-mentioned communication theories and the Lao traditional communication system that still dominates the shaping of the modern Lao society.

The research very clearly shows the relationship between the Nongviengkham community and Buddhist temples and how the temple, as a hub of communication, assists community development. Buddhist temples support community development as well as government development programs via many activities, as mentioned in the discussions in this chapter.

As Muppidi noted, the mass media is supposed to have certain objective effects on society to serve a social purpose. In this study, we have shown that the temple, through its support for training of the novice monks and its role in facilitating communication among the monks, temple, and the village, serves this same purpose. The temple is a conduit for serving a social purpose with intended positive values. While the media may come in the form of a newspaper, radio, or television, the temple's loudspeakers, leaflets, posters as well as direct communication between the monks and the community provide this same facility. In fact, it may be a much more economically viable model of a communication system since this system could function with very little or no funds (money) at all. Needless to say, all over the world, the public broadcasters are crying out for funds all the time. They are still struggling to find an economically viable funding model. The temple's role in nurturing tradition and culture is also a role often attributed to a PSB as one of its major functions.

Another issue that is an important part of the discourse on PSB is its role in raising "civic consciousness" in the society. With the excessive commercialization of the broadcast media in particular, with many of the so-called PSBs in Asia taking the commercial path to economic viability, there is a viewpoint expressed in academic circles that the best argument for public funding of PSBs, especially in the Asian context with the rapid social changes taking place, is for PSBs to play a civic consciousness raising role.

As former All India Radio executive Usha Bhasin (Muppidi and Manvi, 2012: 126) explains:

> Civic consciousness is awareness of one's community. At the very least, it means an individual is aware of the events happening around him. Ideally, it would mean that the individual is involved in the life of the community, understanding their role in the community, and seeking to contribute when they are able to do so. But, it all begins with an awareness of one's community.

The debate is about how the media, especially television, could play that role. In the case of Nongviengkham Village, we can see how Lao Buddhist temples play this communication role creating a "civic consciousness" in the community. It helps community members to live in a positive relationship with each other and also it shows us how Lao Buddhist sangha fulfills its role in the society as a communication or a facilitator of communications. One could argue that the novice-monks' training is partly a public service (communicating) role that covers all fields of community development. The traditional methods of communication between both Buddhist temples and Nongviengkham community work well for this community as well as for the Lao Government development programs, and we need to look at this communication system as modern rather than traditional and old-fashioned. Some technology to improve this communication system may help but not a television station or a radio station in the community that could provide them dreams rather than civic consciousness.

Bibliography

Banerjee, I., and K. Seneviratne., eds. 2006. *Public Service Broadcasting in the Age of Globalisation*. Singapore: AMIC.
Buaphalakone, Bualin. 2015. *Brief History of Nongviengkham Village and Its Temples in Village Report*. Vientiane: Nongviengkham Village Office.
Channiyavong, Khambang. n.d. *Lao Tradition "heed 12-khong 14."* Vientiane.
Luangphasy, Duangsay. 1994. *Social Manners*, 4th ed. Vientiane: State Printing.
Ministry of Propaganda and Culture. 1984. *INTHINGAN SONE LOUK* [Children Moral Advice "INTHINGAN"]. Vientiane: National Fine Arts Research Institution.
Muppidi, Sundeep, and Premila Manvi, eds. 2012. *Public Service Broadcasting and Its Role in Raising Civic Consciousness*. Singapore: AMIC.
Phetmeuangkhuan, Patithin. 2016. "DOs and DON'Ts When Out and About in Laos." *Vientiane Times*, August 31, p. 12.
Phonekasermsouk, Kideang. 2006. *Lao Culture, Living Based on "Heed 12-khong 14."* Vientiane State Printing.
Siebert, F. S., T. Peterson, and W. Schramm. 1963. *Four Theories of the Press*. Chicago: University of Illinois.
Vilaysack, Somphay. 2009. *Lao Culture*. Vientiane: National University of Laos.

Interviews

Phra Achan Khamphan Sengmany, the abbot of Vat Siviengkham Photharam (Vat Ban), dated October 16, 2016.
Phra Achan Vatana Budpasa, the abbot of Vat Pa Samakhi Xayaram (Vat Pa), dated October 16, 2016.
Phra Achan Okad Phetsisanavong, aged 89 years old, one of the elderly monks in Wat Si Meuang temple, dated October 12, 2016.
Mr Bualin Buaphalakone, party secretary-head of Nongviengkham village, dated September 14, 2016.
Mr Khamdone Sanaphone, aged 63 years old, the Head of Lao Front for National Construction of Nongviengkham Village, dated September 14, 2016.
Ms Khammeung Philavan, aged 76 years old, called "MEA TOU MEE", one of the elderly of Nongviengkam village, dated September 15, 2016.
Mr Southi Sythatphouthorn, the vice-director of Dongdok Buddhist High School, dated September 21, 2016.
Mr Phosynoi Khampad, the head of Technology Data Academic Unit of Dongdok Buddhist High School, dated September 21, 2016.
Mr Bouasy Phetthanoulath, the vice-head of student affair office of National University of Laos, dated September 29, 2016.
Ms Kita Keomany, aged 21 years old, student at Archeology Faculty, National University of Laos and lives in SEA Games Village, dated September 30, 2016.
Ms Vongsavanh Duangsavanh, aged 21 years old, a student at Sirimoungkhoun English College and lives in Nongviengkham Village, dated September 30, 2016.

Special Advisor

Professor. Dr Bualy Paphaphanh, Department of Lao Language—Mass Communication, Faculty of Letters, National University of Laos, Vientiane, Laos.

Teamwork

Bounthavone Lathsawat, Department of Lao Language—Mass Communication, Faculty of Letters, National University of Laos, Vientiane, Laos. Phongphasith Southammavong, Department of Lao Language—Mass Communication, Faculty of Letters, National University of Laos, Vientiane, Laos.

17

Cambodia: Mindful Public Relations—From Monastic to Government Communications

Nayheak Khun

Public relations (PR) is something new for Cambodians. Many misunderstand what it is, and what are the roles of spokesperson (Government PR practitioners) and their challenges and responsibilities. Although the phrase "public relations" did not appear until the 20th century, the practice of PR has been evident since the dawn of recorded history (David and Charles, 2000).

However, Cambodia has a long and rich history of Hindu and Buddhist influence of cultures and societies that go as far back as the Pre-Angkor Era— before 802 CE (i.e., Funan—1st century—13 CE, Chenla—8th century—550 CE, Java Invasion—8th century CE, Birth of Angkor 802–834 CE). These influences continued into the Angkor Era (802–1431 ACE) and post-Angkor Era (1431–present day).

There have been many temples (called *wats*) built by Khmer kings to connect and gather people to have solidarity for empowering the country. As Try (1991: 81–82) notes, "a righteous king had been seen as the key stone of the premodern Buddhist polity, and it was virtually impossible for anyone to envisage a non-Khmer as the ultimate protector of the realm." And, as Harris (2005: 131) notes, "monastics often led movements animated by the ideal of freedom from a foreign yoke."

Cambodia is a country that believes in the Theravada Buddhist religion that has been respected by Kings; and it is highlighted in the kingdom's motto that states on the flag "nation, religion, king" which is referring to a monarchical and Buddhist Cambodia promulgated by the constitution (May 1946).[1] Under his reign and his political movement, Sangkum Reastr Niyum (People's Socialist Community), King Norodom Sihanouk was styled as a "great righteous king" (*dhammika mahareach*) of Buddhist socialism-linked

---

[1] The 1993 Constitution of the Kingdom of Cambodia and its Amendments, Available at http://cambodia.ohchr.org/~cambodiaohchr/sites/default/files/Constitution_ENG.pdf (accessed on November 15, 2017).

putatively traditional Khmer values with a full set of Buddhist principles (Harris, 2005: 146), implying his role as the protector of the Buddhist monastic order.

Sihanouk often referred to himself as the king-monk; he tended to avoid any reference to the ancient Khmer concept of the god-king or Buddha-king (*buddharàja*) associated with paradigmatic monarchs such as Jayavarman VII (Harris, 2005: 144).

The King, the Monastery, and the Community

As the symbolic centers for serving their necessary educational, cultural, as well as social functions, until today most of the Cambodian people still preserve these ways of life centered on the *wats* (temples/monasteries). To this day, some 85 percent of the population in Cambodia lives in villages whose symbolic centers remain the *wats*. Thus, the *wat* is not only the moral-religious center of a village community, it also serves the educational, cultural, and social functions.

Until recent times, *wats* were the main centers of learning with schools and libraries where the Khmer culture and language was preserved and transmitted from generation to generation. They also served as culturally, and environmentally, sensitive foci for people-centered development that included, indeed featured, social safety nets for the poor, destitute, and needy (KEAP Project,[2] 1988).

The arrival of Theravada Buddhism from Sri Lanka via Burma in the 12th century CE seem to have contributed to a fundamental shift of Cambodian Buddhism from an aristocratic model influence by the Brahamin caste system to a model that is more grassroots-oriented in which the *wats* play a central role with a populist and antiaristocratic message with Buddhism spreading to rural areas.

As Harris (2006: 27) notes:

> Under its benign influence the peasantry gained a new lease of solidarity and were able to break free from the confines of the "world of local spirits and traditions" to a wider understanding of their place in the historic process.

---

[2] KEAP Project has been doing work to assist Cambodians in their recovery from the Khmer Rouge era since 1988. Available at http://www.keap-net.org/index.html (accessed on October 27, 2017).

This may have contributed to the destruction of the Cambodian-Angkorian caste system (borrowed from Indian Hinduism) though as Harris (2006) points out there is no inscriptional evidence yet found to show that it would have resulted in interethnic or interclass marriages and greater social interactions.

The Theravada ideology of kingship was based on the concept of spiritual maturity as the right to rule. Thus, when a king is appointed his right to rule may not be easily challenged by political expediency.

Since the emergency of Theravada Buddhism as the dominant religious tradition, the Cambodian king was regarded as the "one who has merits" (*neak mean bon*), a notion connected to the doctrine of karma, which sees present worldly merits as a result of the accumulation of beneficial deeds in previous existences (Harris, 2006: 51).

The monastery (*wat*) will typically consist of a group of buildings within an enclosed complex with several entrances. There will be shrine rooms for both to worship the Buddha and tutelary spirits (*neak ta*), an assembly hall or open-sided pavilion for meetings, sermons and chantings/ceremonies, communal housing or individual *kuti* (huts) for monks, a tank or bathing pond for monks, and a kitchen for devotees to cook food for monks. Many temples may also have family monuments on its perimeter to deposit ashes of relatives. The principle structure, however, is the stupa and ceremony hall/vihara. It is at this ceremony hall that many of the communications between the community and the monastery takes place. In both Thailand and Cambodia it is customary for the King to cede this space for the "sangha" (monks) (Harris, 2006).

Khmer Monastic System

The monk traditionally occupied a unique position in the transmission of Khmer culture and values. By his way of life, he provided a living model of the most meritorious behavior a Buddhist could follow. He also provided the laity with many opportunities for gaining merit. For centuries, monks were the only literate people residing in rural communities; they acted as teachers to temple servants, to novices, and to newly ordained monks. Until the 1970s, most literate Cambodian males gained literacy solely through the instruction of the sangha.[3]

---

[3] Available at http://www.photius.com/countries/cambodia/society/cambodia_society_role_of_buddhism_in_-8.html (accessed on October 27, 2017).

Goonatileka (2003) argues that advances in navigational technology between the 4th and 5th centuries helped in the spread of Sri Lankan Sinhalese Buddhism with its focus on the Pali language, Mahavihara tradition of education, and forest monastic systems to spread first to Thailand and then to Cambodia. This helped in the spread of Pali language as a lingua franca of Theravada Buddhism.

The Cambodian monastic system was able to withstand the French colonialism period of the late 19th and the first half of the 20th century. But after independence, young Cambodian intellectuals changed their attitude toward the Buddhist clergy and lost interest in becoming monks in their teenage years, which was a traditional practice until then. During French rule, at intervals, monks have been involved in pro-independence struggle, and in the 1970s, they joined demonstrations against communism. When Khmer Rouge took over Cambodia in the mid-1970s they were hostile to Buddhism, and monks were forced to leave the *wats* and do manual labor in the villages. Many *wats* were destroyed.

As Pannasastra University lecturer Ven. Kou Sopheap noted in a video discussion (Lotus Talks, 2016), "during Pol Pot regime Buddhism apparently disappeared from the land of Cambodia, but in the hearts of the people it never disappeared. That is why, after the regime fell, Buddhism came back."

The monastic system has been restored and the links between the *wat* and the community reestablished since the Khmer Rouge was overthrown in the late 1970s. Pou Sovanchana, lecturer, Pannasastra University of Cambodia, argues (Lotus Talks, 2016):

> There are no questions or doubt about the linkage between society, Buddhism and Cambodia. This is very deep-rooted and inseparable, the constitution of Cambodia states very clearly that "Nation, Religion, and King" are one. These three components are parts of the social family. After the Pol Pot regime fell, sagha was revived and today there are so many monks. They can still be a major force for stabilizing the country, for environment protection, and for bringing and making the livelihood of people better.

And as Ven. Kou Sopheap (Lotus Talks, 2016) recalls, "when I was young, I saw my grandfather try to convince the people to mobilize the power in community to build roads, houses, schools, and communities. From that, I realized that Buddhism plays an important role to stabilizing and mobilizing people."

During the Pol Pot Regime, Buddhism became the biggest target, and between 1975 and 1979, Buddhism was completely destroyed. As Ven. Oeun Sam Art (Lotus Talks, 2016), Voice Dean, Preah Sihanouk Raja Buddhist

University, notes: "(There were) no Buddhist monks in the whole country. Because within Buddhism (monks) work with many scholars and intelligent people. So, they thought that Buddhism (monks) is very influential to the society (and it is) deeply (engrained) in their hearts." In the past, most of the families sent their sons to be the monks for a period of time. It is a "must" because if they were not to be the monks, they also were not giving their daughters in marriage.

> This is one way to build a social fabric, as we were already destroyed during the Pol Pot regime. No one trust[ed] anyone else. They even killed their own parents. So, Buddhism play[ed] a key component in building the social fabric and building connection in teaching people how to love one and another. After the Pol Pot regime (was overthrown) in 1979 we had international support, the local people stand up to build their communities. The monks and the teachers of the villages are the important people in calling people/villagers, if we want to build the roads and the temples. We don't need to pay (for) those people, we just call them, we just make some cakes and play music. And then, they just come and build the roads and ponds together. We built communities together. And, this way Buddhism contributes to rebuild the nation as well as rebuild Buddhism. (Ven. Sopheap, Lotus Talks, 2016)

And Ven. Oeun Sam Art explains (Lotus talks, 2016):

> After Pol Pot regime collapsed in 1979, every community and village started to rebuild the temples on their own. They started to rethink how to restore Buddhism in their own communities. It is not because of the policies of the government. It is because of mentality. And, the people think about the usefulness of Buddhism in society. After the collapse of the Pol Pot regime, the most important factor that rebuilt Cambodian society is Buddhism. We used the Buddhist means, we use the Buddhists teaching to rebuild Cambodian society, like to build hospitals, schools, roads, houses, mentalities, etc. Without Buddhism how could we build society again so quickly, as what we see in the Cambodian society right now? (It is) because most of Cambodian families lost their family members through killing fields. So, the community people knew clearly who killed their families. So, they should have taken revenge from those people who killed their families. When they [want] revenge, how can you make Cambodian society to become peaceful?

> We have seen the teachers of Buddhism say "revenge never finished with revenge." So, Cambodian people understand to forgive and forget with that. We can call this mental reconciliation. We should not take revenge from those people who were violent, or killed your families. That is why, the people who committed bad things, they can live harmoniously and peacefully with those people who are living in communities.

The Community and the Monastery Today

To develop the Buddhist culture and pass it from one generation to another, Cambodian community and the monastery are communicating with each other through Buddhist events and special days, for instance, for celebrating the Khmer New Year (Maha Sangkran) over three days on April 13, 14, and 15 depending on the ancient astrological calendar. The first day of the New Year is called "Maha Sangkran" and all the Cambodian people go to the temple, offer food to the monks, and receive their blessings. And the second day is called "Wanabot"; on this day they offer gifts to parents, grandparents, and elders, and many of them also go to the pagodas and build a mountain of sand to remember their ancestors who have passed away and have the monks give them blessings of happiness and peace. On the third day— called "Leung Sakk"—most of Cambodians go to the temple and perform a ceremony called "Pithi Srang Preah." The purpose is to honor and give a special cleaning to the Buddha statues, to the monks, elders, grandparents, and parents, and to apologize to them for any mistakes one may have made over the past year. "Khmer New Year is not only about festival, joyful, family gathering, and playing traditional games, it is also a good opportunity to pass on the Cambodian traditions to the next generation," Ven. Van Sothoeun,[4] at Sampov Meas pagoda.

In addition, *Pchum Ben* is a religious ceremony, which is celebrated after the full moon in the tenth month of Phatraboth. *Pchum Ben* is the occasion when people remember their ancestors. They prepare the food for offering to monks, light incense and candles, and offer flowers at the pagoda. The monks then offer prayers to the Buddha on behalf of all those who have died.

> Buddhists believe that after we have died our spirit, or mind, will be born again. Those who have led a good life will be born into a happy world, but those who have committed harmful sins will be born into an unhappy world. We call the happy world "heaven," and the unhappy one "hell." (Ven. Nou Rach,[5] at Wat Phnom pagoda)

There are also other special events which help the *wat* to be an integral part of the community, such as house warming, wedding, celebrating the birth of a new baby, and Meak Bochea Day in which the communities connect

---

[4] Ven. Van Sothoeun, interview with the author, recorded on March 4, 2017, at Sampov Meas pagoda.
[5] Ven. Nou Rach, interview with the author, recorded on February 26, 2017, at Wat Phnom pagoda.

and invite monks to give prayers and blessings to them for prosperity, luck, and success. Cambodians believe that the pagoda is not only a place for communities and monks to take part in ceremonies, it is also a learning center where educated monks interact with the community both mentally and psychologically in Buddhist mindful communication and learning.

> They will send their sons to live and study with monks at pagoda if they are not disciplined, don't study, or listen to their parents. I'm very concerning about young people's drug addictions (users), gangsterism ... etc. It is very hard and takes time to teach and lead them to a better life, by changing them through Buddhist lessons. We will try our best to serve as the culturally and environmentally sensitive foci for people-centered development that includes social safety nets for the poor, destitute, and needy. (Ven. Sambath,[6] at Chak Angre pagoda)

Public Relations in Cambodia

PR, as described through mainly Western-centric theories, has more popularity and significance within the government of Cambodia institutions, particularly in recent decades. Since 2010, for every ministry they initiated, they have spokespersons for each province in order to release information from government to the public and the media. Khieu Kanharith, government spokesperson, said at a "spokesperson training" workshop at the Department of Media and Communication of Royal University of Phnom Penh on March 30, 2013:

> Now, we should call spokesperson as the information officer because they work harder than the spokesperson. The role of information officer is not only to wait for (being) given information but also to tell first what is going on. They had better bear the word "WHY" in their mind all the time.

In recent years, we have 24 provinces and municipality spokespersons that we call "Team in charge of Information in municipal/provincial administrations." Thus, it can be seen that the government in Cambodia has started systematization, in particular, relations between PR and the media.

---

[6] Interview with the author "Ven. Sambath" recorded on March 5, 2017 at Chak Angre pagoda.

As Kanharith[7] explained, they selected three spokespersons, representatives of each province and a municipal base using the criteria:

> ... nominated duty governor as the first spokesperson, provincial official as the second spokesperson, and head of information department. The reason we chose them is, they always attended all the government meetings and also they knew clearly about all the information and news updated from the government.

We can see here that when Western concepts of PR creep into the contemporary Cambodian governing system, the role of the *wat* is taken over by municipalities, and provincial and national information departments. For example, the definition of PR by American definitions says (Elliott, 2012; Newsom and Scott, 1985):

> The Public Relations Society of America describes the profession as encompassing "a strategic communication process that builds mutually beneficial relationships between organizations and their publics" (Elliot, 2012: 4). Throughout its development, PR has been recognized as a profession intent on controlling and responding to the communication of various publics while developing favorable attitudes about organizations and the issues they represent.

According to David and Charles (2000), they opt for a 10-word definition:

> The management of communication between an organization and its public.

PR is like a management, leader, or CEO to promote good relationships from one organization/entity to others. We called them "two-way communication" or "multi functions/purposes." Alternatively, the definition of PR as given by Sriramesh and Verčič (2009: 4) is a definition of global PR explicitly addressing the multicultural meaning of it:

> Public relations is the strategic communication that different types of organizations use for establishing and maintaining symbiotic relationships with relevant publics many of whom are increasingly becoming culturally diverse.

Given these some sort of definitions, it seems that PR practitioners can play a role in many situations and functions. They can work with the government,

---

[7] H. E. Kanharith said in the Workshop "spokesperson training" at the Department of Media and Communication of Royal University of Phnom Penh on March 30, 2013.

in corporations, nonprofit organizations, or trade associations, and as independent PR consultants. PR have a direct reporting relationship to senior management by using a two-way symmetrical model, which involves giving messages, receiving messages, and creating a balanced power between the two groups, because they are knowledgeable of the symmetrical and managerial roles and have academic training in PR and professionalism. PR roles are "abstractions of behavior patterns of individuals in organizations" when practicing PR (Dozier, 1992).

But for the journalists, it is about people who are living and working in the society and to report the true news and facts to the public about them. According to Dan and Ilias (1999), journalists work in social groups within a newsroom, to produce stories for their organizations. "There should be a strong journalism—and there is a strong belief among us in the crucial role of journalism in society," said a junior consultant (Larsson, 2009: 135–36). "Everyday work of a journalist is very stressful. So, they often consider contacts with PR agents as useful, if we practice serious work conduct and do no gold digging" (PR Consultant cited in Larsson, 2009: 135).

Red Batario (cited in ADB, 2008) argues that what Asia needs is a problem-solving kind of journalism that requires journalists to be deeply involved with communities and communities to support space for the ordinary voices to be heard. He advocates type of community media, pointing out some examples from the Philippines, where such media have created a forum for citizens, local governments, nongovernmental organizations (NGOs), academe, and business to air their views on community issues and development. He argues that journalists could participate in such community affairs without losing their traditional independence. But for such media (or PR) to succeed, there should be a sound economic model for the community media supported by the community.

However, within the government (local or national), PR plays propagandas role, especially during election campaigns. Every party uses PR as propaganda to increase their popularity within the community/country. Moreover, for every institution of government or NGOs, they hire PR people as spokesperson to answer the press and journalists' questions.

For example, when the former Secretary of State Hillary Clinton was visiting many countries, she used PR skills in her politics strategies to earn popularity, friendship, and support for her country. Clinton (2012) said that "I'm confident that we will continue to solve problems and produce results that make our nations stronger, more peaceful, more secure, more prosperous, and also contribute to doing the same for the world." However, in a presentation to US Congress in 2013,[8] she requested for more funds for her State Department claiming that the US is losing the information war to foreign countries, particularly to Russia's RT Channel and China's CCTV.

In Myanmar, pro-democracy leader Aung San Suu Kyi also used PR skills to gain popularity and votes for her party from the people and support from other countries during her election campaign. She said, "We had good relations with the US and with China. I don't see why we shouldn't continue to" (Bill, 2012).

Four roles of PR were prescribed in the research of Broom and Smith (1979):

1. Firstly, the communication technician's role primarily dealt with the technical aspect of PR spreading from writing news releases and/or feature stories, establishing media contact, commissioning graphic design, compiling website, content development, and employee newsletter writing and editing contents. These are the most common roles that PR practitioners in Cambodia have to perform.
2. Secondly, the expert prescribes a role like PR consultants who can consult top management in dealing with PR matters.
3. Thirdly, the communication facilitator's role is similar to a liaison officer, an interpreter, a mediator, or information source and the official contact between an organization and its public. They are the important people who maintain two-way communication to ensure smooth dialogue and accurate mutual interpretation. On the other hand, they act as the spokesperson for the company or organization, providing information from the company to the public and receive feedback from the public.
4. Lastly, the problem-solving process facilitator acts as a strategic planning team and collaborates with other managers.

Mindful Communications and Public Relations

Mindfulness has become recently "a common topic of discussion in media and popular culture" (as discussed in the Introduction). And, there has been a great popular cultural interest in the philosophical concept of mindfulness and its relevance in the human experience of contemporary society.

---

[8] See Hillary Clinton: US losing information war to alternative media at https://www.youtube.com/watch?v=o23a5UHXabo (accessed on October 27, 2017).

Mindfulness training could play an important role in PR as PR itself is about understanding the person to whom you are communicating a message and crafting the message in such a way that this person understands what you are communicating. As the mindfulness (*Vipassana*) meditation guru S. N. Goenka (Hart, 1991: 40) argues:

> We are influenced by people around us and by our environment, and we keep influencing them as well. If the majority of people, for example, are in favour of violence, then war and destruction occur, causing many to suffer. But if people start to purify their minds, then violence cannot happen. The root of the problem lies in the mind of each individual human being, because society is composed of individuals. If each person starts changing, then society will change, and war and destruction will become rare events.

As Ven. Piyasilo (see Chapter 1) explains, mindfulness is about not getting distracted from your mind the knowledge of a given situation. It is also about paying attention to the present moment and being nonjudgmental.

While mindfulness would seem to have application in the PR workplace, its "ethic of compassion" (Seppala, 2013: 3) might be perceived to conflict with PR practitioners' view of assertive marketplace-based standards of practice. Taking mindfulness-based concepts too far in another direction might allow mindfulness to be construed as some sort of transcendent tool to increase productivity and profits (White and Cooper, 2014).

A core precept of mindfulness is the idea of existence and interrelationships. "We cannot find a true boundary or edge to anything, because all things exist in dependence on other things" (Mattis-Namgyel, 2011: 34). Good recent example is the 2016 US presidential campaign and the way Donald Trump and Hillary Clinton used vastly different methods of PR campaigns to attract the voters. Another example is the Davoa Mayor Rodrigo Duterte's successful presidential campaign in the Philippines in 2016, which used very sophisticated methods of PR to reach the grassroots communities, circumventing the mainstream media and later as president how he used these techniques to dominate the public agenda (see Chapter 21). "In the Philippines, paid trolls, fallacious reasoning, leaps in logic, poisoning the well—these are only some of the propaganda techniques that have helped shift public opinion on key issues," noted Reza (2016) who calls it the "weaponization of the internet."

The perceptions were identified by Wheatley and Frieze on mindfulness listed in five categories of PR communications as shown in the box following (Swanson, 2014).

1. Heroic, Ineffectual Leadership
Wheatley and Frieze contend that a mindful leader does not act like a hero. A hero frequently and foolishly is deluded into thinking the uncontrollable can be unilaterally controlled. In contrast, a mindful leader does not work solo. A mindful leader encourages positive collaboration and participation among followers.

2. Uneasy Interactions
When a workplace professional finds it difficult to initiate interpersonal relationships, some level of mindlessness may be responsible. Uneasy interactions can occur quickly in interpersonal relations; they can occur in a nanosecond via social media. Such was the lesson learned when Internet marketing/PR executive Justine Sacco, en route to Africa, posted a Tweet reading: "Going to Africa. Hope I don't get AIDS. Just kidding. I'm white!" The Tweet instantly went viral. Sacco's uneasy interaction resulted in a swift dismissal from employer IAC before Sacco's aircraft had even reached Africa.

3. Refusal to Embrace New Ideas
Mindlessness in the workplace can be evidenced in a refusal to embrace new ideas or an unrealistic clinging to outmoded approaches. Corporate leaders demonstrate this kind of mindlessness when they oppose change that is outside their control.

4. Atmosphere of Distrust
When a professional cannot engage confidently with a coworker, one or both parties may be approaching the interaction mindlessly. An appearance of untrustworthiness can also be created through media portrayals of celebrities and other prominent public figures.

5. Lack of Accountability
In 2010, former British Petroleum CEO Tony Hayward offered the textbook example of lack of corporate accountability. At the height of BP's Deepwater Horizon oil rig environmental catastrophe, Hayward uttered the mindless comment heard round the world: "I'd like my life back." Hayward's "self-destructive communications" cost him his job.

Relationships Between Journalists and Public Relation Practitioners

The relationship between journalists and PR practitioner is a quite debatable field of communication studies. They are cooperative and fraught with conflict and imply a double negotiation over the exchange of resources and over the rules regulating this exchange. Since their relationships are complex and ambiguous, it is characterized by integrating two dimensions—cooperation and conflict. "Cooperation" means the functional nature of the relationship between two groups. Every day, journalists need sources of information in order to produce newsworthy stories to keep the public informed, push the agendas for public debates, and the creation of public reality. Some sources of those news reports are coming from PR experts who are representatives, in particular, of their institutes/organizations. On the other hand, PR practitioners need journalists to assist their daily works in distributing the source of information that constitute the great game—"news." So, without collaborating with the media, they cannot succeed in reaching out to their target audiences.

Unfortunately, for both of them, the "conflict" might occur every single time they distrusts each other and opposite divergent views control their work. "For journalists, public relations officers symbolize the sources' desire to control their work. Journalistic distrust of 'interested' sources is thus exacerbated when they come in contact with the PR specialist" (Charron, 1989). Due to their relationships, "public relations officers attempt to convince the journalists by adapting their source's message to the journalistic production requirements," to be assured that the journalist is provided with good articles originating from a credible and newsworthy source for dissemination to the public (Charron, 1989). Especially, between the decision-makers (minister/governor) and the spokespersons, they need to have strong internal communication lines because the information dissemination would be at risk of failing without their (good) regular interactions and communication as a team.

In addition, the minister of information (Kannharith) has highlighted the importance of professional communication by government agencies with the media—"the need for decision makers to professionally deal with media and to provide them interesting, relevant and user friendly information through the spokespersons and PR departments" (Ludwig, 2014).

PR in Cambodia Today

The main purpose of PR actors is to work closely and have a continuous relationship with journalists in order to prevent publicity that is hard to control. A research study was undertaken by the author to look into the importance of spokesperson and its PR role in relationship to the public. The study was conducted under the assumption that news journalists have difficulty approaching their counterparts such as spokespersons in the government.

To focus on this issue, the author went to various institutions to learn about people who are working as spokespersons and journalists. Because the resource persons of spokespersons in the government are limited and constrained, I decided to choose a qualitative tool to convince interviewers to actively participate in discussing particular topics, in order to seek "multiple trusts, alternative visions, and critical perspectives" (L'Etang, 2007: 25). In employing qualitative methods it is expected to "examine communication as experienced by people not as something linear and logical but as typically open, complex, and human. They also see communication and social relations as inseparable from their social and historical contexts" (Daymon and Holloway, 2002: 167).

For respondents, I selected 9 journalists and 9 spokespersons from different organizations for in-depth interviews focused on this issue, as well as allowing "participants' interpretations of their experiences and expressed in their own words, using the jargon and speech styles that are meaningful to them" (Daymon and Holloway, 2011: 6). The reason why it led me to choose a qualitative rather than quantitative tool is because I wanted them to address their feelings about how spokespersons are working to deal with journalists (Tables 17.1 and 17.2).

Table 17.1
Government Spokespersons' Information

Position	Institution	Gender	Age	From
Spokesperson	Ministry of Information	Male	>50	Phnom Penh
Spokesperson	Council of Ministers	Male	>50	Phnom Penh
Spokesperson	Ministry of Information	Male	>50	Svay Rieng Province
Spokesperson	Ministry of Information	Male	>50	Ratanakiri Province
Spokesperson	Ministry of Information	Male	>50	Pailin Province
Spokesperson	Ministry of Information	Male	>50	Kampot Province
Spokesperson	Ministry of Information	Male	>50	Preah Vihear Province
Spokesperson	Ministry of Information	Male	>50	Kampong Cham Province
Spokesperson	Ministry of Information	Female	>50	Kratie Province

Source: Interview with the author.

Table 17.2
Journalists' Information

Position	Institution	Gender	From
Editor in Chief	VOA	Male	Radio
Editor	WMC	Male	Radio
Reporter	VOD	Female	Radio
Reporter	Phnom Penh Post	Female	Newspaper
Reporter	Cambodia Daily	Female	Newspaper
Reporter	CEN	Male	Online
Editor	Cambodia News	Male	Online
Reporter	TVK	Male	Television
Reporter	Apsara	Female	Television

Source: Interview with the author.

Result and Discussion

What Role and Responsibility Today's Government Spokespersons Fill

After in-depth interviews with nine spokespersons, the result showed that the municipal spokespersons (two informants in Phnom Penh) understand and have better knowledge and experiences of concepts of communication and spokesperson skills than the provincial spokespersons (seven provinces). It may be because spokespersons in the provinces were just nominated. So, they were unable to explain properly what the roles of a government spokesperson were. Nevertheless, they know the main roles of a good spokesperson such as telling the truth not lies, doing press conferences, or producing press release and transition between government and media (Informants 3, 4, 5, 6, 7, 8, 9).

However, the spokespersons in Phnom Penh are quite aware of their roles.

> Do not force me to say what I do not believe in. I have never told a "lie." Spokespersons are not reactive, but we are always proactive. It means that, we have to do and prevent in advance before those issues happened. We have to follow up with every news and information all the time. We have to work 7 days per week and 24 hours per day. (Informant 1)
>
> To be a good spokesperson, you should understand and know about law, politics and other fields—at least you need to know about law and politics.

Then, the public officers should try to explain the public to know, understand, think and accept what they have said. When they understand and accept our words, they will join us with us as our partners. We don't speak by our own emotion or feeling, but say what has been written in the papers. One more important thing is our characteristics—we should be honest. Lying cannot stay with us for long, but honesty can. In conclusion, public relation officers should try their best on both action and term. We are not the boss, but we are the messengers to the public. Our message is not to mock or look down on others, but we try to explain them in a polite way although they may do bad things to us. We are a messenger for society—our words, actions and characteristics speak to the public and not to only one person. It means that when we speak to someone in an organization our communication is representative of the whole organization. (Informant 02)

Furthermore, as a spokesperson, we have to work for the society and peace. "The main role is to protect our boss—I try my best to protect the government and prime minister. We are not a judge, so we cannot say this side is right or wrong" (Informant 02). He lists three main responsibilities as:

First, I organize such information strategy that I have a clear calendar of what has happened annually. So, I evaluate the event every 12 months. The planning of strategy is not only focusing on what has been happening but trying to tell the society to understand the current situation. For example, now it is near that there is going to be a national election, so I seek a strategy to convey the detail for them to understand. Then, I have a monthly strategy. I will decide what information should be told to the public.

Second, I organize the media training. I train the government officers myself. I need to prepare the documents. I train spokesperson, media and communication officers for government institutions. I separate them in different workshop—workshop for spokesperson, for public officer and media officer.

Third, I have a responsibility for media coverage. It means that I have to listen to radio, read newspaper and be online and watch TV to see what are they focusing on and what is happening. The important responsibility is responding to media and journalist. Answer their questions related to my institution. We are the institution's ambassadors, so we try to prevent any chaos or protest that may occur due to lies or rumor. (Informant 02)

The Challenges of Government Spokespersons

Provincial spokespersons have more challenges such as a lack of human resources and skills, and technical problems than the spokespersons in Phnom

Penh (the capital). At the Ministry of Information in the provinces, there are only a few resource persons with skills to work and to help facilitate smooth release of information to the government and the public. During the interviews, I asked them to estimate the average of how many (in percentages) of the officers are active and inactive in their institutions. And the result showed that around 30 percent of the officers are active and 70 percent inactive. Furthermore, regarding technical problems, they do not have enough equipment to work with for spreading information such as computers, printers, cameras, and Internet (Informants 2, 3, 4, 5, 6, 7, 8, 9).

> I think that we don't have enough resource persons to serve the government and the public. And some of them lack media and communication skills. They don't know how to report, write and get information because their capacity is still limited and we have to improve and train them more. (Informant 06)

In the past, spokespersons always had some challenges while they were working, especially with the journalists. But, now they have become cooperative, after they clearly understood the roles of spokesmen. The big challenge of a spokesperson is "time." They work from the morning till late at night. When news is released without any newsworthy element, they need to spend at least three months explaining to the public so that they understand the truth. So spokesmen must be ready all the time—when journalists have questions, spokespersons will have to reply to them (Informant 02).

Sometimes, the challenges are caused by the public because they do not know and understand the spokespersons.

> When I say something it does not satisfy them, they have abusive words not only for me but also for my family. Anyway, we accept this because we know that we have to work for the pubic and also cannot satisfy all. Sometimes, we received impolite questions from the victim party. (Informant 02)

The Perspectives of Journalists and Government Spokespersons Works

THE JOURNALISTS' PERSPECTIVES

Generally, journalists are always facing difficulty with obtaining interviewees from the government officials. "It is a habit for the government officers to be careful with journalists and it is also difficult and challenging for us to communicate with those officers" (Informants 1, 2, 3, 4, 5, 6, 7, 8, 9).

Most of the government officers are afraid and try to avoid talking to the media. "They try to turn off the telephone, and they say that they are busy. I do not know 'why'." But the journalists cannot wait for them to reply because "[they] have to publish and broadcast, otherwise [their] stories will go rotten. So, we decide to put them to 'off record' and find other sources instead" (Informants 1, 2, 3, 4, 5, 6, 7, 8, 9).

Sometimes, the officers need a formal letter from the journalists' institutions before giving interviews. "It will take a long process if I ask for a formal letter (from my institution). As we know the officer is working so slowly, we think that it is not a good choice" (Informants 1, 3, 4, 8, 9). "We never put the request for a formal letter to them because we think that it does not work" (Informants 2, 5, 6, 7).

Even when there are spokespersons, we can say only a few of them "are happy and welcoming to talk to the journalists. We think that they should improve and try to understand the journalists' situation. It would be better if spokesmen have journalistic backgrounds" (Informants 3, 5, 9).

The Government Spokespersons' Perspectives

It would be dangerous if the officers think that they understand everything. "We must speak the truth but not all the truth that we must speak. We don't tell a lie because it is our major principal. We should be proud of ourselves for being information officers because everything we do is for our society" (Informant 01).

Some officers are not equipped to deal with their field or role; they are more likely to lack capacity and academic ability for work. "The only one solution is 'remove them'. If the officers do not have enough abilities and knowledge of the work, it will lead to reflect the weaknesses of the whole institution" (Informant 01).

Even though we have spokespersons for representing every ministry, the journalists still find it difficult and cannot reach them to verify the news. Every ministry has different policies and systems. So, firstly, the institutions themselves should try to understand the roles of journalists. "For me, if I could not be responsible for my job, I would like to 'resign' immediately" (Informant 01).

For the professional spokespersons, they try to explain and answer the questions to make the citizens understand issues clearly. "A lie and excuse can live only for a very short time, but the truth stays with us for a long time—this is ethics of a spokesman" (Informant 02).

> To gain the media trust, first, we should be modest and behave cordially with our partners—media and audiences. Second, we try to tell them as much as

possible. So, we do not lie to them or try to avoid their questions. One more important thing is that a PR person should listen carefully to the questions from the media, and try our best to answer them. The media officers' task is to try to verify and eliminate the rumors in the society. (Informant 02)

"I regret when I tell the wrong information, and I am happy when I know reporters can write a lot of articles using my words" (Informant 02). "We are happy to talk to and welcome the media. And also we want to get more training as we are new spokespersons" (Informants 3, 4, 5, 6, 7, 8, 9).

Cambodian PR Industry and Traditional Monastic Communication System

Nation–Religion–King is a motto of the Kingdom of Cambodia, which means independent territory, country and nation, and religion, followed with respect for the king. The Cambodian King uses this ideology for protecting and governing the people, and for the unification of the Cambodian Kingdom through Buddhism and its heritage. The king is valuable to the Buddhists as the institution is respected for erecting temples and pagodas. As discussed earlier, these are the places for Cambodian people to join and meet for mediations, education, communication, and consultations. These places are blessed by Buddhist monks as advisors and counselors. So Buddhism plays a very important role in building Cambodian society where people can live peacefully.

> The *wat* was not only the moral-religious center of a village community, but served important educational, cultural, and social functions as well. Until recent times, *wats* were the main centers of learning with schools and libraries where the Khmer culture and language was preserved and transmitted from generation to generation. (Ven. Maha Ghosananda)[9]
>
> In fact, adaptation to a great variety of political contexts—be they colonial, monarchical, socialist, republican, or doctrinaire Marxist—has been a marked feature of its history over the last century and a half.... It may be no exaggeration to assert that an accommodating spirit has been an intrinsic feature of Cambodian Buddhism since its inception. The visible presence of the sangha

---

[9] KEAP Project has been doing work to assist Cambodians in their recovery from the Khmer Rouge era since 1988. Available at http://www.keap-net.org/index.html (accessed on October 27, 2017).

and its unique significance as the only institution able to operate effectively and with high levels of mass support throughout the whole of the country have ensured that almost all governments have felt the need to cultivate the Buddhist sector, whatever their political philosophy. There is little reason to assume that this situation will change in the near future. (Harris, 2005: 230)

Going back to tradition could create a kind of soft communication that makes a connection between communities, monasteries, and governments (Royalists) by using mindful PR tools. It can create an authentic PR system that could bring them altogether to create better harmony in the society.

Conclusions and Recommendations

This study examined the relations between the government spokespersons and the media. In fact, both of them still misunderstand the roles and responsibilities of each other.

Firstly, the government spokespersons are quite unclear with their role and responsibilities. That is why they turn off their phones and avoid talking to the journalists. Somehow, they get pressurized and influenced by the government and political plyers to talk about secret and hot issues to the media and the public. So many people think that they do not perform well and abuse their responsibilities.

In addition, most of the government spokespersons are males. According to Table 17.1, there is only one female spokesperson among nine spokespersons. So it shows that it is still a challenge for females to become active in working as government officers (spokespersons).

Secondly, talking about technology, provincial spokespersons are new to the job and their regions are poor in terms of technical and human resources. They do not have enough access to use those technological tools to spread information to the public and the media faster. Meanwhile, they lack resourceful persons to work with such technology and only a few with such skills are working in the ministries.

Thirdly, sometimes, the relations between spokespersons and journalists are hampered or caused from the political issues and the "freedom of speech issues," because before they speak and give interviews to the journalists, they have to get permission from their bosses. That is why sometimes they are afraid and then avoid talking to the media because they do not want to lose their positions in the government.

To sum up, the government spokespersons in Cambodia have not yet become skilled in this field. They should have more training to improve and develop their performance. And the journalists, before going to interview them, should research and try to understand the nature of the spokesperson's institution, because every institution has different systems and policies.

However, nowadays, we can see that the government spokespersons have developed more human resources than in the past, because as noted, in 1992, there had been only one government spokesperson. In 2010, they had spokespersons representing all ministries in Phnom Penh. And since 2012, there has been "Team in Charge of Information in municipal/provincial administrations." They play the role of provincial government spokespersons.

To recap, the result of this research study comes from the study of just 18 government spokespersons and journalists, with whom I conducted in-depth interviews.

The nine government spokespersons, I felt, did not want to talk and give interviews to me initially. But, after some persuasions, they agreed to let me interview them. Especially, the provincial spokespersons did not have much information to respond to my questions, because it seemed that they were unclear about their positions and roles. Also, all of them did not normally give interviews to the journalists.

However, when I interviewed the journalists, they complained that the government officers do not respond to their requests that well as they try to make excuses and avoid talking to the media. Only a few of them are happy and welcome the press to talk to them. Moreover, the journalists also have a suggestion to the government that they should have an official contact list with short descriptions and background of each government officer and spokesperson, as this will make it easy for everyone to contact them directly.

In conclusion, the government spokespersons have their own arguments and they claim that they are always welcome to talk and give interviews to the journalists. In contrast, the journalists said that it is difficult and hard to contact and interview the government officers, even spokespersons.

This begs the question whether the temples' traditional communication system could be utilized by government institutions to perhaps create a second tier of—may we put it—a less confrontational form of communication between the government and the community.

After completing this study, the researcher found out a new angle related to accessing government information, PR, and media (journalists). The e-government strategies are developing in spreading and accessing information from the government to the public and journalists. Even in the provinces, they also have their own provincial websites, channels, televisions, and radios. However, there is lack of research into Asian PR. Sriramesh (2004: 2) notes "the silent continent" in terms of the limited and inadequate amount of research available.

> Western definitions of public relations assume a democratic political structure where competing groups seek legitimacy and power through public debate and elections, which is not always the norm in many parts of the world, including Asia. Particularly difficult to discern are the "emerging democracies" of Asia where alternative views may be encouraged in theory, but not in practice. As a result, various covert and overt forms of self, social, and government censorship can be seen. (Sriramesh, 2004: 8)

Bibliography

ADB. 2008. *Development Asia: Tackling Asia's Inequality: Creating Opportunities for the Poor.* Manila: ADB.
Ben, W., and A. Pheap. 2012. "Government Spokespersons Get Lessons in Handling the Press." *Cambodia Daily*, November 8: 6.
Bill, K. 2012. "A Conversation with Daw Aung San Suu Kyi." *The New York Times*, September 30. Available at http://keller.blogs.nytimes.com/2012/09/30/a-conversation-with-daw-aung-san- suu-kyi/book? (accessed on October 26, 2017).
Broom, G. M, and G. D. Smith. 1979. "Testing the Practitioners Impact on Clients." *Public Relations Review* 5 (3): 47–59.
Castelli, J. W. 2007. "Government Public Relations: A Quantitative Assessment of Government Public Relations Practitioner Roles and Public Relations Model Usage.*"* Unpublished master's thesis, University of South Florida, United States.
Charron, J. 1989. *Relations Between Journalists and Public Relations Practitioners: Cooperation, Conflict and Negotiation.* Université Laval, Canada. Available at www.cjc-online.ca/index.php/journal/article/download/499/405 (accessed on October 26, 2017).
Clinton, Hillary. 2012. *Remarks at the Opening Plenary of the U.S.–Morocco Strategic Dialogue.* Available at http://www.state.gov/secretary/rm/2012/09/197711.htm (accessed on January 10, 2013).
Dan, B., and H. Ilias. 1999. "Practitioners Roles, Public Relations Education, and Professional Socialization: An Exploratory Study." *Journal of Public Relation Research* 11 (1): 91–103.
David, S. 1998. *A Panacea for Local Government? The Role of PR.* Unpublished master's thesis, The Constitution Unit School of Public Policy, United Kingdom.
David, W. G., and M. Charles. 2000. *Public Relation: A Value-driven Approach.* Boston, MA: Borton Allyn and Bacon.
Daymon, C., and I. Holloway. 2002. *Qualitative Research Methods in Public Relations and Marketing Communications.* London: Routledge.
———. 2011. *Qualitative Research Methods in Public Relations and Marketing Communications* (Second Edition). London: Routledge.

Dozier, D. M. 1992. "The Organizational Roles of Communications and Public Relations Practitioners." In *Excellence in Public Relations and Communication Management*, edited by J. E. Grunig, 327–55. New Jersey: Lawrence Erlbaum Associates.
Elliott, S. 2012. "Public Relations Defined, After an Energetic Public Discussion." *New York Times*, March 1. Available at http://www.nytimes.com/2012/03/02/business/media/public-relations-a-topic-that-is-tricky-to-define.html (accessed on October 28, 2017).
Goonatileka, H. 2003. "Sri Lanka–Cambodia Relations with Special Reference to Period 14–20th Centuries." *Journal of the Royal Asiatic Society of Sri Lanka* XLVII. Available at http://www.lotuscomm.org/lotus-academy/buddhist-history/447-sri-lanka-cambodia-relations-with-special-reference-to-the-period-14th-20th-centuries (accessed on October 26, 2017).
Grunig, L., J. Grunig, and D. Dozier. 2002. *Excellent Public Relations and Effective Organizations*. Mahwah, NJ: Lawrence Erlbaum Associates.
Harris, I. 2005. *Cambodian Buddhism: History and Practice*. Honolulu, HI: University of Hawai'i Press.
———. 2006. *Cambodia Buddhism: History and Practice*. Thailand: Silkworm Books.
Hart, W. 1991. *Vipassana Meditation: The Art of Living as Taught by S.N Goenka*. Nashik: Vipassana Research Institute.
Kaur, K., and H. Shaari. 2006 "Perceptions on the Relationship Between Public Relations Practitioners and Journalists." *Kajian Malaysia* XXIV (1&2): 9–3.
Larsson, L. 2009. "PR and the Media: A Collaborative Relationship?" Book Review. *Nordicom* 30 (1): 147.
L'Etang, J. 2007. *Public Relations: Concepts, Practice and Critique*. London: SAGE Publications.
Lotus Talks. 2016, May 1. "Reviving Cambodia Buddhism After Pol Pot 'Genocide'." Singapore: Lotus Communication Network. Available at www.youtube.com/watch?v=OWeMVk_OJyo&t=1303s (accessed on October 26, 2017).
Ludwig, H. 2014. *How to Work Effectively as a Spokesperson*. Cambodia: Konrad Adenauer Stiftung. Available at http://www.kas.de/kambodscha/en/publications/38751/(accessed on September 1, 2016).
Mattis-Namgyel, E. 2011. *The Power of an Open Question*. Boston, MA: Shambhala Publications.
McCormack, J. 2010. "Get Along with the Boss." *Career World* 38 (5): 15–17.
MyPRSA. 2012. *What Is Public Relations?* New York: Public Relations Society of America. Available at http://www.prsa.org/aboutprsa/publicrelationsdefined/(accessed on October 26, 2017).
Narin, S. 2011. "Counting on Change in the Name of Democracy." *Lift Magazine*, May 25, 12–13.
Newsom, D., and A. Scott. 1985. *This Is PR: The Realities of Public Relations*. Belmont, CA: Wadsworth.
Reporters without borders. *Press Freedom Index 2016*. Available at https://rsf.org/en/ranking (accessed on October 28, 2017).
Reza, Maria. 2016. "Propaganda War: Weaponizing the Internet". *Rappler*, October 7, Philippines. Available at http://www.rappler.com/nation/148007-propaganda-war-weaponizing-internet (accessed on October 26, 2017).
Schelling, Thomas. 1960. *The Strategy of Conflict*. Cambridge, MA: Harvard University Press.
Seppala, E. 2013. "Why Compassion in Business Makes Sense." *Daily Good: News that Inspires*, November 25. Available at http://www.dailygood.org/story/520/why-compassion-in-business-makes-sense-emma-seppala/ (accessed on October 26, 2017).
Sriramesh, K., ed. 2004. *Public Relations in Asia: An Anthology*. Singapore: Thomson Learning.

Sriramesh, K., and D. Verčič., eds. 2009. *The Global Public Relations Handbook: Theory, Research, and Practice.* New York: Routledge.

Sullivan, Marguerite H. 2006. *A Responsible Press Office.* Global Publishing Solutions. Available at http://www.au.af.mil/au/awc/awcgate/state/pressoffice.pdf (accessed on October 26, 2017).

Swanson D. J. 2014. Exploring the Concept of Mindfulness in Public Relations Practice. *Public Relations Journal* 8 (4). Available at http://www.prsa.org/Intelligence/PRJournal/Vol8/No4/ (accesed on October 26, 2017).

Taylor, M. 2000. "Toward a Public Relations Approach to Nationbuilding." *Journal of Public Relations Research* 12 (2): 179–210.

The 1993 Constitution of the Kingdom of Cambodia and its Amendments. Available at http://cambodia.ohchr.org/~cambodiaohchr/sites/default/files/Constitution_ENG.pdf (accessed on October 26, 2017).

Try, Jean-Samuel S. 1991. "Le Bouddhisme Dans La Société Khmère Moderne." ["Buddhism in Modern Khmer Society."] PhD thesis, École Pratique des Hautes Études, Section Sciences Religieuses, Paris.

White, C., and A. Cooper. 2014. "Apple and Amazon's Big Lie: The Rebel Hacker and Hipster Nerd is a Capitalist Stooge." *Salon*, March 8. Available at http://www.salon.com/2014/03/08/apple_and_amazons_big_lie_the_rebel_hacker_and_hipster_nerd_is_a_capitalist_stooge/ (accessed on October 28, 2017).

18

Crossing Panel Borders: Transnational Constrained Comics Composition and Mindful Development Communication

Nicolas Verstappen[1]

Long neglected, the comics[2] medium is increasingly gaining scholarly attention as provider of highly textured and hybrid word-and-image texts. During the last decade, academic institutions across the world have gradually introduced and given more prominence to comics studies in their programs. In addition to the creation of dedicated academic conferences or scholarly publications such as *ImageTexT* launched in 2005, *Studies in Comics* launched in 2010, or *Inks* launched in 2016, the study of comics also led to even more specialized scrutiny.

For instance, the *SANE journal: Sequential Art Narrative in Education* publishes, since 2010, research and practitioner-based articles covering all intersections of comics and education. The use of comics in classrooms—which has recently found an increasing number of proponents (Aleixo, 2017; Aleixo and Noris, 2010; Bakis, 2012; Jacobs, 2007a, 2007b; Scanlon, 2015)—has given some interesting exercises involving the production of comics narratives in graduate education courses (Sousanis, 2015a) or college composition courses (Comer, 2015).

The constrained comics exercise presented in this chapter was developed to serve as a convenient and productive tool for an undergraduate creative writing course composed of Thai students without any particular art formation. Through the constraint of iconic iteration, by duplicating, reframing, and combining a limited number of panels drawn by European cartoonists, and adding textual elements, this exercise was conceived to invite students

---

[1] The author would like to extend his warmest thanks to cartoonists Joseph Falzon, Sacha Goerg, and Pierre Alary who kindly and gracefully provided the graphic writing course with original artwork, making this exercise possible.

[2] Like the term for any medium, comics requires a singular verb. As Chute (2008: 462) notes, "treating comics as a singular has become standard."

to cross or push back formal, modal, cultural, and national boundaries. This chapter discusses in detail the concepts, theories, and the overlapping creative stages that go into producing comic scripts (or writing) and also the transcultural processes.

Through an introduction to the different challenges faced by the students during the complex elaboration of their graphic narratives and the obtained results, the chapter suggests that the constrained comics exercise holds promise as an effective tool in multimodal and transnational collaborative writing that could be adapted to mindful development communication.

Based on the Buddhist practice of *sati*—which "literary means remembering or recollection" (Sivaraksa, 2015: 1)—mindful communication relies on the ability to "see interconnection" (Phap Dung, as quoted in Barclay, 2017) in order to become—according to Bialylew (Malcolm, 2015)—"more aware of what's going on in the world [and feeling] more connected, both to yourself and to other people." Introduced to these concepts through discussions with my colleague Dr Kalinga Seneviratne, and considering troubling resonances between mindfulness and graphic narrative composition as a "way of thinking," the chapter concludes on a discussion on how comics art also holds promise as a tool to raise awareness of our natural and social environments as a living and intimately interwoven fabric, and to foster mindful communication at a broader level.

Method Framework: Course Description and Participants

This study was conducted in the graphic writing segment of a creative writing course proposed to senior students of a four-year bachelor's degree in communication management in the Faculty of Communication Arts of Chulalongkorn University located in Bangkok. The graphic writing section—a 16-week and 3-credit course—aims at the practice and development of writing skills, focusing on visual storytelling and text/image dynamic. As the lecturer of this course, I oriented its content on the study of comics art aesthetics and the use of writing exercises based on the creation of comics-related graphic narratives. As my class was mostly composed of students without any particular drawing formation, the graphic writing exercises relied mainly on the transformation of preexisting artworks through visual substitution, iconic iteration, or other constraints.

The class was composed of 35 students, all Thais expect for one student from the Philippines. Four students had never read a comic book or a manga prior to the course.³ The remaining students were occasional or frequent readers of manga. Only three students expressed particular interest in American comics which were all superhero-related. Students were not familiar at all with Franco-Belgian comics—or *bandes dessinées*—except for the adventures of the Belgian character Tintin mentioned by five students.⁴

Through a series of lectures and research assignments, students were introduced to formal and narrative aspects of comics art and to its global history from the 1830s to the present time; composition assignments—consisting of various comics writing exercises—were given each week. The final project consisted of the creation by each student of five short comics stories of various formats over a 12-week period.

Writing with Pictures: Multimodality, Hybridity, Recollection, and Border Crossing

Royal (2010) claims:

> Given its reliance on symbols and iconography, comic art speaks in a language that is accessible to a wide audience, transcending many of the national, cultural, and linguistic boundaries imposed by other media and giving it a reach that is as democratic as it is immediate.

The creation of a comics narrative, however, implies an elaborate undertaking.

Duncan and Smith (2009: 4) propose to consider that "[a]s an art form, a comic book is a volume in which all aspects of the narrative are represented by pictorial and linguistic images encapsulated in a sequence of juxtaposed panels and pages."

The act of *encapsulation* appears to be a central and multilevel process in the making of comics narratives. One of the most fundamental levels would be the selection by the writer or artist of certain moments of prime action

---

³ The term "manga," used only in the singular form, will be defined as comics originally produced by Japanese publishers, and usually created by Japanese cartoonists.

⁴ Information concerning the students was collected through surveys distributed at the beginning and end of the semester. Students gave their informed written consent, allowing the presentation of the information gathered in this chapter. Because some wished to remain anonymous, I cite these students using pseudonym initials only. I cite student authors using their nicknames only, with their written consent. Their works are reprinted with permission.

from the narrative that will be "encapsulated in a discrete space, which in comics is called a *panel*" (Duncan and Smith, 2009: 10). In the wake of Pierre Fresnault-Deruelle, Benoît Peeters (1998: 22) defines the comics panel "as a picture 'in disequilibrium', quartered between the panels immediately preceding and following, but so too between its aspiration for autonomy and its inclusion in the narrative" (translation).

According to Duncan and Smith (2009: 10), choosing "the sequence of moments to encapsulate is important, because adjacent panels can interact to create a level of meaning that does not exist in individual panels alone." McCloud (2006: 10) also points out the "choice of moment" as the first of five basic types of choices that need to be made in order to create a clear and convincing storytelling in the comics form. It consists in deciding which—and how many—moments "to *include* in a comics story and which to *leave out*." Other basic types of choices are the *choice of frame* where the artist defines "the right *distance* and *angle* to *view* those moments—and where to *trim* them," the *choice of image* or how to render "the characters, objects and environments in those frames *clearly*," the *choice of word* which consists in "picking words that *add valuable information* and *work well* with the images around them," and finally the *choice of flow* to guide "readers *through* and *between* panels on a page or screen."

Inside the physically limited space offered by the page to "be addressed as a unit of containment" (Eisner, 2000: 63), the cartoonist must continuously take into account all these interweaving stages of action while elaborating his or her layout. To give a specific size and place to a panel, for instance, will consequently determine the space left available on the page for the other panels to be displayed. Additionally, the amount of text—whether dialogue in speech balloons, captions, or onomatopoeia—might influence the dimension of the panel in or alongside which it is placed. Speech balloons, for instance, occupy a delineated area seemingly masking or obstructing part of other pictorial elements in the panels. Their size, shape, and specific location have to be considered with attention while establishing the dimension and inner composition of a panel.

The balance between text and image is not to be achieved in the composition only. As Duncan and Smith (2009: 146) argue, "[i]t is the proper emphasis and interaction of pictorial and linguistic that is the basis of effective comic book communication." Defining comics "as a hybrid word-and-image form in which two narrative tracks, one verbal and one visual, register time spatially," scholar Hillary Chute (2008: 452) specifies that:

> comics doesn't blend the visual and the verbal—or use one simply to illustrate the other—but is rather prone to present the two non-synchronously; a reader

of comics not only fills in the gaps between panels but also works with the often disjunctive back-and-forth of reading and looking for meaning.

Commenting on the combination of sequential art and text in comics, Jacobs (2007a: 182) also points out that

> [t]his combination of words and images—what Gunther Kress calls *multimodality*—works to create meaning in very particular and distinctive ways; in a multimodal text, meaning is created through print, visuals, and the combination of the two in order to achieve effects and meanings that would not be possible in either a strictly print or strictly visual text.

Jacobs (2007b: 196) considers that comics engage both creators and readers in "acts of hybridity," "that is by articulating in new ways [...] established practices and conventions within and between different modes of meaning" (New London Group, 2000: 29). Jacobs (2007b: 23) also notes that linguistic, visual, audio, gestural, and spatial elements combine in comics narratives and that, "[t]aken together, these elements form a multimodal system of meaning making."

Building his or her story with a hybrid form and the *encapsulation* of information on several and interfering levels, the cartoonist must yet provide the reader—relying consistently on the forthcoming participation of the latter—with a "sense of continuous experience" (McCloud, 2006: 129), avoiding disjunction to become disruptive. As Duncan and Smith (2009: 12) state, "Perhaps one of the most important standards for the critical evaluation of a comic book is whether or not the encapsulation choices of the writer and artist produced successful closure," the term *closure* referring here to the concept adapted by Scott McCloud from Gestalt psychology. *Closure*—or the "phenomenon of observing the parts but perceiving the whole" (McCloud, 1999: 63/67)—stands as the "grammar" of comics "since our definition of comics hinges on the arrangement of elements," on the juxtaposition of panels usually delineated by their borders or *frames* and isolated by interstitial gaps known as *gutters*.

McCloud (1999: 66) states that "[t]he gutter plays host to much of the magic and mystery that are the very heart of comics [for it is] in the limbo of the gutter [that] human imagination takes two separate images and transforms them into a single idea," into a "continuous story out of discrete panels" (Duncan and Smith, 2009: 12). For his part, Denson (2013: 274) notes that the *frame* marks "a boundary that defines the image as a unit, thus separating it from the space around it, but it also marks a zone of connection and in fact invites the viewer to cross its threshold, to pass into the territory it defines."

Furthermore, Sousanis (2015a: 1) points out that "we make connections not just from one panel to the next, but across the page and back and forth, in all directions." Coined as *iconic solidarity*, Groensteen (2007: 18) defines this principle as "interdependent images that, participating in a series, present the double characteristic of being separated [...] and which are plastically and semantically over-determined by the fact of their coexistence *in praesentia*."

In his dissertation in comics form *Unflattening*, and relying on Groensteen (2007: 146), Sousanis (2015b: 62) also considers that the entire composition of a page is:

> A connected space, not reliant on a chain-like sequence linearly proceeding from point to point.... Rather associations that stretch web-like across the page braiding fragments into a cohesive whole. Each element is thus: one with everything. This spatial interplay of sequential and simultaneous [...] imbues comics with a dual nature [...] both three-like, hierarchical and rhizomatic, interwoven in a single form.

Interestingly enough, the aforementioned quote is originally distributed over six captions and a speech balloon on a comics page depicting a teeming-with-life mangrove setting—allocated over a nine-panel grid as a polyptych—where a meditating Buddha will pronounce the line "one with everything." On the following page, Sousanis (2015b: 63) furthermore invokes the term "awareness" by stating that the comics spatial interplay holds "two distinct kinds of awareness—the sequential and simultaneous."

Sousanis' references to Buddhism and awareness strikingly echo Rupert Gethin's (2001: 39) considerations on mindfulness in the *Milindapañha* account, where *sati* "should be understood as what allows awareness of the full range and extent of *dhammas*; *sati* is an awareness of things in relation to things, and hence an awareness of their relative value." If the word *sati* literary means "remembering" or "recollection to recall something," Gethin (2001: 36) notes that the "Sanskrit root [...] seems to connote two basic ideas, namely 'to remember' and more simply, perhaps, 'to have in mind'," and that in Buddhist literature, "it is the bare aspect of 'remembering' or 'having in mind' that is focused upon to the exclusion of other meanings: memory as the act of remembering, not what is remembered, or, as the commentaries put it, 'memory' in the sense of remembering [...]". This definition of *sati* echoes, in turn, another comics-related statement by Sousanis (2015b: 66):

> When we take the all-over composition into account, form and expression become one. Meaning is thus conveyed not only by what's depicted, but

through structure: the size, shape, placement, and relationship of components—what they're next to and what they're not, matters. (Orientation too.)[5] Art Spiegelman describes each page as an architectonic unit—ideas made spatial.[6] Citing Goethe, Chris Ware likens comics to "frozen music," a space to reconstitute memory.[7] From the forking paths, tangential (and parenthetical), layered and overlapping, intersecting, unbound, moments nested within moments, comics can hold the unflat ways in which thought unfolds.

A space to recollect, or "to reconstitute memory," cartooning is also "the art of turning time back into space," according to *Maus*' author Art Spiegelman (as quoted in Ware, 2015). On the matter, Spiegelman (Conan, 2011: 17) furthermore states:

> Like how does something happen, and ... how does it reverberate through time? And that act of memory is important, and comics are great for memory. Like even when you have a short comic, like a three-panel comic, you've got a past, a present and a future as soon as you look at those three boxes. And that allows you to reflect and compare times.

Facilitating *sati*'s conscious and concomitant acts of "remembering" and "having in mind," comics rhizomatic composition might also "be read as a positive illustration of multiculturalism, where the rhizomatic overtakes the singular, essential root," to reallocate here a statement of Mitsch (1997: 54) on Maryse Condé's novel *Crossing the Mangrove*.

Gutter, panel, or comics page could indeed each serve as an apt metaphor of the *transnational place*, a "space which is defined by movement, porosity and interstitiality, and in an urban and architectural paradigm which is based on openness and inclusiveness" (Bartoloni, 2013: 46). Without covering the same exact notions, terms such as *interstitiality*, *liminality*, *duality*, *hybridity*, or *border crossing* are yet fundamental concepts in both comics and transnational studies which seem to echo each other. For instance, McCloud's (1999: 66) statement that it is "in the limbo of the gutter [that] human imagination takes two separate images and transforms them into a single idea" finds an interesting resonance with Bartoloni's (2013: 53–54) comment that "[t]he space in-between, which is opened up by translation and transnational

---

[5] The original text is distributed over captions on a comics page. The line "(Orientation too.)" is displayed upside down in the original.

[6] Spiegelman quote from Witek, J. (Ed.) (2007). *Art Spiegelman: Conversations*. Jackson: University Press of Mississippi, pp. 276–277.

[7] Ware quote from: Ball, D. M., and Kuhlman, M. B. (Eds.) (2010). *The Comics of Chris Ware: Drawing Is a Way of Thinking*. Jackson: University Press of Mississippi, p. 182.

places, is one of the sites in which a new understanding of the subject can take place" and goes on to state that

> [The new understanding of the subject] can be achieved when confronted with an environment that is at once familiar and unfamiliar. It is this mixture of the known and the unknown that will propel the subject into the realisation of his or her own gaps and of an identity that far from being homogeneous is multifarious and variegated.

These notions of "gap" and "mixture of the known and the unknown" echo Chute's (2008: 452) statement that "[c]omics moves forward in time through the space of the page, through its progressive counter point of presence and absence: packed panels (also called frames) alternating with gutters (empty space)." These remarkable resonances are also to be found between the formal functioning of comics and their own imbrications in transnational exchanges if we consider the suggestion of Denson, Meyer, and Stein (2013: 6):

> In both cases, imagined geographies are constructed, challenged, and brought in contact with one another through dynamic processes that fail to respect the sanctity of "the other's domain" and in which "mutual forbearance on the borders is seldom exercised." Such a process unites the single reader, for whom a narratively coherent world emerges from juxtaposed images and words, with imagined communities of various sorts—the communities of fans, of local and spatially dispersed cultures, and of nations, among which graphic narratives circulate.

In order to conclude this discussion, we still need to introduce the principle of *redundancy* which plays an important role in the emergence of a narratively coherent world from juxtaposed images and words. As the "narrative is segmented into discontinuous units which are aligned sequentially [and] articulated by syntagmatic links," writes scholar Ann Miller (2007a: 88), the "[n]arrative progression depends, therefore, on the conservation of certain elements and the modification of others." She relies here on the conception that "comics are founded on a dialectic of repetition and difference, each image linked to the preceding one by a partial repetition of its contents" (Groensteen, 2007: 115), a principle that Groensteen (2007: 117) yet sees as "far from being an obligatory bridge between two consecutive panels of a narrative sequence". This principle of repetition will be at the core of the constrained exercise presented in this chapter, an exercise inspired by the earliest works of Lewis Trondheim.

OuBaPo and Constraint of Iconic Iteration

In the pages of his minicomic series *ACCI H3319* self-published between 1988 and 1990, then-debuting French cartoonist Lewis Trondheim produced comic strips and single-page comics narratives relying only on the repetition of a photocopied single panel or a highly limited set of different panels. For instance, in the series of strips collected under the title *Le dormeur* (The Sleeper), each strip is built on the juxtaposition of three identical panels presenting, in close-up and frontal view, the minimalist depiction of a bedridden man wearing a nightcap.

Miller (2007b: 119) states that "[t]he repetition of identical panels throughout a strip would seem to be a radical restriction, since it counteracts the sequentiality on which the medium is founded", noting that "the threat of stasis is [however] avoided, since narrative progression is devolved onto the dialogue."

If the pictorial elements remain unaltered in the panels composing *Le dormeur*, it is indeed through the introduction of speech balloons—revealing bitter discussions with his off-panel wife—that the narrative moves forward. If this approach can be considered as a radical restriction, it was also regarded by Trondheim (2009) as a productive one, stating that it was just about the only effective means he found to tell stories without feeling too embarrassed by his drawing abilities. Moreover, amusing himself by "pushing the principle of iconic redundancy to its paroxysm," the French cartoonist explored the interplay of text with an identical image.

With two uneven ovals for the shape of the eyes, simple dots for the irises, and a short horizontal stroke for the mouth, the facial features of the bedridden man are minimal, leading to the difficultly of defining a clear and specific facial expression. A seemingly half-closed eye might confer a sense of weariness to the face. Yet, depending on the content of the dialogues, the identical facial expression tends to be reinterpreted as conveying expressions of sternness or disdain.

Words can then be considered as acting in *Le dormeur* as a textual anchorage. We might, however, note that words are conversely affected by the image. A seemingly enthusiastic comment pronounced by the bedridden man, with a facial expression that does not convey any sense of excitement, tends to be interpreted as being sarcastic. This interplay—here envisioned quite radically—follows the observation of Kukkonen (2011: 39) that, in comics, "the facial expressions of characters can be juxtaposed with the speech bubbles, enabling readers to corroborate what is being said by checking the characters' utterances against what their bodily postures and expressions reveal."

Trondheim's early experiments drew the attention of French cartoonist Jean-Christophe Menu who invited Trondheim to consider collaboration based on a similar experimental process (L'Association, 2007). Menu drew four square panels devoid of any text. The first panel depicted a pensive man sitting on a rock. The second panel presented the same character facing a toad standing in a pound. The third panel portrayed the same man lying in a desert and staring at a night sky. The fourth panel presented a building—whose hardly discernible architecture could evoke a small Greek temple with columns—standing by the sea.

Provided with these imposed panels, repeating and arranging them in sequences, adding speech and thought balloons, Trondheim produced a dozen strips each composed of four panels. Feeling somewhat limited, he asked Menu for four additional panels leading to a set of eight panels.

With this set of eight panels, Trondheim produced a total of 100 four-panel strips. Published in 1991 by L'Association under the title *Moins d'un quart de seconde pour vivre* (Less than a quarter of a second to live), the resulting series of strips presented the metaphysical considerations—through conversations and some soliloquies—of an anguished man, a rock, a toad, a man fully buried in the desert, and a hermit cloistered in his cabin. This cabin, which was not described previously as such, is in fact the building whose hardly discernible architecture evoked a small Greek temple with columns. It is through the textual information introduced by Trondheim that the nature and function of the building will be clearly defined, or anchored. With their tail pointing at the cabin, a series of speech balloons revealed the voice, and by extension the presence, of a hermit cloistered in the building. Speech balloons with their tail pointing to the rock provided the stone with a voice, transforming the supposedly decorative element into a character which discussed extensively with the pensive man. This example highlights the particular interplay of words and pictures in comics, and how the introduction of a simple speech balloon and the disposition of its tail can turn—with much effectiveness and immediacy—an inanimate object or an animal into a talking being, as if the "balloon" was providing it with a "breath," and a "spirit," as denoted in the original root of the Latin word *anima* (Collins' Online Dictionary, n.d.).

Moins d'un quart de seconde pour vivre and the constraint on which it is built foreshadow the works undertaken by the OuBaPo, acronym for *Ouvroir de Bande Dessinée Potentielle* (Workshop for Potential Comics), a committee officially established in France in 1992 and dedicated to create comics under voluntary artistic constraint as a way to push the structural dimension of the medium beyond its alleged boundaries. The group places itself in the lineage of the OuLiPo, acronym for *Ouvroir de Littérature Potentielle* (Workshop for Potential Literature), a committee dedicated "to the use of constraints as a mechanism for the production of literary texts" (Miller, 2007b: 117).

Through the publication in 1997 of a first collection of reflections and works initiated by the OuBaPo in the collective book *OuPus 1*, comics theorist and member of the committee Thierry Groensteen laid down "the theoretical foundations for OuBaPo by listing, and in most cases exemplifying, different types of [...] constraints that have been, or could be, the basis of OuBaPo exercises" (Miller, 2007b: 118). The constraint consisting of producing a graphic narrative based on the repetition of a single panel or a very limited set of panels was listed under the denomination *itération iconique* [iconic iteration] (Groensteen, 1997). The iconic iteration is considered *complete* when the panels are duplicated in their entirety, except for textual alteration, and *partial* when the process of repetition affects only some elements or sections of the panel. A "progressive reframing from one panel to the next" (Miller, 2007b: 119) is an example of *partial* iconic iteration.

The exercise presented later in this chapter exploited both *complete iconic iteration* and *partial iconic iteration*.

Development of the Set of Imposed Panels

The first step of the project consisted of developing a limited set of panels containing pictorial elements but deprived of any text.

Not being a cartoonist myself, I only drew rough sketches of the pictorial elements in the panels (Figure 18.1) with the intention of asking various professional cartoonists to finalize the artwork. The elements encapsulated in the panels evoked features of a crime story as the genre seemed both appealing to young adults and potentially generative of interesting dramatic tensions through moral conflicts. A female character holding a gun and a male character tied to a chair appeared to have a more important position in the panels, being centered in the frames and, presumably, facing each other.

Other elements were added in order to provide the students with more potential characters such as two birds in the cemetery, a rat in the basement, two cockroaches on a barrel in the basement, or a cell phone atop the same barrel. Some other elements were conceived in order to be exploited or

Figure 18.1
Set of Seven Roughly Sketched Panels Used as a Reference for the Three Professional Cartoonists

Source: All rights remain with the author: Nicolas Verstappen.

interpreted in several ways. The repartition of the elements in the two rectangular panels was for instance planned to allow an effective and subsequent reframing of these panels.

After completion, the roughly sketched panels and the project were presented to various mainstream and alternative European professional cartoonists having their own distinctive styles. The objective was to enlist at least three cartoonists in order to provide the students with three different renditions of my original set. Reinterpreted by a different artist, each set would show small variations in the pictorial elements depicted and specific character designs. Each set would also convey a particular mood through the stylistic differences. The goal was to enhance the visual literacy of the students through the observation of these differences and by understanding how these variations might benefit their narratives.

French cartoonist Joseph Falzon, Swiss cartoonist Sacha Goerg, and French artist Pierre Alary agreed to participate in the project. They were left free to reconsider the overall design of the characters but were asked to respect the presence and disposition of particular elements (rat, cell phone, cockroaches, etc.). It resulted in the production of three sets of seven panels (Figure 18.2). The cartoonists agreed that their panels could undergo some specific transformations in order to extend the set from seven panels to 15 panels. For instance, the panel with the smoking gun was duplicated and altered to create another panel in which the smoke was erased.

To this set of 15 panels, two black panels—originally aimed at evoking the obstructed viewpoint of the blindfolded man—were added. It resulted in three sets of 17 panels (Figure 18.3), handed to the students in order to create their final project through the process of iconic iteration.

Instructions for the Exercise

During the fourth class, each student received several copies of the set of 17 panels based on Joseph Falzon's set of seven panels. By cutting, arranging, and pasting different or identical panels, each student had to create a comics page relying on a 3×4-panel grid, a grid where the width stands for three square panels and the height for four square panels. By adding

Figure 18.2
Three Different and Final Sets of Seven Panels

Source: All rights remain with the authors: Joseph Falzon, Sacha Goerg, and Pierre Alary. Used with permission.

Note: Respectively drawn by Joseph Falzon (right), Sacha Goerg (center), and Pierre Alary (left).

Figure 18.3
Extended Set of Limited and Imposed Panels Based on the Original Set of Seven Panels

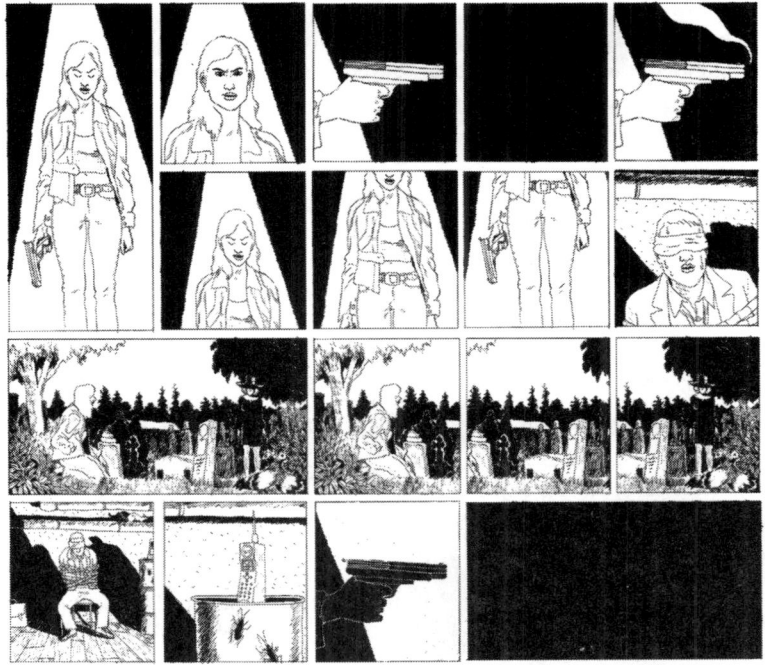

Source: All rights remain with the author: Joseph Falzon. Used with permission.
Note: The panel of the smoking gun has been duplicated to create another panel in which the smoke was erased. This panel was then duplicated and turned into a negative image. The two rectangular panels have been divided into three square panels. Two black panels were added. The final set is then composed of 17 panels.

speech balloons and captions to their page, students finalized their short comics narrative. They were then provided with the sets drawn by Sacha Goerg and Pierre Alary.

They were asked to reproduce the layout of their first narrative with the panels of Goerg and Alary in order to appreciate the potentially exploitable variations of style, mood, and other elements between the sets. On the same principle of iconic iteration and with the same three sets of 17 panels, students were asked to create individually four other stories of various formats over the next 12-week period.

They were allowed to use panels from different artists in a single narrative on the condition that the undertaking was motivated. They were allowed to tilt or reverse panels to create negative versions of the panels, and to use partial iconic iteration by enlarging and reframing portions of panels. One of the stories of the final project had to reach a length of minimum four pages; each page layout was constructed on a 2×3-panel grid. This study would focus only on the stories produced in this longer format as it implied a more abundant repetition of panels.

Results: Multimodal Narratives

In the four-page comics produced as her final project, student Bigbell used only the set of panels drawn by Joseph Falzon (Figure 18.4). Composed of 22 panels spread over four pages, her story was built on the repetition and rearrangement of 10 out of the 17 imposed panels.

Figure 18.4
First Two Pages of the Four-page Comics Produced by Bigbell

Source: All rights remain with the authors: Bigbell and Joseph Falzon. Used with permission.
Note: Based on the iconic iteration of panels drawn by Joseph Falzon.

It relates the story of a female assassin who delivers a long and self-glorifying speech about her skills in front of her future victim. At the end of the story and through a telephone conversation with her employer, she discovers that the captive man is deaf and did not catch, therefore, a single word of her self-flattering monologue. The graphic narrative was cleverly constructed to emphasize the humorous impact of the final twist. In the large horizontal black panel launching the story, Bigbell places the onomatopoeia of footsteps descending a staircase ("tap, tap, tap") and one of a door slamming ("Slam!"). It is interesting to note that the three "tap" sounds are disposed spatially at three different and progressively descending levels to evoke the material presence of a staircase not pictorially represented.

In the second panel, we discover a blindfolded man tied up in a basement. Based on these new elements, the content of the previous panel is reinterpreted; the reader assumes now that the first panel is black because it presents the obstructed point of view of the blindfolded man. The noise of the slamming door seems to have awakened the captive man as he emits the strangled sound "ugh." Yet Bigbell ingeniously misleads the reader.

As we seemingly shared the obstructed point of view of the blindfolded man in the first panel, we assumed that the sounds presented in the panel where those heard by the captive as we assumed they woke him up. Relying upon the fact that we would merge two "narrative tracks, one verbal and one visual" in the constant "back-and-forth of reading and looking for meaning," Bigbell misleads us until the end of the story where we discover that these two tracks were not presenting the auditory and visual perceptions of a single character but sensory perceptions from separate sources.

The narrative composed by Fon relates the story of detective Sarah Holmes who holds a gang lord captive (Figure 18.5). She has the intention to render justice by herself, but the criminal begs for his life. On page 2, after a horizontal panel presenting the detective seemingly reflecting on her decision, the page will be divided vertically by a series of dots into two parallel narratives. Panels in the left column present the "choice A," where the detective kills the criminal in cold blood, and those in the right column depict the "choice B," where Sarah Holmes spares the life of the gang lord.

The vertical separation of the panels in two columns continues on pages 3 and 4, unveiling in two parallel stories the consequences resulting from each choice.[8] The second page offers interesting compositional choices. The first

---

[8] The composition of Fon's narrative was inspired by the short comics—*The Spirit: Two Lives* by American cartoonist Will Eisner, published on December 12, 1948 (Section #446), and it was analyzed during the graphic writing course.

Figure 18.5
Pages 1–3 of the Four-page Comics Produced by Fon

Source: All rights remain with the authors: Fon, Joseph Falzon, and Pierre Alary. Used with permission.
Note: Based on the iconic iteration of panels drawn by Joseph Falzon and Pierre Alary.

panel, originally a square panel presenting the face of the female character with her eyes closed, was enlarged by Fon to cover the full width of the page. It places the detective at the center of the page, right above the line of separation between her two potential choices, accentuating the moral conflict that tears her apart. In the right column, we can also note how the use of the gun as a negative image, reversed by Fon on its horizontal axis, emphasizes the concept of an alternative or opposite choice that mirrors the left column.

These two examples highlight the possibilities and the challenges offered by the multimodal and constrained composition of graphic narratives and tackled by significantly drawing on problem-solving skills.

As mentioned by student K. N. in a survey conducted after the course: In this exercise, "everything was important—story plot, panel arrangement, drawing style."

Results: Transnational Perspective

The three sets of panels devoid of any text, the Western-looking setting by non-Thai cartoonists and the process of redefining the panel boundaries led to some interesting graphic narratives revealing transnational dialogues as well as marginalized or invisible communities.

For instance, Nick composed a story set exclusively in the Père Lachaise cemetery in the direct aftermath of November 2015 Paris terrorist attacks (Figure 18.6). Except for the two black panels, he created his four-page story relying only on the repetition and reframing of the cemetery panel drawn by Pierre Alary. The first three panels on the first page present complete and reframed views of the cemetery where a woman is crying. From the fourth panel, Nick continues his narrative with a series of panels reframing enlarged shots of three different tombstones. Adding speech balloons to these graves and, thus, providing them with an *anima*, Nick reveals the voices of three ghosts residing in the cemetery.

Disturbed and affected by the sorrow of the woman mourning a victim of the attacks, the ghosts of French playwright Molière, Polish composer Chopin, and American singer Jim Morrison start a conversation. Each ghost—through his own cultural prism connected to a different epoch and nation—comments and condemns the frightful event. Their dialogue spreads simultaneously and symbolically across national, cultural, and panel borders. Dead but with a living conscience, in the next world but still observing ours, these ghosts form a transnational and imagined community in the afterlife, a community made visible by the delineation of new borders (enlargement

Figure 18.6
Pages 1, 3, and 4 of the Four-page Comics Produced by Nick

Source: All rights remain with the authors: Nick and Pierre Alary. Used with permission.
Note: Based exclusively on the partial iconic iteration of a single panel drawn by Pierre Alary, except for the use of two black panels in the fourth page.
Disclaimer: This image is for representation purpose only.

and reframing of a panel) and by an "act of hybridity" (inclusion of speech balloons and written text in the image).

A similar observation can be made on the story composed by Top (Figure 18.7). Using panels from the three different sets and reframing the panels to remove all the animals (birds, cockroaches, and rats), Top keeps only the human characters in the first three pages of his six-page graphic narrative. By adding speech balloons with their tails pointing toward the borders of the panels, he suggests the presence of an invisible narrator continuously kept off-panel. Addressing the reader and speaking on behalf of a group, this invisible narrator explains that members of his community are everywhere yet unseen by the humans who destroy their common habitat. From the end of the third page and by presenting the panels without reframing, Top reveals the presence of animals and, therefore, makes visible the animal narrator and its community kept off-panel up to this point.

The imagined community of the animals—pleading for its recognition in the endangered world it shares with humans—is first symbolically kept invisible in the *gutter*, the interstitial gap between the panels, "the space in-between." It leaves the margin to become apparent through the "unframing" of reframed panels, the redefinition of the panel boundaries or *borders*. These two stories highlight how formal aspects of the constrained comics exercise, through "acts of hybridity" and partial iconic iteration, and transnational expressions can be interrelated and mutually reinforcing.

Figure 18.7
Pages 1–4 of the Six-page Comics Produced by Top

Source: All rights remain with the authors: Top, Joseph Falzon, Sacha Goerg, and Pierre Alary. Used with permission.

Note: Based on the iconic iteration of panels from the sets of Joseph Falzon, Sacha Goerg and Pierre Alary.

Cross-cultural Undercurrents of the Exercise

Through the use of silent panels whose "accessible" nature transcends "many of the national, cultural, and linguistic boundaries," the exercise presented in this study enabled a creative collaboration between European and Thai participants and the production of elaborate graphic narratives by students without any particular drawing abilities.

The constraint of partial iconic iteration—through its process of reframing panels and redefining their borders—was exploited by some students to make visible invisible communities and to renegotiate symbolically the boundaries between communities sharing a common space.

The *frame*, as a "boundary" and a "zone of connection," the *gutter*, as a "space in-between" or the hybridization of text and image are other formal elements of the comics medium that were exploited in order to identify and connect these communities. "Acts of hybridity"—consistently undertaken by the students during the multiple and interweaving stages of comics making—also confirmed that this exercise sets itself as an efficient tool to combine "linguistic, visual, audio, gestural, and spatial elements" in "a multimodal system of meaning making."

Adopting Comics Medium to Development Communication

If the acts of reframing and unframing reveal the presence of animals and, therefore, make visible an imagined community long kept off-panel in student Top's short comics, the constrained exercise also forced, beforehand, the writer to consider the animals as potential characters in his narrative. Like Lewis Trondheim considered a stone as an active participant in *Moins d'un quart de seconde pour vivre*, Thai students were invited to explore all the visual resources offered by each panel of the limited set in order to develop their longer graphic narratives. The anecdotal and decorative presence of animals or graves in the original sets had to be reconsidered as provider of more active and important narrative elements. If *sati* "should be understood as [...] an awareness of things in relation to things, and hence an awareness of their relative value," the constraint of *iconic iteration*—as designed here—also led to reconsider the value of centered human characters as relative and that of non-human or invisible entities as significant.

Acting as an anchor with much effectiveness and immediacy, the speech balloon—with its tail and embedded text—provided "inanimate" objects with an *anima*, such as the graves in Nick's comics became—through metonymy—three ghosts discussing November 2015 Paris terrorist attack. Simply talking about, interacting with, or being direct victims of human actions, this unexpected cast resumes its place in the "hugely incomprehensible yet indescribably fine texture of life." Seemingly, encouraging the mindful search for "interconnection" in order to become "more aware of what's going on in the world (and feeling) more connected, both to yourself and to other people" and other entities, the constrained exercise holds promise as a tool to raise awareness of our natural and social environments as a living and intimately interwoven fabric similar to the aforementioned teeming-with-life mangrove polyptych depicted in Sousanis' (2015b: 62) *Unflattening*.

Furthermore, the comics panel is to be meticulously examined not only for the potentially productive details it may contain but also "as a picture 'in disequilibrium', quartered between the panels immediately preceding and following." As aforementioned, choosing "the sequence of moments to encapsulate is important, because adjacent panels can interact to create a level of meaning that does not exist in individual panels alone." The seminal choice of moment—which consists in deciding which, and how many, moments "to include in a comics story and which to leave out" in order to create a sense of continuous experience—invites the author to constantly be aware of the panel's "quartered" nature as an encapsulated "prime action" being both a moment in time and part of a flow of movement. The process echoes the *sati*-related mental faculty of Bare Attention coined by monk Nyanaponika Thera.

Nyanaponika (2005: 32) defines Bare Attention as "the clear and single-minded awareness of what actually happens to us and in us, at the successive moments of perception." Furthermore, Nyanaponika (2005: 44) argues:

> Bare Attention is concerned only with the present. It teaches us what so many have forgotten: to live with full awareness in the Here and Now. [...] Past and future are, for average consciousness, not objects of observation, but of reflection.

Comics composition might then act as an efficient tool to consider past and future as objects of reflection if we invoke once more Spiegleman' statement that "even when you have a short comic, like a three-panel comic, you've got a past, a present and a future as soon as you look at those three boxes.

And that allows you to reflect and compare times." Yet, more strikingly, Nyanaponika's words echo those written by Chris Ware (2015) in his webcomics *Why I Love Comics*, where the artist states:

> We look to "Art" to restore this preadolescent ability to see before the reducing effects of language, forged behind closed eyes, removed us from the immediate present. Spending more and more effort trying to remember and predict our life rather than simply experiencing it, we sense time as moving ever faster, swallowing us in its wake.... And here's where comics come in! Half pictures and half words, comics take the perceptual process of reading and apply it to the comprehension of images ... i.e., one literally reads pictures rather than simply looking at them.... Our minds string these little pictures back together and intuit the hidden "music" that binds them, animating them both in our memories and before our very eyes in a sort of voluntary lucid dream.... Ideally, ultimately even inculcating an empathy with them.... Time, as cut into minute sausage slices and laid out on the page in an array from which larger connections and patterns may be sensed, is the cartoonist's "paint" or "clay." [...] Trying to communicate the hugely incomprehensible yet indescriptibly fine texture of life in little reconstructions sort of mirrors the way we remember it.... Really, when one comes right down to it, in the end, that's all we have: our memories![9]

To remember how to "live with full awareness in the Here and Now" for Nyanaponika, and to experience again "the immediate present" we were removed from in a "voluntary lucid dream" for Ware, mindfulness and comics composition share here similar functionalities. Moreover, they might facilitate the pursuit of a similar goal if we draw an additional parallel between statements by Sousanis and Nyanaponika.

The latter (2005: 44) argues that "Bare Attention, keeping faithfully to its post of observation, watches calmly and without attachment the unceasing march of time;[10] it waits quietly for the things of the future to appear before its eyes, thus to turn into present objects and to vanish again into the past," while Sousanis (2015b: 66–67) states that the comics form, "[t]hrough its multiplicity of approaches for constituting experience, [...] can provide an elevated perspective from which to illuminate the traps of our own making

---

[9] An acrostic sentence formed out of the first words of each panel from Chris Ware's pages reads: "Born before daylight, we spend half our time asleep in darkness trying not to forget ourselves."

[10] This line also echoes aforementioned quote by Sousanis (2015b: 66): "From the forking paths, tangential (and parenthetical), layered and overlapping, intersecting, unbound, moments nested within moments, comics can hold the unflat ways in which thought unfolds."

and offer a means to ... step out." From its post of observation, or elevated perspective, and by learning "to pause, to slow down, and to stop" (Thera, 2005: 42), Bare Attention will also, according to Nyanaponika (2005: 43), "allow us time for the reflection whether in a given situation, activity by deed, word or mental application is necessary or advisable at all."

The aforementioned graphic narrative composed by Thai student Fon offers itself as an apt illustration of this mental process. On her second page, the first panel—originally a square panel presenting the face of the female character with her eyes closed—was enlarged by Fon to cover the full width of the page. It places the detective at top center, with an elevated perspective, right above the line of separation between her two potential choices, accentuating the moral conflict that tears her apart and on which she seems to meditate. Able to display simultaneously, and to draw comparison between, two alternative timelines with much effectiveness and comfort as the nonlinear composition can be "read and appreciated at whatever pace the reader finds most appropriate" (Moore, 2007: 5), Fon fully exploits the principle of *iconic solidarity* defined by Groensteen (2007: 18) as "interdependent images that, participating in a series, present the double characteristic of being separated [...] and which are plastically and semantically over-determined by the fact of their coexistence *in praesentia*" (italic in the original).

Comparing images and alternative choices displayed *in praesentia*, or "in the present time, for the present, of the present position and circumstances" (Lieber and Ramshorn, 1839: 251), readers—and detective Sarah Holmes— somehow experiment mindfulness which is, according to Bialylew (Malcolm, 2015), "really about training our attention to be more present, and through that we develop more awareness about what's going on from moment to moment." Applied to interpersonal communication, it aims at developing the ability "to choose the right words (and actions in a particular) situation," according to Ven. Phuwadol Piyasilo (see Chapter 1).

Applied to engagement with worldly politics, it aims at developing "more inclusiveness to intervene," in not choosing a side as "left and right were never separate," according to Phap Dung (Barclay, 2017). If "Bare Attention brings order into the untidy corners of the mind (by showing) up the numerous and fragmentary perceptions, unfinished lines of thought, confused ideas, stifled emotions, etc., which are daily passing through the mind (as thought-fragments which might) gradually reduce the range and lucidity of consciousness in general, as well as its plasticity, i.e. its capacity of being shaped, transformed and developed" (Thera, 2005: 45), comics composition offers itself as an appropriate tool for "braiding fragments into a cohesive whole," "in a connected space, (where) associations ... stretch web-like across the page" and where "each element is thus: one with everything" (Sousanis, 2015b: 62).

In a survey conducted after the course, student W. S. stated: "I thought that it was easy to create a comic but it's not. We need to think a lot. Think in different dimensions." Sharing with the Buddhist practice of *sati*, the fundamental notion of "recollection," of bringing back to the level of conscious awareness (Recollect, n.d.) what is lost or scattered, comics composition—through its scaffolding and interweaving stages, as a constrained exercise or not—appears then to be a promising tool in developing mindful communication as it foster the ability to think in different dimensions, to be aware of things in relation to things, to reflect and compare times, to reconstitute memory, to "communicate the hugely incomprehensible yet indescriptibly fine texture of life," while—and because—constantly remaining *in praesentia*.

References

Aleixo, P. 2017. "According to a New Study by Researchers at Sheffield Hallam University, Comics Are a Better Educational Resource than Traditional textbooks." (Radio interview), March 2. Available at http://www.bbc.co.uk/programmes/b08hd4ty (accessed on October 26, 2017).

Aleixo, P., and C. Noris. 2010. "The Comic Book Textbook." *Education and Health* 28 (4): 72–74. Available at http://sheu.org.uk/sites/sheu.org.uk/files/imagepicker/1/eh284pa.pdf (accessed on October 26, 2017).

Bakis, M. 2012. *The Graphic Novel Classroom: Powerful Teaching and Learning with Images*. Thousand Oaks, CA: Corwin.

Barclay, E. 2017. *A Buddhist Monk Explains Mindfulness for Times of Conflict*. Available at http://www.vox.com/science-and-health/2016/11/22/13638374/buddhist-monk-mindfulness (accessed on October 26, 2017).

Bartoloni, P. 2013. "The Interstitial Language and Transnational Experience." *Cultural Studies Review* 19 (2): 42–69. Available at https://epress.lib.uts.edu.au/journals/index.php/csrj/article/view/2811/3758 (accessed on October 26, 2017).

Chute, H. 2008. "Comics as Literature? Reading Graphic Narrative." *PMLA* 123 (2): 452–65. Available at http://www.jstor.org/stable/25501865 (accessed on October 26, 2017).

Collins' Online Dictionary. n.d. "Anima." Available at https://www.collinsdictionary.com/dictionary/english/anima (accessed on October 26, 2017).

Comer, K. 2015. "Illustrating Praxis: Comic Composition, Narrative Rhetoric, and Critical Multiliteracies." *Composition Studies* 43 (1): 75–104.

Conan, N. 2011. "'MetaMaus': The Story Behind Spiegelman's Classic." (Radio interview), October 5 Available at http://www.npr.org/2011/10/05/141085597/spiegelmans-metamaus-the-secrets-behind-maus (accessed on October 26, 2017).

Denson, S. 2013. "Afterword: Framing, Unframing, Reframing: Retconning the Transnational Work of Comics." In *Transnational Perspectives on Graphic Narratives: Comics at the*

Crossroads, edited by S. Denson, C. Meyer, and D. Stein, 271–84. London: Bloomsbury Academic.
Denson, S., C. Meyer, and D. Stein. 2013. "Introduction." In *Transnational Perspectives on Graphic Narratives: Comics at the Crossroads*, edited by S. Denson, C. Meyer, and D. Stein, 1–12. London: Bloomsbury Academic.
Duncan, R., and M. J. Smith. 2009. *The Power of Comics: History, Form and Culture*. New York, NY: Continuum.
Eisner, W. 2000. *Comics & Sequential Art*, 19th ed. Tamarac, FL: Poorhouse Press.
Gethin, R. M. L. 2001. *The Buddhist Path to Awakening*. London, UK: Oneworld Publications.
Groensteen, T. 1997. Un premier bouquet de contraintes [A First Bouquet of Constraints]. *OuPus* 1 (1997): 13–58.
———. 2007. *The System of Comics*. Translated by B. Beaty and N. Nguyen. Jackson, MS: University Press of Mississippi. First published in 1999.
Jacobs, D. 2007a. "Marveling at 'The Man Called Nova': Comics as Sponsors of Multimodal Literacy." *College Composition and Communication* 59 (2): 180–205. Available at http://www.jstor.org/stable/20456992 (accessed on October 26, 2017).
———. 2007b. "More than Words: Comics as a Means of Teaching Multiple Literacies." *The English Journal* 96 (3): 19–25. Available at http://www.jstor.org/stable/30047289 (accessed on October 26, 2017).
Kukkonen, K. 2011. "Comics as a Test Case for Transmedial Narratology." *SubStance* 40 (1): 34–52. doi: 10.1353/sub.2011.0005
L'Association. 2007. "Foreword, Mode d'Emploi (Instruction Manual)." In *Moins d'un quart de seconde pour vivre* [Less Than a Quarter of a Second to Live], edited by J. C. Menu and L. Trondheim. France: L'Association.
Lieber, F., and L. Ramshorn. 1839. *Dictionary of Latin Synonymes*. Boston, MA: Charles C. Little and James Brown.
Malcolm, L. 2015. On Being Mindful. ABC.net (Radio interview), May 10. Available at http://www.abc.net.au/radionational/programs/allinthemind/on-being-mindful/6449422 (accessed on October 26, 2017).
McCloud, S. 1999. *Understanding Comics: The Invisible Art*. New York, NY: Paradox Press. First published in 1993.
———. 2006. *Making Comics: Storytelling Secrets of Comics, Manga and Graphic Novels*. New York, NY: HarperCollins.
Miller, A. 2007a. *Reading Bande Dessinée: Critical Approaches to French-language Comic Strip*. Bristol: Intellect Books.
Miller, H. 2007b. "Oubapo: A Verbal/Visual Medium Is Subjected to Constraints." *Word & Image* 23 (2): 117–37. doi: 10.1080/02666286.2007.10435775
Mitsch, R. H. 1997. "Maryse Condé's Mangroves." In *Research in African Literatures* 28/4, 54–70. Bloomington, IN: Indiana University Press.
Moore, A. 2007. *Alan Moore's Writing for Comics*, 4th ed. Rantoul, IL: Avatar Press. First published, Rantoul, IL: Avatar Press, 1993
New London Group. 2000. "A Pedagogy of Multiliteracies: Designing Social Futures." In *Multiliteracies: Literacy Learning and the Design of Social Futures*, edited by B. Cope and M. Kalantzis, 9–37. London, UK: Routledge.
Peeters, B. 1998. *Case, Planche, Récit: Lire la Bande Dessinée* [Panel, Page, Story: Reading Bande Dessinée]. Paris, France: Casterman.
Recollect. n.d. In Merriam-Webster's online dictionary. Available at https://www.merriam-webster.com/dictionary/recollect (accessed on October 26, 2017).

Royal, D. P. 2010. "Foreword." In *Multicultural Comics: From Zap to Blue Beetle*, edited by F. L. Aldama, ix–xi. Austin, TX: University of Texas Press.

Scanlon, M. J. 2015. "The Work of Comics Collaborations: Considerations of Multimodal Composition for Writing Scholarship and Pedagogy." *Composition Studies* 43 (1): 105–30.

Sivaraksa, S. 2015. Edited transcript of his keynote speech at the symposium "Mindful Communication for ASEAN Integration" at Chulalongkorn University, December 14–15, 2015. Available at http://media.wix.com/ugd/cc6e39_0f525005da484afd9a85c65d8a 89c033.pdf (accessed on October 26, 2017).

Sousanis, N. 2015a. "Grids and Gestures: A Comics Making Exercise." *SANE Journal: Sequential Art Narrative in Education* 2 (1, article 8): 1. Available at http://digitalcommons.unl.edu/ sane/vol2/iss1/8/ (accessed on October 26, 2017).

———. 2015b. *Unflattening*. Cambridge, MA: Harvard University Press.

Thera, Nyanaponika. 2005. *The Heart of Buddhist Meditation: A Handbook of Mental Training Based on the Buddha's Way of Mindfulness*. Kandy: Buddhist Publication Society. First published The Word of the Buddha Publishing Committee, 1954; revised ed., London: Rider and Co., 1962.

Trondheim, L. 2009. "Entretien minimaliste." Interview *by L. Massaïa*. Du9, L'autre Bande Dessinée. Available at http://www.du9.org/entretien/entretien-minimaliste-lewis/ (accessed on October 26, 2017).

Ware, C. 2015. "Why I Love Comics." *The New York Times*, October 16. Available at https:// www.nytimes.com/interactive/2014/07/17/books/review/18ware.html?_r=0 (accessed on October 26, 2017).

SECTION E

Mindful Communication and Contemporary Media

19

Practicing Mindful Communication in a Multicultural Society: Case Study of Malaysian News Reporting

Azman Azwan Azmawati, Chai Ming Hock, and Raqib Sofian

After 10 days in detention under the Security Offences (Special Measures) Act (SOSMA), Bersih Chairperson Maria Chin Abdullah was released,[1] but no explanation was given (Kiniroundup, 2016). Maria was detained under Section 4 of SOSMA, to quote the Malaysian Attorney-General Mohamed Apandi Ali, "because she is suspected of being involved in activities that could be detrimental to parliamentary democracy" (Bernama, 2016).

She was detained on November 18, a day before the Bersih 5 rally in Kuala Lumpur, organized by Bersih, an NGO demanding for—among others—a fair and clean election, the very foundation to parliamentary democracy. The news reports in Malaysian newspapers leading up to the rally took a racial undertone, highlighting that the rally was mostly participated by non-Malays (Zulkifli, 2016), with foreign influence (*Utusan Malaysia*, 2016) to challenge the dignity of the Malays. This kind of reporting is expected in Malaysia where almost every issue or event is seen from a racial lens. Of late, this kind of reporting has been even more intense, especially with the current political landscape.

In Malaysia, the state controls the media—both directly and indirectly, through numerous measures—legal, political, and economic. Despite the increased commercialization of the media, which was introduced by former Prime Minister Mahathir Mohamad in mid-1984, the control is still pervasive. Primarily, the Malaysian media industry is still owned, governed, and monopolized by the State.

This chapter looks at religious and political reporting in two Malaysian newspapers—*English* and *Bahasa Malaysia*—a case study within the context of mindful communication versus conflict-driven communication.

---

[1] Available at https://www.malaysiakini.com/news/364446 (accessed on October 27, 2017).

Malaysia, Multiculturalism, and Political Structures

The narrative on Malaysian history often would mention about the multicultural nature of Malaysian society and, often, this nature is simplified into Malay–Chinese–Indian representation. One just needs to observe festive advertisements in the Malaysian media for this simplified representation.

Officially, Malaysia only existed after September 16, 1963, when Malaya, Sabah, Sarawak, and Singapore came together to form Malaysia. Singapore withdrew from the federation in 1965. However, August 31, 1957, was given more prominence in the official narrative of Malaysia, celebrated as the Independence/National Day.

This is important because younger generation of Malaysians were told of a story of how three political parties came together to fight for independence from the British. After all, it was United Malays National Organisation (UMNO), a Malay-based political party, that prevented the British in establishing Malayan Union after World War II. This part of the history is crucial in sustaining the current social and political dominance of the Malays in Malaysian society.

The story goes that not only UMNO managed to prevent the implementation of Malayan Union that would result in the end of the power of the Malay royalty, UMNO also managed to prevent the British from granting all Malayan citizenship based on the principle of jus soli. With the granting of citizenship to limited numbers of non-Malays in Malaya at that time, the political position of the Malays was established.

The question of race is central in any discussion on Malaysia (Crouch, 1980) and would usually touch on the role of the British in the formation of the society. Official narrative would usually discuss about the role of the British in bringing in the Chinese and Indians to support their economic activities, hence changing the composition of the society, which originally consisted of the Malays. This official narrative is important because it is used as a justification for the establishing of Article 153 in the Federal Constitution which enshrined the special positions of the Malays.

This later leads to the implementation of the New Economic Policy (NEP) in 1971, with the "overriding objective to promote national unity through the two-pronged strategy of (a) eradication of poverty by raising income levels and increasing employment opportunities for all Malaysians, irrespective of race, and (b) accelerating the process of restructuring Malaysian society to correct economic imbalance, so as to reduce and eventually eliminate the identification of race with economic function."

In reality, the implementation of NEP and other pro-Malay policies is only possible with the domination of UMNO within Barisan Nasional (BN)—the political coalition that has ruled Malaysia since Independence. BN is a coalition of political parties, spearheaded by UMNO, with other race-based political parties like Malaysian Chinese Association (MCA) and Malaysian Indian Congress (MIC).

After 1971, decisions regarding culture, economy, and politics of Malaysia were no longer decided through compromise within the BN political framework, but decided by UMNO leaders (Von Vors, 1976). The domination of these race-based political parties influenced the public discourse of other facets of the Malaysian life. Each political party represents one major ethnic group in Malaysia, and in each party assembly and general election, race-based demands would be disseminated to their respective supporters. The result of these political arrangements is a highly racialized public discourse during the general election period.

With the media ownership firmly linked to political parties, each political party would speak to their supporters through specific media. For UMNO, their vast network of media and their control of public media through political appointment to ministerial post ensure that their views get prime-time airing and prominent coverage in the press.

In the case of MCA, their commercially successful the *Star* also helps MCA reach their supporters. However, being commercially successful does not necessarily translate to political influence. The *Star* is a pale version of itself since the Ops Lallang in 1987. That year, the publication license of the *Star* was suspended for three months. Since then, the *Star* realized who is their real master.

The sacking of Deputy Prime Minister and Finance Minister Anwar Ibrahim by Prime Minister Mahathir Mohamad in 1998 marked a turning point in the Malaysia political landscape and the beginning of the biggest political crisis for UMNO. Subsequent general elections in 1999, 2004, 2008, and 2013 saw a various degree of success of the opposition political parties in coming together to deny the ruling coalition BN their sacred two-thirds majority in the Parliament. Given the optimism surrounding this *new politics*, critics argue that Malaysian politics had matured and ready to move beyond race-based politics.

Even though there were attempts at introducing a more inclusive political culture when Abdullah Ahmad Badawi took over the leadership from Mahathir Mohamad in 2003, Abdullah later admitted to having had underestimate the resistance for change within UMNO (Welsh and Chin, 2013).

Media in Malaysia

Malaysia has some of the toughest censorship laws in the world. The authorities imposed major control over the media and use "national security" to ensure that "harmony" is maintained in the country. Print and electronics media are subjected to many laws and regulations. The government is keen to insulate the largely Muslim population from what it considers harmful foreign influences. News is subject to censorship; entertainment shows and music videos regularly fall foul of the censors, and scenes featuring swearing and kissing are routinely removed.

The broadcasting system in Malaysia comprises public-funded institutions and private enterprises; however, both are highly aligned to the ruling government and consequently, support all policies including plans stipulated by the ruling parties. Currently, State-owned Radio Television Malaysia (RTM), which is the only public service broadcaster in Malaysia, is under the supervision, control, and ownership of the Ministry of Information, Communications and Culture Malaysia (MICCM) and operates two TV networks and many radio services. Television in Malaysia has always played the role of the state's mouthpiece, and public television has always been used as the government's apparatus for nation-building. This includes the Malay and English newspapers as well as many television channels; it is closely linked to the UMNO, the leading party of the ruling coalition.

Although the print industry generally is dominated by private ownership, the majority of print outlets are controlled either by political parties in the ruling coalition or by businesses with political connections to the BN. Huaren Management, which is associated with another BN member, the MCA, monopolizes Chinese-language newspapers. Despite the BN's insistence that mainstream newspapers are impartial, the owners' political and business interests often lead to self-censorship by journalists (Freedom House, 2015).

The Communications and Multimedia Act (CMA) gives the communications and multimedia minister a large measure of discretionary authority over broadcast licenses. The BN reviewed existing media licensing and censorship laws in 2012, and a resulting amendment to the 1984 Printing Presses and Publications Act (PPPA) repealed a provision that had required all publishers and printing firms to obtain an annual operating permit. However, the revision left all other restrictions in place, including the government's authority to grant or deny license applications and to revoke the required licenses at any time without judicial review. The Home Affairs Ministry may also issue "show cause" letters, which require newspapers to explain certain articles or face suspension or revocation of their permits (Freedom House, 2016).

Conflict-driven Journalism Versus Mindful Journalism: Malaysian Context

Johan Galtung and Mari Holmboe Ruge (1965) is perhaps the most cited work on news values. Their seminal work later leads to these generally and commonly accepted criteria of news values—impact, conflict, timeliness, proximity, prominence, currency, human interest, and the unusual (see, e.g., Conley and Lamble, 2006; Masterton, 2005). In journalism school, students were taught that these news values formed the criteria for selection, and news organization—being a commercial, more than a community entity—would select news with conflict elements in order to sell their newspaper.

In the context of Malaysia, conflict would also include the contest for limited political, economic, and social resources, and hence, lead to news that is promoting the gain of one community over social harmony. This is usually highlighted in newspapers as the role played by politicians in securing these resources, for example, news report on politicians from MCA securing the building of another Chinese language school in Malaysia. This kind of reporting would produce circles of demands from politicians representing other communities, and would continue to be reported so as to establish these politicians' relevance in the ethnocentric political framework in Malaysia.

It is a cliche to say that the media has an important role to play in nation-building. Media is one of the channel in which the ruling elites reinterpret the past and define the future. It makes a big difference between an all-inclusive or an exclusive label in the context of reporting on communities in Malaysia.

In the reporting of election issues in Malaysia, very little is explained; rather, most reasoning was taken as a given. Focus is usually on the ethnic background of the candidates and electorates. Election issues usually involve framing of issues as a challenge and a zero-sum game. The gain of one ethnic group is portrayed as a loss to another ethnic group. This approach of reporting is important in order to build a competitive political environment and to ensure that in this competitive environment, there would be political leaders that would lead the fight for economic good for each ethnic community.

In the reporting, it is often pointed out that the Malay communities are economically inferior due to their past experience with the colonial power. Other ethnic groups are said to have a head start in economic development due to their advantage position being involved in economic activities from the beginning. Even though this simplified account is questionable, this is the narrative being presented to Malaysians in regards to the socioeconomic development as a nation. This narration is being reproduced in order to justify the ongoing affirmative action policies for the Malays and other indigenous people. In every general election held in Malaysia, racialized election issues would form part of the election campaign of the ruling coalition. This form of campaign is expected in a political system which is based on political representation on race. The next section will discuss the racialized reporting of general election issues by the mainstream newspapers—the platform on which the ruling coalition channeled their election campaign to the voters.

Case Studies: Religious and Political Reporting

The 2013 general election (GE13) was the first general election fought by the new prime minister of Malaysia, Mohd Najib Tun Razak, and the 13th since Malaysian independence. Najib, who is also the president of UMNO took over the leadership of the party from Abdullah Ahmad Badawi in 2009 after the ruling coalition BN lost its two-thirds majority in the Parliament during the 2008 general election, prompting the early retirement of Abdullah.

A new leader calls for a new vision. Under Najib, 1Malaysia became the slogan to draw support after the divisive political campaign of the 2008 general election. 1Malaysia is used to reflect a country united in diversity, even though in reality, Malaysian society is much divided along the ethic and religious lines (Chin, 2010). Moreover, 1Malaysia meant different things to different communities. For the non-Malays, 1Malaysia is a signal that the government recognized them as "full citizens," whereas the Malays took it as "maintaining status quo, without changes to the special position and privileges" (Chin, 2012). In the economic front, Najib launched the Economic Transformation Programme (ETP), and together with the 1Malaysia, a series of programs and initiatives were launched. Leading up to the GE13, an advertisement claim that BN had launched over 200 programs under the 1Malaysia umbrella.

Prior to the GE13, the second largest component party in BN—MCA, representing the interest of the Chinese in the BN framework—only managed to win seven parliamentary seats, a pale performance compared to the Chinese majority opposition political party, DAP that managed to secure 38 seats.

Realizing that the challenge to secure votes—regardless of the ethnic background—would be tougher, Najib sought to secure the Chinese and Indians votes directly, even though traditionally these are tasked to MCA and MIC within the BN coalition. The 2008 general election showed that

MCA had lost its legitimacy in representing the interests of the Chinese community (Yeoh, 2010).

In most news reports in Malaysia, the ethnic background of individuals or groups are stated explicitly. Some samples of these news reports include "1,500 Indians admitted to pre-U courses" (*The Star*, 2013a), "Najib can help Indians, says Hindraf" (*New Straits Times*, 2013a), and "Scrapping to woo Indians" (Dorairaj, 2013).

In the 2013 general election campaign, both the ruling coalition and opposition political parties made statements that racialized issues. Generally, issues such as education and business would be linked to Chinese community in Malaysia. In every general election, MCA will use these two issues to remind the Chinese community that their interests would be taken care of if they continue their support to BN. For example, the *Star* reports that "a new Chinese secondary school would be built in Pokok Sena [Kedah] to meet the need of Chinese community" (*The Star*, 2013b). This statement reflects BN's simple assumption that only Chinese students attend Chinese schools; it does not discuss the reason national schools lose out to Chinese schools. That kind of reporting will require more in-depth writing and will produce articles that will not fit into the national narrative such as the popularity of Chinese schools among non-Chinese parents. Hence, the more "acceptable" news reports will be to frame the issue within the need of a specific community, with their political parties "fighting" for their interests. That kind of reporting fits nicely into the tri-ethnic framework of BN.

During the GE13, it is common for newspapers to only mention Malay, Chinese, and Indians in their news reports, and only occasionally highlight other ethnic communities. In their feature articles, newspapers also generalized these communities to be homogeneous, with common and shared views. These assumptions and generalizations by politicians and the media fit into the tri-ethnic framework of BN. Featured articles would discuss the voting pattern of each community separately, with headlines like "More Indians support BN" (*New Straits Times*, 2013b), "Parties singing and dancing to the tune of Indians" (Letchumanan, 2013), "Remember good deeds of government, Chinese urged" (Mail and Chan, 2013), and "Barisan goes all out to woo Chinese voters in Kedah" (*New Straits Times*, 2013c). These kind of articles assumed that each community differs in terms of characters, causes, and supports.

Malaysian Chinese are assumed to be generally pro-opposition. An article written by the *Star* group editor Wong Chun Wai claimed that "80 percent of Chinese community would vote [opposition]" (Wong, 2013). This article is not backed by any objective study and provides no empirical proof to back up such claim. Instead of seeking to understand the Chinese community, the practice of journalism in Malaysia merely makes assertion and generalization. This kind of reporting promotes antagonism, not understanding, and a reinforced racial stereotype that Chinese are generally pro-opposition, and ungrateful to the ruling coalition despite all that was done for them.

Besides being pro-opposition, Chinese community is also portrayed as emotional. The *Star* highlighted a statement by Johor chief minister saying that "tendency of the Chinese community to vote through emotion has reached an unhealthy level" (Kong, 2013). The *Star* confidently declared that "it is obvious that the Chinese community in Johor is not with Barisan Nasional" (Tan, 2013a).

A conflict-driven journalism tends to highlight differences between communities in Malaysia, pitting one community against another. This seems to be a common practice in Malaysian journalism to highlight political alliance of each community, hence, this kind of reporting is not just stereotypical, they are also promoting antagonism between communities. For example, in an article by Joceline Tan of the *Star*, she characterizes political rivalry in Malaysia as Chinese community supporting one side and the Malay community supporting the other side. She claims that "the presence of Chinese at DAP talks had driven Malays back to supporting [BN]" (Tan, 2013b). This unsubstantiated claim implies that the Chinese and Malay communities are at odds with each other. The writer repeats her assertion in another article, claiming that "the wave of Chinese support for the opposition had caused the Malay wave surging towards [BN]" (Tan, 2013c).

Besides highlighting differences between communities, a conflict-driven journalism practiced by the *Star* also promotes threats between communities. For example, the *Star* group editor Wong Chun Wai writes to remind Malay voters that if "there is a dramatic shift of Malay community to [the opposition], this would end BN rule after 56 years" (Wong, 2013). This reminder, together with other statements like opposition political party DAP supporters are "mostly Chinese" and that the opposition are "sure to capture [federal capital] Putrajaya," remind the Malays that their political dominance is under threat.

Another divisive political campaign strategy of the BN is to separately target the same community through two newspapers—*New Straits Times* (NST) owned by UMNO and the *Star* owned by MCA. NST would highlight the failure of Parti Islam SeMalaysia (PAS) to include hudud law in the opposition election manifesto as a sign of PAS conceding to the demand of DAP, hence betraying the aspiration of the Malay community. On the other hand, the *Star* would highlight the persistence of PAS to implement hudud law and this is a mistake for DAP to be part of the opposition political cooperation.

The Malay community is reminded that PAS-DAP cooperation is a loss for them because PAS would be betrayed by DAP and will have to compromise in their struggle. This approach is designed to reduce Malay support toward PAS and DAP. UMNO deputy president, Muhyiddin Yassin, reminded the Malay community that PAS would be played out by DAP, and DAP will dominate the opposition (Sulaiman and Abdullah, 2013). This statement is in stark contrast with MCA president's statement which claims that PAS would lead the opposition—divide and rule at its best.

The *Star* highlighted PAS leader Dr Haron Din's statement that PAS would implement the hudud law if the opposition came into power even if DAP opposed it (Sira et al., 2013). Haron was reported as saying that he was confident that DAP would accept the implementation of hudud law because DAP was prepared to use the PAS party symbol to contest in the GE13 (at this point, DAP was deregistered due to some membership irregularities in their annual general assembly). The following day, the *Star* reported that a few PAS leaders have said that "Islamic jurisdiction have always been a party's agenda" (Farik et al., 2013). To further drive fear into the Chinese community of the opposition and to portray Chinese community as fearing the hudud law, MCA president Chua Soi Lek reminded the Chinese community that "even though we cannot force non-Muslim [community] to accept Islam views, by voting for opposition, the opposition would exactly do that" (*The Star*, 2013c).

Case Study: Church Raid

The incident that occurred on August 3, 2011, had sparked a variety of reactions in the media. It was reported that the Selangor Islamic Affairs Department (JAIS) along with a team of the Royal Malaysian Police (PDRM) carried out an inspection on the church in Damansara Utama on receiving a tip-off.

Based on the information received by a tip-off, there were 12 Muslims attending a dinner to break their day-long fast at the church and there were also some elements of suspicion. For example, words such as "Quran" and "pray" were used during the Church's public sermon session. In addition, attempts were made to prevent the search from being carried out and disposing of evidence according to the Utusan Malaysia report (*Utusan Malaysia*, 2011a, 2011b, 2011c).

The ceremony held at the church was "raided" for allegedly trying to convert Malay Muslims, which is an offense under the country's constitution which states: "Islam is the religion of the Federation but other religions may be practiced in peace and harmony in any part of the Federation" [Article 3 (1)].

In the context of Malaysia, the relation between Islam and Malay, called "Melayu," is very close. It is clearly stated in the Federal Constitution, that "Malay" means "a person who professes the religion of Islam, habitually speaks the Malay language, and conforms to Malay custom" (Article 160 of the Constitution). Thus, in the Constitution, it clearly states that being Malay one must be a Muslim and it is strictly prohibited to profess a religion other than Islam (Johana et al., 2010: 92–93).

Article 11 of the Constitution also provides for two cases: (a) every person has the right to profess and practice his religion and, subject to Clause (4), to propagate it. Clause (4) stated that the State law and in respect of the Federal Territories of Kuala Lumpur and Labuan, federal law may control or restrict the propagation of any religious doctrine or belief among persons professing the religion of Islam (Johana et al., 2010: 96).

In an environment such as in Malaysia, consisting of various races and religions, added with a feeling of "Islamophobia" deep in the current society, especially by the non-Muslims (Rashaad, 2016), such cases may lead to conflicts. Therefore, this section will discuss about how *Utusan Malaysia*, a prominent Malay newspaper, and the *Star*, an English newspaper, reported on this issue.

The Star

As was observed by the author, the *Star* took a moderate approach in reporting on this issue. The *Star* expressed a clear stance in criticizing the actions taken by JAIS, which described it as hasty and had brought trouble to national harmony. JAIS was issuing contradictory statements due to a source that said the event had nothing to do with proselytizing any party but only a HIV charity fund.

> No religious official anywhere should be so inflammatory, much less have the temerity to commit such an outrageous act. That goes double for a multi-racial, multi-cultural and multi-religious Malaysia in the 21st century. (*The Star*, 2011)

> It is unprecedented. The operation by the Selangor state religious department (Jais) on the Damansara Utama Methodist Church on Wednesday is shameful and a blot on our history. (Wong, 2011)

> Riddles from this latest incident may turn into waves of hatred that travel beyond racial borders, and thus threaten our unity. This renders futile ongoing

painstaking efforts to nurture our national solidarity that began a few decades ago. Result: unity remains shaky and elusive. Like it or not, we have to admit this harsh reality. (Ahmad, 2011)

As it turns out, the JAIS operation on Damansara Utama Methodist Church was a grotesque showcase of self-contradictions by the perpetrators. They claimed they had evidence of unlawful proselytising to Muslims, but we know the occasion was a fundraising event for HIV support activities. (*The Star*, 2011)

The *Star* also criticized the state government (then consisting of PAS,[2] Keadilan,[3] and DAP[4]) who were allegedly failing to address the conflict. There were two different opinions; some members in PAS supported the action taken by JAIS, while the others rejected it. In this situation, PAS was seen as being in dilemma whether to gain the support of non-Muslims or champion the Muslims community, especially from the extreme conservatives.

The Selangor Government has considerable explaining to do, besides expressing regret over the incident. Why is such zealotry upheld by a Pakatan Rakyat state councillor, why is Mentri Besar Tan Sri Khalid Ibrahim so clueless, and why are his political allies so disunited in condemning the raid? (*The Star*, 2011)

However, recent events and more, especially PAS', hesitant and divided response to the Selangor Islamic Department (Jais) raid on the DUMC church would suggest that the party is not ready for prime-time. (Karim, 2011)

The former's divided approach—with Selangor exco Hassan Ali supporting the raid and Shah Alam MP Khalid Samad condemning it—indicates that the Islamist party's much-vaunted move to the centre has not been as smooth as their insiders wish us to believe. (Karim, 2011)

PAS wants to get mileage from the incident, keep its more conservative members happy that it is not seen as going after Dr Hassan and at the same time win over the non-Muslim voters that it needs if it is to win in the many mixed constituencies its candidates hope to contest. (Kuppusamy, 2011)

---

[2] The Pan-Malaysian Islamic Party (Malay: Parti Islam Se-Malaysia), commonly known as PAS, is an Islamist and opposition political party in Malaysia.

[3] Parti Keadilan Rakyat, often known simply as Keadilan or PKR, is a centrist multiracial political party in Malaysia formed in 2003 and it was formed for Anwar Ibrahim and his family justice and promotes an agenda with a strong emphasis on social justice and anti-corruption. Anwar Ibrahim is a Malaysian politician who was the leader of the Opposition between 2008 and 2015.

[4] The Democratic Action Party, or DAP is a multiracial, center-left Malaysian political party advocating social democracy and secularism, social justice, social liberalism, progressivism, and multiracialism.

However, the *Star* was seen as playing a big role as a peacemaker in the conflict by publishing articles in the form of advices and lessons to the audience. The *Star* urged the people to think what lessons can be drawn from those cases. The *Star* also called the people to obey the command of the Sultan of Selangor, Sultan Sharafuddin Idris Shah to stop discussing the issue in public and refocus on harmonizing the relationship between the people, especially in the state of Selangor.

> Obviously, the culprits in the present case are the ignorant, the obstinate, the opportunists and the extremists from both Muslim and non-Muslim sides. They must not be allowed to administer or interfere with religious matters if we are to live in peace and harmony. (Ahmad, 2011)

> We must strive to be progressive enough to appreciate that it is good to learn the religions of fellow Malaysians. We can argue about the superiority of one's religion but it is good to be religious and God-fearing regardless of one's belief. (Wong, 2011)

> I call upon all religious leaders and followers to exercise more wisdom and to properly practise their respective religions with mutual love, respect and sincerity. (Ahmad, 2011)

In fact, although the *Star* generally criticized the action taken by JAIS, it published an article (a letter from a reader) which asked the non-Muslims to be sensitive on issues involving Islam with regard to dos and don'ts in Islam.

> I would like to share my experience with fellow Christians and encourage them to exercise both wisdom and restraint when planning and organising activities involving Muslims, even if we feel there's "nothing wrong with it...." As tolerant Malaysians, Christians must realise several important truths with regards to Islam. I learnt from an Islamic scholar from the Institute for Islamic Understanding Malaysia that we should never act in words or deeds that may render a Muslim as "melanggar aqidah" (going against his faith) among his fellow brethren. (Thirunavukkarasu, 2011)

On the same note, the *Star* urged the government to set up a commission, so that such incidents did not recur and everyone get to know the truth. This was because such issues involving religion could cause conflict in a society comprising various races and religions.

> We may urge an independent commission to be set up to conduct a fairer investigation. If this takes place, all parties must extend their utmost cooperation and not hide the minutest details of facts and explanation surrounding the "raid." (Ahmad, 2011)

Utusan Malaysia

Based on the analysis conducted, *Utusan Malaysia* (the mainstream Bahasa Malaysia newspaper) played the political cards by criticizing the state government, especially the Islamic party PAS, which was portrayed as incompetent in championing the Malay Muslims' rights. This opportunity was fully utilized to demonstrate the weaknesses of opposition politicians, especially the Malay Muslims in defending Islam.

Dalam isu JAIS, ternyata kerajaan campuran pembangkang di Selangor gagal menanganinya mengikut semangat perlembagaan negara. Maka jelas, Menteri Besar Selangor, Khalid Ibrahim untuk kesekian kalinya, gagal menjaga kepentingan umat Islam. Dia hanya mengikut telunjuk pemimpin-pemimpin DAP. Dayus sekali. (Utusan Malaysia, 2011a)

(Translation): On the issues of JAIS, the oppositions in Selangor have failed to handle it in accordance to the spirit of the constitution. Clearly, the Chief Minister of Selangor, Khalid Ibrahim, has failed to protect the interests of the Muslim community for the umpteenth time. He only follows the dictates of the DAP leaders. Cowards!

Hamba lazimnya mengelakkan diri daripada menyebut nama, tetapi kali ini keperluan mendesak demi kebenaran. Maka izinkan hamba menyebut nama Menteri Besar Selangor, Tan Sri Khalid Ibrahim dan Ahli Parlimen Shah Alam, Khalid Abdul Samad yang menjadi sasaran utama perhimpunan anti-murtad dan menyokong tindakan JAIS itu. Dalam mencari pengaruh untuk mendapatkan undi pilihan raya, masyarakat Islam yang berpecah belah telah merelakan diri mereka bersahabat karib dan tunduk kepada tuntutan bukan Islam, khususnya orang-orang Kristian. (*Utusan Malaysia*, 2011b)

(Translation): I usually refrain myself from naming names, but this is an urgent time for the truth. So, let me mention the Chief Minister of Selangor, Tan Sri Khalid Ibrahim, and a member of the Shah Alam Parliament, Khalid Abdul Samad, who were the main targets of the anti-apostasy rally and supported JAIS's actions. In seeking votes for the election, the divided Muslims community had volunteered to be friends and bowed to the demands of the non-Muslims, especially the Christians.

Terserlah sejak awal lagi tindakan Menteri Besar, Tan Sri Abdul Khalid Ibrahim terlihat tidak bijak. Dalam nada mempertikai tindakan JAIS itu beliau menyebutnya sebagai serbuan. Sedangkan Exconya, Datuk Dr Hasan Mohd. Ali yang membela tindakan JAIS menakrifnya sebagai pemeriksaan. (Zulkefli, 2011)

(Translation): It can be seen from the beginning that the decision made by the Menteri Besar, Tan Sri Abdul Khalid Ibrahim was not wise. He used the word ambush, while his Excellency, Datuk Dr Hasan Mohd Ali defended JAIS by using the word checking.

Agak terkeliru dan mendukacitakan Menteri Besar Selangor Tan Sri Abdul Khalid Ibrahim dalam keadaan yang tergesa-gesa meminta ampun dan maaf kepada pihak gereja di atas serbuan yang dilakukan oleh pihak JAIS tanpa mengetahui akan perkara sebenar di sebalik kejadian tersebut. (Jamal, 2011)

(Translation): It was somewhat confusing and disappointing when the Chief Minister of Selangor, Tan Sri Abdul Khalid Ibrahim, was in a hurry to ask for forgiveness from the church's authority for the raid that was done by JAIS without knowing the truth behind the incident.

Utusan Malaysia continuously tried to provoke the conflict between the political parties and did not make any attempt to calm the situation. PAS was portrayed as weak and easily being controlled by DAP in handling the issue. *Utusan Malaysia* also attacked politicians from Pakatan Rakyat, especially the Malay Muslims as most of them remained silent on the issue. They were also allegedly failing to fight for Islam in Selangor, particularly on this issue.

Sebelum ini, Pas memberi alasan berkawan dengan DAP kerana ingin berdakwah dan memperkenalkan Islam kepada pemimpin DAP seterusnya mengislamkan mereka dalam masa terdekat. Soalnya Pemimpin DAP mana yang sudah masuk Islam sejak Pas mula menjalin hubungan politk dengan DAP? (Mashitah, 2011)

(Translation): Before this, PAS gave reasons for wanting to be friends with DAP to preach and introduce Islam to the leader of DAP and Islamize them in the near future. The questions is, which DAP leader has converted into Islam since PAS began a relationship with DAP?"

Sepatutnya dalam isu-isu melibatkan kepentingan umat Islam dan Islam kita bersatu. Tetapi sebaliknya, demi untuk meraih undi, kepentingan puak dan parti politik Pas sanggup merugikan kepentingan sendiri, bahkan menjual agama. Lalu kita balik bertanya kepada Pas, apakah tolakan mereka supaya berdamai dan bersatu oleh UMNO, padahal ini sangat diperintahkan oleh Islam, dalam masa yang sama lebih rela bersekongkol dengan pihak yang jelas-jelas ekstrem, iaitu DAP.... (Zaini, 2011)

(Translation): We should be united when it comes to the issues involving the interests of the Muslim community. Instead, in order to win votes, PAS were willing to lose and sell the religion. We need to ask PAS a question, why are they rejecting to stay united and make peace with UMNO, when it is highly ordered in Islam, at the same time, more willingly to collaborate with the extremes, which are the DAP members....

> *Malah yang menyedihkan, para pemimpin utama Pas tunduk membiarkan Islam digugat hanya kerana perhitungan undi dan pilihan raya.* (*Utusan Malaysia*, 2011a)

(Translation): It is sad to see how PAS let Islam to be dictated in the name of elections and votes.

> *Seolah-olah kiblat golongan tersebut adalah DAP, junjungan besar mereka adalah Lim Kit Siang dan agama mereka adalah pluralisme. Pendekatan mereka memudaratkan Islam dan lebih bahaya berbanding pemimpin-pemimpin ajaran sesat seperti Ayah Pin.* (*Utusan Malaysia*, 2011a)

(Translation): It is as though that they worship DAP and Lim Kit Siang, and their religion is pluralisme. Their approach is dangerous to Islam, in fact, worse than the other faith issues such as the case of Ayah Pin.

In this case, *Utusan Malaysia* clearly supported the actions taken by JAIS and criticized the church which was portrayed as not respecting the Malaysia Constitution and did not respect the sensitivity of Muslims. The church was seen as if it was trying to challenge Islam and Muslims by inviting the 12 Malay Muslims to the church, and there were allegations that they were trying to proselytize. This situation led to the existing conflicts becoming more complicated, especially among the Muslims and non-Muslims. *Utusan Malaysia* also was being very biased toward JAIS without giving space to the church to provide clarification on its part on the case.

> *Perlembagaan Persekutuan yang memperuntukkan Islam adalah "agama bagi Persekutuan" dan Perkara 11 (4) yang melarang agama lain disebarkan kepada penganut Islam. Ia sekali gus menimbulkan persoalan mengenai kedudukan Islam sebagai agama rasmi negara. Kontroversi terbaru ini juga boleh menjejaskan keharmonian masyarakat kerana ia termasuk perkara sensitif yang boleh menjejaskan hubungan kaum di negara ini.* (Mohd Ayop, 2011)

(Translation): The Federal Constitution in Malaysia has allocated Islam as the "religion of the Federation" and Article 11 (4) which prohibits the spread of other religions to the Muslims. It then raises the question about the position of Islam as the official religion. This latest controversy could also affect the social harmony as it includes sensitive matters that could affect the race relations in this country.

> *Berdasarkan undang-undang, meskipun kebebasan beragama menjadi hak setiap orang, kebebasan itu tidak boleh dijadikan alasan untuk mempengaruhi orang Islam agar menukarkan agamanya. Berdakwah atau mempengaruhi orang Islam supaya menukarkan agama adalah satu tindakan salah dan boleh didakwa di mahkamah.* (Aziz, 2011)

(Translation): Although the Malaysian law allows its citizens to choose their religion, it is not the reason for the non-Muslims to persuade Muslims to change their religion as it is not allowed in Islam. One can be charged in the Court for doing so.

Gerakan memurtadkan umat Islam telah lama berlaku. Apa yang penting bukannya angka, tetapi percubaan dan keberanian mencabar kedaulatan agama Islam. Kita tahu, tetapi buat-buat tidak tahu. (Mohd Ridhuan, 2011)

(Translation): The movement to proselytize the Muslims has been going for quite some time. What's important now is not the number, but the attempts and bravery have challenged the sovereignty of Islam. We do know, but we pretend to not care about it.

Semua peruntukan tersebut sudah jelas dan sejak awal Perlembagaan Persekutuan dirangka semua kaum telah sepakat menerima peruntukan itu. Malangnya ada kumpulan atau pertubuhan-pertubuhan agama yang menunjukkan kedegilan mereka yang seolah-olah mahu mencabar Perkara 11(4). (Mohd Ayop, 2011)

(Translation): Such provisions are clear, and since the beginning of the Federal Constitution, everyone has agreed to accept the provision. Unfortunately, there are groups or religious organizations that showed their stubbornness which seemed to challenge Article 11 (4).

In essence, all parties were asked to improve the image of JAIS, as its image was alleged to have been tarnished because of the case, but there was no call for the same to the church.

Hakikatnya, tindakan JAIS ke atas Gereja Methodist Damansara Utama di Petaling Jaya itu berlandaskan kepada prinsip dan tanggungjawab agensi penguatkuasaan itu untuk mempertahankan akidah umat Islam serta kesucian agama ini. Akidah bukan bahan dagangan politik, ia tidak boleh dijual beli. (Azman, 2011)

(Translation): Essentially, JAIS's action was to defend the sacredness of Islam as it is the department's responsibilities to protect Islam from any kind of harms, threat and anything of that nature. Faith is not a political trade, it cannot be bought.

Maka JAIS atau mana-mana jabatan agama perlu diberi ruang melaksanakan tugas sebagaimana pemeriksaan dan pemantauan terhadap pelbagai aktiviti lain yang mencurigakan. (*Utusan Malaysia*, 2011c)

(Translation): JAIS or any other religious department must be given the space to check on or observe any activities deemed as dangerous to the faith.

Last but not least, *Utusan Malaysia* also reported on this issue by trying to play the racial sentiment by asking the audience, mainly the Muslim Malays, to unite and fight for Islam. They neglected to mention other races together building a harmonious country. Such reporting could worsen the relationship between the Muslims and non-Muslims as it promoted racism which was not in tandem for citizen's integration efforts by the government.

Tidak kisah kalau kita mahu berbeza fahaman politik, menyertai NGO berlainan atau tidak berada dalam mana-mana kelompok tetapi apabila kedudukan umat Islam mula diganggu gugat kita harus mengarak bersama-sama panji-panji 'Tiada tuhan yang disembah melainkan Allah dan Nabi Muhammad itu pesuruh Allah. (Zulkefli, 2011)

(Translation): It does not matter if we want to have different political ideologies, being in a different NGO or not aligned to any parties but when Islam is being questioned, we must be in solidarity in the name of Allah dan Muhammad.

Inilah masanya untuk mengikuti jejak Fatah dan Hamas yang berdamai, lalu kita pertahankan agama dan perkukuhkan kekuatan kita. Apabila kita bersatu dan teguh percayalah tidak akan ada mana-mana pihak berani bersikap kurang ajar, biadap dan mengambil kesempatan meraup keuntungan. Strategi mereka memang licik dan penyamaran mereka memang halus.Mudah-mudahan kita tidak terus buta! (Zaini, 2011).

(Translation): This is the time to follow the footsteps of Fatah and Hamas (two political parties in Palestine) in making peace, then we defend our faith and strengthen our power. When we are united and firm, do believe that there will not be any party which will dare to be rude and take the opportunity to reap the benefits. Their strategy is cunning and their camouflage is pretty good. Hopefully, we do not continue to be blinded!

Jika orang bukan Islam mahu umat Islam menghormati amalan agama mereka maka mereka juga harus menghormati dan mematuhi agama Islam, khusus Perkara 3 dan Perkara 11 (4) yang terkandung di dalam perlembagaan negara. Mereka seharusnya berasa bersyukur kerana Malaysia adalah di antara negara yang memberikan kebebasan agama kepada orang bukan Islam. (Aziz, 2011)

(Translation): If the non-Muslims want Muslims to respect their religious practices, they must also respect and abide by the religion of Islam, specifically Article 3 and Article 11 (4) of the Constitution. *They* should be grateful that Malaysia is among the countries that provide the freedom of religion to non-Muslims.

Conclusions and Recommendations for Mindful Communication

A conflict-driven journalism which also tends to highlight differences between communities in Malaysia, pitting one community against another, is a common practice in Malaysian journalism. This kind of reporting not only highlights the political alliances of the newspapers, it is also promoting hostility between communities.

As demonstrated by the case studies, the print media must change their approach in reporting if serious nation-building agenda is to be promoted. While the current government is propagating nation-building as the way to move ahead, the media ironically is heading backward resorting to conflict-driven journalism.

As mentioned earlier, the narrative on Malaysian history often talked about the multicultural nature of Malaysian society and often, this nature is simplified into Malay–Chinese–Indian representation. In terms of ownership and control, the state mostly controls the media—both directly and indirectly—through numerous measures, legal, political, and economic. Primarily, the Malaysian media industry is still owned, governed, and monopolized by the state. With the media ownership firmly linked to political parties, each political party would speak to their supporters through specific media.

This, in turn, results into racial-based reporting which eventually promotes antagonism between communities as demonstrated by the political and religious reporting. The Malay newspapers playing the racial sentiment by asking the readers, mainly the Muslim Malays, to unite and fight for Islam is mostly the order of the day. They neglected to include other races together building a harmonious country. Such reporting could worsen the relationship between the Muslims and non-Muslims as it promotes racism which is not the government's aspiration for citizen's integration.

Malaysian journalists must be educated to take the approach of mindful journalism in their profession in order to represent harmonious perspectives. The conflict-driven approach which has become the norm in the Malaysian religious and political reporting must be changed to become a routine in the daily process of truth reporting. Journalists must abide by the ethical codes and principles which mostly are guided by good religious teaching. Informed journalism practice will help to create a better media environment domestically and in the world, generally.

Journalism oriented toward peace, humanity, truth, and solutions are attributions that help to foster a harmonious environment. The framework of ethical values, as opposed to "what sells, sell" value, will accommodate more to a better mindful society. Mindfulness is no more an alien concept but a normal daily concept in many areas which must be inculcated in the journalism practices too.

As much as we are aware and understand the constraints of the invisible hands exerting their power in the media, the media itself must be aware and advocate peace and mindful journalism in enhancing the growth for others. Media definitely has played many roles in the post-independent Malaysian journey in becoming a progressive and developing nation, and hence the role of public informer/educator to maintain harmony and eliminate racial tension among ethnics must be heightened. Media as a catalyst for public discussion is critical for public policies that are not only relevant to ethnic communities but the nation as a whole, as the country is aiming to achieve its Vision 2020 of becoming a developed nation, which is around the corner.

Media as the public platform in ensuring further growth of Malaysia in terms of politics, economy, and society must self-realize that for a healthy environment to grow, its roles are very crucial and pertinent. The two newspapers studied, demonstrated that conflict-driven journalism is still the practice. And that must be changed through its own policies as an information provider and educator to the Malaysian society. Mindful journalism will not only create one harmonious society but also a multiracial society with high level of tolerance and respect for each other. It is obvious that with the state ownership and controlling factor, the opportunity to make certain changes will be challenging but the journalists can start by doing their part continuously with "mindfulness" in their spirit and daily practices.

References

Ahmad, Wan Azhar Wan. 2011. "Let Wisdom and Reason Prevail." *The Star*, August 30. Available at https://www.thestar.com.my/opinion/columnists/ikim-views/2011/08/30/let-wisdom-and-reason-prevail/ (accessed on October 25, 2016).

Aziz, Jamaludin Mhd Tahir. 2011. "Sederhana Selesai Kemelut." *Utusan Malaysia*, August 12. Available at http://ww1.utusan.com.my/utusan/info.asp?y=2011&dt=0812&pub=Utusan_Malaysia&sec=Rencana&pg=re_01.htm (accessed on October 12, 2016).

Azman, Anuar. 2011. "Waspada, Wujud Usaha Memurtadkan Umat Islam Di Selangor." *Utusan Malaysia*, October 11. Available at http://ww1.utusan.com.my/utusan/info.asp?y=2011&dt=1011&pub=Utusan_Malaysia&sec=Rencana&pg=re_05.htm (accessed on November 11, 2016).

Bernama. 2016. "A-G: Maria's Detention in Accordance With Law." *The Star*, Malaysia, November 25. Available at http://www.thestar.com.my/news/nation/2016/11/25/apandi-maria-detention-in-accordance-with-law/ (accessed on December 25, 2016).

Chin, James. 2010. "Malaysian Chinese Association Politics a Year Later: Crisis of Political Legitimacy." *The Round Table* 99 (407): 153–62.

———. 2012. "Malaysia Politics: Anwar and Najib's Moment of Truth." *The Round Table* 101 (03): 271–74.

Conley, D., and S. Lamble. 2006. *The Daily Miracle: An Introduction to Journalism*, 3rd ed. Melbourne: Oxford University Press.

Crouch, Harold. 1980. "From Alliance to Barisan Nasional." In *Malaysian Politics and the 1978 Election*, edited by Harold Crouch, Lee Kam Hing, and Michael Ong, 1975–77. Kuala Lumpur: Oxford University Press.

Dorairaj, Nadason. 2013. "Scrapping to Woo Indians." *The Star*, May 3.

Farik Z., H. Sira, P. Y. Foong, X. Y. Yee, and L. Regina.. 2013. "No Letting Up On Hudud." *The Star*, April 25.

Freedom House. 2015. *Individual Country Ratings and Status, 1973–2016*. New York: Freedom House.

Galtung, J., and M. H. Ruge. 1965. "The Structure of Foreign News." *Journal of International Peace Research* 2 (1): 64–90.

Jamal L. J. 2011. "Tubuh Suruhanjaya Siasat Isu Murtad." *Utusan Malaysia*, August 9, Available at http://ww1.utusan.com.my/utusan/info.asp?y=2011&dt=0809&pub=Utusan_Malaysia&sec=Forum&pg=fo_01.htm (accessed on October 24, 2016).

Johana Mohd Taib, Amir Husin Mohd Nor, Muhammad Nazir Alias, and Amir Fazlim Yusoff. 2010. "Peruntukan Undang-undang Berkaitan Kesalahan Jenayah Aqidah di Malaysia." In *Kesalahan Jenayah Aqidah, Menurut Kerangka Perundangan di Malaysia*, edited by Amir Husin Mohd Nor, Amir Fazlim Yusoff, Muhammad Nazir Alias. Selangor: Universiti Kebangsaan Malaysia.

Karim Raslan. 2011. "PAS Goes on Soul-searching Trip." *The Star*, August 9.

Kiniroundup. 2016. "Maria Freed; PAS' Tit-for-tat Threat; Pasir Salak Mob Released." *Malaysiakini, Malaysia* November 29. Available at https://www.malaysiakini.com/news/364473#ixzz4RqB7t4Rs (accessed on October 26, 2017).

Kong See Hoh. 2013. "Greater Challenge for BN This Time." *The Sun*, May 3.

Kuppusamy, Baradan. 2011. "Red Faces in Pakatan." *The Star*, August 9. Available at https://www.thestar.com.my/opinion/letters/2011/08/09/red-faces-in-pakatan/ (accessed on October 25, 2016).

Letchumanan, A. 2013. "Parties Singing and Dancing to the Tunes of Indians." *The Star*, April 29.

Mail, R., and Z. Chan. 2013. "Remember Good Deeds of Government, Chinese Urged." *The Star*, April 28.

Mashitah Ibrahim. 2011 "Pas: Parti Aloh Sokmo." *Utusan Malaysia*, August 8. Available at http://ww1.utusan.com.my/utusan/info.asp?y=2011&dt=0808&pub=Utusan_Malaysia&sec=Rencana&pg=re_02.htm (accessed on September 24, 2016).

Masterton, M. 2005. "Asian Journalists Seek Values Worth Preserving." *Asia Pacific Media Educator* 16 (6): 41–48. Available at http://ro.uow.edu.au/apme/vol1/iss16/6. (accessed on October 26, 2017).

Mohd Ayop Abd Razid. 2011. "Patuhi Peruntukan Kebebasan Beragama." *Utusan Malaysia*, August 18.Available at http://ww1.utusan.com.my/utusan/info.asp?y=2011&dt=0818&pub=Utusan_Malaysia&sec=Rencana&pg=re_08.htm (accessed on October 26, 2016).

Mohd Ridhuan Tee Abdullah. 2011. "Selamatkan Akidah Umat Islam!" *Utusan Malaysia*, October 17.Available at http://ww1.utusan.com.my/utusan/info.asp?y=2011&dt=1017&pub=utusan_malaysia&sec=Rencana&pg=re_01.htm&arc=hive (accessed on December 24, 2016).

New Straits Times. 2013a. "Najib Can Help Indians, says Hindraf." *New Straits Times*, May 3.
———. 2013b. "More Indians Support BN." *New Straits Times*, May 1.
———. 2013c. "Barisan Goes All Out to Woo Chinese Voters in Kedah." *New Straits Times*, May 1.
Rashaad, Ali. 2016. "Minorities Push Against the State's Race Policies and Politics. The Threat to UMNO Posed by Malaysia's Rising Islamophobia." *Today Online*, April 19.
Sira, Habibu, Martin Carvalho, Kow Kwan Yee, and Josephine Jalleh. 2013. "Hudud if Pakatan Comes to Power." *The Star*, April 24.
Sulaiman, J., and N. I. Abdullah. 2013. "DPM: DAP Strongest in Pakatan." *New Straits Times*, May 2.
Tan, Joceline. 2013a. "Whose Way Will it Be in Gelang Patah?" *The Star*, May 3.
———. 2013b. "The Mother of All Battles." *The Star*, May, 5, 27.
———. 2013c. "Perfect Storms Brewing Over Putrajaya." *The Star*, April, 30, 26.
The Star. 2011. "The Trespass That Was Not a Social Call." *The Star*, August 7. Available at https://www.thestar.com.my/opinion/letters/2011/08/07/the-trespass-that-was-not-a-social-call/ (accessed on October 15, 2016).
———. 2013a. "1,500 Indians Admitted to Pre-U Courses." *The Star*, May 3.
———. 2013b. "New Chinese School for Pokok Sena." *The Star*, May 1.
———. 2013c. "Chua: DAP Was All Set to Accept PAS Symbol and Hudud." *The Star*, April 25.
Thirunavukkarasu Jr. 2011. "Be Sensitive to Muslim Beliefs." *The Star*, August 7. Available at https://www.thestar.com.my/opinion/letters/2011/08/07/be-sensitive-to-muslim-beliefs/ (accessed on October 17, 2016).
Utusan Malaysia. 2011a. "Pas gugat Islam?" *Utusan Malaysia*, August 14. Available at http://ww1.utusan.com.my/utusan/info.asp?y=2011&dt=0814&pub=Utusan_Malaysia&sec=Rencana&pg=re_03.htm (accessed December 14, 2016).
———. 2011b. "Apa Nak Jadi Kepada Umat Islam Malaysia?" *Utusan Malaysia*, August 14. Available at http://ww1.utusan.com.my/utusan/info.asp?y=2011&dt=0814&pub=Utusan_Malaysia&sec=Rencana&pg=re_02.htm (accessed on September 17, 2016).
———. 2011c. "JAIS, Murtad Dan Persoalan Undi." *Utusan Malaysia*, August 7. Available at http://ww1.utusan.com.my/utusan/info.asp?y=2011&dt=0807&pub=Utusan_Malaysia&sec=Rencana&pg=re_04.htm (accessed on December 17, 2016).
———. 2016. "Penahanan Maria Chin Di Bawah SOSMA Wajar." *Utusan Online*, Malaysia, November 22. Available at http://www.utusan.com.my/berita/nasional/penahanan-maria-chin-di-bawah-sosma-wajar-1.410551 (accessed on December 24, 2016).
Von Vorys, Karl. 1976. *Democracy Without Consensus: Communalism and Political Stability In Malaysia*. Kuala Lumpur: Oxford University Press.
Welsh, B., and J. Chin, eds. 2013. *Awakening: The Abdullah Badawi Years in Malaysia*, 3–38. Petaling Jaya: SIRD.
Wong Chun Wai. 2011. "Let's Fight to Keep Malaysia Moderate." *The Star*, August 7. Available at https://www.thestar.com.my/opinion/letters/2011/08/07/lets-fight-to-keep-malaysia-moderate/ (accessed on September 17, 2016).
———. 2013. "Caught Up in the Frenzy." *The Star*, May 5.
Yeoh, Seng Guan. 2010. "Editorial: Post 'Political Tsunami'." *The Round Table* 99 (407): 125–29.
Zaini, Hassan. 2011. "Murtad: Mudah-mudahan Kita Tidak Terus Buta Perut!" *Utusan Malaysia*, August 10. Available at http://ww1.utusan.com.my/utusan/info.asp?y=2011&dt=0810&pub=utusan_malaysia&sec=Rencana&pg=re_02.htm&arc=hive (accessed on September 10, 2016).

Zulkefli, Hamzah. 2011. "Memilih Lorong Gelap Demi Kekuasaan Politik." *Utusan Malaysia*, August 16. Available at http://ww1.utusan.com.my/utusan/info.asp?y=2011&dt=0816&pub=Utusan_Malaysia&sec=Rencana&pg=re_03.htm (accessed on December 16, 2016).

Zulkiflee, Bakar. 2011. "Antara Kuasa Dan Akidah." *Utusan Malaysia*, August 15. Available at http://ww1.utusan.com.my/utusan/info.asp?y=2011&dt=0815&pub=Utusan_Malaysia&sec=Rencana&pg=re_01.htm (accessed on November 16, 2016).

Zulkifli, Jalil. 2016. "Biarkan Bersih 5.0 Ditunggang DAP." *Utusan Malaysia*, October 13. Available at http://www.utusan.com.my/berita/politik/biarkan-bersih-5-0-ditunggang-dap-1.394216. (accessed on December 14, 2016).

20

Philippines: Beyond the Body Count—Mindful Journalism and the Human-centric Approach to Reporting the Drug War

Therese Patricia C. San Diego

> If I become president, there's [sic] no such thing as bloodless cleansing. I propose to get rid of the drugs within three to six months. And maybe I can do it.
>
> —Rodrigo R. Duterte

The above statement by Rodrigo R. Duterte was spoken on January 20, 2016, at a university forum organized by online news outfit Rappler, which sought to help students assess candidates for the coming Philippine national elections (Palma, 2016; Ranada, 2016). Duterte, then mayor of Davao City in the Mindanao region, was a presidential aspirant whose platform of government included his commitment to eradicate illegal drugs.

In May 2016, he won the elections by a plurality of over 39 percent of the total vote (Doronila, 2016) and became the country's first Mindanaoan[1] president (Presidential Communications Operations Office, 2016). Soon after his inauguration on June 30, 2016, the Philippine National Police (PNP) started to implement the new administration's campaign against illegal drugs.

On July 1, 2016, PNP chief Ronald M. dela Rosa signed Command Memorandum Circular No. 16-2016, which sets the "guidelines, procedures and tasks of police officers/units/stations" in carrying out "Project: Double Barrel" under the PNP Anti-Illegal Drugs Campaign Plan (Office of the Chief, Philippine National Police, 2016: 1). This supports the "Barangay Drug Clearing Strategy of the government and the neutralization of illegal drug personalities nationwide."

---

[1] Mindanao is the southernmost island group in the Philippines.

The Drug War: Numbers Game

News outlets in the Philippines and across the globe published updates on the number of drug-related deaths based on PNP reports. Inconsistencies in PNP data added to the complexity in covering the drug war.

For instance, in October 2016, four months after Duterte assumed office, Reuters received two different sets of data from the PNP. On October 5, 2016, the police shared with Reuters an estimate of 3,652 deaths since Duterte's June 30 inauguration, inclusive of nearly 2,000 cases under investigation.

On October 12, 2016, however, PNP spokesperson Dionardo Carlos informed Reuters that based on recent investigations, it was discovered that 1,566 drug suspects were killed in police operations while 722 deaths were either under investigation or had already been investigated (Morales, 2016).

According to another article from GMA News, PNP reported that from July 1, 2016, to October 15, 2016, 1,645 drug suspects were killed in police operations while 1,967 more drug-related deaths are under investigation (Colcol, 2016). The same PNP data on the number of drug suspects as of October 15 was reported in *The Manila Times* (Vargas, 2016) and in the *Manila Standard* (2016).

While human rights groups attribute the "deaths under investigation" or DUIs to vigilante killings (Marshall and Morales, 2016), the PNP spokesperson notes that the DUIs are "murder and homicide cases still under investigation," which may not necessarily be extrajudicial or vigilante killings (Merueñas, 2016, para. 5).

In January 2017, following the discovery of the October 2016 kidnapping and killing of a South Korean national by rogue police officers inside the PNP headquarters (Esmaquel, 2017), the anti-illegal drug units of the PNP were deactivated (De Jesus, 2017; Gonzales, 2017).

On February 16, 2017, the *Philippine Daily Inquirer* reported its "last update" on the drug war killings after the suspension of the anti-narcotics campaign (Inquirer.net, 2016/2017). From June 30, 2016 to February 16, 2017, 2,127 were reportedly killed in the operations, with 1,104 by the police and 1,022 by unidentified men.

The war on drugs, however, soon resumed. In February 2017, the president asked the Armed Forces of the Philippines (AFP) to support the Philippine Drug Enforcement Agency (PDEA) by organizing a new task force for the operations against "high-level drug syndicates" (but not "street pushers"), according to AFP Chief General Eduardo Año (dela Cruz and Mogato,

2017). The PNP then launched "Double Barrel Reloaded" in March 2017, which PNP chief dela Rosa described to be "more extensive, aggressive and well-coordinated, with built-in systems that guarantee full accountability and instill internal discipline among all personnel" (Philippine National Police, 2017). When the PNP chief briefed the House of Representatives on its implementation, he noted that citizens should "expect" the new operations to be "less bloody" (Cayabyab, 2017), but more deaths of drug suspects in police operations have since been reported (Mogato, 2017).

Church leaders and Philippine Vice President Maria Leonor "Leni" Gerona Robredo are among the citizens who have lamented the lack of public outcry against the killings in the war on drugs (Dizon, 2016; Gonzales, 2016).

In a pastoral statement, bishops from Negros Island wrote, "While we commend the government for its political will and determination in addressing the terrible drug problem menace that has long plagued our country, we strongly urge that this be done within the bounds of the law and with full respect for human rights" (Gonzales, 2016). The bishops pointed out "the seeming apathy and indifference of the general public in the face of these extrajudicial killings" and added that they are "deeply concerned that this alarming insensitivity could lead to a deadening conscience and the dawning of a culture of death."

What could be the cause of this apparent apathy over the thousands of deaths connected to the war on drugs? Could this be attributed to the kind of reporting that dominates the Philippine news media?

The Stories Behind the Statistics: Current Practices, Gaps, and Opportunities

What are the stories behind the numbers? Apart from the hard news articles on the number of drug suspects killed, are there stories that seek to shed more light on each case? Where are the real-life accounts of the killings that can illustrate to the public the truth about the deaths? What do Filipino journalists, editors, and journalism experts think about adopting mindful journalism as a framework for reporting on the war on drugs?

This chapter explores how human-centric, mindful journalism can provide a framework for reporting on the drug war. It consists of a review of literature on mindful journalism and similar forms of journalism; a qualitative content analysis of selected news articles on the war on drugs from October to November 2016; and interviews with Filipino journalists, editors, and journalism scholars about their views on the necessity and feasibility of applying mindful journalism in the Philippine context, particularly in reporting on the killings in the war on drugs.

Mindful Journalism vis-à-vis Other Similar Forms of Reporting in the Philippines

In July 2016, Chulalongkorn University invited communication and journalism trainers from ASEAN and neighboring countries to a workshop on "Mindful Communication for ASEAN Integration," which introduced mindful communication and journalism training curricula based on Asia's age-old philosophies. This project was funded by the UNESCO International Programme for the Development of Communication (IPDC).

One course curriculum presented during the training was on "Human-centered Journalism," described to take a "humanistic approach" in teaching investigative journalism.

Its main objective is to equip students with the knowledge and skills in "mindful conceptualizing, researching and writing human-centred journalistic stories" by familiarizing them with the "framework of deep listening and dialogical interviewing techniques, mindful investigative research methods and humanistic interpretation of surveys, as well as different forms of narrative techniques for human-centred journalism" (see Chapter 8).

Other forms of journalism in the Philippines share similarities with mindful journalism. These are development journalism, public or civic journalism, and peace journalism.

Development Journalism

In 1968, the Philippine News Service and the Philippine Press Institute started gathering reporters who can work on "development stories," and this reportedly "marked the first serious attempt of the working press to cover news topics hitherto been largely ignored" (Jamias, 1991: 38). Development journalism is characterized by its focus on "stories that can enhance people's lives particularly the poor" and "the effect of events on the poor" (Jamias, 1991: 41).

Other qualities of development journalists that set them apart from conventional reporters are their attitudes and behavior in information gathering, information processing, information transformation, and information distribution.

Jamias (1991) notes that development journalists use multiple information sources, explore unfamiliar beats, use available materials but establish more information links and gather information from the community. Apart from ensuring balance, objectivity, and accuracy in their reports, development journalists also weigh news against criteria of development, such as access, participation, and appropriateness. They write follow-up stories for policy action and immediate decisions, and they find balance in terms of presenting different sides of a story, while being "prescriptive in favor of development criteria and indicators" (Jamias, 1991: 46).

Subjects covered in development journalism are not limited to agriculture, community development, environment, health, and social welfare; crime is also among its concerns. When development journalists report on crime, they look into "investigative reports on causes, extent; policies and programs of government; evaluation of police activities and reform measures; social and psychological basis of crime; penal conditions, juvenile delinquency, drug problems" (Jamias, 1991: 52).

Public or Civic Journalism

In the Philippines, public journalism, also referred to as civic journalism, was introduced in 1995 through a workshop series by then Evelio B. Javier Foundation, which later became the Center for Community Journalism and Development or CCJD (Batario, 2012).

According to CCJD President and Executive Director Victor Redmond "Red" Batario (2012: 2), the Center "redefined public journalism in the context of enhanced citizen participation in governance and the role of journalists in this kind of environment." He also notes that this form of journalism "debunks the idea of many journalists that the purpose of the story is the story itself" and that it "invites a new approach to setting the news agenda and covering the news: by offering opportunities for public discussion and debate over what community issues should be top priority and how these can be solved or addressed" (Batario, 2012: 1).

Veteran journalist and Center for Media Freedom and Responsibility (CMFR) trustee Vergel O. Santos (as cited in Opiniano et al., 2015: 32) explains that civic journalism "attacks local gut issues with such focus and thoroughness as it engages every sector of the locality." He notes that civic journalism "turns the news media into a catalyst for community action, thus promising the community a distinct identity and sense of self-reliance."

Peace Journalism

According to Lee and Maslog (2005: 311), the three "most salient indicators" of peace journalism are "avoidance of demonizing language, a nonpartisan approach, and a multiparty orientation."

In Lee and Maslog's study (as cited in Gunaratne, Pearson, and Senarath, 2015: 220), the authors noted:

> [Peace journalism] like public journalism and developmental journalism ... is grounded in communication philosophy—namely the commitment to the idea of civic participation, the understanding of social justice as a moral imperative, and the view that the value and the sacredness of the individual are realized only in and through communities.

According to CMFR Executive Director Melinda Quintos de Jesus, Filipino journalists explored "peace news" in the early 1990s by organizing seminar workshops that discussed the government's peace program and NGOs' peace efforts, and provided a venue for the discussion on difficulties in covering the peace process. Such learning opportunities are needed by journalists, given the complexity of peace issues. As de Jesus (2000: 233) pointed out, when journalists are faced with a deadline, it is easier to "count the casualties and the dead bodies," but learning more about peace issues would equip them with the knowledge and capability to identify new sources and find fresh perspectives that have not been covered before.

Qualitative Content Analysis on a Series of Articles on the War on Drugs: Is the Mindful Approach Applied?

The common thread that runs through mindful journalism, development journalism, public or civic journalism, and peace journalism may explain why the philosophy behind mindful, human-centric reporting appears to resonate with Filipino journalists.

Though the mindful approach is not always applied in the Philippine news coverage of the war on drugs, there are efforts among local news media outfits to produce more in-depth articles on the topic that go beyond mere statistics.

An example is "War on Drugs: The Unheard Voices" by the ABS-CBN Investigative and Research Group (2016), which CMFR (2016) describes as a news article series that "humanizes the drug war." The six-part series is based on stories of 50 of the drug suspects killed in the drug war, randomly selected from over 1,700 reported victims of police operations in the four months since President Duterte assumed office. ABS-CBN, one of the largest mainstream news organizations in the country, began to publish the series on its website on October 27, 2016.

How, then, do these articles follow the mindful, human-centric approach illustrated through (a) engagement of ordinary citizens, including those from marginalized communities, as information sources; (b) development of profiles on human sources; (c) acquisition and reporting of diverse points of view; and (d) reporting on human rights?

Six reports were chosen for this project's qualitative content analysis, which aim to explore whether or not and how the human-centric approach is used in each of the six reports.

Given the qualitative design of the study, the coding frame was developed based on non-frequency indicators. The qualitative content analysis was conducted through the classification of the material as "instances of the categories of a coding frame" (Schreier, 2012: 8). Below is a narrative discussion of the findings based on the four indicators listed above.

Engagement of Ordinary Citizens as Information Sources

In the first article, Ballaran (2016a) gathered information from ordinary citizens including female relatives of two men slain—a mother and a daughter. One information source, described as a "relative" of a father and son who were killed in their sleep, was unidentified.

The second article, also by Ballaran (2016b), featured an unidentified male relative and seven female kin—a neighbor, two sisters, and mothers of the four different persons slain. Other unnamed sources were neighbors and witnesses.

In the third article, authored by Reyes and Cervantes (2016), the ordinary citizens interviewed were two mothers and two former partners or girlfriends of the persons killed. The experiences of a six-year-old boy and a one-year-old girl—children of two of the drug suspects slain—were also described.

The ordinary citizens featured in the fourth article include a woman witness who requested to be unidentified; the "relatives" of a suspect, also unidentified; and the female younger cousin and 67-year-old grandmother of another drug suspect who was slain during a buy-bust operation (Gonzales and Cabigao, 2016).

In the fifth article, by Navallo (2016), the only ordinary citizen interviewed was the wife of a police officer who was killed during a shootout. In the sixth article, authored by Bonquin (2016), no ordinary citizen was interviewed.

Most of the ordinary citizens interviewed were either relatives or witnesses to the killings. The sex and age of some of the information sources were not specified, but among those who were identified, most were female. In contrast, there was only one identified male ordinary citizen among the interviewees.

Though there were no reported interviews with children and youth, one report shared information about a young boy's experience after his father was slain. There was also one report that featured the views of a senior citizen—the grandmother of a drug suspect who was killed.

Development of Profiles on Human Sources

None of the six articles provided comprehensive profiles on any of the persons killed or the families left behind. In fact, among the ordinary citizens, several were unidentified. This could be attributed to limitations during data gathering, such as journalists' need to protect interviewees' privacy, the hesitation of witnesses and families to be interviewed, and the lack of time during fieldwork.

Acquisition and Reporting of Diverse Points of View

The first two articles presented the viewpoints of the relatives of slain drug suspects and witnesses to the killings, as well as reports from the police.

The stories of the relatives and witnesses contradicted what was written in the police reports, with family members of 43 out of the 50 suspects covered in the ABS-CBN team's research saying the suspects "did not fight back." Out of the 43 persons slain, "about 16 ... were heard begging for their lives before they were shot to death" (Ballaran, 2016a). The article also highlighted how the drug suspects suffered multiple gunshots during police operations and how relatives described these as "inhumane killing" (Ballaran, 2016a).

On the other hand, the third article featured information from police reports; the interviews with the former girlfriend of a slain suspect, the mother of another, and the "live-in girlfriend" of yet another; the observations about two children who lost their fathers in the drug war; the deputy director of the Children's Rehabilitation Center; and the secretary of the Operations and Programs Group-Protective Programs of the Department of Social Welfare and Development (DSWD).

In addition to the discrepancies between the stories of the relatives and the police reports, the third article also told the stories of the families that the slain drug suspects left behind. The experiences of the six-year-old boy and the one-year-old girl after their fathers were killed, for instance, were relayed by the relatives who were interviewed. According to the deputy director of the Children's Rehabilitation Center, orphans need "psychosocial processing" to help them recover from the trauma of the sudden loss. The interviewee from DSWD noted that the Local Social Welfare and Development Officers have the "primary responsibility" of providing support to the families of those slain. She noted that DSWD has social workers and psychologists trained on psychosocial support provisions.

In the series, the fourth article appeared to have the most diverse sources as the writers gathered information from a police report and other documents from the PNP; families of two slain drug suspects, including one suspect's "relatives" and the female cousin and grandmother of another; a female witness to one of the killings; the spokesperson of a human rights group; and interviews conducted by the ABS-CBN news team with the PNP spokesperson and barangay chairpersons. The barangay chairpersons are the ones who prepare lists of drug pushers and users based on reports of their "concerned constituents" (Gonzales and Cabigao, 2016).

The fifth article focused on the side of the police—specifically, perspectives from the Caloocan Police team that lost a police officer during a shootout, the wife of the officer killed, and the PNP spokesperson.

The perspectives featured in the final article in the series were limited to those of the PNP spokesperson, a human rights lawyer, and the deputy director of the Children's Rehabilitation Center. The PNP spokesperson emphasized the supposed decrease in "petty crimes happening on the streets" (Bonquin, 2016). Rene Saguisag, human rights lawyer and former senator, was quoted to have raised the need to "review" if the killings are "really the way to go" given that "the hardline policy [against illegal drugs] is a failed one and should be replaced by another policy" (Bonquin, 2016). Eilek Renes Manano, deputy director of the Children's Rehabilitation Center, emphasized that the causes of early drug addiction among children should be determined.

Reporting on Human Rights

Though "human rights" per se are not explicitly discussed in half of the articles, the entire series exposed human rights violations.

The first article, for example, reported that no warrants of arrest were issued, and one of the persons slain in the drug war was already detained and handcuffed when he was shot dead. One was begging for his life when the police shot him four times. The issue of collateral damage was also raised; there was a case where the companions of the suspected drug addict were also killed. The same article points out inconsistencies between police reports and accounts of witnesses and relatives.

The second article explicitly stated that "many" of the families of the persons slain want to "sue the police for depriving their relatives of their right to due process" (Ballaran, 2016b). Apart from this, the article also pointed out that under Chapter III, Article 13, Paragraph 7 of the Revised Penal Code, one's criminal liability is mitigated if the offender voluntarily surrenders to a person in authority or its agents. Relatives of those slain in the drug war describe the killings to be "inhumane," as many of the individuals killed suffered multiple gunshots.

In the third article, an interviewee emphasized that citizens who make mistakes should be punished, but not killed. The lack of due process was once again underlined. It also discussed the availability of psychosocial support provisions for the children who have witnessed the drug war.

The fourth article again highlighted cases where police reports show that the drug suspects opened fire, while witnesses say the suspects begged for their lives and did not even own a gun. There was also a case in which the grandmother of the person slain said her grandson "was still alive for thirty minutes" but the police did not listen to her when she asked them to bring him to the hospital (Gonzales and Cabigao, 2016).

The fifth article focused on the plight of a police officer who was killed while serving an arrest warrant to a drug suspect. According to the police, the gunman tried to escape but was later cornered and shot by the police when he allegedly resisted arrest. The article also pointed out that according to the wife of the slain police officer, her husband was not wearing a bulletproof vest when he was shot. The article indicated that according to PNP data, 13 officers have been killed while 36 others were wounded during anti-drug police operations from July 1 to September 29, and these cases "could have been prevented if they were each issued a [sic] protective gear" (Navallo, 2016). According to the PNP spokesperson, the PNP chief acknowledged the necessity of providing protective gear to police officers, but as of the article's writing, the gear had not yet been issued.

At the end of the sixth article, excerpts from the Universal Declaration on Human Rights were presented. On the other hand, in the main body of the article, the quotes from Saguisag emphasized violations of the rule of law in the drug war.

Summary

The most prominent mindful journalism indicators observed in the articles are (a) the engagement of female ordinary citizens as information sources, and (b) the discussion on human rights, though implicitly.

Ordinary citizens that still need to be engaged as information sources include males; members of the lesbian, gay, bisexual, transgender, queer or questioning, and intersex (LGBTQI) community; children and youth; senior citizens; persons with disability; and indigenous peoples.

There is room for more overt discussions on human rights—not only the rights violated, but also the consequences of such violations on the affected families and society as a whole.

There is a need for more in-depth profiles on interviewees. More resources may be necessary to enable journalists to develop such profiles. It must be noted, however, that privacy issues should be considered when covering cases where interviewees might be in danger.

Though the range of information sources cited in each article varied, the series as a whole covered diverse perspectives. The presentation of each of the different points of view, however, was brief; this could be due to the limitations of the digital medium. While more space can be allotted for web articles, concise and easily digestible content is recommended in order to hold the reader's attention.

Mindful Journalism: A Framework for Reporting on the War on Drugs?

Eight interviews were conducted with Filipino journalists, editors, and journalism scholars who shared their thoughts on the need for and feasibility of using the mindful approach in reporting on the war on drugs.

Perspectives on the Role of Journalists in Covering the Drug War

Jhoanna Ballaran,[2] author of the first two articles in the series, "War on Drugs: The Unheard Voices," says the press should give a face and a voice to the victims and their families, demand accountability from the government, and promote human rights. Marilou Guieb,[3] a journalist from the *Baguio Chronicle*, likewise believes that journalists need to write stories that "serve as records and testimonies that can help the public decipher the humanity or inhumanity of the (anti-drug) operations, and to voice out their sentiments on the matter."

Ballaran recognizes the "tremendous effort" of the Philippine media in terms of going "beyond the numbers" and reporting both the human and social cost of the drug war, with the publication and broadcast of stories on the families the slain drug suspects left behind.

On the other hand, Ed Karlon Rama,[4] National Coordinator of the Peace and Conflict Journalism Network (PECOJON) in the Philippines, points out that though national media outfits are "successful in raising awareness" about the war on drugs, they "sometimes [fall] short of facilitating understanding because of the nature of their coverage and the volume of stories at the national level." He notes that the "running tally of the casualties" combined with statements from "thought leaders in both mainstream and social media" and the "poor media literacy of the audience" are limiting the conversation among citizens to "a duality—okay or not okay—and its various configurations: moral or immoral, human rights of criminals or peace and order, Yellowtards or Dutertards."

Rama adds:

> This is the problem when journalists (a) fail to provide context; (b) limit the framing of their narratives to direct violence and omit structural and cultural causations in the storytelling; (c) limit themselves to elite sources and fail to consider other views, especially the ones on the ground; and (d) fail to spot and instead convey the propaganda as truths.

Serafin I. Plotria,[5] chairperson of KBP Negros Occidental and station manager of DYHT-FM under the Radio Mindanao Network, also says journalists

---

[2] Interview with the author, March 13, 2017, Manila.
[3] Email interview with the author, February 14, 2017.
[4] Email interview with the author, March 4, 2017.
[5] Email interview with the author, February 11, 2017.

must provide context in their stories and "get out from the volley of two parties out-staging each other." He adds, "Today's journalists' reportage should focus on building comprehensible and objective information (on which the) public may base their choices."

Victor Redmond Batario,[6] president and executive director of the CCJD, also believes in the role of journalists in equipping the public with the information they need to participate in decision-making. He says, "Journalists should ask themselves whether their reporting exacerbates the phenomenon or provides citizens with a better understanding of what is happening around them … thus (enabling citizens) to make better-informed decisions and take action."

Similarly, Ramon R. Tuazon,[7] president of the Asian Institute of Journalism and Communication (AIJC) and secretary general of the Asian Media Information and Communication Centre (AMIC), points out that journalists should "explain not just what is happening but why these are happening [as well as] the impact of the killings on the individual, the family, and the society." He notes that beyond sharing facts, the news media should "make citizens reflect, ask questions, and be critical" about the anti-drug operations, and that journalists need to study the root causes of the issue such as the "failure of the criminal justice system, which is being used to 'rationalize' the killing."

Tuazon adds that the "culture of death" and the issue of impunity should be discussed in the media. Francis Allan L. Angelo,[8] editor-in-chief of the *Daily Guardian*, shares the same sentiments. He says that one of the "ultimate aims of deeper reporting into the killings" is to "prevent the culture of impunity and unabated killings which could affect journalists and other crusaders of human rights and other civil liberties."

Tuazon also believes that journalists have the responsibility to sustain public interest in the subject. He notes, "After the initial grief subsides, people tend to turn away in collective amnesia." Ballaran likewise notes that journalists need to be "more creative" in sharing stories on the drug war as citizens may get tired of hearing the same stories every day.

Marites D. Vitug,[9] president of the Journalism for Nation Building Foundation (JNBF) and Rappler editor at large, acknowledges the same challenge and recommends finding new story angles and expanding the context of the news coverage to keep the public engaged. She notes, "Of

---

[6] Interview with the author, January 5, 2017, Manila.
[7] Interview with the author, December 28, 2016, Manila.
[8] Email interview with the author, February 10, 2017.
[9] Interview with the author, January 28, 2017, Iloilo City.

course, people sometimes get tired ... but we should just keep doing our job. Maybe mindful journalism can ... remind the reader that this issue will not go away and ... that there's something wrong."

According to Rama, "The litmus test for good journalism is the quality of conversations that happen in the community as a result of the audience's consumption of the news." He adds, "What journalists need to aspire for in their storytelling should therefore be to cause more intelligent conversations and, hopefully, decision-making among people."

Perceived Advantages and Disadvantages of Engaging Ordinary Citizens and Marginalized Groups as Information Sources and Reporting Diverse Points of View

Guieb notes that in covering the killings, "the context that needs to be analyzed (is) embedded in the emotional stories of the victims and their families—their life situations that can help get to the root of the problem."

Ballaran shares that gathering information from the field adds "authenticity" to stories as ordinary citizens candidly share their experiences and express their emotions during interviews. Fieldwork also helps flesh out the details for investigative reports; comparisons can be made between official police records and accounts from witnesses. Ballaran adds that journalists often find more than what they were originally looking for, such as new angles for future stories. She recognizes that it is important to "immerse" oneself in the field, which she also refers to as "a sea of possible stories."

Plotria points out that in order to provide context and to show the "sentiments of the greater public," journalists "should include various voices coming from top to bottom in their reporting."

Moreover, Rama notes that "engaging citizens can also mean engaging an organized movement of people that is advocating a particular agenda." He adds that it would be "good" if such an agenda would provide a "new dimension that widens the people's perspectives and improves conversations, as opposed to simply fueling the existing polarity."

However, the interviewees note the challenges such as detecting propaganda and evaluating the credibility of sources.

According to Angelo:

> In an era of fake news, parodies, and propaganda, reporters should take the time to verify the background of the source, their intent, and the veracity of their claims. More often than not, the marginalized sector is more likely to

tell the truth as they are the first victims and stand to lose more when there are abuse and lawlessness.

Plotria recommends profiling of interviewees to identify "extended sources" as well as "creating layers of sources to be included in stories."

In addition, Tuazon underlines the possibility of exposing ordinary citizens to danger if journalists tap them as information sources in the drug war coverage. Guieb recommends practicing sensitivity when interviewing the grieving families.

There is also the possibility of not being granted an interview by citizens out of fear. "The challenge is [journalists] may not get the information they need because the people are scared [to] be the next victims," Vitug notes.

Ballaran says there are also families of the persons slain in the drug war who declined interviews because of their desire to move on. When this happens, she respects the interviewee's decision but tries to explain that she wishes to cover the story in order to give the person the opportunity to air his or her side. Ballaran notes that it is important to answer the question, "What's in it for me?"

Limited funding is another challenge. Batario notes this is often a problem for the community press, but even for Ballaran, who works for a national media organization, logistical requirements are a disadvantage. She notes, however, that the pros of doing fieldwork outweigh the cons.

While Tuazon agrees that journalists should "present other viewpoints beyond the traditional sources," he also suggests looking into whether or not and how citizens are able to "process" what is happening. He adds that journalists should engage ordinary citizens not only to gather stories but also to "educate" them by encouraging them to think critically about the drug war and to ask their own questions.

Reporting in the Context of Human Rights

All of the interviewees agree that journalists should frame reports on the killings in the war on drugs within the context of human rights.

According to Plotria, stories should highlight the violation of not only the rights of the persons killed but also the rights of those who survived and the families left behind. He says:

> It is imperative that life should be preserved, protected, nurtured, and upheld by no less than the state. The state should never condemn its people who went wayward and suffered out of its government's failure to provide better alternatives towards a more desirable and meaningful life.

Rama notes that there should be more reports on the "structural and cultural conditions" that paved the way for the drug war. He adds that the means of addressing the drug issue—without violating human rights—should be discussed. Vitug, on the other hand, recommends looking at the health and economic aspects of the drug problem.

Ballaran says another role of the journalists is to communicate the importance of respecting due process and respecting the right to life of each person, including those involved in drugs. They should not only give a voice to ordinary citizens, but they should also address the culture of violence and encourage the public to demand accountability and justice.

"When journalists write from a human rights perspective they bring to bear not only the principles of good journalism but also open up another dimension in the public's understanding of the phenomenon's impact and relationship with them and their lives," Batario explains. "It is not enough to report the killings as a result of an anti-illegal drugs campaign given not only the blatant brutality with which these are perpetrated but [also] the culture of impunity that the killings further strengthen."

Deep Listening, Structural Violence, and Mindful Reporting

In Chapter 8, Supaporn Phokaew argues that a key criterion for the media in order to practice mindful communication is "deep listening," which could create an "open mindfulness" toward reporting and generating stories. She says, "the aim of mindful communication is that we should facilitate change and that at the end we have to reduce the state of suffering for the people in the society." She further notes the need to "first understand suffering and then find the way to solve it."

In Chapter 2, Sulak Sivaraksa notes that the poisons of greed, hatred, and delusion are the root causes of personal suffering. He further notes that more attention should be paid to the "structural violence" of economic and political systems, and for "deeper understanding of the nature of modern institutions and social structures."

In this connection, he emphasizes that "proper education" is necessary:

> People are not taught the truth about things like climate change, structural violence and solutions to deforestation. In a world of lies and deceit, individuals must be able to distinguish facts from fiction, so that they could skilfully work through the solution rather than offering propaganda.

He further notes, "Mindfulness is not enough; rather through contemplative meditation on ethics and the rest of the Noble Eightfold Path the poisons can be rooted out and lead us into generosity, loving kindness and wisdom."

The "war on drugs" has a clear relationship with what Sivaraksa described as "structural violence" in the Philippine socioeconomic context. The news media must therefore persist in listening to the people involved in and affected by this campaign.

How can the Philippine media continue to address such issues with mindful reporting principles? What different news angles could be generated by listening deeply to people?

Sources and Angles for Exploration

The journalists, editors, and journalism scholars interviewed for this chapter cited sources and story angles that the news media should explore in the drug war coverage.

Health and the Nature of Drug Addiction

Plotria, Vitug, and Ballaran suggest interviews with health experts. According to Vitug and Ballaran, there has not been enough coverage about the reasons behind drug addiction. Plotria shares his approach to covering the drug war: "I look at the perspective of the clinical expert on the nature of addiction ... [and] public health professionals on the effect of illegal drug use to [one's] health."

Economy, Social Inequity, and Drug Use

Vitug suggests interviews with economists on how the drug issue is linked with the bigger society in terms of social inequity. "Why do these poor people use drugs? Because they want to escape," she points out. "Why do they want to escape? Because of the harsh realities.... [There is a need to] improve social services, the economy ... but that's hardly written about."

Ballaran adds that social workers can help explain why the drug problem exists in the first place. They should also be interviewed about the economic impact of the killings on victims' families and the help they receive from DSWD.

The Police Perspective

Though Tuazon and Batario note that much of the news coverage has been dominated by points of view of the police and other state actors, Vitug and Ballaran recommend interviewing the police and those who come up with the list of suspects in order to determine where they get the drug suspects' names and how the list is drafted and vetted.

Ballaran and Tuazon also suggest interviewing the PNP foot soldiers who execute the operations. Tuazon raises questions on how they "justify or rationalize" the killings, and their "possible effects or impact" on those who shoot the drug suspects, with the aim of gathering responses that do not "present a single (imposed) frame or explanation following official line."

Angelo likewise recommends obtaining the views of the police on issues that "affect the credibility" of the campaign against illegal drugs, particularly "how the drug war pressures the police and other law enforcement agencies in doing 'extra-judicial' actions (like evidence planting) to fulfill their 'quotas.'"

Angelo, however, points out a challenge: "If we reach out to the police to get their views on pressures caused by the drug war, they decline to be quoted which makes for a very weak and even dubious story." The solution? Angelo says,

> We try to reach as many relevant sources as possible. If they don't want to be quoted, we make sure that we take down notes or even record their statements (if they allow us) as insurance. For police officers who don't want to speak in [the] open, our strategy is to confront the higher ups who normally respond and address the issue.

Guieb notes, however, that "one must sharpen the ear for expected biased statements."

Batario raised another possible obstacle for journalists: "how to overcome the intransigence of the government (read: President Duterte, the police, Congress, Cabinet) in brushing aside criticisms or opposing points of view." In order to address this, he notes that "journalists must constantly report with context and from a human rights perspective."

The Stigmatization of Human Rights and the Cycle of Violence

While all of the interviewees agree that journalists should frame reports on the drug war in the context of human rights, they acknowledge what seems to be the desensitization of the people to such stories.

According to Ballaran, the human rights activists she has interviewed say they are put on the defensive because they are being portrayed by the government as an "obstacle" to the "success" of the war on drugs. She reiterates the need for creativity on the part of the journalists in helping citizens understand the importance of human rights and how violating these rights can lead to widespread violence and invasion of privacy. "Due process must be followed, however complicated that is," she argues.

"The death of one diminishes us all," Ballaran quotes the introduction of the "War on Drugs: The Unheard Voices." She points out the cycle of violence that can occur when people continue to be killed without due process. "It is normal to hear from families of slain drug suspects that they want to avenge the deaths of their family members," she shares in Filipino. "We need to realize that revenge is a reality. Five, ten, fifteen years from now, they could become the problem—the children who witnessed their parents being killed."

The Families Left Behind

Tuazon, Batario, and Guieb point out that the news media should continue to give a voice to victims' families and discuss how the killings target the poor. Ballaran says reports should cover the trauma experienced by the wives, children, and parents of those slain.

Guieb stresses, however, that apart from the difficulty in accessing these sources, another concern for journalists is practicing "sensitivity to the present emotions and grief ... of the victim's loved ones."

Such requires a journalist's judgment call. Guieb notes, "It might be more sensitive to read into the body language of the grieving [family] rather than to intrude into their private grief, unless it might seem like their speaking out helps them ventilate their suffering." She adds, "But even in such cases, a reporter must be sensitive on what to include in the report as in many instances, many [statements given] at the height of emotions can violate [the interviewee's] dignity and privacy...."

A Holistic View on the Drug War

On the other hand, Plotria argues that journalists should look at the drug war as the "tip of the iceberg." He notes that it is a "social issue" and its coverage should go beyond the "victim–perpetrator, aggrieved–offender point of view" and the perspectives of "those who lost a father, sister, mother, or brother as victim."

According to Plotria, reporting "multiple voices" is crucial now more than ever as such stories open discussions on the potential long-term impact of the drug war and other related crimes that may emerge from it. "The more it is in the public space for discussion, more options in dealing with it will surface," he says.

Vitug highlights the role of editors in guiding journalists in the coverage of the war on drugs as they can see the bigger picture amid the numerous issues related to it that come out daily. She recommends "team reporting" where editors assign reporters to cover various aspects of the issue such as the Philippine economy, livelihood and development, social inequality, and health.

As the drug war continues, it seems that mindful, human-centric reporting is precisely the kind of journalism the country needs. Alongside traditional journalism principles and ethics, the news media should be encouraged to engage ordinary citizens as information sources, develop profiles on human sources, cover diverse points of view, and report in the context of human rights.

From the ordinary citizens to the authorities, every subject should equally benefit from deep listening. Such can lead to increased understanding of the different perspectives on the issue, which can inform strategic decision-making toward possible mutual agreements that can help address the drug problem in the country while protecting human rights and the rule of law.

References

ABS-CBN Investigative and Research Group. 2016, October. *War on Drugs: The Unheard Voices.* Available at http://news.abs-cbn.com/war-on-drugs (accessed on October 26, 2017).

Balana, C. D. 2017. *PNP Starts War on Bad Cops. Philippine Daily Inquirer, January 31.* Available at http://newsinfo.inquirer.net/866695/pnp-starts-war-on-bad-cops (accessed on October 26, 2017).

Ballaran, J. 2016a. *Cops Gun Down Suspects Begging for Their Lives.* ABS-CBN News. Available at http://news.abs-cbn.com/war-on-drugs/part1 (accessed on October 26, 2017).

———. 2016b. *They Surrendered—and Got Killed.* ABS-CBN News. Available at http://news.abs-cbn.com/war-on-drugs/part2 (accessed on October 26, 2017).

Batario, R. 2012. *Public Journalism: A New Approach to Setting the News Agenda.* Available at https://ccjdphils.files.wordpress.com/2012/06/what-is-pj1.pdf (accessed on October 26, 2017).

Bonquin, C. 2016. *Thousands Have Died, Thousands More to Follow?* ABS-CBN News. Available at http://news.abs-cbn.com/war-on-drugs/part6 (accessed on October 26, 2017).

Cayabyab, M. J. 2017, March 14. *Dela Rosa Briefs Solon on "Double Barrel" Campaign.* Available at http://newsinfo.inquirer.net/880716/dela-rosa-briefs-solon-on-double-barrel-campaign (accessed on October 26, 2017).

Center for Community Journalism and Development. 2012, May 31. *The Visayas Examiner's Experiment with Public Journalism.* Available at https://ccjdphils.wordpress.com/2012/05/31/the-visayas-examiners-experiment-with-public-journalism/ (accessed on October 26, 2017).

Center for Media Freedom and Responsibility. 2016, November 4. *"Unheard Voices": Humanizing the War on Drugs.* Available at http://cmfr-phil.org/media-ethics-responsibility/journalism-review/unheard-voices-humanizing-the-war-on-drugs/ (accessed on October 26, 2017).

Colcol, E. 2016. "PNP: 1,645 Drug Suspects Killed, 1,967 Deaths Under Investigation Since July 1." *GMA News Online*, 15 October. Available at http://www.gmanetwork.com/news/story/585128/news/nation/pnp-1-645-drug-suspects-killed-1-967-deaths-under-investigation-since-july-1#sthash.ayPQxJfq.dpuf (accessed on October 26, 2017).

De Jesus, J. L. 2017. "Police Can No Longer Conduct Drug Operations." *Philippine Daily Inquirer,* January 31. Available at http://newsinfo.inquirer.net/866984/police-can-no-longer-conduct-drug-operations (accessed on October 26, 2017).

De Jesus, M. Q. 2000. "Media's Role in the Creation of a Culture of Peace." In *The Media and Peace Reporting: Perspectives on Media and Peace Reportage,* 227–34. Pasig City: Office of the Presidential Adviser on the Peace Process.

Dela Cruz, E., and M. Mogato. 2017. "Philippine Army to Create Task Force to Chase Big Drug Syndicates." *Reuters,* Manila February 19. Available at http://ca.reuters.com/article/topNews/idCAKBN15Y051 (accessed on October 26, 2017).

Dizon, N. 2016. "Leni Laments Lack of Public Outcry vs Drug Killings." *Philippine Daily Inquirer,* August 5. Available at http://newsinfo.inquirer.net/803133/leni-laments-lack-of-outcry-vs-drug-killings#ixzz4Z9X9fiYE (accessed on October 26, 2017).

Doronila, A. 2016. "Turbulent Transition for Rody." *Philippine Daily Inquirer,* June 13. Available at http://opinion.inquirer.net/95191/turbulent-transition-for-rody (accessed on October 26, 2017).

Esmaquel, P. 2017. "Important to Punish Korean's Murderers, U.S. Envoy Says." *Rappler,* January 25, Philippines. Available at http://www.rappler.com/nation/159398-punish-south-korean-jee-murderers-us-ambassador (accessed on October 26, 2017).

Gonzales, Y. V. 2016. "Negros Bishops Hit Gov't Inaction, Public Apathy over Killings." *Philippine Daily Inquirer,* October 12. Available at http://newsinfo.inquirer.net/824543/negros-bishops-hit-govt-inaction-public-apathy-over-killings (accessed on October 26, 2017).

———. 2017. "PNP: War on Drugs Suspended, Purge of Bad Cops on." *Philippine Daily Inquirer,* January 30. Available at http://newsinfo.inquirer.net/866507/pnp-war-on-drugs-suspended-purge-of-bad-cops-on (accessed on October 26, 2017).

Gonzales, J., and F. J. Cabigao. 2016. "'Oplan Tokhang': From Tagging to Killing." ABS-CBN News Available at http://news.abs-cbn.com/war-on-drugs/part4 (accessed on October 26, 2017).

Gunaratne, S. A., M. Pearson, and S. Senarath. 2015. *Mindful Journalism and News Ethics in the Digital Era: A Buddhist Approach.* New York: Routledge.

Inquirer.net. 2017. "The Kill List." *Philippine Daily Inquirer,* February 16. Available at http://newsinfo.inquirer.net/794598/kill-list-drugs-duterte (Original article published 2016) (accessed on October 26, 2017).

Jamias, J. F. 1991. *Writing for Development: Focus on Specialized Reporting Areas.* Los Baños: College of Agriculture, University of the Philippines, Los Baños.

Lee, S. T., and C. C. Maslog. 2005, June. "War or Peace Journalism? Asian Newspaper Coverage of Conflicts (Abstract). *Journal of Communication*, 55(2): 311–29. doi: 10.1111/j.1460-2466.2005.tb02674.x

Manila Standard. 2016. "PNP Reports Toll in Drug War." *Manila Standard*, October 16. Available at http://thestandard.com.ph/mobile/article/218936 (accessed on October 26, 2017).

Marshall, A. R. C., and N. J. Morales. 2016. "Duterte's Enforcer Says 'We Are at War', Has No Regrets About Killings." *Reuters*, October 4. Available at http://www.reuters.com/article/us-philippines-duterte-policechief-insig-idUSKCN1240F0 (accessed on October 26, 2017).

Merueñas, M. 2016, October 2. "PNP: Deaths 'Under Investigation' Now at 1,745; Cases Filed at 321." Available at http://www.gmanetwork.com/news/story/583522/news/nation/pnp-deaths-under-investigation-now-at-1-745-cases-filed-at-321 (accessed on October 26, 2017).

Mogato, M. 2017. "Four Drug Suspects Killed as Philippine Police Resume Drugs War Operations." *Reuters*, Manila, March 7. Available at http://www.reuters.com/article/us-philippines-drugs-idUSKBN16E0HI?il=0 (accessed on October 26, 2017).

Morales, N. J. 2016. "Philippine Police Lower Death Toll in Drugs War to Below 2, 300." *Reuters*, Manila, October 13. Available at http://www.reuters.com/article/us-philippines-drugs-toll-idUSKCN12D0R1 (accessed on October 26, 2017).

Navallo, M. 2016. "No Cop Should Die Fighting Drugs." ABS-CBN News. Available at http://news.abs-cbn.com/war-on-drugs/part5 (accessed on October 26, 2017).

Office of the Chief, Philippine National Police. 2016, July 1. *Command Memorandum Circular No. 16-2016*. Available at http://didm.pnp.gov.ph/Command%20Memorandum%20Circulars/CMC%202016-16%20PNP%20ANTI-ILLEGAL%20DRUGS%20CAMPAIGN%20PLAN%20%E2%80%93%20PROJECT%20DOUBLE%20BARREL.pdf (accessed on October 26, 2017).

Opiniano, J., J. E. Arcalas, M. R. Mallari, and J. P. Tuazon. 2015, March. "Philippine Community Journalism: Roles, Status and Prospects." *Grassroots Editor & Community Journalism* 56 (1): 29–36.

Palma, P. 2016, January 21. *Duterte Vows to Eradicate Illegal Drugs*. Available at http://cnnphilippines.com/news/2016/01/21/rodrigo-duterte-illegal-drugs-elections-2016.html (accessed on October 26, 2017).

Philippine National Police. 2017, March 7. *PNP Activates Drug Enforcement Group; Double Barrel Reloaded, Tokhang Revisited*. Available at http://www.pnp.gov.ph/news-and-information/news/773-pnp-activates-drug-enforcement-group-double-barrel-reloaded-tokhang-revisited (accessed on October 26, 2017).

Presidential Communications Operations Office. 2016, June 30. *Duterte to take historic oath as first Mindanaoan President*. Available at https://pcoo.gov.ph/transition/duturte-to-take-historic-oath-as-first-mindanaoan-president/ (accessed on November 15, 2017).

Ranada, P. 2016. "Duterte: No 'Bloodless Cleansing' vs Crime." *Rappler*, Philippines, January 20. Available at http://www.rappler.com/nation/politics/elections/2016/119688-rodrigo-duterte-no-bloodless-cleansing-crime (accessed on October 26, 2017).

Reyes, A. M., and R. Cervantes. 2016. "War Leaves Too Many Widows, Orphans." ABS-CBN News. Available at http://news.abs-cbn.com/war-on-drugs/part3 (accessed on October 26, 2017).

Schreier, M. 2012. *Qualitative Content Analysis in Practice*. Thousand Oaks, CA: SAGE Publications.

Vargas, A. 2016. "Civilians Constitute Bulk of Drug Fatalities—PNP." *Manila Times*, October 15. Available at http://www.manilatimes.net/civilians-constitute-bulk-drug-fatalities-pnp/291417/ (accessed on October 26, 2017).

List of Interviewees

1. Ramon R. Tuazon
   President, Asian Institute of Journalism and Communication (AIJC)
   Secretary General, Asian Media Information and Communication Center (AMIC)
   Chairperson, Commission on Higher Education (CHED) Technical Committee for Communication
   December 28, 2016
2. Victor Redmond Batario
   President and Executive Director, Center for Community Journalism and Development
   January 5, 2017
3. Marites D. Vitug
   Award-winning author and journalist
   President, Journalism for Nation Building Foundation
   Editor at large, Rappler
   January 28, 2017
4. Francis Allan L. Angelo
   Editor-in-Chief, *The Daily Guardian*
   February 10, 2017 (via email)
5. Serafin I. Plotria
   Chairperson, KBP Negros Occidental
   Station manager, DYHT-FM, Radio Mindanao Network
   February 11, 2017 (via email)
6. Marilou Guieb
   Editorial staff, *Baguio Chronicle*
   February 14, 2017 (via email)
7. Ed Karlon N. Rama
   National Coordinator (Philippines), The Peace and Conflict Journalism Network (PECOJON)
   March 4, 2017 (via email)
8. Jhoanna Ballaran
   News Researcher, ABS-CBN Investigative and Research Group
   March 13, 2017

21

South Korea: Compassionate Approach to Journalism—Buddhist True Network

Emi Hayakawa

Buddhism was introduced to Korea from China in approximately 372 CE. Buddhism was adopted as the official state religion in the Goguryeo, Silla, and Baekje Kingdoms during the Three Kingdoms period (57–668), and the Unified Silla kingdom (665–918) succeeded in applying Buddhism as the psychological force for the unification of the peninsula.

According to the Jogye Order of Korea Buddhism, during the Unified Silla Period, Buddhism played a preeminent role in cultural development, resulting in the construction of the presently UNESCO world heritage sites as Bulguksa Temple and Sokguram Grotto in Gyeongju.

Furthermore, in 918, the King Taejo (r. 918–943) took control of a new government and gradually established the Goryeo dynasty (918–1392). Korean Buddhism blossomed and became a "religion of the state" in a very thorough manner, receiving extensive support and privileges, while at the same time involving itself deeply with the ruling family and powerful members of the court, and Buddhism became a unifying factor and the grounds for further national and cultural flourishing.

The Goryeo Dynasty followed the teachings of Unified Silla National Monk, Master Doseon (827–898), as important temples were constructed on the great mountains across the peninsula, adding further impetus to the propagation of the dharma. The number of Buddhist orders diversified and flourished and became a "religion of the state." Furthermore, it was during the Goryeo Dynasty that the Tripitaka Koreana was carved into 80,000 woodblocks as an offering for national protection from outside forces and invasion during this time.

Henceforth, Buddhist ideas and ideals have guided and influenced the Korean culture since its introduction in the Korean peninsula, and the 1,700 years old Korean Buddhist teachings are deeply embedded within the traditional Korean culture. Thus, Korean Buddhism has been considered a cultural background rather than a formal religion.

At the end of the 20th century, Korean Buddhism needed a revival with the advancement of technology and media playing a big role in it. Thus, in

1994, Buddhist True Network (BTN), was established as the first Buddhist propagation media in Korea. Since its inception, BTN has dedicated itself to propagating the beautiful ancient Buddhist traditions not just among the Korean people but also across the globe.

Birth and Mission of Buddhist True Network (BTN)

The BTN is the world's only non-sectarian 24-hour Buddhist TV channel that was established by the Korean Buddhist community in 1994 and began nationwide broadcast in 1995. It is both a TV and radio network channel devoted to Buddhism. Since its establishment, BTN has been creating and broadcasting a wide variety of inspirational contents to further inspire awakening of hearts and minds through Buddhism. Moreover, the channel extends its utmost respect to the triple gem[1] and has aimed to propagate the Buddha Dharma across the globe via both TV and radio, and operates on all digital platforms, from cable TV to satellite platforms to smartphones.

BTN contents include original programming with diverse cultural documentaries; dharma talks and teachings; talk shows and interviews; educational programs and children's programs; holistic health programs; and BTN NEWS, the daily news digests.

As a Buddhist media, BTN implements mindful journalism as a means to broadcast the current headlines and news digests. BTN NEWS bureau believe that both Buddhism and journalism are investigations of the understanding of the truth, the reasons behind those truths, the possibility of change, and the way of life that can lead to a life free of suffering.

In general, news programs are developed by the mass media team to provide viewers with factual information they need to make the best possible decisions about their lives, their communities, their societies, and their governments. As American reporter Doug Mcgill states, Buddhism and journalism, properly understood, are methods of investigation aimed at producing transformative insight.

Sri Lankan–American journalist Shelton Gunaratne (Gunaratne, Pearson, and Senarath, 2015: 5) argues that guided by the Buddhist path (*magga*) "mindful journalism could establish a set of norms that perceptive human beings could use to compare and contrast with the traits of commodity-oriented news served in a hurry with all its warts or defilements."

---

[1] Triple gem is the three pillars of Buddhism—Buddha (the teacher), *Dhamma* (his teachings), and sangha (his disciples).

The Buddha has realized the concept of *samsara*, our suffering nature. He emphasized that one should always note that suffering, differences, and problems will always be there, but suffering can be eliminated. This is the teaching of the Four Noble Truths which are the foundation of Buddhist philosophy:

1. Life brings suffering (*dukkha*).
2. Suffering is a part of living (*samudaya*).
3. Suffering can be ended (*nirodha*).
4. There is a path that leads to the end of suffering (*magga*).

In the first two Noble Truths, the Buddha diagnosed the problem (suffering) and identified its cause. The third Noble Truth is the realization that there is a cure, which is the Eightfold Path, the prescription, and the way to achieve a release from suffering.

As discussed in the Introduction, the Four Noble Truths provide us the guide to understand the dependent originations of the SDGs and the need to understand the causation of poverty (suffering). So the role of a journalist (communicator) is to understand all these, be mindful of the situation on the ground and set about to compile reports that encourage or advocate policies that will lead to the eradication of poverty and suffering. This would lead you to practice compassion and loving kindness.

BTN NEWS and Path to Eradicating Suffering

BTN NEWS focuses on the role that Buddhism plays in the cessation of suffering. BTN does this by imparting factual accuracy and motivating Buddhist values such as compassion, loving kindness, and a sense of healing to viewers.

For example, on April 16, 2014, the SEWOL FERRY capsized off South Korea's southern coast killing 304 people, mostly high school students, in one of South Korea's most high-profile maritime disasters.

On April 17, 2014, KBS news,[2] South Korea's leading terrestrial channel, reported the harrowing experiences and the difficult situation of rescue plans due to the rain, wind, and fog, highlighting the death and a count of the missing. They showed the suffering of the families who were not able to hold their loved ones in their arms. They showed images of the victims

---

[2] https://www.youtube.com/watch?v=3j03TltnfpI) (accessed on November 3, 2015).

in body bags stating that there were much more dead and reported that the few survivors will be needing much psychiatric therapy for the emotional damage that was caused by this tragic disaster. The Korean society (TV audience) that had watched this felt devastated by this situation and most of the nation wept in heartache.

Visibly, although mass media news provide the latest headlines based on factual accuracy of the tragedy, they highlight the sufferings of the situation by focusing on the devastation of the situation by their continual use of provocative words in their headlines.

McGill (2008) calls these vocabularies on suffering as "verbal steroids" and recalled that, as a journalist, how he tended to get hooked on such provocative words because his stories and byline sucked in viewers as his piece shot straight onto the front page as the main news.

Looking at the coverage of the 2004 Asian Tsunami 2 years after it hit South and Southeast Asian coats, Kalinga Seneviratne (2006) commented on the back cover of the book *Media's Challenge: Asian Tsunami and Beyond*:

> The tsunami demonstrated that modern journalism can do more than just bring unfolding stories to the world. One of the biggest lessons of the tsunami that is unravelling is that modern journalist can also help to heal communities, rebuilt lives, keep families intact and raise funds. The media should also keep an eye on government and relief agencies, helping to ensure that aid gets to the people who need it, and that those who deliver the goods remain accountable to the donors and practice ethical standards of aid delivery.

Going back to the story above, in contrast, on the same date, on April 17, 2014, BTN NEWS[3] opened with a comment stating that BTN prays for the news of reuniting of survivors and began by reporting the current situation of the tragic Sewol Ferry disaster, but focused more on the process of healing.

BTN reported on how most of the Korean Buddhist monasteries had begun a prayer ceremony for the safe return of the victims, and where Jogyesa temple, the head temple of the Jogye Order, had held a dharma event and prayer ceremony along with 500 lay people for the safe return of all victims of the ferry disaster. Then it reported on all plans of actions for consolation for the families, rescue plans, and support plans from the Jogye Order, the president of Jogye Order, and the president of Korea that they will continue all forms of support.

---

[3] BTNNEWS.TV: http://www.btnnews.tv/news/view.asp?idx=28139&msection=2&ssection=8&page=18) (accessed on November 3, 2015).

Showing the Buddhist community, including sangha, and lay people nationwide having gathered together to pray and aid the situation gave viewers a sense of hope. In Buddhism, we call this *bodhicitta*.

Bodhicitta Path to Journalism

Bodhicitta is a core concept of Mahayana Buddhism, meaning the compassionate wish to reach enlightenment for the benefit of others. It is referred to as the path of selfless enlightenment. Its trademark is a strong commitment to profound compassion or love for others. The essence of *bodhicitta* basically means having compassion and loving kindness. Another meaning is that you help others when you are able.

Currently in Korea, forms of violence out of anger and impulsive rage crimes are on the rise. According to research in 2015 by the Korean Association of Psychiatric Practitioners, about 50 percent of Korean adults have experienced symptoms of impulse control disorder at least once, and about 10 percent of them needed treatment. So then why is a society that emphasizes group harmony and respect prone to rage and anger?

We believe that the media plays a key role. In general, news reporting from across the world regularly exposes viewers to crime news reports, where the media portrays the hard facts of our society very realistically and makes an endeavor not to leave any factual stone unturned. Consequently, it re-enacts the crime scene and the viewers end up learning much more about the crime than they had intended to.

When BTN journalists encounter such news, instead of focusing on the crime scene, we place our focus on finding a compassionate alternative for the problem in a way that will benefit society. Moreover, in the case of violent crimes, we, in particular Buddhists, do not believe that the offenders held such violent personalities from birth.

The 14th Dalai Lama[4] explains in his statement on compassion that

> Since a child cannot survive without the care of others, love is its most important nourishment. The happiness of childhood, the allaying of the child's many fears and the healthy development of its self-confidence all depend directly upon love. If they do not receive proper affection, in later life they will rarely love their parents and, not infrequently, will find it hard to love others.

---

[4] Refer to https://www.dalailama.com/messages/compassion-and-human-values/compassion (accessed on October 27, 2017).

To broadcast such news, on January 24, 2016, BTN[5] focused on broadcasting the importance of loving families, portraying how building positive communities can prevent violence out of anger and impulsive rage crimes that are on the rise by reporting on various cultural events for young people and dharma events geared for young children and families.

Ultimately, the need of love lies at the very foundation of human existence. Therefore, BTN sought the answer in the importance of healthy communities and families, placing strong emphasis on the importance of family, domestic happiness, and communities that support each other as the alternative to violent crimes.

And, coincidentally, looking at the coverage of the outbreak of South Korean bird flu that was raised to high alert in the end of 2016, we can find a similar example.

During these massive outbreaks of avian influenza, general news programs and newspapers reported on the severity of the outbreak, the rapid spread, the areas quarantined, and how many birds had been culled and the effects of the outbreak on our society. Various news programs approached the news using statistics and hard evidences establishing facts.

Consequently, according to Reuters (2016), one of the largest international news agency, the Agriculture Ministry of South Korea ordered the culling of 16 million birds, or almost one-fifth of the poultry population. They went on to report the perils and dangers of the virus on people, the areas quarantined, and the effects of increase of prices in poultry and eggs, and re-emphasized that previously 14 million birds were culled until that outbreak was finally brought under control in November 2015.

However, BTN NEWS took a different perspective. BTN journalists informed viewers of the catastrophic outbreak but gathered items based on the Buddhist concept of investigating the importance of lives of all sentient beings. Instead of focusing the perspective upon human society, we emphasized the fact that one-fifth of the entire poultry population was very easily eradicated since our society do not see the bird population as living creatures but only as food stock to feed our hunger. Thus, on the NEWS piece broadcast on January 3, 2017, and February 14 and 15, 2017, we highlighted the importance of all lives by capturing the various Buddhist rituals held across the nation to venerate and appease the spirits of the dead birds and called out to the society for the desperate need to find an alternative to culling.

As we all know from our experiences, words, information, and updates can change the way you look at any situation. Buddhism is making a way

---

[5] BTNNEWS.TV: http://www.btnnews.tv/news/articleView.html?idxno=35073 (accessed on February 15, 2017).

for every single human being to look at life from a different and positive perspective. Although many general mass media companies put their focal point on powerful and provocative images and headlines, BTN NEWS aims to focus on motivating *bodhicitta* and compassion in viewers.

Thus, in order to do this, BTN journalists must understand the fundamentals of Buddhism in conjunction with their role as journalists, because, to BTN, the ultimate purpose of both Buddhism and journalism is to serve and benefit humanity.

BTN CEO, Madame Bonil Koo, concludes, "Until now, BTN has fulfilled it's duties as the leading Buddhist media propagation channel…. BTN will continue to be a broadcaster with it's core philosophy on loving kindness and happiness for the path of practice and spiritual development of all sentient beings."

References

Gunaratne, S. A., M. Pearson, and S. Senarath. eds. 2015. *Mindful Journalism and News Ethics in the Digital Era*. New York, NY: Routledge.
Mcgill, Douglas. 2008. "The Buddha, the Dharma and the Media." *Mcgill Report*, February 19.
Seneviratne, K., ed. 2006. *Media's Challenge: Asian Tsunami and Beyond*. Singapore: AMIC.
Reuters. 2016. "South Korea Orders Record Cull of Poultry to Contain Bird Flu." Reuters, December 16. Available at http://www.reuters.com/article/us-health-birdflu-southkorea-idUSKBN1450CF (accessed on October 25, 2017).

22

Sri Lanka: Mindful Communication and Reconciliation

Ariyarathna Athugala

Mindfulness is the gentle effort to focus continuously on the experiences occurring at the present moment. The objective of "Mindful Communication for ASEAN Integration" was to debate the feasibility of alternative models of journalism to the prevailing Western paradigm. Rather, it is an acknowledgment that the basis of one of the world's major religions can offer guidance in identifying a secular moral compass that might guide our mindful journalism practice, as technology and globalization place mindful models under stress.

Buddhist psychology divides consciousness into two parts. One part is mind consciousness and the other is store consciousness. Mind consciousness is our active awareness. Store consciousness is the base of our consciousness. Store consciousness has the capacity to learn and to process.

Human moral principles from key religious teachings like the Noble Eightfold Path (NEFP; in Buddhism) could form the basis of a more relevant and broadly applicable model for the practice of "mindful journalism." This is the foundation of mindful journalism, within which one locates the space for media to promote reconciliation. Reconciliation is understood to be processes that use culture, religion, caste, language, storytelling, and communication in a very broad sense to grapple with the meaning of traumatic events.

Communication experts are starting to devote more attention to reconciliation, but mindful research on reconciliation is still in its infancy. Some Asian research and theories are developing, but much theory is still to be found in other fields, such as communication and theology.

Drawing from literature on reconciliation in divided communities as a framework, this chapter will discuss the perceptions Sri Lankans hold about the definition of reconciliation, the initiatives that can be used to promote reconciliation in Sri Lanka. Overall, this chapter seeks to present an alternative to conventional mindful communication that characterizes the current discourse about the Sri Lankan-related environment by encouraging creative approaches to reconciliation.

Historic Context

Sri Lanka is one of the few countries that successfully ended a long running armed conflict by defeating a terrorist organization, the Liberation Tigers of Tamil Eelam (LTTE). Sri Lanka experienced a 26-year long civil war from 1983 to 2009. Sri Lanka's political, social, and economic development was constrained by ethnic conflict and war between the government and the LTTE, also known as the Tamil Tigers. The protracted nature of the conflict inflicted deeply felt consequences at human, social, physical, and institutional levels.

After the conflict was over, the country had to face numerous challenges in terms of post-conflict recovery and nation-building. Post-conflict nation-building was not very successful, because it failed in building the hearts and minds of the grassroots level people who were really affected by the dispute. However, in the past few years (after the conflict ended in 2009), many efforts were taken to enhance mindfulness and social harmony. Meanwhile, commitments have been made to develop Sri Lanka as a better nation for every citizen to live.

While addressing some of the potential challenges faced by the country in connection with the practice of reconciliation, promotion of mindful communication between communities could be a very useful tool if properly implemented. It could be an essential tool to strengthen the social unity and integrity of the public. With these objectives in mind, this article analyses the necessity of promoting mindful reconciliation in the post-conflict era through journalism and communication. Promoting mindful reconciliation is therefore the communication of political, social, and economic reconciliation collectively.

Sri Lanka's ethnic conflict has been characterized by the growing distance that separates Sinhalese Buddhists from Tamil Hindus. A look at the Catholic Church of any county shows that a similar lack of communication and indifference exists within the same community united by religious faith but separated by politics, language, and culture.

Currently, the country is in the midst of a reconciliation process, which aims to knit together the divided communities and ethnic groups. This is a complex exercise, which demands inclusion of a host of groups with various interests; it includes the creation of a national and inclusive vision for the future, political and economic reforms, and significant attitudinal changes.

In 2015, the Government of Sri Lanka set up the Office for National Unity and Reconciliation (ONUR) headed by the former President

Chandrika Bandaranaike Kumaratunga. Its vision[1] statement toward a national agenda says:

> A strong, stable, progressive, inclusive and peace-loving nation where all Sri Lankans co-exist in harmony and unity, while diversity and national identity is respected and celebrated with a guarantee of equal opportunity in economic, social, cultural and political spheres for every citizen.

While its mission states:

> Promote and provide for a society that respects fundamental rights, freedom, rule of law, equality and diversity; treat and respect all citizens with dignity and non-discrimination irrespective of ethnicity, religion, language, caste, age, gender, sexual orientation, birthplace, political opinion.

In January 2017, Mrs Kumaratunga,[2] while addressing a school function, said that reconciliation will soon be included in the school curriculum. "Education is not merely about learning subjects such as languages, religions and sciences. We should take a holistic approach to education. The children should also learn about the society in general," she said. "They should learn about the prevailing social issues, the solutions to overcome such issues and about what we should do. They should study these things in-depth."

Background and History of the Conflict

Sinhalese have historically felt a sense of deprivation at the hands of European colonial rulers and the minorities' failure to explore comprehensively the implications of any actions that could address the Sinhalese grievances. Similarly, any solution meant to resolve the problems of Tamils and Muslims now must not be at the expense of the Sinhalese. That would not only be unfair and unjust, but it would make such a solution unsustainable in the long run.

The root causes of the three-decade conflict in Sri Lanka can be traced back to unequal treatment of the Tamils and perceived discrimination by the State. The Tamil community's campaign was against State structures and policies that were considered discriminatory to the Tamils. The failure of

---

[1] See http://www.onur.gov.lk/index.php/en/about-onur (accessed on October 27, 2017).
[2] Refer to http://dailynews.lk/2017/01/23/local/105428/%E2%80%98reconciliatio n%E2%80%99-will-be-included-school-curriculum-chandrika (accessed on October 27, 2017).

the dominant sections of the polity to address these grievances, the failure to rigorously examine changes to the policies and practices by successive governments, and the subsequent creation of a Tamil political leadership permitted the growth of unrealistic expectations amongst the Tamil youth. Finally, the democratic Tamil political leadership lost control and the LTTE monopolized the Tamil struggle, with disastrous consequences for Tamils as well as for the country as a whole. The Muslims, though not direct protagonists in the armed conflict between the LTTE and the Sri Lankan State, have undergone considerable suffering during the years of fighting in the North and East of the island.

The balance to be found must be perceived upon the common need for reconciliation and mindful coexistence. Here exists a trust deficit which has subscribed to the view that as the minority moves toward communicating geographical separation, any concession by the State will be detrimental to the majority (Sinhalese) community. But the Tamil minority lacks confidence and trust as a result of failed aspirations and expectations.

Sri Lanka is faced with unique opportunity to foster mindful environment, unity, and national reconciliation.

As a result of the long-time strife and struggle, two key challenges remain to be addressed so as to propel the country toward enduring reconciliation and mindfulness. The root causes for division in the society need mindful solutions that would be satisfactory to all the communities and peoples of Sri Lanka.

As Ven Piyasilo noted in Chapter 1, "in the Buddhist philosophy the real meaning of mindfulness is to remember something in any given situation." There is much in the collective memory of Sri Lankans in the past half a century that can be recalled and used to analyze the current moment. The thoughts and emotions that arise from these memories could be applied to the present situation to develop strategies without getting distracted from the present moment.

There remains a need to take further steps so that reconciliation achievements may be translated into mindful and cooperative benefits that will have an impact on the life of every Sri Lankan.

Many who appeared before the Lessons Learnt and Reconciliation Commission (LLRC) emphasized that what had been achieved by the security forces should be invested in a political process. The commission again found significant common ground among a broad spectrum of persons who made representations that this task can and should be achieved whilst upholding the territorial integrity and sovereignty of the nation and safeguarding the long-cherished Sri Lankan values of democracy, tolerance, and power sharing (LLRC, 2010).

Mindful communication is inherently a complex process where specific aspects of the reconciliation may gain attention and importance, undermining the overall outcome that is sought. In any reconciliation environment, mindful journalism is utilized as a dominant tool of propaganda.

The implementation arrangements should then ensure widest participation to promote public awareness for journalistic actions in a manner that brings about the widest mindful communication of the people in the implementation of the reconciliation. In the Sri Lankan context, both the State and the LTTE have used the audio and visual mediums in different degrees to propagate their ideologies.

What Is Mindfulness?

The Pali word for "mindfulness" is sati. Sati can also mean "recollection," or "alertness." Mindfulness is a whole body and mind awareness of the present moment as explained in the Introduction.

"Mindfulness" is an important word that cannot be readily dismissed now as "mystic." Today, meditation is practiced worldwide as part of mental development. The Sanskrit word for meditation, *bhavana*, means "mental culture," and all forms of meditation involve mindfulness. In recent years there has been a growing interest in mindfulness meditation as part of psychotherapy.

The Buddha said that there are four frames of reference in mindfulness:

1. Mindfulness of body (*kayasati*).
2. Mindfulness of feelings or sensations (*vedanasati*).
3. Mindfulness of mind or mental processes (*cittasati*).
4. Mindfulness of mental objects or qualities (*dhammasati*).

Ven. Gunaratana (1994) says that mindfulness comprises three fundamental activities.

1. Mindfulness reminds us of what we are supposed to be doing. If we are sitting in meditation, it brings us back to the focus of meditation. If we are washing dishes, it reminds us to pay full attention to the washing of the dishes.
2. In mindfulness, we see things as they really are. Our thoughts tend to cloud reality, and concepts and ideas distort what we experience.
3. Mindfulness sees the true nature of phenomena. Through mindfulness we directly see the three characteristics or marks of existence—it is imperfect, temporary, and egoless.

Zen teachers say that if you miss the moment, you miss your life. How much of our lives are we to be mindful of?

Mindfulness also means observing and releasing habits of mind. Being fully mindful means being fully attentive to everything as it is, not filtering everything through our subjective opinions. Ven. Henepola Gunaratana (1994), a Theravada Buddhist monk, explains in the book *Voices of Insight* that mindfulness is essential to help us see beyond symbols and concepts. "Mindfulness is pre-symbolic. It is not shackled to logic," he says. "The actual experience lies beyond the words and above the symbols."

Reconciliation

Reconciliation is a fairly new concept that became internationally focused with the Argentinean Truth Commission in 1984. The Latin verb *reconciliare* means "reestablish peace or friendship." Reconciliation has been defined in many ways, and the meaning of the term is by no means clear. According to Encyclopedia Britannica, reconciliation refers to (a) the action of reconciling, and (b) the state of being reconciled. Whereas reconstruction primarily refers to the restoration of economic, political, and physical infrastructure, reconciliation concerns the social fabric. Reconciliation also refers to a Roman Catholic sacrament, and is a theological term frequently used in Christian theology. As such, the term carries strong religious connotations. Reconciliation is defined by its Hebrew root word *Tikuum Olam* which means a three-part process of heal, repair, and transform.

In order to "heal" the impact of tribal or ethnic division, civil war, and violence, a process of acknowledging the evils that have been committed is essential. "Repairing" the structures involves ensuring that those wounds do not reoccur in today's society and ensuring resistance toward structural violence. "Transformation" lies in the process of creating a national identity and a sense of belonging for all.

Bar-Tal and Bennink (2004) emphasize the importance of the outcome of the conflict resolution on the reconciliation process. He identifies two main outcomes of conflict resolution:

1. Solution where two or more conflicting groups continue to live within the same system, and
2. Solution where the conflicting parties will live in separate states.

While the second form requires reconciliation between two different states, the first form necessitates the establishment of a new system that incorporates the past rivals on equal premises. In this case, the very creation of such systems—educational, political, cultural, economic, and legal—has great impact on the reconciliation process. Reconciliation refers to the restoration of fractured relationships by overcoming grief, pain, and anger. It is a societal process that involves mutual acknowledgment of past suffering into constructive relationships toward mindfulness.

Reconciliation can occur in every sphere of human experience, including individual and community levels. We will explore these common yet complicated aspects of our human existence, describe their importance for personal and community mindfulness, with many real-life stories of how they might be applied in positive ways to heal and strengthen both individuals and communities.

Reconciliation can be seen as a four-level process, including:

1. Developing a shared vision of an interdependent and mindful society
2. Building human-centric relationships
3. Facilitating significant cultural and attitudinal changes
4. Enabling substantial social, economic, and political changes

By engaging in the reconciliation process (community level)

- Promoting forgiveness on community level
- Ways to build and rebuild relationships

  - Cultivating public sphere dialogue
  - Starting grassroots mindful initiatives
  - Utilizing the healing power of sharing stories and mindful meditation

Enabling people to embrace tensions in the process of reconciliation and dialogue is the starting point. In a similar manner, reconciliation must actively involve in rebuilding relationships by creating mindful awareness for people to engage with each other through talking, entertaining, and gathering. In order to rebuild relationships, there must be platforms to develop understanding between groups and communities. Dialogue can be practiced in schools and corporate institutions.

While mindfulness can be practiced quite well without Buddhism, Buddhism cannot be practiced without mindfulness. In its Buddhist context, mindfulness meditation has three overarching purposes: knowing the mind, training the mind, and freeing the mind.

The principles of the NEFP in Buddhism for eradicating suffering could be applied in a secular fashion to the reconciliation process. The first "truth"—the reality of *dukkha* (suffering)—is seen as part of a conditioned existence. It could be seen in terms of subtle inner conflicts that lead to mental pain and torment.

The second "truth" is the casual arising of grasping, clinging, and aversion. As Buddhanet[3] explains:

> On one hand it is trying to control anything and everything by grabbing onto or trying to pin them down. On the other hand it is control by pushing away or pushing down and running away or flinching away from things. It is the process of identification through which we try to make internal and external things and experiences into "me and mine" or wholly "other" than Me. Because all conditioned existence is impermanent it gives rise to Dukkha, and this means that in conditioned existence there is no unchanging and permanent Self. There is nothing to grasp onto and also in reality, nothing or no "one" to do the grasping! We grab onto or try to push away ever changing dynamic processes. These attempts to control, limit us to little definitions of who we are.

The third "truth" is the end of *dukkha* which is nirvana that is beyond grasping, control, and conditional existence. The fourth "truth" is the path that leads you to nirvana. Path is ultimately unlearning rather than learning. Awakening, your true nature, is already always present. We are just not awake to this reality. Clinging to limitation and attempts to control the ceaseless flow of phenomena and process obscure our true nature. The Buddha called his teaching a raft. To cross a turbulent river, we may need to build a raft. When built, we single-mindedly and with great energy make our way across. Once across we do not need to cart the raft around with us. In other words, do not cling to anything including the teachings.[4]

This raft could be the process of reconciliation and the various institutions/programs we create to reach that destination. So what are the inner conflicts that various segments of the society face vis-à-vis coexistence with others? And when we come to the second truth, what are the ideas, perceptions, and fears we hold about each other? Why are we clinging onto them? Can we let go of those grasping which is the third truth that leads to the path—the raft? These are questions policy planners need to address before they build the raft

---

[3] Refer to http://www.buddhanet.net/e-learning/8foldpath.htm (accessed on October 27, 2017).

[4] Refer to http://www.buddhanet.net/ (accessed on October 27, 2017).

which will aid institutions and programs to reach the ultimate "nirvana" of reconciliation.

Let us now look at some experiences of Sri Lanka's reconciliation process.

Bringing Tamils and Sinhalese Together

We invited a large number of journalists in Jaffna (Tamil) and Madawachchi (Sinhala) to come and practice with us. Both groups had a lot of suspicion, anger, and fear, because both groups had suffered so much during the conflict period. They were of the opinion that by practicing mindful thinking and mindful writing, they could overcome their sufferings and fears and try calming down their negative feelings. However, in the beginning, the practice and the energy of mindfulness that you generate is not powerful enough to embrace the huge amount of fear, anger, and suspicion. You need to invigorate the collective energy of mindfulness to be strong enough to recognize and hold the energy of fear, anger, and suspicion.

The mindfulness training included the following:

- Attention training to cultivate qualities of concentration, clarity, and equanimity; the common thread connecting all other skills
- Relaxation
- Techniques to elicit the relaxation response in mind and body

Mindful awareness is a cultivable skill with broad applications through all aspects of society, including education, living systems, politics, creative work and even the institutional relations.

> Similarly, physical diseases, in addition to the familiar somatic signs and symptoms, also manifest with psychological, social and spiritual symptomatology. It is understandable that a person with a chronic arthritis or incurable cancer will have sadness, hopelessness and resentment. They may go on to develop frank Reactive Depression. Spiritually, they may lose faith or contrariwise may develop added faith in their religion. It is now well established that a person with chronic physical illnesses are benefited from psychological forms of treatment such as counselling and relaxation exercises. Spiritual solace may be also helpful.[5]

---

[5] Professor C. Sivagnanasundram Oration 2013, By: Dr Daya Somasundaram, September 26, 2013, HNB Auditorium, Jaffna. Refer to http://shanthiham.lk/wp-content/uploads/2014/11/Oration-Psychosocial-Rehabilitation-Daya-Somasundaram.pdf

Sri Lanka faces the challenge of instituting a credible and meaningful process of reconciliation involving two broad areas—addressing the structural and social drivers of conflict and mindful communication that generates confidence and is resilient at the level of communities and individual people.

Tools to Promote Reconciliation

Mechanisms for promoting reconciliation include a proposal to set up a "reconciliation commission," and Sri Lankans were asked to comment during the interviews conducted on their perceptions of such a commission and what mechanisms could be used to spread reconciliation in the country. In addition to training of journalists, workplace and working groups were put forward as tools to promote reconciliation.

Based on the variety of tools suggested, Sri Lanka reflects on the following issues:

- Encourage greater discussion about reconciliation between Sinhala, Tamil, and Muslim communities,
- The creation of initiatives that can help print media promote reconciliation,
- Establish a committee to clarify various perspectives on the ethnic and post-war issues with mutual acknowledgment,
- Focus on education,
- Reforming the media studies curriculum and promoting mindful communication that encourages creative and critical thinking and honest exploration of the future from a variety of perspectives,
- Initiate a mindful media campaign about reconciliation and different perspectives on the social problems,
- Develop and implement mindful training and seminars to prepare people to work together when country is reunified.

Icons for Reconciliation

It is an opportune time to consider some icons from the past that could be utilized for the reconciliation process. They have reached out to the majority Buddhist community respecting the national cultural identity.

Pansale Piyathuma (Catholic Priest of the Temple)[6]

Fr. Marcelline Jayakody (June 3, 1902–January 15, 1998) was a Sri Lankan Catholic priest, musician, lyricist, author, and journalist and an exponent of indigenous culture.

> Religion is for belief. What we believe is our religion. Religion is based on morality and precepts. It is by practicing religion that one can lead a good life. Nobody can definitely say my religion is the only true religion and the others are false.

This was what Rev. Fr. Mercelline Jayakody told when he was interviewed by Buddhist monk Pandit Ven. Ittepana Dhammaloka Thera to write a book about the Catholic priest under the title of "Pansale Piyathuma." At a time of chaos and confusion over religious identity, Fr. Jayakody's preaching has to be honored and appreciated.

Fr. Jayakody was one of the few Sri Lankans who won the Ramon Magsaysay Award, which is also called as the "Asian Nobel Prize." He wrote hymns and carols, lullabies and songs, Buddhist Vesak and Poson Bakthi Geetha that attracted both Buddhists and Catholics. One such song had these lyrics:

> *Netha Yana Thena Veherak Peniyan*
> *Veherak Nethi Thena Veherak Theniyan*
> *In Ena Pamovudaya Nuwanata Deniyan*
> *Dutu Vita Sitha Thula Sil Gamiyan*

> [Where ever you go you may see a temple,
> If there is no temple there, may they build a temple,
> The lesson which comes from it may go the heart,
> Whenever we see it, peace may fill our heart.]

Muslim Singer of Buddhist Songs

Mohideen Baig (December 5, 1919–November 4, 1991) was a notable Sri Lankan musician known particularly for his Buddhist devotional songs. A Muslim who moved to Sri Lanka from Salem in Tamil Nadu, he was not forgotten in his time.

---

[6] See Fernando (2001).

In 1956, then Prime Minister S. W. R. D. Bandaranaike conferred a Distinguished Citizenship on him. In 1967, he was considered as a highly influential multicultural/multireligious figure in the country's arts history.

Mohideen was followed into the music industry by his son Ishak, who also achieved considerable success. He won the Kalasuri (artistic great) titles twice, in 1983 and in 1987.

Mohideen got the opportunity to appear at Sri Lanka's first Independence Day ceremony and at the 1974 Non-Aligned Summit in Colombo.

Globalization and Open Markets

While the above two icons of Sri Lankan coexistence belong to a bygone era before the advent of globalization and open market economics, the current efforts of reconciliation between ethnic and religious groups may well be more complicated with cultural flows from outside threatening local communities, cultures, and identities.

In a nutshell, nationalist poet, novelists, and social activist Dr Gunadasa Amarasekera's (Wijewardena, 2012) message is as follows:

> Sri Lanka has been subject to the forceful power of globalisation and free market economy system in the last three and a half decades or so. This force has destroyed the country's rich cultural heritage of which the core has been founded on Sinhalese Buddhism. This has in fact generated disastrous results for the future of the country. The path, which the country would have taken to avert this disaster, would have been the revival of the nationalistic movement which the late Anagarika Dharmapala had started in 1930s when the country was still under the British rule.

Thus, Wijewardena notes that in a "sense" what is required is nothing but redesigning Sri Lanka's value system and goals based on Amarasekera's words, "the core of our civilisational heritage which has escaped our minds so far, with disastrous results."

Journalism and Its Moral Compass

The recent inquiries triggered by digital journalism and ethical practices have demonstrated that journalism within the mindful model appears to have lost its moral compass, and we need to explore new ways to recapture this. We should educate journalists, serious bloggers, and citizen journalists to adopt a mindful approach to their news and commentary accommodating a reflection upon the implications of their work on reconciliation and harmony as a routine part of the process.

The media plays a major role in shaping societal consciousness, and since Buddhism and other religious thoughts have a stake in expressing its teachings to as large an audience as possible, the debate over how to create mindful journalism is one in which Buddhism can actively participate but should not be seen to be dominating.

There are many ways in which media can help in the process of reconciliation. The creation of safe spaces in the form of newspaper supplements and web discussions that are reported in provincial media, the promotion of ethnic diversity in television programming, reporting stories with a mindful mindset, supporting reconciliation in language media by journalists collaborating in reporting exercises, sharing and translating content, using new digital media to capture and strengthen voices that may have been hitherto marginalized are some methods that media can adopt toward initiatives in support of wider discourse on reconciliation.

To transform media into one that promotes reconciliation requires us to look at the way media works. Mindful stories of human interest are often submerged in a deluge of stories that report on negative events in a reconciliation process. Reconciliation is not a single event.

The distinction between an event and a process is an important one to always bear in mind. A reconciliation process is the apotheosis of the aspirations of all peoples to coexist in a society founded upon principles of democracy and justice.

We should recognize and be mindful to build on examples of the reconciliation process, particularly through focusing on communities and organizations. Without alternative sources of mindful reconciliation stories, people are led to blame Sri Lankans for their own circumstances. It is essential that the reconciliation process, while mindful of the need to overcome miscommunication, highlights the "mindful news" which is emerging through better evidence of creative activity and effective partnerships. It must also remind Sri Lankans of their role in reconciliation.

An exercise inextricably linked to the promotion of reconciliation, this requires mindful journalism to highlight voices that examine reconciliation mechanisms and understandings on a provincial, district, and national level, even when partisan politics and official negotiations marginalize such processes.

The ability to create Sinhala, Tamil, and English content in support of reconciliation remains a significant challenge but one that needs to be addressed if discussions on reconciliation are to move from minority circles into the conscience of ethnic communities and those in the hinterlands of conflict.

One of the problems with emerging citizen journalism and news websites is that their proponents do not necessarily ascribe to mindful journalists' ethical codes. Their advocacy roles for certain causes or communities without being mindful of how it could be seen and reacted to by the larger community may hinder mindful journalism practice toward reconciliation. However, codes of ethics have often failed to work effectively in guiding the ethics of the journalists for whom they were designed, let alone the litany of new hybrids including citizen journalists and the avid users of other emerging news platforms.

Bibliography

Bar-Tal, Daniel, and Gemma Bennink. 2004. "The Nature of Reconciliation as an Outcome and as a Process." In *From Conflict Resolution to Reconciliation*, edited by Yaacov Bar-Siman-Tov, 11–39. Oxford: Oxford University Press.

Cantacuzino, M. 2013. *Transforming Lives Through the Power of Personal Narrative*. London: Winston Churchill Memorial Trust.

———. 2015. The Forgiveness Project: Stories for a Vengeful Age. London and Philadelphia: Jessica Kingsley Publishers.

De Mel, N., P. Peiris, and Shyamala Gomez. 2013. *Broadening Gender: Why Masculinities Matter: Attitudes, Practices and Gender-based Violence in Four Districts in Sri Lanka*. CARE international.

De Mel, N., and R. Venugopal. 2016. *Peace Building Context Assessment: Sri Lanka*. London School of Economics and Political Science. Available at http://lk.one.un.org/wp-content/uploads/2016/04/Peacebuilding-Context-Assessment-Draft-1-single-pages.pdf (accessed on October 25, 2017).

De Silva, J. 2006. Dr. Maya Gunasekera (1961–2006). *Journal of the National Science Foundation of Sri Lanka* 34 (3), DOI:http://doi.org/10.4038/jnsfsr.v34i3.3650.

Enright, R. 2008. *Forgiveness Is a Choice*. Washington, DC: American Psychological Association.

Fernando, Susitha R. 2001. "'Pansale Piyathuma'—103 years old." Available at http://www.sundaytimes.lk/050821/tv/3.html (accessed on October 27, 2017).

Gunaratana Mahathera, H. (Venerable). 1994. *Mindfulness in Plain English*. High View, WV: H. Gunaratana Mahathera Bhavana Society. Available at http://www.bhavanasociety.org/ (accessed on October 28, 2017).

Gunaratne, S. A. 2009. "A Buddhist View of Journalism: Emphasis on Mutual Causality." *Javnost: The Public* 16 (2): 61–75.

Lynch, J. 2010. "Peace Journalism." In *The Routledge Companion to News and Journalism*, edited by S. Allan, 542–53. London: Routledge.

Radhakrishnan, R. K. 2011. "The Report of the Lessons Learnt and Reconciliation Commission of Sri Lanka May Lack Credibility in International Fora." *Frontline*. The Hindu Group, 28 (25).
Thaheer, M., P. Peiris, and Kasun Pathiraja. 2013. *Feeling of Safety' in Reconciliation in Sri Lanka: Voices from the Former War Zones*. Colombo: ICES.
Wijewardena, W. A. 2012. "Globalisation According to Gunadasa Amarasekere: The Scholar Who Has Refused to Change." *Colombo Telegraph*, May 12. Available at https://www.colombotelegraph.com/index.php/globalisation-according-to-dr-gunadasa-amarasekera-the-scholar-who-has-refused-to-change/ (accessed on October 25, 2017).

23

Mindful Communication for Sustainable Development: A New Asian Communication Paradigm

Kalinga Seneviratne

Mass Media is one of the most powerful tools in modern society. Even without its present-day proliferations into digital media, and sharing in social media, its influence on the course of history had often been manifested—the US lost the Vietnam War because its own mass media turned the tide of American public opinion. As wielders of this tool with power to pave the path of conflict and suffering, or the path of understanding and peace, journalists should have clear awareness that this power bears with it both responsibility and accountability—"Responsibility" in doing your job of gathering, screening and giving information; "Accountability" in following up on the results with integrity and balance.

The use of bye-line in journalism is for the purpose of accountability. On the other hand, it can also foster egoism and worse, egocentrism, resulting in sensational rather than rational style of communication, drawing the attention and attachment of mass audience to the individual journalist.

With the mindfulness of Sila, Samathi, *Panna*, a journalist's individualism will naturally channel itself from the sphere of egoism to that of altruism which involves taking into account the full picture of each situation and asking oneself: "What will be the short- and long-term benefits and drawbacks of what I am about to do? Will my action affect a smaller or larger number of individuals?"

With mindfulness of the users, the powerful tool of mass communication can become an effective agent in the building of an unselfish and constructive society, integration of and collaboration between ASEAN countries, and a more harmonious world.

As the above comments from the award-winning Thai writer and social media personality Khunying Chamnongsri Hanchanlash[1] reflects, mass media is a powerful tool in modern society, which could either make or break a society. In today's Internet age, "what exactly is the mass media?" is a question

---

[1] Excerpts from a talk given at a seminar "Mindful Communication for ASEAN Integration" at Chulalongkorn University, Bangkok, in December 2015.

many are still debating. Thus, this is why in this book we have tried to take a broader look at the mass media and various tools at its disposal to assist in communicating for sustainable development.

In exploring mindful communication for sustainable development (MC4SD), we have drawn heavily from the Buddhist philosophy. But, we have also made it clear that you do not need to be a Buddhist to practice or adopt these ideas/concepts, even making a comparison to the work of Catholic priests (Chapter 12). We have also explored some innovative ideas such as using Japanese "silent" communication strategies (Chapter 15) and "mindful comic writing" for sustainable development communication (Chapter 18). In Chapters 16 and 17 we have examined how modern public relations could benefit from drawing in from traditional communication methodologies of Buddhist societies, for example in Laos and Cambodia.

If we are going to look at MC4SD as a new Asian Sustainable Communication paradigm, it is imperative that we challenge some of the existing Western-centric communication theories as we have tried to do in Chapters 1 to 6. We have also introduced new ideas (some of them are old ideas in a new dressing) such as deep listening, human-centric reporting, and middle path journalism.

The United Nations Economic and Social Commission for Asia and the Pacific (UNESCAP) in its "Economic and Social Survey of Asia and the Pacific 2017" said in its executive summary[2]:

> Governance quality has been defined in various ways by different organizations and institutions. In the Survey for 2017 political dimensions, such as democratic accountability, are avoided, and governance is framed in terms of how power is exercised instead of how it is acquired. This approach respects the diversity of cultures, historical experiences and levels of development that countries in the Asia-Pacific region share. A more functional definition of governance enables the focus of the Survey for 2017 to be on transmission mechanisms—mobilization and allocation of fiscal resources—through which governance affects various aspects of sustainable development.

ESCAP's chief macroeconomist, Hamza Ali Malik, at a media conference during its launch said:

> We should not be telling governments what type of democratic systems they should be or not be running. Governments should be deciding that for themselves. We are more interested in analysing how the power is exercised in terms of delivery of public services rather than how it is acquired. That is what we are focusing on.

---

[2] Available at http://www.unescap.org/sites/default/files/Executive%20Summary-Survey2017.pdf (accessed on October 27, 2017).

He added:

> If you look at our region there has been a range of cultural experiences, history, development models that interact with democracy and it offers a range of arrangements of how development can be pursued by phases, so we are not getting into the determinance of governance in that sense. (Seneviratne, 2017)

In Chapters 9 and 13, in particular, we have looked at how this diversity of political systems and ways of exercising power could be monitored and facilitated by the media, rather than it playing an adversarial role of a watchdog.

As Pipope Panitchpakdi (Chapter 9) noted, "news has to be critical, but being critical doesn't have to be confrontational. Being critical is looking at it objectively but the approach of doing it doesn't have to be negative." Giving a number of examples, he discussed how this approach could be developed.

Sugath Senarath (Chapter 13) argued taking a Buddhist perspective that good governance is more than economic development; it should also lead to moral development. Such moral dimensions require the journalist to analyze how power is exercised once it is acquired. This will also require consulting the views of people on how they see this power being exercised for the sustainable development of their society.

Curriculum

Here we have listed four curricula that we have developed for the IPDC-UNESCO-funded project designed for offering at tertiary level and also in journalism training programs in Asia. These could also be offered in other areas with minor modifications to bring in local/regional resource material. The curricula were developed with the clear intention of weaning away Asian journalism teachers/trainers from too much dependency on western (usually American) material and offering them resource material from closer to home that could be more relevant to local environment/culture/society.

Media and Society

This 12-week semester-long course curriculum takes a critical approach to the study of the role of the media in society. It takes a value-based approach to the production and consumption of mass media, with a special emphasis on the role of media in community building and promoting social harmony.

Traditional Asian philosophical approaches to social interaction, governance, and stability will be explored and compared with contemporary ideas of the media acting as a democratization tool.

The course tries to give a broader perspective of the development of mass communication and communication theory and balance the freedom of expression concepts with media's role in the society as a harmonizing tool. It also looks at media's economic models, its role in shaping culture, captivating/colonizing the mind, environmental awareness, social media in society, and reporting conflicts and assisting to build a peaceful society.

Human-centered Journalism

Human-centered journalism course is recommended for offering in the first year of a 3-year bachelor course in mass communication/journalism. This course takes a humanistic approach to train students in investigative journalism. The main objective is to help them develop thinking and skills in mindful conceptualizing, researching, and writing human-centered journalistic stories. The course will focus on the roles of humanity in the analysis and the practice of complex storytelling. Students will be familiarized with the framework of deep listening and dialogical interviewing techniques, mindful investigative research methods and humanistic interpretation of surveys as well as different forms of narrative techniques for human-centered journalism.

This is a 12-week course with 4 hours (two 2-hour classes per week) of a combination of lectures, contemplative workshops and dialogues, seminars, extensive fieldworks, individual assignments, and tutorial.

In the first week of the course, students will be trained to listen to one's inner voice and engaging with the mind and body based on mindful meditation techniques. In week 2, students will be introduced to traditional Asian and Western philosophical approaches to humanity, and they will also be introduced to the art of listening to others with contradicting points of view, with compassion. In week 3, students will be guided to interpret data from a humanistic perspective as a journalistic exercise.

Week 4 will include a practical exercise with a series of field trips to a site of potential final assignment reporting. Students will be advised to observe the situation and human interaction on site, as well as to talk to as many people as possible. In week 5, students will view a movie, followed by a discussion on their emotions, insights, and experience after seeing the movie. Then, they will be guided to discuss different ways in which human-centered storytelling can be combined with data journalism.

Weeks 6–8 will focus on anatomy of human-centered storytelling with a lecture followed by class exercises of read and critique of stories, as well as pitching a story idea to the lecturer for approval for final exercise. Weeks 9–11 will include fieldwork, and writing of first and final draft. In week 12, the final copy will be presented to the class in a seminar style with a discussion on the exercise. The grading for the final assignment will include a reflective essay on the exercise as well.

Development Journalism

This course is designed to develop specialized reporting skills of a journalism student in reporting issues dealing with various aspects of development. The traditional concept of development itself would be challenged in this course and new ideas would be examined and explored that are specific to the Asian environment.

To be offered as a final year elective, traditional Asian wisdom will be considered in the context of developing new paradigms of development reporting. Lecturers are encouraged to source sample story ideas for each week from their own country or the immediate neighborhood. The semester-long 12-week course will be presented in 3-hour weekly blocks of workshop style lectures and class exercises.

The week 1 lecture will examine contemporary news values in reporting development issues and give an overview of the construction of news values, function of news agencies, the global flow of news, and its role in shaping development news. In weeks 2 and 3, we will look at the definitions and philosophies of development, historical context, what is development journalism, and how it should be structured.

In week 4, we will explore the challenges development journalism faces due to commercialization and globalization of the media, which makes sensationalism and dramatization important aspects of news reporting, and why development journalism should be about reporting a process. Reporting of the 2004 Asian Tsunami will be closely examined as a case study. Week 5 will be devoted to looking at the craft of doing development features both for print and broadcast.

Weeks 6–8 will cover different genres of development reporting. In week 6, we will look at economic reporting and examine Asian concepts such as sufficiency economics and gross national happiness, while in week 7 we look at arts and entertainment as development issues, especially in the Asian context where cultural identity and protecting cultural heritage have socioeconomic connotations. In week 8, we examine the role of the development journalist in covering environmental issues and supporting Sustainable Development Goals.

In week 10, we look at the issue of cross-border development reporting in the age of globalization such as labor migration, human trafficking, asylum seeking, and money laundering. In the final two weeks, students will also examine new paradigms of development reporting using new media technology, social media and community media avenues, as well as the role of the citizen journalist in development reporting with examples drawn from across Asia.

Sufficiency Economics and Business Reporting

Bachelor-level final year special project/elective of an undergraduate degree in journalism or mass communication, this workshop could be incorporated into specialized reporting electives such as development reporting or economic-business reporting or human-centric reporting modules or it could be a final year specialist reporting project.

The earlier curricula which are designed for a semester-long course could also be modified to offer shorter workshops or a series of workshops under the theme/topic.

What Is the Difference—East Versus West Battle

One is entitled to ask what would differentiate these curricula from the existing ones. Is this an exercise in the East versus the West battle? It is certainly not and challenging the West is not trying to create conflict. Using the eastern metaphor—this is an exercise in developing *panna* (wisdom) to gain insights and be enlightened about the diversity of perspectives available for communicating in today's information-rich society.

Today, we are at an age where the West is going gaga about adopting mindfulness for improving its health services and stressful lifestyles. As we have discussed in the Introduction, mindfulness is at the root of the ancient Asian philosophical approach to a healthy enlightened lifestyle, which the Buddha taught over 2,500 years ago. But the Asians have forgotten it, perhaps as a result of 500 years of European colonization and indoctrination that makes them feel inferior in the face of *panna* to the West.

Over 2 decades ago, Petras (1993) said that western "cultural imperialism plays a major role in disassociating people from their cultural roots and traditions of solidarity, replacing them with media-created 'needs' which change with every public campaign." He went on to discuss the role CNN, Hollywood, Disney, etc., play in shaping peoples' perspectives and tastes. These curricula are designed to draw people back into their communities and associate themselves with traditions and customs that are made relevant to 21st century living with mindful communication practices assisting in this transformation.

Be it Asian communication scholars uncritically adopting theories of communication that have been framed and developed in a western social context; or Thai media reporting uncritically on their front page how local football fans turned up in thousands to welcome the British football champions, Leicester City, to Bangkok because it is owned by a Thai tycoon; or Asian media carrying pictures and reports from western media sources of President Obama being mobbed by Vietnamese youth in Ho Chi Minh City without asking the question "why couldn't Obama apologise for American war crimes in Vietnam such as using napalm bombs," dropped not that far from the city; all these point to what one may call the impact of cultural imperialism on the Asian mindset.

New Journalism for an Emerging Asia

What Asia needs today is a new journalism for an emerging Asia that is able to rid Asians of this hangover of cultural imperialism and critically examine and assess itself as well as the outside world, especially the news and information coming from the West.

What this curriculum aim to do is to develop journalism training programs in the region where Asians draw inspiration from their own traditional wisdom—as we have tried to do in this book—and feel proud and confident to adopt these to craft a model of journalism which, while not been overly adversarial, will not be overtly uncritically supporting the status quo in order to protect social harmony.

The Buddha proposed a middle path to guide your lives, and that is what we hope we will be able to achieve in developing a system of human-centric news journalism for an emerging Asia, the framework of which was discussed by Dorji Wangchuck in Chapter 11.

The Buddha attributed peoples' unhappiness (*dukkha*) to three defilements—desire (*tanha*) and clinging (*upadana*) fostered by ignorance (*avijja*). If you take any topic for reporting, these three elements are there, especially so in economic or developmental reporting. To achieve sustainable development, the craft of journalism and development communication needs to dismantle these three defilements.

We hope this book has provided some food for thought as well as assisted in developing strategies for practice so that the media could assist in achieving what the United Nations call the "2030 Agenda" of sustainable development.

References

Petras, J. 1993. "Cultural Imperialism in the late 20th Century." *Third World Resurgence* 39: 28–32.
Seneviratne, K. 2017. Exercising Power More Fairly More Important SDG Yardstick than Democratic Accountability. *IDN-INPS*, May 3. Available at http://www.indepthnews.net/index.php/global-governance/un-insider/1118-exercising-power-fairly-more-important-sdg-yardstick-than-democratic-accountability (accessed on October 25, 2017).

Links to Full Curricula

- Media and Society: http://docs.wixstatic.com/ugd/cc6e39_7bf32b0cadf541d18839f28147a87060.pdf
- Human-Centred Journalism: http://docs.wixstatic.com/ugd/cc6e39_f19f40fa5cf246b9aba97c1418ca5b96.pdf
- Development Journalism: http://docs.wixstatic.com/ugd/cc6e39_f6e1827f0db64116a140b20597406e33.pdf
- Sufficiency Economics and Business Reporting: http://docs.wixstatic.com/ugd/cc6e39_fa111a7f63bb4624bb587d694bf6d082.pdf

About the Editor and Contributors

Editor

Kalinga Seneviratne is Lecturer in the Faculty of Communication Arts, Chulalongkorn University, Bangkok. He is a media analyst with many years of experience in journalism. He was the Australia and South Pacific correspondent for the Inter Press Service news agency. From 2005 to 2012, he was the Head of Research at the Asian Media Information and Communication Centre, Singapore. Dr Seneviratne has been an award-winning radio broadcaster in Sydney. He received the Media Peace Award (1987) from the United Nations Association of Australia and the Educational Award (1992) from the Community Broadcasting Association of Australia. He writes for several news services and has several published works to his credit. Before joining the Faculty of Communication Arts at Chulalongkorn University, Dr Seneviratne taught development journalism and international communications at Macquarie University, Sydney; University of Technology Sydney; Ngee Ann Polytechnic, Singapore; and Nanyang Technological University, Singapore.

Contributors

Binod C. Agarwal worked at the Space Applications Centre, Indian Space Research Organisation. He is an expert in international communications, and for his contributions he was awarded the Asian Communication Award (2009) by the Asian Media Information and Communication Centre, Singapore.

Ariyarathna Athugala is Senior Professor in the Department of Mass Communication, University of Kelaniya, Sri Lanka. He is the former Chairman of Sri Lanka's national broadcaster Rupavahini and also the former Director General of Department of Government Information, Sri Lanka.

Azman Azwan Azmawati is Associate Professor in the School of Communication, Universiti Sains Malaysia. She holds a PhD in Economic Journalism and a Master's in International Relations. She is the President for Asian Congress for Media and Communication (ACMC).

Lim Kooi Fong is the founder and managing publisher of the web-based news site "The Buddhist Channel" (buddhistchannel.tv) and BuddhisTravel.com. He is the CEO of Chegoo World, an ePublishing company based in Kuala Lumpur.

Emi Hayakawa is the Head of Global Operations of the Korea-based television channel Buddhist True Network. She is also a radio broadcaster.

Chai Ming Hock is a faculty member, School of Communication, Universiti Sains Malaysia. He teaches journalism, newspaper publication, and photojournalism.

Nayheak Khun has been working as a reporter and an editor for many years. She is a member of the Club of Cambodian Journalists and Konrad-Adenauer-Stiftung Female Legal Youth Network.

Ananda Kumaraseri has authored several books on the cultivation of human values, personal development, holistic education, holistic parenting, childcare and development, and peace. He is a well-known speaker whose interests lie in the application of Buddhist teachings in daily life.

Pipope Panitchpakdi is a journalist, radio broadcaster, and television producer. He studied political theater at San Jose State University and journalism and mass communication at Bangkok University.

Kwangsoo Park is Professor, Department of Won-Buddhism, and Director of the Research Centre for Religions, Wonkwang University, South Korea. He is also the Vice President of the Korean Association for the History of Religions.

Hommala Phensisanavong is a lecturer and the Deputy Head of Mass Communication Department, Faculty of Letters, National University of Laos, Vientiane, Laos. She holds a Master's of Educational Studies in Applied Linguistics. Her research focus is in the area of communicative language in use.

Supaporn Phokaew is Senior Lecturer in the Faculty of Communication Arts at Chulalongkorn University, Bangkok. Her research focus is in the areas of media for children, community media, communication for local empowerment, and communication for disaster mitigation.

Venerable Phuwadol Piyasilo is a monk at the Yen Boon Forest Monastery in Thailand. He is a mass communication graduate from Chulalongkorn University, Bangkok, and has many years of experience in journalism.

Sanjay Ranade founded the Department of Communication and Journalism at the University of Mumbai in 2003. His research interests include religious communication, therapeutic communication, music, drama, and intrapersonal communication design.

Therese Patricia C. San Diego is Program Officer at the Asian Institute of Journalism and Communication in Manila, Philippines, where she conducts research in the areas of communication for development, health communication, child rights, and safety of journalists and media workers.

Sugath Mahinda Senarath is Senior Lecturer in Mass Media in the Department of Mass Media, University of Colombo, Sri Lanka. He has a PhD from the School of Journalism and Communication, Wuhan University, China.

Jirayudh Sinthuphan is Director of the South Asia Research Center, and Lecturer in the Faculty of Communication Arts at Chulalongkorn University, Bangkok. He has a PhD in drama and performance practice from the University of Exeter, UK.

Sulak Sivaraksa is a social critic, and for his social work, he received the Right Livelihood Award in 1995. He is the founder of the International Network of Engaged Buddhists along with the Dalai Lama, Vietnamese monk Thich Nhat Hanh, and Cambodian monk Maha Ghosananda.

Raqib Sofian is pursuing a PhD at the School of Communication, Universiti Sains Malaysia. His research interest is in media and politics, media and religion, and representation in the media.

Cho Cho Thwin is Associate Professor in the Department of Journalism, National Management Degree College, Yangon, Myanmar. She has a PhD in geography from Yangon University and is an expert in assessing media development with respect to agriculture and rural development.

Nicolas Verstappen is Lecturer for the Communication Management International Program, Faculty of Communication Arts, Chulalongkorn University, Bangkok. He teaches courses focusing mainly on graphic narrative composition, history, and aesthetics.

Dorji Wangchuck is a documentary filmmaker and journalist and is currently pursuing a PhD in communication studies at the University of Macau, China. He has led major projects with the Bhutan Broadcasting Service in order to introduce television and FM radio in the country.

Kanako Watanabe studied at the Tokyo University of Foreign Studies and later at the University of Bath, UK. She is an expert in Japanese–English translation and was involved in research projects at Chulalongkorn University, Bangkok.

Evans Rosauro I. Yonson is Chairman of the Development Communication Department of Xavier University, Ateneo de Cagayan in Cagayan de Oro, Philippines. His interests are in migration of ASEAN higher education students, rural radio broadcasting, and capacity building of indigenous youth.

Index

acceptance of differences, 98
advertising, 31
   culture, 136
agricultural revolution, 173
Al Jazeera, 96
All India Radio, 66, 69
Ambedkar, B. R., 71
Anderson, Benedict, 87
Annual Status of Education Report (ASER) survey 2011, 61
Anukaran (doing after), 76
Anukirtan (saying after), 76
Apauruseya, 74
Arakan Army (AA), 118
Arakan Liberation Army (ALA), 118
Argentinean Truth Commission (1984), 322
Armed Forces of the Philippines (AFP), 288
Arya Samaj, 70
ASEAN
   citizenship, 85–87
   communication revolution in, 37
   goal of, 81
   journalism in, 40
   media practice as research, 85
   media role in, 40
   task ahead, 84
Asian Conference on Religion and Peace, 46
Asian financial crisis, 47
Asian Institute of Journalism and Communication (AIJC), 299
Asian Media Information and Communication Center (AMIC), 299
Asian values, 58, 98
atamsamishan (self-retrospection of soul), 35

bad lending, 49
bad news, 97
bhavana, 174
Baig, Mohideen, 327

Bandaranaike, S. W. R. D., 328
Bhagvad Gita, 76
bhava (sentiments or emotional states), 75
Bhutan
   earthquake in 2009, 134
   population of, 134
   values in society, 142
Bhutan Broadcasting Service (BBS), 135
Bhutanese media, 133
   genesis of, 134
   new era and responsibility of, 135–38
   role of, 139
Bhutan Media Foundation (BMF), 133
Bhutan Times, 138
bias-free communication, 44
Birth and Mission of Buddhist True Network (BTN)
   eradication of suffering, path for, 312–14
   establishment of, 311–12
   journalists, 314, 316
   mindful journalism, implementation of, 311
   news, 314, 315
Bodhichitta, concept of, 314–16
border crossing, 242
Border Guard Force (BGF), 118
Brahmo, 70
brain or mind (*mana/manasa*), 161
British Broadcasting Corporation (BBC), 66, 121
Buddha, 71
   advise on designing of religious enquiry, 54
   community growth, conditions for, 55
   Four Noble Truths of, 312
   framework for overcoming mundane human problems, 171
   importance of living, working and cooperating, 55
   individualized property, 173

Index   345

instructions in *Satipatthana Sutta*, 109
middle way approach, 339
opposition to prevailing rituals and sacrifices, 35
religious freedom, advocacy of, 54
teachings, critical aspect, 31
Buddhism, 34, 41, 89, 91, 104, 139
  Aggana Sutta of *Digha Nikaya*, 162
  all beings (*sabbe sattā*), 163
  believes in innate goodness, 162
  Dasa Raja Dharma principle, 164
  facilitation between extremes, 57
  human affairs, measurement of, 165
  in China, introduction of, 310
  Kalama Sutta in, 99
  negative traits or characteristics of mind, 167
  Noble Eight Fold Path (NEFP) in, 324
  on balanced way of life, 166
  philosophical tenets of, 56
  upholding of democracy, 164
Buddhist, 70
  attitude toward legal dispensation, 168
  legal system, 147
  path of enlightenment, 30
  soteriology, 36
  view of human rights and religion liberty, 52
  way of life, 166
Buddhahood, 31
Burke, Edmund, 136

Cakkavatti Sihanada Sutta, 164
Cambodia, 82
  Angkorian caste system, 214
  believes in Theravada Buddhist religion, 213
  challenges faced by government spokespersons, 228
  community and monastery, communication between, 218
  government spokespersons, role and responsibility, 227
  Hindu and Buddhist cultures and societies, 212
  journalists and public relations practitioners, relationship between, 224
  journalists perspectives, 229

  Khmer monastic system, 216
  mindful communications, 230
  monasteries in, 214
  perspective of government spokespersons, 230
  public relations in, 221, 226
  symbolic centers, 213
  Theravada ideology of kingship, 214
  traditional monastic communication system, 231
celebrating blissfulness, 98
Center for Community Journalism and Development (CCJD), Philippines, 291, 299
Center for Industrial Technology, 152
Central Public Information Officer (CPIO), 70
Christian, 70, 103
  missionaries, 39, 63
Chuangtzu, 47
Chulalongkorn University, 45
Chute, Hillary, 239
civil rights, 57
climate change, 173
coercion, 98
collective reasons, 162
College of Agriculture, 152
College of Medicine, 152
color printing, 65
comic art, 238
comic composition, 236
  adopting to development communication, 255–59
  cross cultural undercurrents, 255
  instructions for exercise, 250
  multimodal narratives, results of, 252–54
commitment, 147
communication
  definition of, 44
  importance of, 108
  strategy, approaches for, 111
Communications and Multimedia Act (CMA), Malaysia, 268
Communist Party of Burma (CPB), 118
community, 144–45
  media, 105, 106, 220
  story, 105
  TV, 106
  wellbeing, 58

compassion, 93, 98, 145–46
concentration, 110
conformist society, 95–97
Confucius, 44, 46, 50
contemplation, 36
contentment, 143–44
convergence of communication technology, 37
corporate CEOs, training for mindfulness, 30
critical (mindful) thinking, 32
cultural attitudes of East and West, difference between, 83
cultural diversity, 113
cultural heritages, 86
cultural imperialism, 338
culturalization, 114
culture contact, 41
culture of death, 299
curriculum
   economics and business reporting, 337
   human-centerd journalism, 335–36
   journalism, development of, 336–37
   media and society, 335

Daesh terror group, 56
Dalai Lama, 314
Dan'gun myth, 45
Daoist teachings, 46
declaration of human rights, 58
deep ecology, 172
deep listening, 94, 303
delusion, 32
Democratic Karen Benevolent Army (DKBA), 118
Democratic Voice of Burma (DVB), 121
Deshimaru, Taisen, 184
development communication (DC 20), 155
development communication (DevCom) program
   aim of, 152
   definition of, 152
   of Xavier University, 155–58
dhammas, 241
dharma or righteousness, concept of, 35
digital storytelling, 82, 85, 86
dignity
   human, 58, 164
   of human person, 53–56
   of Malays, 265
direct to home (DTH) television, 40
Doordarshan, 66
   three-tier program service, 69
duality, 242
Duterte, Rodrigo R., 287

east vs west, difference between, 337–38
ecological degradation, 173
economic cooperation, 51
economic growth, 90
education system in world, 177
egohood, 31
empathetic listening, 156
encapsulation act, 239
energy, 110
environmental degradation, 173
epics, 73
epic story telling, 100
epistemology, India, 71–73
equanimity, 110
escapism, 29
ethical perfection, 165
ethics, 29, 30, 113, 125
   contemplative meditation on, 32
   definition of, 113
   global, 46, 58
   public, 44
ethnic media, 121

Facebook, 106
fairy tale, 73
filming, 100
financial crisis
   current, causes of, 48–49
   symptoms of, 48
Fisher, Walter, 87
folk tale, 73
Fourth Estate concept, 136
freedom of expression (FOE), 95
free speech, 100
fundamental Buddhist ethical principle, 52–53

gaebyeok thought, 45
Gandhi, Indira, 65
General Assemblies of the Parliament of World Religions (India 1993, Australia 2009), 46
Gethin, Rupert, 241

global financial crisis, 47
globalization, 50
    positive potential of, 43
Gochiso-sama, 183
Goenka, S. N., 110
good governance
    and Buddhism, 169
    and Buddhist thinking, 166–68
    characteristics of, 161
    definition of, 161
goodness of human beings, 44
Goryeo Dynasty, 310
governance, genesis of, 161
Grameen Bank, 50
graphic writing, 238
greed, 32
green growth, 89, 90
Gross National Happiness (GNH), 133
    definition of, 141
    vision of, 139–41
Gunawardene, Nalaka, 101

Hall, Edward T., 181
Hanchanlash, Khunying Chamnongsri, 332
happiness, 53
Harakah al-Yaqin (Faith Movement, HaY), 120
hatred, 32
high-context (HC) communication or message, 181
Hindu Code Bill (1951), 71
Hindu Marriage Act 1955, 70
Hindus/Hinduism, 34
    definition of, 70–71
    ritualism, 34
    structural basis of, 35
    values, 70–71
holistic effective approach, 171
human beings, 76, 173
    and sustainable development, 91
    as individuals, 52
    destiny, 52
    goodness of, 44
    need to understand, 176
human-centered journalism, 335–36
human development, 91–92
human greed, 173
human-interest stories, 106

human rights, 57–58
Hutanuwatr, Pracha, 84
Hutchins Commission Report (1947), 64
hybridity, 242

iconic iteration, constraint of, 244–46
iconic solidarity, 241
ideal society, vision and goals of, 84
ignatian pedagogy, 154, 156, 159
Indian communication, sustainability of, 75–76
Indian Penal Code in 1860, 64
individualization, 100
individual liberty, 57
Indonesia, 82
    one state ideology, 84
industrialization, in West, 97
information-education-communication (IEC), 157
inner happiness, 92
Institute for the Development of Educational Administrators, 152
International Crisis Group (ICG), 120
International Media Support (IMS), 123
International Programme for the Development of Communication (IPDC), 290
Internews, 123
inter-personal communication, 26
interstitiality, 242
investigation of *Dhamma*, 110
Isan, 27
Ishin-denshin, 183
ISIS, 56
Islam, 84, 115, 274, 276, 279
Islamophobia, 274
Itadakimasu, 183

Jain/Jainism, 34, 35, 70
Japanese
    communication, 181
    novels, 181
Japanese culture, 181
    gift giving in, 184–85
    Shinto and Buddhism in, 182–84
    wrapping culture and environment, 185–86
Jati Pratha (or caste system), 35
jen, 44

Jesuits or Society of Jesus
  compassionate engagement with community, 158–59
  educational system, 150
  education, goal of, 154
  genesis of, 150
  in Philippines and Mindanao, 151–52
  school graduate, 154
  The Characteristics of Jesuit Education document, 151
Jogye Order of Korea Buddhism, 310
Josephson, Michael, 112
journalism, 89
  Asian thought to practice of, 46
  curriculum in, 38
  financial reform, role during, 49–51
  goal of, 50
  in contemporary era, 51
  need for research, 41–42
  publicness of, 45
  role in ASEAN countries, 39–40
  values in India, 63–66
Journalism for Nation Building Foundation (JNBF), 299
journalists, 100
  duty to care about people, 105
  need for, 105–06
  role of, 44, 45–48
joy or rapture, 110
Judo-Christian method of teaching journalism, 36
Jyodo Shinshu, 183

Kabat-Zinn, Jon, 30
Kachin Independence Army (KIA), 118, 119
Kachin Independence Organization (KIO), 118, 120
Kalamas (a group of critically-minded people), 54
Kalama Sutta, 54, 55, 99–100
Karen insurgents, 119
Karen National Union (KNU), 118, 119
Karen newspaper, 121
Karenni Nationalities Progressive Party (KNPP), 118
karuna (compassion or loving kindness), 28, 93

Kikokusijyo, 181
kindness, 93, 98
knowledge, attitude, and practices (KAP) survey, 155
knowledge, Indian philosophical approaches to, 72
Koo, Madame Bonil, 316
Kress, Gunther, 240
Kumaraseiri, Ananda, 114
Kumaratunga, Chandrika Bandaranaike, 319
Kuuki Yomenai, 182

Labayen, Julio Xavier, 84
Laos, 82
  Buddhist nation, 192
  community temple building fund, 197–98
  nature of people, 192
  nearby educational institutions, 205–06
  Nongviengkham jungle temple, 195–96
  Nongviengkham village, 192–94
  Nongviengkham village temple, 194–95
  novice monks and continuity as communicators, 203–05
  novice monk students, 199–200
  public service broadcasting vs traditional communication methods, 208–10
  small community temple, 197
  traditional methods of communication, 208–10
Leonor, Maria, 289
Liberal Arts Program (LAP) of undergraduate students, in Myanmar, 123
Liberation Tigers of Tamil Eelam (LTTE) or Tamil Tigers, 318
liminality, 242
Lingayat, 70
low-context (LC) communication, 181

MacBride Commission Report (1980), 64, 65
madyama pratipada (or middle way), 91
magis, 158
Mahasammata (the Great Elected), 162
Mahatma Gandhi, 137
Mahavir
  and Buddha difference between, 35
  denied God existence, 35

Mahavira, 71
Mahayana Buddhism, 314
mainstream TV, 106
majjhima patipada, 173
Malayan Union, 266
Malays, 82
Malaysia
    Church raid incident (2011), 273–74
    independence of, 266
    journalism, conflict-driven, 269–70
    media role in, 268
    mindful journalism, 269–70
    New Economic Policy (NEP) of 1971, implementation of, 266
    racial riots in 1969, 81
    recommendations for mindful communication, 282–83
    religious and political reporting, 270–73
    Star newspaper, 274–76
Malaysian Chinese Association (MCA), 267
Malaysian Indian Congress (MIC), 267
Malik, Hamza Ali, 333
manga, 238
Manussa, 161
mass media, 60, 108, 332
    Mahatma Gandhi views on, 137
mass news media, 63–66
Maulmain Chronicle, 121
McKeough Marine Center, 152
media, 37–39
    practice as research, 85
    promotion of mindfulness, 94
    training, 109
media mindful communication education, 41
Meiji period (1868–1912), 183
mental disposition, 72
metta (compassion or loving kindness), 28, 93
middle path journalism, concept of, 133
    definition of, 138, 139
    dimensions of, 142–47
    principles of, 138
middle path (*majjhima patipada*), 166
Milinda Panha, 164
millennium development goals (MDGs), 89

mind
    and media, relationship between, 176
    cultivation from fetal stage, 174–75
    mental culture development, 174
Mindanao, 153
mindful
    behavior, 112
    definition of, 35
    journalism, 37–39, 112
    reporting, 302–03
    training, 94, 326
mindful communication, 89, 90, 93, 97, 101, 111–15
    aim of, 94
    medium for development, 114
    teaching programme of, 113
mindful communication for sustainable development (MC4SD), 333
mindfulness, 110
    activities of, 321
    Buddhist meaning of, 36–37
    building of egos, 31
    definition of, 35, 319–21
    frames of, 321
    growing popularity in Europe and North America, 29
    in Asia, meaning of, 30
    in Buddhist philosophy, 1, 25
    in communication, 25
    in communication field, 109
    inter-religious understanding, 36
    origin of, 35
    practices in West, 26
    through contemplative meditation on ethics, 32
    training, 115, 325
Ministry of Information, Communications and Culture Malaysia (MICCM), 268
mobile digital devices, 65
mobile phones, 106
mobile phones use by India, significance of, 68
modernity, characteristics of, 43
Mohamad, Mahathir, 81, 267
Moksha, 35
monarchy, concept of, 97
Mon newspaper, 121
mortgage crisis, 47

multimodality, 240
Muslim, 70
Myanmar, 82
  curriculum development, 124–26
  ethnic armed groups, challenges for, 118
  government, major conflicts faced by, 118–20
  media sector development in, 121–23
  media training in, 123
  mindful communication, importance of, 116–18
  Muslims, struggle and sufferings, 115
  nationwide ceasefires agreement, 120
  religious freedom for non-Buddhists, limitations on, 115
  role in popularity of insight meditation, 109–11
  Theravada Buddhism in, 109
Myanmar Journalism Institute (MJI), 124, 125
Myanmar Media Development Center (MMDC), 124, 125
myth, 45

Nahdlatul Ulama (Rise of Islamic Scholars), 84
narratology, Indian, 73–74
National League for Democracy (NLD), 118
National Management Degree College (NMDC), 124
National Races TV Channel (NRC), 122
National Youth Association of Bhutan (NYAB) radio, 134
Nationwide Ceasefires Agreement (NCA), 120
Natyashastra, 73, 75
new journalism, for emergent Asia, 339
New Mon State Party(NMSP), 118
news, 95–97
  values, 95
Noble Eight Fold Path (NEFP), 30–32, 303, 324
non-judgmental, 98
non-wholesome, 31
Nyaya, 72

Office for National Unity and Reconciliation (ONUR), 318

One World, 43
oral communication, 41
Origami technique
  art and symbolism of, 187–88
  mindfulness, development of, 189–91
Ortiz, Fernando, 86
OuBaPo, 244–46

Panchasila, 84
Panchatantra, 73
Panitchpakdi, Pipope, 334
panna (wisdom), 26, 165, 337
Pansale Piyathuma (Catholic Priest of the Temple), 327
Pa-O National Army (PNA), 118
Parekh, Bhikkhu, 58
Parinibbana Sutta, 55
past retrieval, to improve present, 147
Paticcasamupada, 91
pedagogy, 177
personal suffering
  roots of, 32
Pheu Thai Party, Thailand, 96
Philippine Daily Inquirer, 288
Philippine National Police (PNP), 287, 288
Philippines, 82
  development journalism in, 291
  mindful journalism in, 290
  ordinary citizens engagement as information sources, 294
  peace journalism in, 292
  profiles on human sources, development of, 294
  public or civic journalism in, 292
Philippines drug war
  acquisition and reporting of diverse viewpoint, 294–95
  engagement of ordinary citizens in, advantages and disadvantages, 300–01
  exploration, sources and angles for, 303–06
  human rights violations, reporting on, 296–97, 302
  journalists role, perspectives in covering, 298–300
  mindful journalism, framework for reporting, 297
  PNP role in, 289

qualitative content analysis on articles on, 292–93
stories on, 290
pictorial elements, development of set, 246–49
picture writing, 238–43
political extremism, 43
political rights, 57
political tumult, 96
Poorva Mimansa, 72
pragmatism, 98
pramāṇa, 72
Prarthana, 70
Printing Presses and Publications Act (PPPA) 1984, Malaysia, 268
print media companies, 41
private satellite television, 41
propriety, 44
public, 44
public awareness, 108
publicness, concept of
 definition of, 44
 Korean myths about, 45
 Korean religions, core to, 45
 of journalism, 45
public opinion, 65
public sector, 44
pun pun pun, TV program, 105
puranas, 73

Radio Free Asia (RFA) Burmese services, 121
Radio Television Malaysia (RTM), 268
Rakhine Buddhists, 119
Rakhines community, 115
Ramayana, 97
Rasa theory, 74, 75, 76
rebellious thoughts, 34
reconciliation
 at community level, 323
 definition of, 322
 icons for, 326–28
 levels of, 323
 outcomes of conflict, 322
reconstruction, definition of, 322
red shirts conflict, 96
regional media, 114
religious extremism, 43

religious propagation, 37
reporting
 as process, 100–03
 challenges about structure, 104–05
 on human rights and democracy, 114
 role of religious charities, 103–04
repose, 110
right action or right conduct (*Samma Kammanta*), 109, 166
right concentration (*Samma Samadhi*), 109, 166
right effort (*Samma Vayama*), 31, 109, 166
right living or livelihood, 109
right mindfulness (*Samma Sati*), 109, 166
right motivation, 31
right speech, 31, 109
right thinking or resolution, 109
right thought (*Samma Sankappa*), 166
right understanding (*Samma Ditthi*), 166
right view, 109
Rohingya community, in Myanmar, 115
 Muslims, 119

sacrifice, 34
Sahridaya (being of similar heart or of one heart), 75, 76
Samadhi (Mental Culture), 165
samma sati, 31
Sampasadaniya Sutta, 52
samsara, concept of, 312
saṃskāra, 72
Sanatan Dharma, 34, 35
Sankhya, 72
sati practice, 34, 36
 meaning of, 30
Sayadaw, Mahasi, 110
Scheduled Tribes, 70
Sein, Thein, 122
self-awareness, 26
semi identity of Indians, 71
Sen, Amartya, 57
Senarath, Sugath, 334
sense of happiness, 98
serenity meditation, 36
Shan newspaper, 121
Shan State Army-South (SSA-S), 118, 120
Shan State National Army (SSNA), 118
Shinawatra, Thaksin, 96

Shinto religion, in Japan, 182–84
Sigāla-Sutta, 165
Sikh, 70
Sikh Gurus, 71
sila (morality), 31, 165
Silavat (village-temple coordinator), 206
Singapore, 82, 266
Singapore Strait Times, 114
Singh, Sardar Hukum, 71
smart phones, 106
smriti, 34
social crisis, 90
social media, 26, 100, 133
social responsibility, 113
Southeast Asia Rural Social Leadership Institute (SEARSOLIN), 152
spiritual development, 93
spiritual unrest, 34
Sri Dhammananda, 163
Sri Lanka
  armed conflict with LTTE, 318
  background and history of conflict with LTTE, 319–21
  ethnic conflict in, 318
  globalization impact on, 328
  journalism role in, 328–30
  open market economics, 328
  reconciliation, tools for promotion of, 326
  Tamil and Sinhalese, bringing together, 325–26
structural violence, 33, 302–03
suffering from misunderstanding, 28
sustainable development, 172–73
  communicating for, 90
  is about human beings, 92
  missing elements in, 91
Sustainable Development Goals (SDGs), 90
Suvarnabhumi culture, 99
Swincer, Graeme, 115
Swiss peace report, 115

Tamil Hindus., 318
Tathagatagarba, concept of, 137
teacher-learner relationship, 155
television, 65

Thai Buddhist traditions, 29
Thai Development Research Institute (TDRI), 104, 105
Thailand, 25, 27, 35
  absorb Western concepts, 83
  adversarial model of journalism, 97
  Asian financial crisis in, 47
  diverse cultures, existence of, 98
  forest monks impact on people lives, 93
  industrialization era, 99
  journalism, 97
  military coup in 2006, 96
  natural calamities in, 106
  red and yellow shirts conflicts in, 96
Thai Public Broadcasting Service (TPBS), 105
The Daily Guardian, 299
The Manila Times, 288
Theravada Buddhism, 36, 109
togetherness, 44
transcultural connectedness or transculturalism, definition of, 85, 86
transcultural media
  education, 85
  practice of, 86, 87
transnational place, 242
Trondheim, Lewis, 244
Tuazon, Ramon R., 299

UNESCO, 38, 290
UNESCO International Symposium on Media Education (1982), Germany, 108
Unified Silla National Monk, 310
Unified Silla Period, 310
Union Solidarity and Development Party (USDP), 118
United Malays National Organization (UMNO), 266, 268
United Nations Economic and Social Commission for Asia and the Pacific (UNESCAP), 161, 333
unity in inequality, 60–2
Universal Declaration of Human Rights Article 1 of, 52
universal love (*metta*), 53
U.S. Federal Reserve, 47

Uttar Mimansa, 72
Utusan Malaysia newspaper, 277–81

Vaisheshika, 72
vedas, 73
Vedic Brahmins, 71
Vietnam, 82, 106
Vipassana meditation, 36, 110
Virashaiva, 70
Voice of America (VOA), 121

Wahid, Abdurrahman, 83
Washi Japanese paper, 186–87
wasteful consumerism, 84
Wat Dhammakaya, Buddhist temple, 104
wats, 212
western liberalism, 58
western media, 100
wholesome state of mind, 31
WIPRO-EI Quality Education Study 2011, 61

wisdom, 31, 32, 44, 303
  Buddhist, 126
  conventional, 142
  factors of, 110
World Conference on Religion and Peace (Religions for Peace), 46
World Trade Center (September 2011), terrorist attacks on, 43
World Wide Web (www), 65

Xavier University, 152, 155–58

yellow shirts conflict, 96
Yoga, 72
Yogashastra, 73, 76
YouTube, 68
Yunus, Muhammad, 50

Zen Buddhism, 183
Zen training, 30